The European Sectoral Social Dialogue

Actors, Developments and Challenges

P.I.E. Peter Lang

Bruxelles · Bern · Berlin · Frankfurt am Main · New York · Oxford · Wien

SALTSA

A Joint Programme for Working Life Research in Europe

SALTSA is a programme of partnership in European working life research run by the Swedish National Institute for Working Life (NIWL/ALI) and the Swedish Confederations of Trade Unions (LO), Professional Employees (TCO) and Professional Associations (SACO).

The aim of SALTSA is to generate applicable research results of a high academic standard and relevance. Research is largely project-based.

Research is carried out in three areas:
* the labour market
* work organisation
* the work environment

The Labour Market Programme

Labour market research is predominantly based on projects in collaboration with European researchers and research institutes. The focus is on ongoing and/or social partner related processes in Europe.

Aims include providing a foundation for ongoing debate, current political issues and processes involving social partners in the European labour market.

Chairman of the SALTSA Programme is Lars Magnusson and Programme Secretary is Torbjörn Strandberg.

website: www.niwl.se/saltsa

Anne DUFRESNE, Christophe DEGRYSE
and Philippe POCHET (eds.)

The European Sectoral Social Dialogue

Actors, Developments and Challenges

SALTSA — JOINT PROGRAMME
FOR WORKING LIFE RESEARCH IN EUROPE
The National Institute for Working Life and The Swedish Trade Unions in Co-operation

observatoire
social
européen
•
osservatorio
sociale
europeo

"Work & Society"
No.55

Éditions scientifiques internationales
Brussels, 2006
1 avenue Maurice, B-1050 Brussels, Belgium
info@peterlang.com; www.peterlang.com

ISSN 1376-0955
ISBN 13: 978-90-5201-052-6
ISBN 10: 90-5201-052-8
US ISBN 13: 978-0-8204-6698-9
D/2006/5678/52

Printed in Germany

Bibliographic information published by "Die Deutsche Bibliothek"
"Die Deutsche Bibliothek" lists this publication in the "Deutsche Nationalbibliografie"; detailed bibliographic data is available in the Internet at <http://dnb.ddb.de>.

CIP available from the British Library, GB and the Library of Congress, USA.

Table of Contents

Acknowledgements

This volume is the product of a collective effort. It would not have been possible without the support and open-mindedness of several parties.

We should like to thank all the European sectoral and cross-industry social partners who gave of their valuable time to grant us the formal or less formal interviews we conducted in the course of our investigations. We are also indebted to the officials at DG Employment and Social Affairs, Ann Branch and Jackie Morin, who greatly facilitated our task and shared with us their vision of social dialogue. We should also like to thank those of our correspondents who preferred to remain anonymous: their responses improved our understanding of the implications of European cross-industry or sectoral social dialogue. We extend our gratitude to the AIAS (Amsterdam Institute for Advanced Labour Studies) research team directed by Jelle Visser which had previously created a database on the sectoral dialogue and agreed to share it with us.

We had a very fruitful seminar to discuss some of our first results and received useful comments from Stefan Clauwaert, Christian Dufour, Adelheid Hege, Otto Jacobi and Bernd Keller. Anne Dufresne wishes in addition to express a particular word of gratitude to Bernard Friot, Corinne Gobin and Annette Jobert for their careful scrutiny of her chapters and judicious comments.

We ourselves of course take full responsibility for the views put forward in this volume.

Our thanks also go to Lars Magnusson and Torbjörn Strandberg of the National Institute for Working Life and The Swedish Trade Unions in Co-operation (SALTSA) for their readiness to cooperate with us in yet another fruitful joint project.

Finally, we are hugely indebted to Valérie Cotulelli for having formatted the text with her customary patience and skill. Special thanks to Dominique Jadot for retrieving the documents and to Renaud Smoes for preparing the tables of the quantitative analysis (chapter 3) and the chapter on social dialogue in UNI-Europa sectors (chapter 6).

Translated into English by Janet Altman and her team (except chapters 10 and 11).

Brussels 2006

Foreword

In Europe of today we face many challenges. One is how to achieve increased growth and move in the direction of full employment. Another is to develop a better understanding, and practice of what can be described as "social Europe". These two phenomena are often regarded as contradictory. In neo-liberal discourse increased growth can only be achieved through the dismantling of the social dimension in European political economy. However, is this really accurate? Might there be a possibility that economic growth and generous welfare schemes can be combined with each other?

Another part of the neo-liberal gospel is that there is a radical rupture between growth and increased employment on one hand and social dialogue on the other. According to this view social dialogue is a blocking stone to innovation, entrepreneurship and flexibility – and therefore to increased growth. Its implication is to preserve an obsolete welfare state, less flexible industrial relations and stickiness in the labour market. However, such views do not take account of a more complex and multidimensional social dialogue which have evolved, especially on the sectoral level during the last decade or so. The different essays in this volume show more than anything else to what extent the social partners *de facto* are taking part in an important social dialogue and struggle which seems crucial to both societal and economic development in Europe in a near future. Here is raised the questions of how to achieve life-long learning (so much needed in the "new economy" which evolves perhaps to slowly but steadily), how to face the demographic challenge of an ageing Europe, how to find means to combine security with flexibility in the labour market and how to combine structural adjustment with social justice to build a better society for the future. For such important issues there is without doubt a need to even further develop a kind of social dialogue which is presented in this important volume, not to abandon it. For in the end the legitimacy for growth induced globalisation in the longer run is determined by how it is possible to combine economic growth with what is understood in a European historical perspective as social justice. If this fails we might be looking forward to a decade or so of economic nationalism, protection and egotism.

Lars MAGNUSSON
Vice rector of Uppsala University and
Chairman of the SALTSA programme

Introduction

Anne DUFRESNE and Philippe POCHET

Why write a book about European-level sectoral social dialogue? There are two justifications for doing so. The first and more obvious one is that the sectoral level is the most important tier of collective bargaining in most EU Member States. At Community level, however, sector-specific social dialogue took a back seat for a very long time, with attention focused primarily on cross-industry social dialogue. This state of affairs is now changing. On the one hand, the European Commission is taking a growing interest in sectoral dialogue, as is clear from its publication of several Communications referring explicitly to the sectoral level (CEC, 1998a, 1998b, 2002, 2004). On the other, from an academic point of view, articles on the subject appeared in 2005 in three of the major industrial relations journals (Industrial and Economic Democracy, Transfer (special issue) and Journal of European Industrial Relations). Various doctoral theses and other works have likewise been published in this field (Sörries, 1999; Sisson and Marginson, 2000; Dubbins, 2002; Hilal, 2005). The present volume is intended as a contribution to this new political and academic debate, with the aim of adding to the existing empirical knowledge about recent developments.

The second justification is that industrial relations or social dialogue (as we shall see, these two terms are not synonymous) form part of European social policy. The debate about the social dimension of European integration dates back many years: it existed even before the European Economic Community was founded. Indeed, a report of the International Labour Organisation (ILO) (ILO, 1956), examining the role of social policy in the future European Economic Community, predicted as early as 1956 that economic integration would bring about social integration[1]. This is the original idea of the anticipated knock-on effect from economic to social policy: functional "spill-over". It is true that every stage of economic integration since the start of the European integration project (the Single Act in 1987, Maastricht in 1992, Amsterdam in 1997, Nice in 2000) has been matched by progress in social integration, but not on the same scale as the progress made in economic

[1] We shall not cover the ECSC here; see Gobin (1996).

integration. Whereas the role of social policy has been debated continually throughout the history of European integration (Majone, 1992; Liebfried and Pierson, 1995; Falkner, 1997 and 2005; Ferrera, 2005 etc.), the themes addressed and the methods used have evolved over time (Pochet, 2005; Goetschy, 2006). So have the main players. Whilst the Member States and the Commission were the key players at the outset, the debate about subsidiarity and about allocating competence to the different levels (European, national, regional, local) made the European social partners take centre-stage. Subsidiarity in fact requires that non-State players (i.e. in this instance the two sides of industry) must take precedence over State players (governments and, in the case of Europe, the Commission and Council). Our volume should equally be seen in the light of this general rethink of Social Europe and its stakeholders.

Turning now to the structure of this Introduction, it comprises four sections. The first will put into context the emergence and evolution of "European social dialogue", both cross-industry and sectoral, by giving a rapid overview of its players and institutions and the ways in which they have evolved. Section II will investigate the nature of the social dialogue, highlighting diverse interpretations of this ambiguous concept. Section III will explain the originality of our chosen approach and describe the specific material and methodology which made this volume possible. Our fourth and final section will explain the main themes covered and the arguments defended by each of the authors.

I. European "Social Dialogue": Evolution and Debates

The concept of "social dialogue" did not appear in European Community jargon until the mid-1980s. As soon as Jacques Delors arrived at the Commission in January 1985, he launched a series of meetings with social partner representatives recognised at European cross-industry level, thereby initiating the system and method of social dialogue. We shall however look back further into the history of cross-industry and sectoral industrial relations – dealing with both types in parallel – to chart the chronology of events ever since the 1960s. We shall describe here four main phases of social dialogue: first moves, running-in, consolidation, and lastly autonomy or decline.

A. First Moves

At the very inception of the original six-member European Economic Community (EEC), a first group of six *joint committees*, composed of members appointed by the Commission (with an equal number of employers and employees) was established in the sectors covered by the "integrated" common policies: mines (1952), agriculture (1974), road transport (1965), inland waterways (1967), fishing (1974) and railways (1972). The exception was the sugar sector which, created an initial informal working group as early as 1968/1969 (see chapter 2).

At cross-industry level, the origins of social dialogue – although the term was not used in those days – can be traced back to the Standing Committee on Employment, which brought together the Council, the Commission and representatives of the social partners from the early 1970s onwards. The Committee's task was to organise dialogue, concertation and consultation between the European institutions and the two sides of industry in order to facilitate the coordination of economic policies in the Member States by harmonising them with Community objectives. These consultations developed over the course of several tripartite conferences held from 1970 to 1978, where declarations were adopted committing governments and the social partners to act in the same vein. However, no tangible initiatives were taken with a view to going beyond the stage of declarations of intent.

B. Running-in

The Single Act (1985), which acknowledged the possibility of developing contractual relations if management and labour so desired, marked the start of a structured social dialogue. This produced a dozen or so "joint opinions" between 1985 and the early 1990s (see chapter 1). The collective players became well established at European level during this period (Groux *et al.*, 1993; Dølvik, 1999). The ETUC was keen to go a step further and conclude European framework agreements. It achieved satisfaction on this point during the 1990s (Degryse, 2006).

Concerning the sectoral social dialogue, a second group of joint committees took shape in the late 1980s and early 1990s in the following sectors: sea transport (1987), civil aviation (1990), telecommunications (1990) and postal services (1994). It rapidly became apparent during the course of the 1980s that the initial goals pursued by the joint committees – namely to help build a European system of industrial relations and promote collective bargaining – were over-ambitious. The time was not ripe for establishing a Community-level bargaining policy.

Moreover, following the example set by the sugar sector in the late 1960s, a number of *informal working groups* (IWGs) were established during the 1980s with the Commission's backing. They were intended to promote a more pragmatic and flexible form of social dialogue in several sectors: Horeca (1983), commerce (1985), insurance (1987), banking (1990), etc. These committees sought to forge mutual understanding and trust between the two sides of industry. Just like UNICE (Union of Industrial and Employers' Confederations of Europe), the sectoral employers' representatives did not wish to take dialogue any further than that at the time.

C. Consolidation

In 1991, the governments negotiated a project for political union to accompany economic and monetary union (the future Maastricht Treaty). Europe's social partners, for their part, successfully completed negotiations on their own contribution only at the eleventh hour. On 31 October 1991, UNICE (under pressure from the European Parliament), CEEP and the ETUC reached an agreement on the development of European social dialogue (Degimbe, 1999; Degryse, 2006). They laid down rules of the game concerning not only the way in which the Commission would consult them on its initiatives, but also concerning the implementation of any Community-level agreements reached between the social partners. Eleven of the twelve EU Member States committed themselves to an "Agreement on Social Policy", annexed to the Maastricht Treaty, while the United Kingdom refused to endorse it (the UK finally ratified the Agreement at the time of the Amsterdam Treaty in 1997). The Agreement is virtually a carbon copy of the social partners' contribution. It gives them a fully-fledged role in the Community decision-making process, since they now are in a position to conclude social policy agreements among themselves which then need only to be approved (or rejected)[2] by the Council of the European Union.

Thus the 1990s were the period when the social partners' role in building a Social Europe was recognised (Braud and Rehfeldt, 1998). Joint opinions nevertheless continued to be issued until 1996. Not until the mid-1990s was the first of three framework agreements concluded between UNICE, the ETUC and CEEP, each of which gave rise to a Community directive. The first relates to parental leave (1995), the second to part-time work (1997) and the third to fixed-term employment contracts (1999) (Degryse, 2000). There has been a succession of failures in cross-industry negotiations since the turn of the millennium: on employee information and consultation at national level (October 1998), and on temporary work (2002). (The latter agreement was to complete a trio with those on fixed-term contracts and part-time work.) Whereas a directive has since been adopted on national-level information/consul-

---

[2] Article 138 of the Treaty gives the social partners the right to be consulted in two stages: firstly, on the advisability, general thrust and content of a proposal (Pochet, 2003). Following this consultation, the organisations consulted may forward an opinion or a recommendation to the Commission. Secondly, they may alternatively inform the Commission of their intention to open negotiations on the topic discussed in the consultations. In that case, management and labour are granted an initial nine-month period in which to reach an agreement. If they fail to take an initiative, the Commission resumes control.

tation (CEC, 2002), the issue of temporary work is still pending before the Council.

At sectoral level, following its framework decision of 20 May 1998 (CEC, 1998), the Commission decided on 1 January 1999 to harmonise the system, replacing both of the former types of body with *Sectoral Social Dialogue Committees* (SSDCs), "intended to promote dialogue between the social partners at European level". Thus sectoral social dialogue was put on an institutional footing as an extension of the cross-industry social dialogue initiated at Val Duchesse in 1985. Whereas the ETUC (European Trade Union Confederation) went along with the Commission in this reform process, UNICE (Union of Industrial and Employers' Confederations of Europe) objected to the perceived loss of social partner autonomy. SSDCs are formed by joint request of the two sides of industry and ultimately approved by the Commission on the basis of their representativeness.

The number of SSDCs has grown since the reform: the sectors organised into Committees increased from 20 in 1997 (just before SSDCs began to be created) to 31 in 2004. More precisely, ten joint committees and 16 informal working groups were transformed into SSDCs, while five sectors established new-style Committees directly: live performance (1999), temporary workers (1999), furniture (2001), shipbuilding (2003), audiovisual (2004) and local and regional government (2004) (see table 3 in chapter 2). It is noticeable that two sectors with a tradition of national collective bargaining are not on the list as yet: metalworking and public services (for more details see chapter 8).

D. Next Stage: Autonomy or Decline?

Ten years after Maastricht, the cross-industry social partners were keen to assert their autonomy *vis-à-vis* the European institutions, especially the Commission. This shared concern was not based on the same premise in the case of employers' and employees' organisations. For the trade unions, it derived from a reassessment of the Commission's role. The Commission had in fact asserted its desire to promote the "open method of coordination" in the social dialogue, and appeared increasingly reluctant to fulfil its role of drafting legislative initiatives in the social policy field. Hence it echoed the trade unions' demands to a much lesser extent than in the past. For the employers, on the other hand, it was a means of shaking off once and for all the pressure exerted by the Commission (Arcq *et al.*, 2003; Branch and Greenwood, 2001). "Legislative" framework agreements gradually gave way to so-called "voluntary" agreements, where matters such as status and follow-up remain quite nebulous – as in the case of those on telework (2002) and stress (2004) (Branch, 2005). This development was accompanied by the gradual introduction of the open method of coordination, inaugurated at

Lisbon, into the social dialogue itself. In 2002 the social partners adopted a three-year work programme (2003-2005) which confirmed the absence of legally binding proposals by promoting "frameworks for action"[3]. In 2005 the social partners – a weak ETUC and a still non-committal UNICE – negotiated a second programme of action (2006-2008).

At sectoral level, the present configuration of the various players' roles corresponds to the post-1993 situation in the cross-industry dialogue: the Commission still plays an active part in general. There is however a growing trend towards increased autonomy. This evolution in the Commission's role has been matched by an evolution in the very definition of the role and content of social dialogue over the course of the four Communications which the Commission has devoted to social dialogue (1996, 1998, 2002 and 2004). Overall, therefore, between 1996 and 2004 the Commission called on the social partners to consolidate their practices, to broaden their field of action in parallel with EU policy developments, and to progress from a role which could be dubbed reactive to a truly proactive role in keeping with the Lisbon policy priorities. This meant in effect that the Commission implicitly refused to continue exerting legislative pressure, thereby making it impossible to conclude framework agreements for the Council to transpose into directives.

This development in the *role* leads to a development in the *methods*, *instruments* and *results*: the social partners are expected to widen their range of practices (notably by introducing the open method of coordination) and to improve the follow-up and implementation of their negotiated outcomes. Finally, having equipped the sectoral social dialogue with an institutional structure by establishing SSDCs, the Commission asked the social partners to define the status and follow-up provisions of their documents more clearly. Thus the aim is to lend structure to social dialogue outcomes by setting out "categories" of joint texts and organising their content. The 2004 Communication endeavours more specifically to clarify the outcomes of social dialogue. In it, the Commission reviews developments in both the cross-industry and sectoral social dialogues, along with the challenges confronting it, especially enlargement (technical capacity of the social partners in the new Member States, national systems of industrial relations, an increased variety of existing traditions, etc.) and the management of economic and social change, which it believes to be the prime purpose of European social dialogue. The Commission starts from the premise that many social dialogue texts contain vague, imprecise follow-up provisions. Moreover,

---

[3] We would mention among others the frameworks for action on lifelong learning and on gender equality.

the significance and status of the documents adopted are often unclear. For this reason it proposes some new terminology which the social partners are invited to draw on when producing their texts. Four broad categories are set out: agreements (implemented in accordance with Article 139(2)); "process-oriented" texts (encompassing frameworks of action, guidelines, codes of conduct and policy orientations); joint opinions and tools; and lastly procedural texts (laying down rules for bipartite dialogue and rules of procedure for SSDCs)[4].

II. Social Dialogue: Varying Interpretations

The history of European social dialogue, described in the previous paragraphs as a process consisting of different phases, may seem to readers to represent a gradual institutionalisation potentially leading to the creation of transnational players able to build a well-structured system of multi-level collective bargaining. This is how some of the academic literature has interpreted the development of social dialogue: as an embryonic European system of properly structured, or even neo-corporatist, industrial relations (Falkner, 1998 and 2004). "At the European level, the fragmented EU system encompasses significant differences among policy areas, including [...] corporatist patterns. It seems that corporatist governance still has a role to play, especially in the context of legitimising the politics of EMU" (Falkner, 1999). The identification of particular players, procedures and rules, coupled with the output of joint documents, causes some authors (among others Jacobi, 1995; Dølvik, 1999; Didry and Mias, 2005), to interpret these recent developments as the true beginnings of such an industrial relations system.

But there are at least two other possible interpretations. Some commentators believe that, since the procedures cannot produce sufficient results to have a real impact on working conditions in the Member States (Keller, 2005), social dialogue remains an institution devoid of substance for the time being. This second approach is implicitly or explicitly based on a German or Scandinavian view of collective bargaining, which for the most part takes place autonomously between trade unions and employers (the State intervenes only indirectly, if at all). It emphasises the divergence in terminology used at Community level and at national level, even if the two levels do interact. Indeed, apparently similar terminology does mask some very different concepts

4 Annex 3 of this Communication consists of a "Drafting checklist for new generation social partner texts". The Commission asks the social partners to provide certain items of information for every text adopted, such as to whom it is addressed, its status and purpose, the deadline by which the provisions should be implemented; how the text will be implemented and promoted at national level, etc.

and dynamics. For this reason, what happens at European level is at best a distortion of proper collective bargaining (according to the German or Scandinavian model); at worst it constitutes a betrayal because it leads to different practices (conflict-free cooperation, partnership) and involves different players (Commission, NGOs, etc.). This general diagnosis of social dialogue as an empty vessel may also be based on a political analysis of the European system, in terms of both the functioning of its institutions and its dominant ideology (neo-liberalism), which leads to the belief that the trade union movement – and with it the political idea of transforming capitalism along progressive lines – is structurally marginalised (Gobin, 1996).

The third and final approach lays greater emphasis on the co-opting and lobbying roles of the social partners. Thus Lo Faro (2000) regards the social dialogue not as a genuine product of collective autonomy but, rather, as an alternative Community source of regulation and legitimacy. The same idea has more recently been developed by the backers of "symbolic Euro-corporatism" (Schulten, 2004; Erne, 2001), who believe that the role of social dialogue is more one of involving the trade unions on the Community scene in order to ensure their general political support for the EU integration project. Similarly, according to de Boer *et al.* (2005), social dialogue does not constitute a European-level system of industrial relations but in actual fact serves the social partners concerned as an alternative means of lobbying. According to this lobbyist vision of social dialogue, "the true value of the ESD seems to lie in the entry into the European policy process it provides the social partners" (de Boer *et al.*, 2005: 67).

At this stage we shall not choose between the three approaches. We think it more interesting to identify the intrinsic characteristics of the European model and infer that it does not replicate national history. The history of trade unionism at national level could be summed up very schematically as the following sequence of events: local collective action gradually created national collective players who, in turn and with varying degrees of support from the State, created collective bargaining institutions, some of them more centralised than others. In other words, collective action created the structures which then enabled it to develop. National achievements in the social policy field were made thanks to the mobilisation of trade unions and citizens. As is aptly pointed out by L. Turner (1996), one important feature of the Europeanisation process was that the structures predated the action. That is to say, at European level the normal sequence was inverted: European structures were put in place bit by bit (e.g. the social dialogue committees) with the intention of helping to create European collective players. The next step might, logically, have been for these parties to take collective action strengthening the previously created structures. But that has not happened. Attempts to promote industrial action across borders have in fact remained limited, apart from tentative moves made for instance in the Renault-Vilvoorde case. Six-monthly demonstrations ahead of European Council meetings are not enough to build a transnational power base, and contribute only marginally to the emergence and reinforcement of Europe's collective players. Based on their extensive database on EU social protests, Doug and Tarrow (2001) note that struggles and protest movements remain essentially national for the time being.

We, for our part, draw a clear distinction between social dialogue and national collective bargaining. We would define the former as: a set of functions (joint action, consultation by the Commission and negotiation between the partners) and "institutional frameworks", both cross-industry and sectoral, which provide the players with strategic resources in terms of power, influence and finance. These institutions make it possible for the "European social partners" to be involved in European decision-making and, perhaps, to negotiate agreements whose content is binding to a greater or lesser extent.

III. Originality of the Approach: Material and Methodology

The Observatoire social européen has been actively engaged in research in this area for many years. In the late 1980s and early 1990s, we worked closely with the European industry federation for agriculture. Thereafter, we monitored developments in the cross-industry social dialogue from the time of the Single Act, especially the changes during the 1990s connected with the Maastricht Treaty and its Social Policy Agreement. In the late 1990s, in cooperation with the French research institute IRES, we focused on specific sectors (textiles, construction, graphical industry – see Dufresne, 2000, 2001, 2002). The OSE has more recently carried out a study for the European Commission (OSE, 2004) aimed at obtaining an overview of the sectoral social dialogue as a whole[5]. Further work in that same area has spawned other reports and articles (Pochet, 2005; Pochet and Degryse, 2005).

As a result of these various projects, the Observatoire now possesses an original and essential tool with which to study the social dialogue.

5 The study consisted of two parts: first, collecting together all the SSD joint documents signed between 1997 and 2003 so as to form a database; second, highlighting the dynamics which underpin – or do not underpin – the development of SSD by devising an overall typology. Cf. Final report "Sectoral social dialogue", Contract VC/2003/0400 – SI2.365647.

We have in fact created a database[6] consisting of more than 400 joint documents, signed by the social partners, emanating from officially recognised European Sectoral Social Dialogue Committees (SSDCs – 31 in 2005) and from the cross-industry social dialogue. This database is updated regularly whenever there are any new documents, and also new committees. Thus, for the first time ever, all documents produced by the sectoral social dialogue since its inception have now been analysed and classified into newly devised categories[7].

The originality of this book, therefore, is that it explores for the first time all the documents produced by the sectoral social dialogue. We have used a neutral term to designate them: "joint documents". The nature of these joint documents varies enormously, ranging from a letter sent jointly to the European Commission, to a joint declaration on enlargement or a recommendation on telework, through to a training tool. This neutral label enables us to avoid the inaccurate term "collective agreement".

These joint documents are linked to what we refer to in our typology (chapter 4) as the "external" and "internal" drivers of social dialogue. The two drivers correspond to the two respective functions of social dialogue: the external driver corresponds to the function of consultation by the Commission and promotes the output of "common positions" addressed to the European institutions. The internal driver corresponds to that of joint activities[8] (or even negotiation) and promotes the output of other types of texts, which we have called "reciprocal commitments" between the social partners. These are addressed to national organisations and fall into five categories:

a) binding agreements
b) recommendations
c) declarations

6 We are grateful to the team in Amsterdam who shared their data with us and assisted us in building our database. The database was coordinated by Anne Dufresne with the aid of Dominique Jadot (documentalist) and Renaud Smoes (webmaster). It is based on the reading and classification of all 'agreements' signed since 1978. The analysis of agreements concluded between 1978 and 1996 and for the years 2004 and 2005 was conducted by Philippe Pochet and Christophe Degryse, and for the period 1997 to 2003 by Philippe Pochet, Anne Dufresne and Christophe Degryse. These documents were previously scattered among the different organisations and the Commission.

7 It should be noted that the Commission has put online all the agreements concluded since 1997, using categories slightly different from our own (http://ec.europa.eu/employment_social/social_dialogue/index_en.htm).

8 Joint activities comprise joint action (conferences, round tables etc.) as well as the generation of texts based on neither consultation nor negotiation.

d) training and information tools

e) rules of procedure (cf. definitions in chapter 3).

Quantitative analysis has demonstrated that the social dialogue has resulted more often in common positions than in reciprocal commitments. Thus the vast majority of joint documents are addressed solely to the European institutions and do not commit national organisations to anything at all. Their purpose is to influence European policy-making rather than to negotiate autonomous agreements on social matters. That is why it can be said that "the added value of the ESD for employers and employees seems to be the entry it provides into the policy process in the EU" (de Boer *et al.*, 2005: 60). As to whether or not a shift is occurring towards more reciprocal commitments and agreements of a more binding nature, on the whole this question can be answered in the affirmative, as we shall see, but a high degree of ambiguity still remains (see chapter 3).

In addition to systematically collecting and categorising the documents, we conducted sixty or so interviews covering all the sectors and, in most cases, the employers, trade unions and European officials responsible for those different sectors. This caused us to draw up a typology of six broad categories of sectors, based on external determinants as well as on the intrinsic logic of the players' strategies and the nature of their exchanges. To a certain extent, the typology answers the difficult question as to what prompts the compromises made by the players and what causes them to engage in dialogue.

The information flowing from these different studies is therefore very valuable and complex at the same time. It is valuable, first of all, in that the large body of research material at our disposal has thrown up the same questions in the minds of all those who initiated this volume: what do we mean by sectoral social dialogue? How does it differ, if at all, from the cross-industry social dialogue? What policy issues lie behind this emergence of new players, the numerous sectoral organisations?

The information is complex, secondly, because each sector is a world unto itself. This, moreover, partly explains the analytical void apparent nationally and also at Community level concerning the sectoral level as such. We shall see that the sectors described in this volume, where the two sides of industry have constituted SSDCs, are very heterogeneous as concerns the number of enterprises and also of jobs[9]. In order to over-

9 Some of them (e.g. civil aviation, tanning/leather) have only a few thousand enterprises – or even a few hundred in the case of the railways – whereas others (commerce, Horeca, construction) have several million. The same applies to jobs: the number ranges from some 20,000 employees in inland waterways to over 20 million in commerce (see Annex).

come this difficulty, we have endeavoured to strike a balance in the volume's structure between the first part, which paints a general picture of the 31 sectors concerned, and the second, which deals with specific cases in three types of sector.

IV. Structure of the Volume

This book is divided into three main parts. The first, consisting of chapters 1 to 4, puts the social dialogue into perspective across the entire range of sectors constituted into Committees. Christophe Degryse outlines the history of cross-industry social dialogue (chapter 1), identifying the milestones in European integration represented by successive Treaties. Next, Anne Dufresne traces the development of sectoral industrial relations structures as such (chapter 2). In essence, she demonstrates the two conditions which have favoured the development of SSD: the existence of common policies (agriculture, transport), and the more recent introduction of liberalisation policies with the need to offset their social consequences (postal services, telecommunications etc.). Philippe Pochet adds to these historical analyses of institutional developments a quantitative analysis of the joint documents contained in the already-mentioned database (chapter 3), before establishing a typology of five categories of sectors crossed with five categories of documents produced (chapter 4).

Part two is devoted to sector-specific case studies. Nadia Hilal considers the case of rail freight (chapter 5), the only sector to have concluded a fully-fledged agreement. Meanwhile Philippe Pochet looks at two very different types of sector: firstly sectors in decline and under pressure from international regulations (textiles and sugar, chapter 6); secondly, with Christophe Degryse, the entire range of private services grouped together in the Europe-wide trade union organisation UNI-Europa (chapter 7). Chapter 8 analyses three major sectors thus far excluded from the social dialogue: metalworking, chemicals and public administration (Dufresne, Degryse, Pochet).

Part three looks to the future. The strategies of European employers' federations (chapter 9), analysed here as being lobbying partners, are crucial to understanding the evolution of SSD. So is the implementation of joint documents nationally, a subject which is covered here specifically in the case of Sweden (chapter 10). Finally, the research team at the Institut du Travail of Louvain-La-Neuve University, which specialises in the social partners' representative status with the European Commission, examines the radical reappraisal of the merits of developing European sectoral dialogue in view of enlargement to take in the central and Eastern European countries, where industrial relations systems are a far cry from those of countries in the west (chapter 11).

References

Benedictus, H., de Boer, R., van der Meer, M., Salverda, W., Visser, J. and Zijl, M. (2003), *The European Social Dialogue: Development, Sectoral Variation and Prospects*, Reed Business Information, Doentinchem.

Béthoux, E. and Jobert, A. (2004), "Regards sur les relations professionnelles nord-américaines et européennes: évolutions et perspectives", Note critique, *Sociologie du Travail*, Vol.46, No.2, April-June 2004, pp.261-270.

Branch, A. (2005), "The Evolution of the European Social Dialogue towards Greater Autonomy: Challenges and Potential Benefits", *The International Journal of Comparative Labour Law and Industrial Relations*, No.21, pp.321-346

CEC (1993), Communication concerning the Application of the Agreement on Social Policy presented by the Commission to the Council and the European Parliament, COM (93) 600, Brussels.

CEC (1996), Communication from the Commission concerning the Development of the Social Dialogue at Community Level, COM (96) 448 final of 18 September 1996.

CEC (1998a), Commission Decision 98/500/EC of 20 May 1998 on the Establishment of Sectoral Dialogue Committees Promoting the Dialogue between the Social Partners at European Level, OJ L 225 of 12 August 1998, pp.0027-0028.

CEC (1998b), Communication from the Commission "Adapting and Promoting the Social Dialogue at Community Level", COM (98) 322 final of 20 May 1998.

CEC (2002), Communication from the Commission "The European Social Dialogue, a Force for Innovation and Change", COM (2002) 341 final of 26 June 2002.

CEC (2004), Communication from the Commission, "Partnership for Change in an Enlarged Europe – Enhancing the Contribution of European Social Dialogue", COM (2004) 557 final of 12 August 2004.

de Boer, R., Benedictus, H. and van der Meer, M. (2005), "Broadening Without Intensification: The Added Value of the European Social and Sectoral Dialogue", *European Journal of Industrial Relations*, Vol.11, No.1, pp.51-70.

de la Porte, C. and Pochet, P. (2002), *Building Social Europe through the Open Method of Co-ordination*, P.I.E.-Peter Lang, Brussels.

Didry, C. and Mias, A. (2005), *Le Moment Delors. Les syndicats au cœur de l'Europe sociale*, P.I.E.-Peter Lang, Brussels.

Dubbins, S. (2002), *Towards Euro-Corporatism? A Study of Relations between Trade Unions and Employers' Organisation at the European Sectoral Level*, Thesis, Institut européen, Florence, March 2002.

Dufresne, A. (2000), "L'état des négociations collectives au plan européen dans les secteurs du textile et de l'habillement", in Ministère de l'Emploi et de la Solidarité (ed.), *La négociation collective en 1999*, Vol.III: Les dossiers, Dossier No.1: La négociation collective dans les pays de l'Union européenne, Éditions législatives et Ministère de l'Emploi et de la Solidarité, Paris, pp.45-73.

Dufresne, A. (2001), "La négociation collective dans les pays de l'Union européenne: Le chantier de la coordination syndicale: l'état des négociations collectives au plan européen dans le secteur de la construction", in Ministère de l'Emploi et de la Solidarité (ed.), *La négociation collective en 2000*, Vol.III: Les dossiers, Éditions législatives et Ministère de l'Emploi et de la Solidarité, Paris, pp.20-45.

Dufresne, A. (2002), "La négociation collective dans les pays de l'Union européenne: L'état des négociations collectives au plan européen dans le secteur du graphisme", in Ministère de l'Emploi et de la Solidarité (ed.), *La négociation collective en 2001*, Vol.I: Tendance et dossiers, Dossier No.1: La négociation collective dans les pays de l'Union européenne, Éditions législatives et Ministère de l'Emploi et de la Solidarité, Paris, pp.223-243.

Erne, R. (2001), *Organized Labour – An Actor of Euro-democratisation, Euro-technocracy or (Re)nationalization*, Paper for the 6th IIRA (International Industrial Relations Association) European Congress, Oslo, 26-29 July 2001.

ETUI-REHS (2005), "Sectoral Social Dialogue", *Transfer*, Special Issue on Sectoral Social Dialogue, Vol.11, No.3, Autumn 2005.

Fajertag, G. and Pochet, P. (1997), *Social Pacts in Europe*, European Trade Union Institute and Observatoire social européen, Brussels.

Fajertag, G. and Pochet, P. (2000), *Social Pacts in Europe – New Dynamics*, European Trade Union Institute and Observatoire social européen, Brussels.

Falkner, G. (1998), *EU Social Policy in the 1990s: Towards a Corporatist Policy Community*, European Public Policy Series, Routledge, London.

Falkner, G., Treib, O., Hartlapp, M. and Leiber, S. (2005), *Complying with Europe. Theory and Practice of Minimum Harmonisation and Soft Law in the Multilevel System*, Cambridge University Press, Cambridge.

Gobin C. (1996), "Consultation et concertation sociales à l'échelle de la CEE. Etudes des positions et stratégies de la Confédération européenne des syndicats (1958-1991)", *Doctoral thesis*, Université libre de Bruxelles.

Gobin, C. (1997), *L'Europe syndicale*, Labor, Brussels.

Hilal, N. (2005), "La naissance d'une coordination syndicale européenne: les mobilisations sociales dans le secteur des transports ferroviaires et routiers", *thèse de doctorat*, May 2005.

ILO (1956), "Social Aspects of European Economic Co-operation", Report by a group of experts, International Labour Office, Genève.

Jacobi, O. (1995), "Der Soziale Dialog in der Europäischen Union", in Mesch, M. (ed.), *Sozialpartnerschaft und Arbeitsbeziehungen in Europa*, Manz-Verlag, Wien.

Jobert, A. (2000, 2e édition 2002), *Les espaces de la négociation collective, branches et territoires*, Octarès, Toulouse.

Jobert, A. (ed.) (2005), "Les nouveaux cadres du dialogue social: l'espace européen et les territories", *Final report for the Commissariat général du plan*, Convention No.2003/10, Paris.

Keller, B. (2005), Europeanisation at Sectoral Level. Empirical Results and Missing Perspectives", *Transfer*, Vol.11, No.3, Autumn 2005, pp.397-408.

Lo Faro, A. (2000), *Regulating Social Europe: Reality and Myth of Collective Bargaining in the EC Legal Order*, Hart Publishing, Oxford-Portland, Oregon.

Lyon-Caen, G. (1972), *A la recherche de la convention collective européenne*, Study for the Commission of the European Communities, Brussels.

Marginson, P. and Sisson, K. (2004), *Europeanisation, Integration and Industrial Relations. Multilevel Governance in the Making*, Palgrave Macmillan, Houndmills.

Marginson, P. and Traxler, F. (2005), "After Enlargement: Preconditions and Prospects for Bargaining Coordination", *Transfer*, Vol.11, No.3, Autumn 2005, pp.423-438.

OSE (2004), "Dialogue social sectoriel 1997-2004", Final report produced for the European Commission, DG Employment and Social Affairs, Brussels, March 2004 (http://europa.eu.int/comm/employment_social/social_dialogue/docs/rapport_final_dss_fr.pdf).

Pochet, P. (2003), "Subsidiarity, Social Dialogue and the Open Method of Coordination: The Role of the Trade Unions", in Foster, D. and Scott, P. (eds.), *Trade Unions in Europe. Meeting the Challenges*, P.I.E.-Peter Lang, Brussels, pp.87-113.

Pochet, P. (2005), "Le dialogue social dans le secteur du textile et des vêtements: l'expérience européenne", in Sajhau, J.-P. (ed.), *Promoting Fair Globalization in Textiles and Clothing in a Post-MFA Environment*, Report for discussion at the Tripartite Meeting on Promoting Fair Globalization in Textiles and Clothing in a Post-MFA Environment, International Labour Organisation, Geneva, pp.60-64.

Pochet, P. and Degryse, C. (2005), "Social Dialogue at UNI-Europa", report presented at the 7th meeting of the UNI-Europa Executive Committee in Berlin, 12 and 13 May 2005.

Rosamond, B. (2000), *Theories of European Integration*, Palgrave, New York.

Schulten, T. (2004), *Solidarische Lohnpolitik in Europa*, VSA-Verlag, Hamburg.

Sisson, K. and Marginson, P. (2000), *The Impact of Economic and Monetary Union on Industrial Relations: A Sectoral and Company View*, European Foundation for the Improvement of Living and Working Conditions, Dublin.

Sörries, B. (1999), *Europäisierung der Arbeitsbeziehungen, der soziale Dialog und seine Akteure*, Mehring, München.

Supiot, A. (2001), "Vers un ordre social international? Observations liminaires sur les 'nouvelles régulations' du travail, de l'emploi et de la protection sociale", Conférence sur l'avenir du travail, de l'emploi et de la protection sociale, Annecy, 18-19 January 2001.

Turner, L. (1996), "The Europeanization of Labour: Structure before Action", *European Journal of Industrial Relations*, Vol.2, No.3, November 1996, pp.325-344.

Annex. Table: Number of Jobs per Sector (to the Nearest Hundred Thousand)

It is important to bear in mind that the 31 sectors are anything but homogeneous in terms of the number of enterprises and of jobs. Some of them (e.g. civil aviation, tanning and leather) comprise only a few thousand enterprises – or only a few hundred in the case of the railways – whereas others (commerce, Horeca, construction) encompass several million. The same goes for jobs: the figure ranges from around 20,000 in the inland waterways sector to over 20 million in commerce. This table gives an indication of the workforce in each sector. It should be read as a general guide rather than a set of hard-and-fast data.

More than 20,000,000	
Commerce	23,500,000 (2002)
More than 10,000,000	
Construction	11,800,000 (2002)
Local and regional government	8,000,000 (2004) (3)
Horeca/tourism	6,400,000 (2001)
More than 5,000,000	
Agriculture	5,500,000 (2004) (1) (2)
More than 3,000,000	
Banking	3,400,000 (2000)
More than 2,000,000	
Temporary work	2,800,000 (2004)
Live performance	2,700,000 to 3,900,000 (2002)
Road transport	2,600,000 (2000)
Cleaning industry	2,600,000 (2001)
Textiles/clothing	2,200,000 (2004)
More than 1,000,000	
Chemical industry	2,000,000 (2004) (3)
Postal services	1,700,000 (2004)
Railways	1,300,000 (2002)
Telecommunications	1,300,000 (2000)
Insurance	1,000,000 (2002)
Personal services	1,000,000 (2001)
Private security	1,000,000 (2004)
More than 500,000	
Furniture	850,000 (2003)
Audiovisual	700,000 (2004) (3)
Electricity	500,000 (2000)
More than 100,000	
Civil aviation	400,000 (2000)
Woodworking	350,000 (no date)
Shipbuilding	350,000 (2002)
Footwear (manufacturing)	300,000 (2002)
Sea transport	200,000 (2003)
Sea fishing	100,000 (1996)
Mines	100,000 (2003)
Between 0 and 100,000	
Tanning and leather	50,000 (2002)
Sugar	30,000 (2004)
Inland waterways	20,000 (2002)

(1) One million permanent employees and 4.5 million seasonal workers.

(2) The figures followed by (2004) come from data gathered from the questionnaires sent out to federations.

(3) According to the words of Ms Odile Quintin at the inaugural meetings of the new committees.

Part I

Panorama of Social Dialogue

CHAPTER 1

Historical and Institutional Background to the Cross-industry Social Dialogue

Christophe DEGRYSE

Introduction

The European-level cross-industry social dialogue has developed in fits and starts since the early 1990s. The Maastricht and Amsterdam Treaties conferred quasi-legislative powers on the Community's social partners (UNICE/ UEAPME, ETUC and CEEP), by enabling them to conclude contractual agreements which can subsequently be transformed into directives by the Council of the Union. This possibility of initiating "negotiated legislation" makes the two sides of industry at least partially responsible for developing a "Social Europe". Their input has evolved in the historical, political and economic context of European integration, which has itself gathered pace and lost momentum at different points in time. The evolving parts played by all concerned must therefore be viewed in this historical setting, whose major stages can be described as follows[1].

I. The 1950s

In the years following the establishment of the European Coal and Steel Community (ECSC), debate about "vertical" European integration (the creation of distinct sectoral Communities) versus "horizontal" integration (the creation of a single Community encompassing those different sectors) gave rise to two new European Communities in 1958, one sectoral – the European Atomic Energy Community – and the other "horizontal" – the European Economic Community (EEC). While the former did not set itself any specific goals in the social policy field, apart from laying down uniform safety standards to protect the health of

[1] Concerning the establishment of the first coal and steel consultation bodies related to the ECSC, see the article by Anne Dufresne on the background to the sectoral social dialogue in this volume.

workers and the population at large, the latter set itself the explicit goal of improving workers' job opportunities and of helping to raise their standard of living. It was the EEC which later set up the European Social Fund (ESF), one of Europe's main social policy funding mechanisms. And Article 118 of the EEC Treaty added the very first social aspects to the building of Europe, which was to be an economic construct but one whose integration, it was thought, would naturally bring about an improvement in living and working conditions; so says the Preamble to the Treaty. The Treaty of Rome entered into force on 1 January 1958. It led in the 1960s to a new dynamic of social partner consultations (as compared with what was already happening within the ECSC) and initiated what later became the cross-industry social dialogue. It is worth noting that at that time there were not yet any unitary European organisations of either employers or employees. UNICE came into being in 1958; the ETUC in 1973. The Economic and Social Committee, a forum for exchanges of views between the European Commission and the social partners, was established as early as 1958. The Committee was the Commission's first formal socio-economic partner in dialogue, but it had difficulty right from the outset in influencing Council decisions.

Articles Relating to Social Dialogue in the Treaty of Rome (1957)

The Commission shall have the task of promoting close cooperation between Member States in the social field, particularly in matters relating to […] the right of association, and collective bargaining between employers and workers" (Article 118). An Economic and Social Committee was established. It shall consist of representatives of the various categories of economic and social activity, in particular, representatives of producers, farmers, carriers, workers, dealers, craftsmen, professional occupations and representatives of the general public (Article 193).

II. The 1960s

During the 1960s the building of Europe was still overshadowed by a debate between champions of European-style federalism and advocates of national sovereignty. Readers will remember, for example, the "empty chair" crisis of 1965, when General De Gaulle's France disagreed with its partners about extending the powers of Community bodies and decided to recall to Paris its permanent representative to the Community. French officials were forbidden to attend any of the various committees and working groups in Brussels. According to Didry and Mias, that crisis weakened the European Commission *vis-à-vis* the Council, especially in its ability to launch new legislative proposals in the social policy field (Didry and Mias, 2005: 43).

Some trade union observers point out that whenever workers' organisations wished to make their voices heard at European level they would attempt to influence national decision-making bodies rather than the European institutions themselves (Dølvik, 1999: 24). We should not forget that, apart from the European regional organisation of the ICFTU, there was still no dedicated Community-wide trade union structure (the ETUC was not founded until 1973); nor were there any clearly defined European trade union strategies. It is also worth noting that the 1960s were not a period of any major concern in terms of jobs, unemployment or social security; after all, they were the "swinging sixties".

A process of consultations between the two sides of industry and the European institutions did nevertheless take shape in the 1960s, on a range of matters such as vocational training, free movement for workers, monitoring the activities of the European Social Fund, etc. These consultations were held in "cross-industry advisory committees", bringing together representatives of governments, trade unions and employers' organisations[2]. There was limited involvement of the social partners, who were merely asked to give their views about Community policies.

"Joint committees" were in addition established at sectoral level. These were consulted by the Commission and drew up opinions on the sectoral policies pursued by the Community (see article by Anne Dufresne). The Commission's attempt to create cross-industry joint groups to work on social policy harmonisation was defeated, around 1965, by the diplomatic crisis over the "empty chair" as well as by the lack of any tangible results (Didry and Mias, 2005: 42).

The Vice-President of the European Commission, Raymond Barre, did however establish the practice in the late 1960s of holding meetings with the leaders of European employers' and trade union confederations at Val Duchesse Priory for regular, albeit informal, exchanges of views.

III. The 1970s

The Hague European Summit of 1969 drew up a plan to reinvigorate the Community and ushered in a promising decade. The 1970s saw an increase in political cooperation among the Six, an agreement on autonomous Community funding, the creation of the monetary Snake and the achievement – in principle – of the first stages of monetary union, as well as enlargement to take in the United Kingdom, Ireland

2 An advisory committee on vocational training was formed on 2 April 1963 and another on the free movement of workers on 15 October 1968. Later, advisory committees were established on the social security of migrant workers (14 June 1971), health and safety at the workplace (27 June 1974), and equal opportunities of men and women (1982).

and Denmark. Yet even though the European Community appeared to be a success story in the 1970s, it nevertheless became sucked into the global economic crisis following on from the first oil shock.

A Standing Committee on Employment bringing together the Council, Commission and social partner representatives was formed in December 1970. Its remit was to organise dialogue, concertation and consultation between the European institutions and the two sides of industry, with a view to facilitating the coordination of Member States' employment policies by aligning them with Community objectives. The directive on collective redundancies, for example, was negotiated within this Committee.

As a result of the oil crisis the Member States experienced a sudden rise in unemployment in the mid 1970s, when their public finances were confronted by a slowdown in revenue growth and an increase in expenditure. It was the beginning of the end of the post-war boom. These difficulties curbed the impetus gained at The Hague and caused the plans for economic and monetary union to be put on ice. The Nine turned their attention back to domestic concerns.

However, it was amidst this mood of "Europessimism" that the first social action programme came into being. At the Paris European Summit of October 1972, just two months before the accession of the UK, Ireland and Denmark, the six Heads of State and Government agreed to strengthen the social dimension of the Community and tasked the Commission with drawing up a programme of action. That programme hinged on three themes: full employment and quality of employment, achieving more equal progress on living and working conditions, and involving the social partners in the Community's economic decision-making and employees in the life of their companies. This programme was adopted in 1974. It coincided with the establishment of the ETUC and led to the adoption of a number of directives and decisions in the social policy field[3]. From this point of view the 1970s proved to be a favourable period, especially since there also began to be a more "committed" dialogue between the social partners and the European institutions, known as "concertation". The purpose of concertation was for the players in the social dialogue to make reciprocal commitments, the underlying idea being that the two sides of industry could share responsibility with the Council in areas such as employment policy.

---

[3] On equal pay for men and women (75/117/EEC), collective redundancies (75/129/EEC), equal treatment as regards access to employment (76/207/EEC), equal treatment in matters of social security (79/7/EEC), the safeguarding of employees' rights in the event of transfers of undertakings (77/187/EEC), as well as a series of directives on health and safety protection for workers (Council of the European Communities, 1975a and 1975b; 1976; 1977 and 1979).

Concertation was further developed at a series of tripartite conferences held between 1970 and 1978[4]. The declarations adopted at these conferences, attended by representatives of governments, the Commission and the social partners, committed governments and social partners to act along the same lines. Yet little was done in practice to develop a true process of European social dialogue.

IV. The 1980s

The first half of the 1980s did not produce any major political, economic or social upheavals on the European scene. The newly elected French President, François Mitterrand, did call for the creation of a "European social area" at the Luxembourg Summit in June 1981, and this idea of consolidating Social Europe remained on the table. But the Europe of Ten (with the arrival of Greece in January 1981) had not yet emerged from the doldrums of the 1970s. The Community had little on its agenda. Apart from the establishment of the European monetary system and the ecu, and the first direct elections to the European Parliament in 1979, no large-scale political initiatives were launched in the early 1980s. This was the time when Margaret Thatcher's Conservative Party came to power in London, with its instinctive opposition to any directives pertaining to labour law.

The tables turned in the second half of the decade. The former French Finance Minister, Jacques Delors, became President of the European Commission and a revival of European integration got under way. The Ten decided in 1985 to undertake a review of the Treaty of Rome. That reform led in the following year to the Single European Act, which in turn paved the way for completion of the single market in 1992. As far as social dialogue was concerned, the Single Act inserted a brief addition into the Treaty of Rome, evoking the possibility of establishing contractual relations between the two sides of industry. But no specific negotiating procedures were laid down, and more importantly the status and scope of any European-level agreements reached between the social partners were not defined (Degimbe, 1999: 216). The Commission was admittedly entrusted with a new task – namely to "develop" social dialogue – which opened up a new field of activity, but the Treaty remained highly cautious and timid on this point. The improvement of working conditions was still exclusively dependent on legislative initiatives, provided for in Article 118a.

---

[4] Brussels tripartite conference of 16 December 1974 on the prospects for European social policy, Brussels tripartite conference of 18 November 1975 on the economic and social situation in the Community, Luxembourg tripartite conference of 24 June 1976 on re-establishing full employment and stability in the Community, Luxembourg tripartite conference of 27 June 1977 on growth, stability and employment.

Article Relating to Social Dialogue Resulting from the Single European Act (1986)

> "The Commission shall endeavour to develop the dialogue between management and labour at European level which could, if the two sides consider it desirable, lead to relations based on agreement" (Article 118b).

Spain and Portugal acceded to the Community in that same year, 1986. This enlargement, along with the one to include Greece five years earlier, strengthened the Mediterranean dimension of the Community. Efforts to step up economic and social cohesion were redoubled. In 1988 the Twelve tasked a committee known as the "Delors Committee" with laying the foundations for economic and monetary union (EMU). They decided in the following year to convene an intergovernmental conference in order to get EMU up and running. That conference negotiated the content of the Maastricht Treaty. Eleven of the twelve countries approved the Community Charter of the Fundamental Social Rights of Workers in late 1989, which led to the adoption of several social policy directives in the 1990s. The accelerating pace of European integration was accompanied by geopolitical upheavals in Central and Eastern Europe (the collapse of the Berlin wall), impelling Europe to strengthen its political dimension, albeit imperfectly. This new lease of life was beneficial to a consolidation of the European social area.

When he arrived at the helm of the Commission in 1985, Jacques Delors decided to hold a meeting of the two sides of industry at Val Duchesse, in the suburbs of Brussels. That was the first European social dialogue summit. The idea behind the meeting was to enable the European social partners to meet around a table and make commitments among themselves, autonomously, in much the same way as they do in social dialogue within Member States (CEC, 1996a). This new form of negotiation was however different from national practices, in that as yet the European social partners had no policy instruments for influencing Community decision-making. Nevertheless, from 1985 to 1990 the dialogue between them resulted in the adoption of a dozen "joint opinions" on a range of topics: vocational training, new technology, mobility[5], etc.

---

5 In particular on social dialogue and new technology (12 November 1985), the growth and employment cooperation strategy (6 November 1986), training and motivation, information and consultation (6 March 1987), the 1987-1988 annual economic report (26 November 1987), the European area of occupational and geographical mobility (13 February 1990), basic education and initial training and adult vocational training (19 June 1990), the transition from school to adult working life (6 November 1990),

What value did these opinions have? According to the former Secretary General of UNICE, Zygmunt Tyszkiewicz, they were "constructive and objective" documents whose main merit was to show the national social partners that the Member States' employers and trade unions could "sit down around the same negotiating table and listen to each others' views on sensitive matters of social policy in a European context" (CEC, n.d.). In other words their value was mainly demonstrative. The CEEP likewise felt that the joint opinions "demonstrate the social partners' capacity to act together", but expressed its desire to go further. Its former Secretary General, Werner Ellerkmann, called for a strengthening of contractual mechanisms (CEC, n.d.). The ETUC's reaction was rather less clear-cut. Its then Secretary General, Mathias Hinterscheid, stressed the inherent potential of the opinions and their political significance, but pointed out the inadequacies of this form of social dialogue "owing to the lack of dynamism of these statements [and] the weakness of the commitment made by the social partners" (CEC, n.d.). He called for an additional step to be taken: the conclusion of European framework agreements and European collective agreements.

The importance of the years 1985 to 1989 lies not so much in the content of the joint opinions adopted and their limited scope (Didry and Mias, 2005: 201) as in the establishment of procedures for regular dialogue. Another social dialogue summit in 1989 adopted "internal conclusions for future work", which resulted in the setting up of a steering group comprising the chairpersons, general secretaries and senior representatives of UNICE, CEEP and ETUC. The group set itself the task of lending structure to the social dialogue and giving it momentum (Degimbe, 1999: 217).

V. The 1990s

1989 and the early 1990s were an extremely turbulent period. The Berlin Wall came down, the trade union Solidarnosc won the first partially democratic legislative elections in Poland, Hungary applied for membership of the Council of Europe, Vaclav Havel became Head of State in Czechoslovakia and a pluralist government was formed – and so the list goes on. All the indications were that Eastern and Western Europe were heading towards unification after forty years of Cold War. For the European Community this translated into a need to strengthen the political part of the edifice, and in 1991 the governments negotiated a plan for political union to accompany economic and monetary union.

---

and new technology and work organisation and labour market adaptability (10 January 1991).

These two components together were to comprise the Treaty of Maastricht.

The European social partners' steering group (see above) decided in January 1991 to set up an *ad hoc* group tasked with examining what contribution they could made to the future Maastricht Treaty and, in particular, how they wished the social dialogue to develop in this embryonic institutional framework. Some very close-fought negotiations took place between February and October 1991 (Dølvik, 1999), with the talks made highly complex by the trade unions' and the employers' different aims and difficult interaction – both between their European confederations and their national organisations – and by the strategies of the Commission, the European Parliament and certain governments (especially that of the UK). But a deal was clinched in the nick of time. On 31 October 1991, just one and a half months before the Maastricht Summit, an agreement on progressing the social dialogue was reached by UNICE (under pressure from the European Parliament and despite strong internal opposition), CEEP and the ETUC. The agreement laid down rules of the game on consultations between the two sides of industry about Commission initiatives, on the role to be played by the two sides, and on the method for implementing possible social partner agreements Community-wide. This contribution took the form of three draft Treaty articles: Articles 118(4), 118a and 118b. However, since the UK refused to ratify the text, only eleven of the twelve Community Member States signed up to the "Agreement on Social Policy" which was eventually annexed to the Treaty. The Agreement reproduces the social partners' contribution more or less verbatim. It makes provision for promoting dialogue and consulting the two sides of industry on the possible direction of EU social initiatives, as well as giving them a quasi-legislative role, in that they can call on the European institutions to transform their agreements into directives. Furthermore, a newly created social dialogue committee was given responsibility for implementing and improving the Community procedures for dialogue, consultation and negotiation laid down by the Agreement. Thus the social partners became a new protagonist in the Community's decision-making process.

Articles Relating to Social Dialogue Resulting from the Maastricht Treaty

"The Commission shall have the task of promoting the consultation of management and labour at Community level and shall take any relevant measure to facilitate their dialogue by ensuring balanced support for the parties. To this end, before submitting proposals in the social policy field, the Commission shall consult management and labour on the possible direction of Community action. If, after such consultation, the Commission considers Community action advisable, it shall consult management and labour on the content of the envisaged proposal. Management and labour shall forward to the Commission an opinion or, where appropriate, a recommendation. On the occasion of such consultation, management and labour may inform the Commission of their wish to initiate the process provided for in Article 4 (Article 3 of the Social Policy Agreement annexed to the Maastricht Treaty, which became Article 118a of the Amsterdam Treaty).

"Should management and labour so desire, the dialogue between them at Community level may lead to contractual relations, including agreements. Agreements concluded at Community level shall be implemented either in accordance with the procedures and practices specific to management and labour and the Member States or [...] by a Council decision on a proposal from the Commission" (Article 4 of the Social Policy Agreement annexed to the Maastricht Treaty, which became Article 118b of the Amsterdam Treaty).

The Maastricht Social Agreement (MSA) initially gave rise to different readings and numerous conflicts of interpretation over the import of what had been agreed, its transposition into European law, its implementation, etc. There were grounds for believing that the social partners did not quite know what the implications of their contribution would be (Dølvik, 1999: 189). According to Dølvik, "the impact of the MSA [on the future of European social dialogue] would hinge not so much on its legal deficiencies as on the political will and ability of the social partners to make use of the new institutional framework". In view of the fact that UNICE, and more particularly some of its national federations (British, Portuguese and Greek), had held out against it until the last moment, some commentators concluded that "by giving employers formal participation rights regardless of whether they want actively to use them, the new arrangement offers them rich opportunities to obstruct political and institutional development [...]" (Streeck, 1994: 169). Be that as it may, there was in theory scope for fresh momentum in the interplay between European legislation and negotiation.

When the Maastricht Treaty entered into force in 1993, the United Kingdom had a special status in respect of social policy. This opt-out did not last long, however, because once the Amsterdam Treaty came to be drafted, in 1997, the (new) UK government finally endorsed the Social Policy Agreement. It therefore moved from its position as an annex to being incorporated in the body of the Amsterdam Treaty. Moreover, that Treaty contained a new Title devoted to European-level employment policy coordination: for the first time, the fifteen EU Member States regarded employment as a "matter of common interest" and consequently resolved to devise coordinated job promotion strategies. The strengthening of the social partners' role had an impact on that of the Commission with regard to the social dialogue, causing the executive body to take a slight step backwards. Whereas under the Single Act the Commission was expected to try to "develop dialogue between management and labour", under the Amsterdam Treaty its task is merely to "facilitate their dialogue".

Thus the 1990s were the decade when the role of the two sides of industry in building Social Europe was recognised. The European Commission devoted several Communications to this role (in 1993, 1996b, 1998 and then in 2002 and 2004).

In the second half of the 1990s, UNICE, the ETUC and CEEP embarked on several rounds of negotiations with a view to reaching framework agreements, as envisaged in the Social Policy Agreement. The first round culminated in 1995 in the signing of a framework agreement on parental leave. A second round resulted in another agreement, on part-time work, in 1997. The first setback came in 1998 when UNICE refused to engage in negotiations on employee information and consultation. The social partners signed their third framework agreement in 1999, on fixed-term contracts. All three of the agreements reached were transformed into Community directives. Along with a draft agreement on temporary work, which fell through in 2001 (see below), these initial negotiations served to demonstrate the social partners' ability to reconcile their views on the balance to be struck between labour market flexibility and safeguarding employees' interests. It was a tit-for-tat scenario: greater flexibility, yes, but more closely circumscribed.

Contrary to predictions by those who interpreted the Maastricht Social Agreement in a pessimistic fashion, this new social dialogue seemed to be operating satisfactorily so far. And yet the deficiencies of the Agreement did begin to show through in 1999: "Another likely medium- or long-term risk of an expanded role for the social partners is of their being left to their own devices in what is still an inherently unequal power relationship" (Degryse, 2000: 18). This power relationship had undoubtedly been unequal from the outset, but it had in part been compensated for by some non-partisan alliances (in particular between the ETUC and several senior Commission officials). "UNICE seems resolved only to bargain under the threat of legislation, and only then where it is a credible threat" (Degryse, 2000: 18). In fact, the political climate of the years since 2000 is now gradually banishing this "threat" of legislation, especially due to the emergence of the open method of coordination.

VI. The Years Since 2000

Three major political events have influenced the development of social dialogue since the turn of the millennium: the introduction of the euro, the Lisbon European Summit of 2000 – and the "Lisbon strategy" associated with it – and the enlargement of the European Union to take in ten new Member States[6]. The European social dialogue gained greater recognition from the Community institutions in this new context, at least officially, especially in respect of the "*economic and social modernisation*" part of the Lisbon strategy, but also as an element of democratic governance (as defined by the Commission). At the Barcelona Spring Summit in 2002, the Heads of State and Government particularly stressed "the need to strengthen the role of the social partners in modernising the organisation of work, improving its quality, vocational training and access to and durability of employment" (European Council, 2002: 46). They also pointed out that

> the social partners share responsibility for finding a balance between flexibility and security in employment and making it possible for enterprises to be adaptable. They must above all play the principal role in anticipating and managing change and achieving the balance which will safeguard the way enterprises operate as well as the interests of workers (European Council, 2002: 46).

This recognition – or exploitation – of the social dialogue went a stage further in 2003, with the introduction of a Tripartite Social Summit aiming "to ensure [...] that there is a continuous concertation between the Council, the Commission and the social partners" (Council of the European Union, 2003: 32). The Summit "will enable the social partners at European level to contribute, in the context of their social dialogue, to the various components of the integrated economic and social strategy, including the sustainable development dimension as launched at he Lisbon European Council in March 2000 and supplemented by the Göteborg European Council in June 2001" (Council of the European Union, 2003: 32).

6 We might also mention the elaboration of the draft constitutional Treaty.

The Treaty of Nice

> "A Member State may entrust management and labour, at their joint request, with the implementation of directives adopted pursuant to paragraph 2. In this case, it shall ensure that, no later than the date on which a directive must be transposed [...], management and labour have introduced the necessary measures by agreement, the Member State concerned being required to take any necessary measure enabling it at any time to be in a position to guarantee the results imposed by that directive" (Article 137).

This trend towards greater recognition has paradoxically been accompanied by a growing tendency to decry what is described as "excessive European regulation". Admittedly, the emergence of the open method of coordination (OMC) linked to the Lisbon strategy has broadened the scope of European social policy. The European Union is beginning to take an interest in topics such as the future of pensions, healthcare, social exclusion etc. But the tools used by the OMC to tackle these issues are anything but binding (drawing up guidelines, evaluation reports and recommendations), certainly by comparison with the legislative arsenal which can be invoked in court. Europe's social partners are themselves increasingly being expected to use the tools of the OMC in their negotiations (see below). All of this is happening in a political context of calls for less red-tape at Community level, as is evident above all from the "better regulation" initiative of Commission President José Manuel Barroso[7].

The first few years after 2000 were a key period as concerns the development of social dialogue practices. Implementation of the Maastricht Social Agreement, which had resulted in negotiated legislation in the latter half of the 1990s, gradually seemed to taking different forms. The last attempt to reach a "legislative" framework agreement, on temporary work, came to nought in 2001. After that there was a move away from such agreements and towards "voluntary" agreements, whose status and follow-up remains largely unclear. Such agreements are no longer implemented through Community legislation, but through procedures and practices specific to the social partners and the Member States. An autonomous agreement on telework was signed in 2002 and another on stress at work in 2004. However, it seems that one big weakness of this type of agreement is uneven implementation, ranging from merely informing the two sides of industry in one Member State to the conclusion of collective agreements in others.

---

7 This initiative aims to withdraw more than seventy European legislative proposals regarded by the Commission as obsolete (CEC, 2005).

As stated above, this development has been accompanied by the gradual introduction of the "open method of coordination" into the social dialogue. The High-Level Group on the Future of Industrial Relations produced a series of recommendations in 2002, which included a suggestion that the social partners should draw inspiration from the OMC and define indicators to measure progress made in respect of the quality of industrial relations. The Commission issued a Communication along similar lines, which states that "the use of machinery based on the open method of coordination [is] an extremely promising way forward" (CEC, 2002: 19). The two sides of industry could, in the Commission's view, implement some of their non-regulatory agreements by identifying European-level objectives or guidelines, basing themselves on periodical national implementation reports and carrying out regular assessments of the progress made. To this end it calls on the social partners to "adapt the open method of coordination to their relations in all appropriate areas; prepare monitoring reports on implementation in the Member States of these frameworks for action; introduce peer review machinery appropriate to the social dialogue" (CEC, 2002: 19).

This second development led to the adoption by the social partners of two "frameworks of action", the first relating to competencies and qualifications in 2002 and the second to gender equality in 2005. It is important to note that during this period UNICE refused to negotiate on a number of topics, such as the protection of employees' personal data and the portability of supplementary pension rights.

Lastly, the social partners began to assert their autonomy from the European institutions, especially in the first few years of the new millennium. This resulted in the adoption of their own "work programmes", the first one covering the period 2003-2005 and the second (probably) 2006-2008, in which the two sides of industry set out their own priorities and negotiating agenda. As might be imagined, this desire for autonomy is not based on the same rationale in the minds of employers and employees. The former hope that autonomy will be a means of avoiding pressure from the European institutions and any threat of legislation, while the latter hope that autonomy will enable them to address new topics of negotiation, independently of the Community agenda, but with the European Commission still "behind the door" of the negotiating room.

VII. A Partial Analysis

An interim assessment in 2005 would no doubt conclude that the Maastricht Social Agreement has exhausted its potential: not on account of its technical and/or legal deficiencies, but due to the strategies of the economic, social, political and institutional players. Since the last framework agreement was signed and transposed into legislation in 1999, only so-called "voluntary" or legally non-binding documents have been adopted. One could question whether UNICE really wants the social dialogue to become an instrument for defining and enforcing social standards throughout Europe. Enlargement, and all the concerns it raises in terms of the representativeness of the social partners especially in the Eastern European countries, coupled with a political climate where excessive Community regulation is under fire, seems to be damaging the role of the social partners. They, especially on the employers' side, now seem to regard the social dialogue more as a lobbying tool than as a forum for negotiation and reciprocal commitments. And where such commitments do exist, a question mark still hangs over their follow-up and implementation. The shifting alliances between players also have a not inconsiderable impact on the quality of the social dialogue. Whereas historically the European Commission has been a staunch ally of the ETUC, in its role of promoting social dialogue and initiating legislation, that no longer appears to be the case today. The social partners' proclaimed autonomy and the "better (or rather *less*) regulation" initiative are causing the Commission to pull back from that role ("the shadow of the law"), thereby isolating the ETUC whose call for a fully-fledged system of European collective bargaining now sounds like a cry in the wilderness.

The Draft European Constitutional Treaty

The main benefit of the draft constitutional Treaty would have been formal recognition of the social partners and of the autonomous social dialogue. Part I of the draft states: "The Union recognises and promotes the role of the social partners at its level, taking into account the diversity of national systems. It shall facilitate dialogue between the social partners, respecting their autonomy. The Tripartite Social Summit for Growth and Employment shall contribute to social dialogue" (Article I-48).

Furthermore, Part III on the policies of the Union stipulates that, among other things, the Union and its Member States

> "shall have as their objectives the promotion of employment, improved living and working conditions, so as to make possible their harmonisation while the improvement is being maintained, proper social protection, dialogue between management and labour, the development of human resources with a view to lasting high employment and the combating of exclusion" (Article III-209).

This draft Treaty does not substantially alter the procedures of the European social dialogue, but it does acknowledge the importance of its role in building the social dimension of Europe.

Conclusions

This overview of the history of European cross-industry social dialogue has brought to light several factors which determine the quality of this dialogue: the general political context ("windows of opportunity"), the protagonists' political will, organisations' strategies, shifting alliances and power politics. The emergence of social dialogue in Europe has been a lengthy, gradual process of advances and setbacks. First of all there needed to be an awareness of the European issues at stake, above all on the trade union side. Next came a phase when real European-level social partners began to emerge. Then there was a period of experimenting with a dialogue which was still rather unproductive and unambitious but did build up a relatively trusting relationship among all concerned. After that came the "Delors moment" (Didry and Mias, 2005) when the social dialogue procedures were institutionalised, leading up to the signature of the Maastricht Social Policy Agreement. The output of negotiated legislation lasted for only a short while owing to the employers' reluctance to go any further down that road. Today the social partners are beginning to diversify their tools of action and to replace their role as producers of standards with one of spreading good practice.

It could be said that UNICE views the social dialogue merely as a strategy for avoiding the imposition of legislation on employers. At the opposite end of the spectrum, the ETUC is arguing in favour of a fully-fledged system of European collective bargaining capable of regulating the social aspects of European integration. The European Commission expanded its role in the social dialogue bit by bit until the years immediately after 2000, when it took note of the social partners' desire for autonomy and began to retreat from its role of initiating legislation. At the same time, "excessive European regulation" came under fire in the name of European competitiveness and enlargement, and "hard" legislation started to lose ground to "softer" instruments inspired by the open method of coordination. Amidst these recent changes, the ETUC seems increasingly isolated in its wish to create a European system of collective bargaining.

One may well wonder today what future the European social dialogue has. It now appears to be in crisis following the heady days of 1995 to 1999. All the stakeholders, be they institutional, political or social, appear to be running out of steam. The desire to transform the social partners into co-legislators is waning, and the very purpose of European social dialogue as a means of defining and enforcing a set of Community-wide social standards has been cast into doubt.

References

CEC (no date), Dialogue social européen. Série documentaire. Les avis communs, European Commission, DGV.

CEC (1993), Communication from the Commission concerning the Application of the Agreement on Social Policy Presented by the Commission to the Council and to the European Parliament, COM (93) 600 of 14 December 1993.

CCE (1996a), Europe sociale, "Dialogue social: le bilan communautaire en 1995", Office for Official Publications of the European Communities, Luxembourg.

CEC (1996b), Commission Communication concerning the Development of the Social Dialogue at Community Level, COM (96) 448 final of 18 September 1996.

CEC (1998), Communication from the Commission "Adapting and Promoting the Social Dialogue at Community Level", COM (98) 322 final of 20 May 1998.

CEC (2002), Communication from the Commission "The European Social Dialogue, a Force for Innovation and Change, COM (2002) 341 final of 26 June 2002.

CEC (2004), Communication from the Commission "Partnership for Change in an Enlarged Europe – Enhancing the Contribution of European Social Dialogue", COM (2004) 557 final of 12 August 2004.

CEC (2005), Communication from the Commission "Outcome of the Screening of Legislative Proposals Pending before the Legislator", COM (2005) 462 final of 27 September 2005 (http://europa.eu.int/eur-lex/lex/LexUriServ/site/en/com/2005/com2005_0462en01.pdf).

Council of the European Communities (1975a), Council Directive 75/117/EEC of 10 February 1975 on the Approximation of the Laws of the Member States Relating to the Application of the Principle of Equal Pay for Men and Women, OJ L 45 of 19 February 1975, pp.0019-0020.

Council of the European Communities (1975b), Council Directive 75/129/EEC of 17 February 1975 on the Approximation of the Laws of the Member States Relating to Collective Redundancies, OJ L 048 of 22 February 1975, pp.0029-0030.

Council of the European Communities (1976), Council Directive 76/207/EEC of 9 February 1976 on the Implementation of the Principle of Equal Treatment for Men and Women as Regards Access to Employment, Vocational Training and Promotion, and Working Conditions, OJ L 039 of 14 February 1976, pp.0040-0042.

Council of the European Communities (1977), Council Directive 77/187/EEC of 14 February 1977 on the Approximation of the Laws of the Member States Relating to the Safeguarding of Employees' Rights in the Event of Transfers of Undertakings, Businesses or Parts of Businesses, OJ L 061 of 5 March 1977, pp.0026-0028.

Council of the European Communities (1979), Council Directive 79/7/EEC of 19 December 1978 on the Progressive Implementation of the Principle of Equal Treatment for Men and Women in Matters of Social Security, OJ L 006 of 10 January 1979, pp.0024-0025.

Council of the European Union (2003), Council Decision 2003/175/EC of 6 March 2003 Establishing a Tripartite Social Summit for Growth and Employment, OJ L 70 of 14 March 2003, pp.0031-0033 (http://europa.eu.int/eur-lex/pri/en/oj/dat/2003/l_070/l_07020030314en00310033.pdf).

Degimbe J. (1999), *La politique sociale européenne. Du traité de Rome au traité d'Amsterdam*, European Trade Union Institute, Brussels.

Degryse, C. (2000), "European Social Dialogue: A Mixed Picture", *Discussion Working Paper*, No.2000.01.02, European Trade Union Institute, Brussels.

Didry, C. and Mias, A. (2005), *Le Moment Delors. Les syndicats au cœur de l'Europe sociale*, P.I.E.-Peter Lang, Brussels.

Dølvik, J. E. (1999), *An Emerging Island? ETUC, Social Dialogue and the Europeanisation of the Trade Unions in the 1990s*, European Trade Union Institute, Brussels.

European Council (2002), Barcelona European Council, *Presidency Conclusions*, 15-16 March 2002.

Streeck, W. (1994), "European Social Policy After Maastricht: The 'Social Dialogue' and 'Subsidiarity'", *Economic and Industrial Democracy*, Vol.15, No.2, pp.151-177.

CHAPTER 2

The Evolution of Sectoral Industrial Relations Structures in Europe

Anne DUFRESNE

The history of sectoral industrial relations in Europe is virtually uncharted territory. Although this makes it interesting, the paucity of relevant sources – both primary and analytical documents[1] – makes the course of events difficult to recount. Indeed, what limited literature does exist on the subject focuses on the more recent period since Maastricht (post-1993)[2] and accordingly deals with the sectoral level only by comparison with the cross-industry level. In this chapter we shall concentrate primarily on the pre-Maastricht period, looking more briefly at more recent times.

The history of sectoral industrial relations – not yet referred to as "social dialogue" – at Community level is much more complex than that of cross-industry relations owing to the diversity of sectors involved. It dates back to the signature of the Treaty establishing the European Coal and Steel Community (ECSC) on 18 April 1951, and can for the most part be described as an institutional response to evolving economic integration in Europe. As we shall see, the two conditions favouring the development of the precursor to sectoral social dialogue (SSD) are the existence of common policies (agriculture, transport, etc.) on the one hand and, on the other, the more recent introduction of liberalisation

1 Gérard Lyon-Caen (1972) gives the only legal description of the first joint committees during the period 1961-1972, while Corinne Gobin (1996a) details the origins of the ECSC. The European Trade Union Institute (ETUI) has also taken stock of "sectoral-level experiences" at the time when the Maastricht Treaty was signed (ETUI, 1993). As for primary documents, DG V (Employment and Social Affairs) published on the subject mainly in the late 1990s: in 1995 an important document summarised the players involved in each sector and their joint activities (CEC, 1995), while important episodes in the dialogues underway are examined in fifteen monthly instalments of the Social Dialogue Newsletter (CEC, 1997-2000) and three annual special editions.

2 We would mention, among others, Keller and Sörries (1998), Sörries (1999), Nunin (2001) and Dufresne (2002).

policies and the need to attenuate their social consequences (postal services, telecommunications etc.).

We shall examine below the sectoral structures bringing together organisations representing trade unions and employers at Community level since their inception. The annex to this chapter will provide an interesting degree of detail about these little-known bodies. Diverse though they may be, they can be grouped in broad categories which took shape with the passage of time: following the formation of an initial atypical structure, the ECSC Consultative Committee in the 1950s (I), there came two generations of joint committees – those in common policy sectors during the 1960s (II), and then those in sectors undergoing liberalisation in the late 1980s (III). Informal working parties did not appear until the late 1980s/early 1990s (IV). We shall also look at the committees in the transport sector. Transport was in fact excluded from a directive on working time (1993), which created the unusual situation of having to negotiate its implementation for each sub-sector individually (roads, railways, etc.) (V). Our last section (VI) will deal with the belated institutionalisation of sectoral-level social dialogue, i.e. the establishment of Sectoral Social Dialogue Committees (SSDCs) in 1998.

Our account of this distant era will enable us to make the following assertion about the functions assigned to the social dialogue: the prime purpose of all these types of bodies has, from the very start, been consultation by the European Commission, while autonomous bipartite negotiations between the players has materialised in only a very few cases. This will lead us to reflect, in conclusion, on what we shall call the "original functional ambiguity" of social dialogue in this protracted process, straddling the line between consultation and negotiation.

I. The ECSC Consultative Committee, a One-off Case

From the launch of the European Coal and Steel Community (ECSC) in 1952, worker and employer representatives played an important role in the process, owing to the nature of these industries and in particular the national governments' degree of involvement in them. Article 18 of the ECSC Treaty instituted a Consultative Committee attached to the High Authority (the European executive), which comprised "equal numbers of producers, of workers and of consumers and dealers". In the case of workers and producers, these members were appointed by the Council of Ministers from a list drawn up by the organisations representing them. Consultation of the Committee was mandatory concerning general objectives and programmes, and the High Authority was duty-bound to keep it informed of the broad lines of its action with regard to competition policy. The Committee's composition and purpose remain unique by comparison with all other bodies established thereafter[3].

The ECSC Consultative Committee differed from the future cross-industry advisory committees (see chapter 1), in that it did not comprise representatives of Member States and its scope was not exclusively social but also (and above all) economic. Although sectoral, it also differed from the future sectoral joint committees whose main purpose was to give opinions on the social consequences of sectoral policies.

In 1955, following a resolution passed by the Consultative Committee, the High Authority instituted two joint committees (one for steel, the other for coal) known as "Mixed Committees for the harmonisation of working conditions and the standard of living" in these sectors. At that time the trade union movement

> [...] sought in this way to compensate for the legal vacuum in the Treaty and, given the High Authority's very limited scope to intervene in the social policy field, to hand over the initiative in this field to trade union organisations. It hoped to be able to negotiate European collective agreements directly with the employers, face-to-face and on the basis of true parity, with a view to harmonising working conditions for miners and steel workers across all six countries (Gobin, 1996a: 179).

In actual fact, that never happened. The principal activity of the steel mixed committee was to gather comparative documentation on pay and social security contributions, while in the coal industry efforts to achieve a "miner's statute" came to nothing[4]. These disappointing outcomes arose out of the employers' abiding belief that social harmonisation in these sectors would occur automatically as a result of economic integration.

Even though these bipartite bodies did not really function properly, it is interesting to note the two-stage institutionalisation of social dialogue in these industries. In the first phase, the Consultative Committee played a key role in overseeing the introduction of an industrial policy through proposals emanating from the High Authority, thereby keeping control over the social consequences of these policies. Then, in a second phase, those policies were addressed more specifically by mixed committees with equal employee/employer representation. In that their work was basically geared to social affairs, these two committees prefigured the future joint committees established in other industries, even though they

---

3 The Committee in fact subsequently served as a model for the Economic and Social Committee of the European Economic Community.

4 The European miner's statute was never adopted, due to objections from employers and Member States who challenged the competence of the ECSC High Authority (Lyon-Caen, 1972: 50).

were different in nature. For example, the advisory committees established in the agriculture and fisheries sectors under the European Economic Community (EEC) served a very different purpose. They were set up after the joint committees in the sectors concerned and in no way constituted the bedrock of those sectors. Rather, they replaced the joint committees as advisory bodies sometimes deemed more "appropriate" by the Commission.

These advisory committees (see details in Annex) were managed by Directorates General of the Commission other than DGV (formerly DG Employment and Social Affairs). They differed from joint committees in that they could be consulted about all social problems encountered in the sector apart from those directly affecting employment relations between employers and workers. These advisory committees were not based on employer/employee parity: one half always comprised producer representatives, while the other half was split between a minority of worker representatives along with other miscellaneous groups of representatives such as consumers, dealers, distributors and even banks and financial institutions (especially for fisheries).

To conclude about the ECSC, it is worth noting that the members of the Consultative Committee seem with hindsight to have been very satisfied with the way their dialogue functioned. In 1995, 40 years on, they voted (almost unanimously) on a memorandum stating that "the rules, procedures and institutions [of the social dialogue] produced very satisfactory results". Accordingly, they called for these arrangements to "continue to be applied as normal until the expiry of the ECSC Treaty in 2002"[5].

We shall now describe the two generations of joint committees. Following the launch of the six-member EEC in 1958, a first wave of five "joint committees on social problems" was instituted between 1963 and 1974 in the sectors where "integrated" common policies were being developed: transport (road transport, inland waterways and railways) and the primary sector (agriculture and fisheries). In those days, the 1960s and early 1970s, this was the predominant form of social dialogue[6].

Then, after the completion of the internal market in 1985, a second wave of four joint committees was added to the first between 1987 and 1994. Two types of sectors constituted joint committees at that time: firstly, the missing sub-sectors of the transport sector (sea transport and

---

5 On the transformation of the Consultative Committee into a sectoral social dialogue committee in 2002, see chapter 8.

6 The sugar sector constitutes an exception in that the very first informal working group was created in this sector back in 1968-1969, at the request of the representative socio-professional organisations. This type of body subsequently became widespread (see below).

civil aviation) and, secondly, new sectors distinguished by the fact that they were in the early stages of liberalisation (telecommunications and postal services). We shall highlight the specific features of each type of body by going into the details of certain exemplary sectors.

Table 1 below lists the two generations of joint committees set up between 1963 and 1994[7].

Table 1: Two Generations of Joint Committees (1963-1994)[8]

Five first-generation joint committees	Four second-generation joint committees
– agriculture (1963/1974*) – road transport (1965) – inland waterways (1967/1980*) – fisheries (1968/1974*) – railways (1972)	– sea transport (1987) – civil aviation (1990) – telecommunications (1990) – postal services (1994)

* For sectors where two dates are shown, the first corresponds to the establishment of a joint advisory committee, later institutionalised as a joint committee.

II. The First Generation: Common Policy Sectors

For our detailed examination of the emergence of the first-generation joint committees, we shall draw on the distinction made by Gérard Lyon-Caen (1972). He placed these committees in two categories – "institutional" and "semi-institutional" – depending on their degree of formalisation and their likelihood of becoming a negotiating forum. This classification can be likened to our typology (see chapter 4 in this volume), which posits two drivers for the social dialogue, "external" and "internal", corresponding to the two functions of social dialogue. The external driver corresponds to the function of consultation by the Commission and contributes to the output of "common positions" addressed to the European institutions. The internal driver corresponds to the function of joint activities (or even negotiations) and contributes to the output of other types of text, which we refer to as "reciprocal commitments" between the social partners and addressed to national organisations. In this context, the so-called institutional committees are those propelled by an external driver, while the semi-institutional ones have an internal driver in addition, lending them greater autonomy. Let us now see how this applies to the various sectors.

7 For more information on each of these committees – background to decisions taken, exact composition, working groups – see Annex.

8 The dates shown here correspond to the initial Commission decisions establishing the committees, even though in most instances those decisions were amended several times by a succession of other decisions prior to the finalisation of documents setting out a new composition or a new function for a committee in the wake of lengthy inactivity or renewed rules of procedure (cf. Annex).

a) The first category – "institutional" committees – encompasses the first three joint advisory committees for *transport*, in very specific European common policy sectors: road transport (1965), inland waterways (1967) and railways (1972)[9]. The establishment of all three was a requirement of the Treaty. We shall take the road transport sector as an example.

In this sector, the European Commission intended from the outset to pursue a policy of harmonising working conditions, as was evident from its decision of 13 May 1965[10]. Harmonisation therefore did not take the form of negotiations resulting in an agreement. It was a matter of standardising the composition of crews, rest periods and working time, overtime arrangements and the introduction of a control book. The Council adopted a first regulation (Council of the European Communities, 1969) on 25 March 1969, laying down rules on these four matters, after discussions in the joint committee established in the meantime by a decision of 5 July 1965. This committee, a study and information forum providing opinions on working documents drawn up by the European Commission, was split into factions: "the work of the committee was imbued with a certain amount of ambiguity, fluctuating between a desire simply to eliminate distortions of competition and a desire to align working conditions on the most favourable ones" (Lyon-Caen, 1972: 57). The 1969 regulation met with resistance from the employers at first but was finally implemented. The joint committee did continue operating, albeit with difficulty. After a lull in its activities it was reinvigorated in 1985[11] (see above). This first example reveals the difficulty of achieving standardisation through regulation alone.

Without detailing all of their respective features, it can be said on the basis of the above example that, on the whole, the first three joint committees in the transport sector were very "official and institutional" in nature, and that the results they achieved were attributable solely to the fact that the common transport policy was enshrined in the Treaty. Their original intention had been to draw up Community standards, yet they were well and truly sidelined into an advisory role.

b) The second category – so-called "semi-institutional" committees – comprises the agriculture (1963) and fisheries (1968) sectors, the first of which we shall look out in detail.

---

9 The railways are likewise considered to be a sector undergoing liberalisation, as we shall see below.

10 This mode of transport was in fact the only one covered by so-called "social" legislation for which DG VII (Transport) was responsible.

11 More generally, in other sectors too, there was a hiatus in the work of sectoral committees around the end of the 1970s. In railways, for instance, the hiatus lasted from 1976 until 1982.

With regard to *agriculture*, the creation of a joint body on social aspects of the common agricultural policy (CAP) was recommended at a conference held in Rome in September 1961. This body was established in 1963 and was the first joint advisory committee, tasked with investigating the harmonisation of living and working conditions in the sector. Although the objective was the same as for other sectors, the singularity of agriculture was that "there is a common policy which has resulted in prices for principal agricultural products being laid down at European level. Thus there is a pressing need to lay down identical working conditions[12]" (Lyon-Caen, 1972: 52).

A working group was established to examine working time developments. It concluded that harmonisation in this area should only be sought through collective bargaining, as happens nationally. For want of any proper Community-wide collective agreements, a recommendation was drawn up in the form of an "accord" and heralded as a major achievement of European collective bargaining on working time. Thereafter two agreements were signed: the first (on 8 June 1968) setting a 45-hour working week for agricultural workers permanently employed in the arable farming sector; and the second (in 1971) extending the first agreement to the livestock farming sector. Then, by a decision of 25 July 1974, the committee was institutionalised as a joint committee. The main task it set itself was to update these agreements, this time reducing the duration of weekly working time to 40 hours (Agriculture, 1978 and 1980). Interestingly, the working group of this committee was also called upon to look into wages and social security contributions, and extended the scope of this work by drawing up a sort of permanent table of contractual provisions on working hours and wages, with a view to making harmonisation proposals[13].

But now, to put into perspective this very positive assessment of the social dialogue, we shall quote what the General Secretary of the European Federation of Agricultural Workers' Unions (EFA) said about that turbulent period in an interview conducted by Corinne Gobin in 1996. The organisations representing trade unions (EFA) and employers (COPA/Committee of Professional Agricultural Organisations in the European Union) "stood before the Community institutions, united and indivisible, begging for subsidies" (E. Klöcker, in Gobin 1996b: 163). In 1991, judging that it had been mistaken, EFA decided "to stop tacitly endorsing the employers' policy [...] without obtaining any satisfaction

[12] This harmonisation was later extended to self-employed farmers, whose social protection is obviously connected with that of employees.

[13] Similar methods were deployed within the fisheries committee, where proposals resulted in a full programme of harmonisation, elaborated by means of negotiation (Sea fisheries, 1972).

at all for the workers in return", particularly with regard to employment. The verdict in 1995 was as follows: "We were pioneers at European level, always for the sake of jobs, and when you take stock at the end of the day we haven't got jobs and we're also lagging behind on the social front" (*Ibid.*: 164). The then General Secretary considers that "the Commission went to excessive lengths in the early 1960s. [...] We were an integral part of the Commission, we were a body of the Commission. [...] Now, we just want it to confine itself to maintaining this joint committee and we, those of us who sit on it, we have to gain the upper hand to force a change of direction" (*Ibid.*: 165).

More recently, and without there necessarily being a causal link with the above quotation, the dynamism of social dialogue in this sector, based on the long tradition described in the foregoing, has been illustrated by three recommendation framework agreements on the improvement of paid employment in agriculture in the EU Member States (Agriculture, 1997), training (Agriculture, 2002) and health/safety (Agriculture, 2005). The 1997 agreement was the first voluntary European-level agreement not to have arisen out of a previous Commission consultation, pursuant to Article 138 of the Treaty[14]. This autonomous negotiating process falls within the strict purview of Article 139 of the Treaty: "It shows that, at European level, the social partners can create and exploit a real autonomous contractual area provided the political will is there" (CEC, 2000: 22). Always a pioneer, the agriculture sector was likewise one of the first in the early 1990s to adopt a very proactive strategy towards the candidate countries, a major source of potential members.

In sum, the aim of this "semi-institutional" committee (and the same label could be applied to its fisheries counterpart) was to draw up "accords", i.e. joint recommendations signed by the social partners. At that time, "those in charge of these committees intended, on the basis of a general programme, to achieve some form of ongoing negotiations broaching different aspects of the status of workers in the industry as they became ripe for debate" (Lyon-Caen, 1972: 60). Unlike the so-called "institutional" committees in the transport sector, the Community authorities had no intention or scope to act unilaterally. No Community rules were enacted. These committees therefore acted under their own initiative, which – subject to the reservations expressed above – makes

14 Council Directive 93/104 of 23 November 1993 laid down a number of measures on the organisation of working time (Council of the European Union, 1993) (see section IV). The general directive had included several derogations, in particular for the agriculture sector, and this agreement now plugged the remaining gaps in respect of daily rest periods, breaks, weekly rest periods and working hours at night. It also determined maximum annual working time.

their work quite exemplary in terms of autonomous European collective bargaining.

We therefore see that a necessary precondition for the development of dialogue in the first-generation joint committees, be they institutional (transport) or semi-institutional (agriculture and fisheries), was the existence of a European common policy.

III. The Second Generation: Sectors Undergoing Liberalisation

The driving force behind the creation of the second-generation joint committees – sea transport, civil aviation, telecommunications and postal services – in the 1980s and 1990s was the need for sectoral regulation in the face of the prevailing trend towards liberalisation[15] or deregulation. Thus, although the official purpose of all the joint committees (of both generations) was to assist the European Commission in devising and implementing Community social policy "aimed at improving and harmonising living and working conditions"[16] in the sector concerned, it is interesting to note that an economic objective was explicitly spelled out only in the decisions instituting the four second-generation committees: "improving the economic and competitive position"[17] of each of these sectors.

We shall now recount the responses to liberalisation in the four sectors concerned, to which we would add the railway sector. Even though the railways belong to the first generation (see below), they likewise share the characteristics of the second in that the sector has been opened up to competition over the past few years[18]. We shall begin with the postal services and telecommunications sectors, before moving on to the three transport sectors in section V. While the transport sectors are also currently being liberalised, they constitute a particular sub-group owing

---

15 It is important not to confuse liberalisation with privatisation. Y. Salesse (2001: 63-64) explains that "Liberalising means opening up to competition, i.e. in essence abolishing a monopoly or a policy of protection. That is not privatisation. An enterprise is not private because it is in a competitive sector [...]. Nevertheless, liberalisation is often viewed as the first step on the way to privatisation".

16 This wording appears in Article 2 of all the Decisions establishing joint committees (see references in Annex).

17 In addition to the above form of words, this phrase can be found in Article 2 of all the following Decisions: Decision 87/467/EEC for sea transport (CEC, 1987a), 90/450/EEC for telecommunications (CEC, 1990a), 90/449/CEE for civil aviation (CEC, 1990b) and 94/595/EC for postal services (CEC, 1994).

18 See in particular Directives 91/440/EEC and 96/48/EC (Council of the European Union, 1991 and 1996) and Directives 2001/12/EC and 2001/16/EC (European Parliament and Council of the European Union, 2001a and 2001b).

to the fact that they were directly affected by the negotiations on working time.

The telecommunications and postal services committees were each set up after the publication of the Green Paper on the development of their sector: telecommunications in 1987 (CEC, 1987b) and postal services in 1991 (CEC, 1991). The postal services committee was in fact modelled on the one already existing for telecoms, not least because the same European organisations represent workers in both sectors.

The joint committee in the *telecommunications* sector was established in 1990, the year of adoption of two directives marking the first stage in the sector's opening-up to competition. Thirty or so common positions were produced by this committee between 1992 and 1999, a figure higher than that of any other committee (see chapter 3 in this volume). Then, in 2001, the signature of "guidelines" on telework[19] lent a fresh dimension to the social dialogue: negotiation in the true sense of the term (Jobert *et al.*, 2005).

As to the *postal services* sector, the market liberalisation affecting it led to the formation of a joint committee in 1994. The liberalisation process has further gathered pace since 1997 (Council of the European Union, 1997). Traditional national public-sector operators are now facing competition from private operators, which are increasingly creaming off high added-value segments of the market (e.g. express mail, small packages). The social partners in the postal sector have been monitoring developments connected with mounting competition in the sector, and have expressed their views in a large number of common positions. However, since not all countries are deregulating their markets at the same pace – privatisation is progressing much more rapidly in some than in others – it is very difficult to speak with one voice. According to a French employers' representative responsible for social dialogue, "there is no unanimity on defining social policy rules at European level, and it is very hard to get beyond exchanges of good practice" (PostEurop interview, 2004).

Thus the chronological evolution in the type of texts adopted in these two sectors is fairly indicative of a two-stage development in the dynamic of social dialogue. These sectors have moved on from producing common positions mainly centred on measures proposed by the European Commission to a proactive role seeking to promote employment, health/safety, training and equal opportunities. The stimulus for social dialogue, therefore, is the shared interest of employers and trade unions when confronted with the threat of liberalisation. Indeed, "Employers

[19] This recommendation served, moreover, as an incentive for joint documents to be signed in the commerce sector and at cross-industry level.

fear a loss of competitiveness for their own (formerly monopolistic and public) companies, while the unions fear a loss of employment as a result of strong competition from new entrants. [...]. The added value of the ESD for employers and employees seems to be the entry it provides into the policy process in the EU" (de Boer *et al.*, 2005: 60).

IV. Informal Working Parties

It soon became apparent during the 1980s that Community-level collective bargaining was not a viable proposition. For this reason, alongside the establishment of the second-generation joint committees (see section III), there appeared another form of social dialogue which was less institutionalised, "more pragmatic and more flexible" (CEC, 1995: 26): informal working parties. These bodies arose in the context of the Commission's 1984 social action programme, which spelled out the role of the social partners in promoting social policy and encouraged the relevant organisations to set up such bodies. With backing from the Commission, informal working parties were established in 14 sectors between 1983 and 1999, taking their lead from the example set by the sugar sector in the late 1960s.

Table 2: Fourteen (Joint) Informal Working Parties

Sugar (1969)	**Textiles and clothing** (1992)
Horeca (1983)	Cleaning industry (1992)
Commerce – retail (1985) and wholesale (1987)	Private security (1993)
Insurance (1987)	Woodworking (1994)
Banking (1990)	Electricity (1996)
Footwear (1991)	Personal services (1998)
Construction (1992)	Tanning and leather (1999)

* The sectors in bold type are the ones serving as examples in this chapter.

Particularly on account of the employers' reluctance to become organised as a representative political partner in European-level dialogue[20], the main objective of these informal working parties was to "create links based on trust and mutual understanding" (CEC, 1995: 27) between the two sides of industry. In the early stages their main *raison d'être* was to analyse employment and training in the sectors concerned. Being informal and free from any pressure exerted by Community policy (unlike other sectors: transport, agriculture and services undergoing liberalisation), they very often developed on the basis of interests shared between the social partners.

---

[20] As was the case for UNICE (the Union of Industrial and Employers' Confederations of Europe) at that time, the sectoral employers' representatives had no wish to go beyond this stage of dialogue (see chapter 9).

Since we cannot be exhaustive here, we shall mention the trail-blazing sugar industry and then give the examples of two significant sectors: construction and textiles/clothing.

In the *sugar industry*, economic change back in the early 1960s had such an impact that both sides had a shared interest in solving their problems by similar means. For this reason the social partners voluntarily established direct contacts without an intermediary. Dialogue centred around an in-depth exchange of information but excluded negotiations. A study was carried out as long ago as 1969 on the length of the working week in collective agreements, overtime, paid time-off during working hours, mergers/concentrations and their social consequences[21].

The *construction* sector first embarked on dialogue (without an identified structure) in the 1970s. At that time the social partners were in contact with departments of the European Commission regarding two points: specific employment problems, and the preservation of employees' entitlements under supplementary pension, social security and unemployment benefit schemes. More recently, the two representative organisations in the sector – the European Construction Industry Federation (FIEC)[22] and the European Federation of Building and Woodworkers (EFBWW) embarked on sectoral dialogue long before it was institutionalised, and independently of the European Commission. Their talks began in March 1990, and they instituted two plenaries per year as well as meetings on topics such as health/safety and training. They were subsequently recognised by the European Commission as "sectoral partners" in the context of the social dialogue (CEC, 1993). Thus the two sides of industry were officially involved in informal working parties from 1992 onwards and, since 1998, in an SSDC (see below, section VI). It is worth pointing out that these institutional changes have made no substantial difference to the quality of the dialogue initiated at the outset.

The real driving force behind dialogue was the "posting of workers" issue. This issue has put considerable pressure on the sector within the EU, the risk being that competing sets of legislation could apply in the same country. A lengthy legislative process eventually resulted in the adoption of a directive on this subject in December 1996 (European Parliament and Council of the European Union, 1996). Taking as a starting point their common position on posted workers, adopted in November 1993, the social partners in the sector (FIEC and EFBWW) signed a joint declaration on the application of the directive in Septem-

---

21 For more up-to-date information about this sector, see chapter 7 in this volume.

22 FIEC was able to engage in dialogue because it was sufficiently independent of UNICE, which disapproved of the establishment of SSDCs (for details of FIEC's strategy, see chapter 9).

ber 1997 (Construction, 1997). The posting of workers was without doubt the issue that triggered debate between the two sides of industry and strengthened their mutual trust while the dialogue was getting underway. The talks were then extended to other themes[23] (see what we refer to as "pragmatism based on parity" in chapter 9).

In the *textile/clothing* sector[24], the commonality of interest in social dialogue essentially derived from the threat to production structures posed by competition from third countries. In fact the first joint round-table talks on this subject took place back in 1963. At that stage, the only measures taken were ones designed to give the industry economic safeguards, since the employers never agreed to discuss social problems. It is worth examining the historical continuity in the players' relationship and in the themes addressed.

Owing above all to the early internationalisation of this sector (described in chapter 7), the two sides of industry (ETUF:TCL/European Trade Union Federation: Textiles, Clothing, Leather – and Euratex/ European Apparel and Textile Organisation) engaged in regular social dialogue from 5 February 1992 onwards. This took the form of an informal working party (IWP) holding regular plenary meetings. The topics addressed on these occasions corresponded to those examined at cross-industry level between the European Trade Union Confederation (ETUC) and UNICE, whenever it was felt that the sector could contribute added value. This was the case with "employment", "vocational training" especially for women, given the high concentration of female labour (Textiles, 1994), and "economic and/or sectoral policies". Nevertheless, the initial aim of this IWP had been nothing more than to foster "links of mutual understanding" between the social partners. Indeed, Euratex – or more precisely the national employers' organisations, especially in the Nordic countries – were unwilling to go any further in the IWP than a dialogue free from regulatory constraint. Even today they still reject all European interference in the social component of their national policies (see chapter 8). As in the construction sector, the conversion of the IWP into an SSDC in 1999 (see next section) did not accelerate the process. The informal working parties did of course receive a negotiating mandate on being transformed into SSDCs but, contrary to trade union expectations, that transformation did not bring about a step-change leading to European-level bargaining.

23 Recommendations on health and safety have been drawn up jointly. A joint forum on European training in the sector was established in 1995.

24 This sector is described in detail in chapter 7 as regards the link with international regulations, and in chapter 8 as regards the point of view of the employers' organisation Euratex.

The two sides of industry signed a joint contribution to the Lisbon summit on 1 March 2000. In it they confirmed that they were still undertaking initiatives to tackle the same topics as those previously dealt with by the informal working parties (Textiles, 2000). For instance, they provided encouragement for an extensive "programme for the coordination of TC companies' planned investments in new technology". With respect to training, a "study on changes in qualitative and quantitative employment and training needs" aimed to achieve a better match between supply and demand for employment and training in the sector. It sought to improve workers' adaptability to the new requirements of the information and knowledge-based society, since workers have a "duty to maintain their own employability". In actual fact, all of these sectoral demands reflected the concerns of the then Portuguese presidency, namely to improve competitiveness and employment by means of the existing Community method. The similarity between the discourse of the IWP in the sector and that of the European Commission is striking.

We now move on to our analysis of the various transport sectors which, even though they too are in the process of being liberalised (see section III above), are in the unusual position of having had to respond to the Commission's demands concerning the regulation of working time.

V. The Transport Sector, a Separate Case: Negotiations on Working Time

Developments affecting the committees in the various transport subsectors are directly related to the "Directive concerning certain aspects of the organisation of working time" (Council of the European Union, 1993). Although its purpose was to regulate this matter in most fields, the directive's scope excluded certain specific sectors. Transport was the main one of these so-called "excluded" sectors[25]. It is interesting to note that this directive was adopted in the very month when the Maastricht Treaty entered into force (1 November 1993). In actual fact, the Social Policy Agreement annexed to the Treaty

> extends the role of invention by the social partners beyond the collective bargaining potential opened up by the directive [...]. Basing itself on the Agreement, the Commission [embarked on] consultations with the sectoral joint committees affected by this exclusion (Didry and Mias, 2005: 108).

---

25 The excluded sectors encompass more than 5 million workers, not least because of the large number of mobile workers in these sectors. They comprise all the transport sectors (road, railway, sea, aviation and inland waterways), fisheries, other offshore activities and trainee doctors.

A White Paper (CEC, 1997) devoted to these sectors was published in July 1997. Its aim was to find a way of ensuring the same conditions for all workers, taking account of the specific characteristics and requirements of these diverse sectors. The Commission put forward a basis for discussion between the social partners and invited them to make recommendations, within joint committees, on ways of adapting the principles of the directive to their respective sectors. These principles mainly concerned daily and weekly rest periods, breaks and annual leave, as well as particular provisions on night work[26].

Then, on 31 March 1998, the Commission launched a second round of consultations of the transport sector social partners. This comprised two aspects: they were asked on the one hand to amend the directive with a view to extending all of its rules to non-mobile workers in the excluded sectors and, on the other, to provide "the necessary sectoral legislation to give sufficient protection to the health and safety of mobile and offshore workers" (CEC, 1998a: 2).

In so doing, the Commission was using the Social Policy Agreement to exert pressure so as to elicit negotiations "in the shadow of the law": a scenario well known at cross-industry level but little used in individual sectors. Ultimately these proposals did revive negotiations in the sectors concerned. According to Keller and Bansbach (2000: 120), "All that we have is the filling of an existing regulatory gap in a specific sector, with the initiative taken by the Commission and not by the social partners". Three sectors did achieve agreements under the threat of legislation: railways and sea transport in 1998, then civil aviation in 2000. The committees concerned were second-generation joint committees, or else akin to this category (see below)[27], although no causal link can be proved. We shall now describe the liberalisation context in each sector, before looking at their respective negotiations.

The *sea transport* sector was by its very nature the first to experience globalisation. Competition is fierce: the fleet flying the flags of EU Member States declined by 30% from 1985 to 1995 as a result of competition from vessels flying third-country flags. Such were the circumstances surrounding the formation of the sector's joint committee in

---

26 To be more precise, the most significant measures contained in the directive are as follows: a minimum daily rest period of 11 consecutive hours out of 24, a minimum uninterrupted rest period of one day per week, a maximum average working week of 48 hours (overtime included), four weeks of paid leave and night work confined to 8 hours out of 24.

27 By contrast, negotiations were unsuccessful in two sectors corresponding to first-generation committees: inland waterways and road transport (cf. chapter 9 in this volume for a detailed account of the failed negotiations. The stillborn agreement was subsequently converted into proposals to the Council and resulted in the adoption of a directive in 2002).

1987[28]. Company mergers have increased since then, as has the trend towards deregulation. Ten years on, negotiations on working time took place in a context where Europe's employers and trade unions were equally aware of the threat to their sector. They "wished to ensure that any provisions agreed would not render Community ships less competitive *vis-à-vis* their non-EU competitors" (Weber, 2001: 147).

The sea transport sector was the first to sign an agreement, later transposed into a directive by a Council decision (pursuant to Article 4 of the Social Policy Agreement). This success can largely be attributed to a particular set of circumstances, namely the negotiation – at the same time and by the same people – of international rules on working time. We can refer here to a multi-layer legislative process. Because this sector is so very internationalised, there is an unusually high degree of interaction between international rules and Community legislation[29]. In 1996, the International Labour Organisation (ILO) adopted Convention No.180 which lays down maximum working hours and minimum rest periods. The Commission's 1997 White Paper provoked intensive debate between FST (Federation of Transport Workers' Unions in the European Union) and ECSA (European Community Shipowners' Association), leading to an agreement enshrining the ILO recommendation (Sea transport, 1998)[30]. On 25 May 1999, this agreement was transposed into a directive applying to all seafarers employed on board vessels registered in an EU Member State (Council of the European Union, 1999). The agreement was also flanked by other legal instruments serving to enforce implementation of the ILO Convention by vessels registered outside of the EU which berth in Member States' ports. One of our interviewees assured us that "the working time agreement is being monitored" (ETF interview, 2004a).

The *railway* sector was not affected by European deregulation policy until the 1990s. Initially, and for many years, the two representative organisations – ETF (European Transport Workers' Federation) and CER (Community of European Railway and Infrastructure Companies) – were united in opposing liberalisation of the sector and produced a large number of joint declarations (e.g. Railways, 1997a, 1997b and

28 A working group on working time was set up as soon as the committee was established (cf. Annex).

29 The European social partners keep under review the ILO's efforts to consolidate all the existing maritime conventions. The law governing sea transport derives largely from international conventions, including those drawn up by the ILO.

30 The agreement reached specifies a normal working day of 8 hours in principle, one day off per week, no work on public holidays and at least 4 weeks of annual paid leave. Lastly, it stipulates that working hours must not exceed 14 in any 24-hour period and 72 hours in any 7-day period. As for rest periods, these are set at a minimum of 10 hours in every 24 and 77 hours in each 6-day period.

1999). All these texts commented on very specific measures associated with the growing liberalisation of the sector brought about by successive railway "packages" (see chapter 5 in this volume). For the social partners it was a matter of anticipating the social consequences and regulating liberalisation by incorporating issues such as health/safety and training. Then, in 1999, the employers' representatives (CER) decided to stop opposing liberalisation, but to engage actively in lobbying to influence the legislation being drafted. Thus the two organisations operated as separate lobbies until 15 March 2003, when the first railway package (the infrastructure package) liberalised international freight, i.e. opened up the market to competition.

The railway sector, while undergoing liberalisation, at the same time falls under the "working time" directive. In 1996 and 1997 the two representative organisations, ETF and CER, had already produced two common positions (Railways, 1996 and 1997c) on the subject, in which they called on the Commission to table a legislative proposal applying the provisions of the 1993 general directive to mobile and non-mobile workers in the rail sector. This stance was firmed up a year later, following a consultation process, when the two sides reached an agreement (Railways, 1998): this was not transposed into a directive but did include some specific derogations for mobile staff. These derogations were subsequently written into the horizontal directive of 2000 (see above). The success of negotiations in this sector can be attributed to two factors in particular: the unity among the European employers' representatives within CER, and the national traditions of social partnership in public enterprises.

The *civil aviation* committee took a while to become established, the main impediment being the fragmentation of interests in the sector. This is illustrated by the division of the employers into five organisations (ACI-Europe – Airports Council International, AEA – Association of European Airlines, ERA – European Regions Airline Association, IACA – International Association of Charter Airlines, and CANSO – Civil Air Navigation Services Organisation[31]). Besides, the airlines disagree with one another about the financial implications of liberalisation. Indeed, civil aviation is in crisis owing to the growing liberalisation of the sector and its economic effects: mergers and competition from low-cost carriers. The employers in this sector, as in others, took steps to lobby the European institutions through informal advisory committees, with the

[31] There are clear demarcation lines between the five organisations in this highly fragmented sector: IACA represents charter airlines; ERA, regional airlines; AEA, European airlines; ACI-Europe, airport authorities; and finally CANSO, flight crews. All these organisations have to cooperate with one another when conducting dialogue/ negotiations with the trade unions.

aim of advancing their respective interests. As for the trade union organisations, they too sought to exert influence upstream of political decision-making. The outcomes of dialogue have been very modest, when all is said and done, apart from the agreement of working time.

The working time agreement was signed in 2000 (Civil aviation, 2000) and then implemented by a Council decision in the same year (Council of the European Union, 2000). It lays down minimum conditions: flying time is limited to 900 hours and annual working time to 2,000 hours (as against 2,304 in the general directive). Minimum numbers of monthly and annual rest days are specified. No distinction is drawn between night workers and day workers. According to an ETF trade union official, "this directive is a 'lifejacket' for airlines that don't have collective agreements" (ETF interview, 2004b). It entered into force on 1 December 2003. Following the signature of this agreement, the two organisations representing the workforce, ETF and ECA (European Cockpit Association), demanded additional FTL (flight time limitation) rules in view of the fatigue caused by the duration of long-haul flights and jet lag. Their counterparts on the employers' side refused.

At the end of a second round of consultations launched in 1998, and following negotiations in the sectors mentioned, this process eventually led to the adoption of a new "horizontal" directive (CEC, 2002) covering all the excluded sectors. This directive extends all the provisions of the 1993 directive to all non-mobile workers in the excluded sectors and to mobile railway workers – subject to the derogations laid down in the directive. It also ensures that all mobile workers in these sectors are covered by four provisions: a maximum annual number of working hours, annual paid leave, guaranteed adequate rest periods and health checks for night workers.

So, taking stock of all the former structures prior to their standardisation in 1998, we have seen that – despite the diversity from one sector to another – three major categories of bodies were established in turn. First came the one-off case of the ECSC Consultative Committee in the 1950s; second, the joint committees in the common policy sectors during the 1960s and then in the sectors undergoing liberalisation in the late 1980s (with the transport sectors, unusually, having had to negotiate on working time); and third, the informal working parties of the late 1980s and early 1990s. Table 3 below shows the establishment of these sectoral bodies since 1954 in chronological order.

Table 3: Chronology of Community-level Sectoral Bodies (Joint Committees and Informal Working Parties) Transformed into Officially Constituted Sectoral Social Dialogue Committees (Table Updated to 31 December 2005)

Joint Committees	Informal Working Parties	SSDCs *	Sectors
1954[32]		X	Mines
1963		X	Agriculture
1965		X	Road transport
1967		X	Inland waterways
1968		X	Sea fisheries
	1969	X	Sugar
1972		X	Railways
(1977)[33]	1982	X	Footwear
	1983	X	Horeca/Tourism
	1985	X	Commerce
1987		X	Sea transport
	1987	X	Insurance
1990		X	Telecommunications
1990		X	Civil aviation
	1990	X	Banking
	1992	X	Construction
	1992	X	Cleaning industry
	1992	X	Textile and clothing
	1993	X	Private security
1994		X	Postal services
	1994	X	Woodworking
	1996	X	Electricity
	1998	X	Personal services (hairdressing)
	1999	X	Tanning
		1999	Culture
		1999	Temporary work
		2001	Furniture
		2003	Shipbuilding
		2004	Audiovisual
		2004	Chemical industry
		2004	Local and regional government
9 JCs	14 IWPs	7 new	31 sectors

* In column 3, the year of establishment of the SSDC is given only for the seven sectors directly constituted in this form from 1999 onwards. The cross in other cases indicates that the 10 joint committees and the 14 informal working parties concerned were all transformed into SSDCs between 1999 and 2001 (except Mines – 2002).

32 The "Mines" joint committee referred to in the table corresponds to the "Coal" mixed committee mentioned earlier.

33 The creation of a Footwear joint committee in 1977 was not followed by an official decision published in the OJEC. This committee therefore operated informally and wound up its activities in 1988 (Gobin, 1996a: 610).

Our next section examines the belated institutionalisation of sectoral-level social dialogue, i.e. the establishment of the Sectoral Social Dialogue Committees (SSDCs) in 1998.

VI. Establishment of the Sectoral Social Dialogue Committees in 1998

Even though bodies representing individual sectors – detailed in the previous sections – already dated back over 30 years, it is worth noting that the initial Social Policy Agreement signed by the cross-industry players in 1991 (see chapter 1), meant to apply both across industry as a whole and to the various sectors, made no specific reference to this level. Nor did the ensuing Commission Communication of 1993 (CEC, 1993), which merely listed in an annex the sectoral organisations (of employers and trade unions) deemed to meet the representativeness criteria[34]. Only more recently did the Commission begin to signal the importance of the sectoral level, beginning in effect with its 1996 Communication on "the development of the social dialogue" (CEC, 1996), where, for the first time, it devoted an entire section to sectoral dialogue.

We shall now describe the way in which the European Commission's definition of the role of sectoral social dialogue evolved in the course of the two Communications preceding the establishment of the new committees (CEC, 1996 and 1998b). The proposals contained in the 1996 Communication mainly relate to the holding of consultations and the operational reforms to be carried out (including the question of the representativeness of European organisations).

With regard to the holding of these consultations, the Commission considers that it "has been well-informed about the positions of the partners on the objectives and content of its proposals" [concerning legislation or regulations with implications for their own sector of activity] (CEC, 1996: 6). It does however regret that the potential of the joint committees and informal working parties as consultative bodies has not been used to the full outside of mandatory consultations[35]. And when their opinions have been sought, according to the Commission, "the sectoral bodies have often been unable to give their opinion until after the Commission has adopted the text in question (point 31)" (CEC, 1996: 6).

One explanation for these shortcomings is that the committees' terms of reference are restricted to the social aspects of Community policies. "The compartmentalisation between social and economic aspects is

---

34 For details of these criteria, see Box 1 in chapter 9.

35 The Commission is obliged to consult the social partners only in the case of social policies for which official procedures are laid down in Article 3.

artificial, usually to the detriment of social policy considerations, which tend to be neglected (point 32)" (CEC, 1996: 6). In order to bridge the gap between social policy and the social effects of sectoral policy, the European Commission proposes

> to move some of the tasks relating to the JCs and IWPs from DGV to the relevant sectoral DGs [...]. Under this system, which aims for a rationalisation of consultative bodies, the responsibility and administrative structure, at least for the Joint Committees which cover a Common Policy of the EU, would involve the relevant Directorate General more directly, with DG V retaining responsibility for coordination, for dialogue on social policy and for monitoring the effectiveness of social dialogue and its input into employment policies (point 38) (CEC, 1996: 7-8).

Finally, in 1998, the respondents to the 1996 consultation urged the Commission to "improve the co-ordination of work within its departments as far as the consultation procedures are concerned; however, they generally prefer that overall responsibility for the sectoral dialogue remain with DGV" (CEC, 1998c: 9).

Concerning operational reforms and a review of procedures, the Commission believes that "these bodies impose a heavy budgetary and administrative burden" (CEC, 1996: 6)[36]. Consequently the objective of the reform undertaken was to streamline dialogue, in other words to:

- reduce the number of members of each committee (point 40);
- cover all strategic sectors (point 36);
- improve inter-sectoral information and coordination (points 34 and 42).

On the first point, the Communication states that "the sectoral Joint Committees cannot continue to expand exponentially with every enlargement" (CEC, 1996: 8). Moreover, a study of the representativeness of sector-specific social partner organisations was launched in the same year as the Communication (1996), making it possible to adjust the composition of attendance at meetings. Operational reforms were also designed "to operate in a more flexible manner and under a restricted linguistic regime, in order to make consultation in advance more feasible" (CEC, 1996: 8), the idea being to make greater use of new technology in order to increase the ability of European organisations to communicate with their national membership.

Concerning the second point, the Commission believes that sectoral dialogue should relate to "strategic" issues and sectors, although this

[36] This burden was due to the large number of meetings held every year. In 1994, for example, each of the 130 annual meetings was attended by between 24 and 50 participants.

term is not clearly defined. Strategic sectors may, in the Commission's opinion, be those "where the social partners are clearly active"; as for strategic issues, "these priority issues should cover the social implications of the relevant social policy as well as questions of general interest to the sectoral social partners" (CEC, 1996: 7).

As for the third point, the Communication notes that links between sectors or with the cross-industry dialogue have been few and far between. It proposes "bringing together representatives from the different sectoral dialogues for information from the Commission on the initiatives likely to interest them" (CEC, 1996: 8).

The reform of the sectoral social dialogue establishing the SSDCs happened relatively rapidly. It was in the aftermath of its framework decision of 20 May 1998 that the European Commission decided, on 1 January 1999, to harmonise the system. Both former types of sectoral body were replaced by Sectoral Social Dialogue Committees (SSDCs), with the intention of promoting dialogue between the social partners at European level (CEC, 1998b).

New rules of the game were thus applied to all the former bodies. The SSDCs were set up by joint request of the social partners and ultimately subject to approval by the Commission according to representativeness criteria (see Box 1 in chapter 9).

Each new committee comprises a maximum of 40 representatives (with an equal number on both sides)[37]. Each European sectoral organisation has a designated number of seats and composes its delegation according to its internal procedures. This alters the nature of representation: SSDC members are now regarded as representatives of their European organisation (and not as individuals appointed by the Council, as was the case for the ECSC Committee, or by the European Commission as happened for the two earlier types of committee). Plenary meetings are chaired either by a representative of the social partners or, at their joint request, by a Commission representative. The meeting secretary is always a Commission representative.

Each committee is expected to adopt its own rules of procedure in association with the Commission (according to our information, 24 of the 31 committees have published their rules of procedure) and its work programme, which is usually annual[38]. At least one plenary meeting is held every year, and more specific issues are dealt with at enlarged

37 Meeting expenses are reimbursed for a maximum of 30 representatives, i.e. one representative for each of the 15 (old) Member States on the trade union and employers' sides respectively.

38 The work programme corresponds to the annual policy guidelines of the former joint committees.

secretariat meetings or in restricted working groups. The social partners may also organise symposiums and seminars, carry out studies, sponsor exchange schemes and provide training. The Commission does not procure a negotiating mandate, which comes directly from national organisations, nor does it lay down any predetermined rules on the manner in which joint texts are to be approved[39].

Since the reform, the number of sectors constituted as committees rose from 20 to 31 between 1997 – just before the SSDCs came into being – and 2004. More precisely, 10 joint committees and 14 informal working parties were converted into SSDCs, while seven sectors set themselves up directly in the new mould: live performance and temporary work (1999), furniture (2001), shipbuilding (2003), audiovisual, local and regional government, and chemicals (2004) (see Table above).

Concluding Observations on the "Original Functional Ambiguity" of Social Dialogue: Consultation or Negotiation?

We have seen from this detailed account of the evolution of European sectoral bodies that all of them, since the very outset, have served the basic purpose of consultation by the European executive. Bipartite autonomous negotiations between the players, on the other hand, have materialised only in a very few cases. This causes us to reflect on the key role of the Commission in this lengthy process, and on what we might call the "original ambiguity" of social dialogue. Which is it, consultation or negotiation?

A simplified definition of sectoral social dialogue might be that it is a set of "frameworks" (joint committees, informal working parties and then SSDCs) and functions (joint action, consultation and negotiation[40]) serving to involve the social partners in European-level decision-making. Having charted the history of the social dialogue bodies, or "frameworks", we shall now take a moment to compare the actual execution of its two main functions (consultation and negotiation), in an effort to better understand its continuity, beyond what is immediately apparent. As we have seen, the Commission considers it essential that workers' and employers' representatives be consulted by the European institutions, this being the founding principle for all the sectoral structures described in this chapter. Not only does consultation lend support

---

[39] A typology of the agreements implemented is given in the 2004 Communication (CEC, 2004).

[40] We shall not refer here to another possible function of dialogue: concertation, which is of more relevance at cross-industry level.

and legitimacy to Community policies; it also contributes the expertise of the many national organisations concerned.

In historical terms, we should remember that "although joint action and consultation have developed gradually throughout the 40 years of existence of the Community (without necessarily using these terms), the concept of negotiation was accepted only much later in Article 118a of the Single Act" (Degimbe, 1999: 190). This article stipulates that "The Commission shall endeavour to develop the dialogue between management and labour at European level which could, if the two sides consider it desirable, lead to relations based on agreement". The two sides do not in fact seem to have considered it desirable, given the paucity of agreements signed between the social partners where we could refer to contractual relations. Rather, the description given in this chapter has revealed that in actual fact most sectoral bodies have almost exclusively pursued their consultative remit. Only in a small number of very specific sectors (basically the Agriculture joint committee) has a more autonomous dialogue developed. This is not spelled out in Commission texts, however, since the Commission has always been somewhat ambivalent about the blurred line between consultation and negotiation.

It should be pointed out that, interestingly, this ambiguity as to the function of social dialogue has existed since the outset. The Commission has always held that the two former types of sectoral committee (joint and informal) "fulfilled the same role and the same functions *mutatis mutandis*" (CEC, 1995: 27). In its view, these bodies had two main aims: as a focal point for potential consultations on social policy matters, and to initiate their own joint activities or even sectoral negotiations. This "potential" for negotiation can be found in all subsequent documents on the social dialogue.

The establishment of the new committees from 1998 onwards has changed nothing from a qualitative point of view. The underlying principle has always been that the social partners desire to meet for these same two reasons: consultation and (potential) negotiation. This fundamental ambiguity seems not to have been resolved, in the meantime, by the signature of the Social Policy Agreement in 1991, even though its provisions set out the specific procedures for each of these two functions at Community level.

What is even more interesting is the fact that, even when agreements actually are negotiated between the social partners, this still occurs in the context of consultation by the Commission. Indeed, the interpretation of Article 4(139)(1) of the Social Policy Agreement given in the 1993 Communication concerning its application reveals that the negotiation in question must take place as part of a procedure which is undoubtedly original but nonetheless remains a consultation procedure.

The ambiguity persists today, with most of the SSDCs still prioritising the consultative dimension of their activities rather than the autonomous dimension, while keeping alive hopes of negotiation.

Finally, as we have shown, the enduring potential of autonomous negotiation is largely overshadowed by the reality of consultation about Community policies, mainly but not exclusively in the field of social affairs.

References

Benedictus, H., de Boer, R., van der Meer, M., Salverda, W., Visser, J. and Zijl, M. (2002), "The European Social Dialogue: Development, Sectoral Variation and Prospects", report to the Ministry of Social Affairs and Employment, Amsterdam Institute for Advanced Labour Studies, The Hague, December 2002.

Bercusson, B. (1998), "The Treaty of Amsterdam: Strengthening Social Dialogue and EC Labour Law", in Gabaglio, E. and Hoffmann, R. (eds.), *European Trade Union Yearbook 1997*, European Trade Union Institute, Brussels, pp.45-66.

CEC (1987a), Commission Decision 87/467/EEC of 31 July 1987 Setting up a Joint Committee on Maritime Transport, OJ L 253 of 4 September 1987, pp.0020-0022.

CEC (1987b), "Towards a Dynamic European Economy", Green Paper on the Development of the Common Market for Telecommunications Services and Equipment, COM (87) 290, June 1987.

CEC (1990a), Commission Decision 90/450/EEC of 30 July 1990 Setting up a Joint Committee on Telecommunications Services, OJ L 230 of 24 August 1990, pp.0025-0027.

CEC (1990b), Commission Decision 90/449/EEC of 30 July 1990 Setting up a Joint Committee on Civil Aviation, OJ L 230 of 24 August 1990, pp.0022-0024.

CEC (1991), Green Paper on the Development of the Single Market for Postal Services (Commission Communication), COM (91) 476, June 1991.

CEC (1992), "Le dialogue social sectoriel", Internal Commission Document, DG Employment, Industrial Relations and Social Affairs, 17 July 1992.

CEC (1993), Communication concerning the Application of the Agreement on Social Policy Presented by the Commission, COM (93) 600 final of 14 December 1993 (http://europa.eu.int/comm/employment_social/ social_dialogue/docs/comm1993_en.pdf).

CEC (1994), Commission Decision 94/595/EC of 27 July 1994 Setting up a Joint Committee on Postal Services, OJ L 225 of 31 August 1994, pp.0031-0033.

CEC (1995), *Dialogue social: le bilan communautaire en 1995*, Directorate General for Employment, Industrial Relations and Social Affairs, Luxembourg.

CEC (1996), Commission Communication concerning the Development of the Social Dialogue at Community Level, COM (96) 448 final of 18 September

1996 (http://europa.eu.int/comm/employment_social/social_dialogue/docs/com_96_448_en.pdf).

CEC (1997), White Paper on Sectors and Activities Excluded from the Working Time Directive, COM (97) 334 final of 15 July 1997.

CEC (1997-2000), "European Social Dialogue", Newsletter from the European Commission, DGV/D, Nos.1 to 15.

CEC (1998a), "European Social Dialogue", "Working Time and Excluded Sectors", Newsletter from the European Commission, DGV/D, No.7 (http://europa.eu.int/comm/employment_social/social_dialogue/newsletter/news7_en.pdf).

CEC (1998b), Commission Decision of 20 May 1998 on the Establishment of Sectoral Dialogue Committees Promoting the Dialogue between the Social Partners at European Level, OJ L 225 of 12 August 1998, pp.0027-0028.

CEC (1998c), Commission Communication "Adapting and Promoting the Social Dialogue at Community Level", COM (98) 322 of 20 May 1998 (http://europa.eu.int/comm/employment_social/social_dialogue/docs/com322_en.pdf).

CEC (2000), *Industrial Relations in Europe – 2000*, Office of Official Publications of the European Communities, Luxembourg (http://europa.eu.int/comm/employment_social/social_dialogue/docs/report2000_en.pdf).

CEC (2004), Communication from the Commission "Partnership for Change in an Enlarged Europe – Enhancing the Contribution of European Social Dialogue", COM (2004) 557 final of 12 August 2004 (http://europa.eu.int/comm/employment_social/news/2004/aug/com_final_en.pdf).

Council of the European Communities (1969), Regulation (EEC) No.543/69 of the Council of 25 March 1969 on the Harmonisation of Certain Social Legislation relating to Road Transport, OJ L 77 of 29 March 1969, pp.0049-0060.

Council of the European Communities (1991), Council Directive 91/440/EEC of 29 July 1991 on the Development of the Community's Railways, OJ L 237 of 24 August 1991, pp.0025-0028.

Council of the European Union (1993), Council Directive 93/104/EC of 23 November 1993 concerning Certain Aspects of the Organisation of Working Time, OJ L 307 of 13 December 1993, pp.0018-0024.

Council of the European Union (1996), Council Directive 96/48/EC of 23 July 1996 on the Interoperability of the Trans-European High-speed Rail System, OJ L 235 of 17 September 1996, pp.0006-0024.

Council of the European Union (1997), Directive 97/67/EC of the European Parliament and of the Council of 15 December 1997 on Common Rules for the Development of the Internal Market of Community Postal Services and the Improvement of Quality of Service, OJ L 15 of 21 January 1998, pp.0014-0025.

Council of the European Union (1999), Council Directive 1999/63/EC of 21 June 1999 concerning the Agreement on the Organisation of Working Time of Seafarers Concluded by the European Community Shipowners' Association (ECSA) and the Federation of Transport Workers' Unions in the European Union (FST) – Annex: European Agreement on the Organisation of Working Time of Seafarers, OJ L 167 of 2 July 1999, pp.0033-0037.

Council of the European Union (2000), Council Directive 2000/79/EC of 27 November 2000 concerning the European Agreement on the Organisation of Working Time of Mobile Workers in Civil Aviation Concluded by the Association of European Airlines (AEA), the European Transport Workers' Federation (ETF), the European Cockpit Association (ECA), the European Regions Airline Association (ERA) and the International Air Carrier Association (IACA), OJ L 302 of 1st December 2000, pp.0057-0060.

De Boer, R., Benedictus, H. and van der Meer, M. (2005), "Broadening without Intensification: The Added Value of the European Social and Sectoral Dialogue", *European Journal of Industrial Relations*, Vol.11, No.1, pp.51-70.

Degimbe, J. (1999), *La politique sociale européenne, du traité de Rome au traité d'Amsterdam*, European Trade Union Institute, Brussels.

Didry, C. and Mias, A. (2005), "Au-delà des politiques de l'emploi: le temps de travail à la recherche d'une représentation des travailleurs", in Laulom, S. (ed.), *Recomposition des systèmes de représentation des salariés en Europe*, Université de Saint-Étienne, Saint-Étienne, pp.81-112.

Dufresne, A. (2002), "La branche, niveau stratégique de la coordination des négociations collectives?", *Chronique Internationale de l'IRES*, No.74, January 2002, pp.59-70.

ETUI (1993), *Les comités syndicaux européens et le dialogue social: expériences au niveau des secteur et dans les multinationales*, European Trade Union Institute, September 1993, Brussels.

European Parliament and Council of the European Union (1996), Directive 96/71/EC of the European Parliament and of the Council of 16 December 1996 concerning the Posting of Workers in the Framework of the Provision of Services, OJ L 18 of 21 January 1997, pp.0001-0006.

European Parliament and Council of the European Union (2000), Directive 2000/34/EC of the European Parliament and of the Council of 22 June 2000 Amending Council Directive 93/104/EC concerning Certain Aspects of the Organisation of Working Time to Cover Sectors and Activities Excluded from that Directive, OJ L 195 of 1st August 2000, pp.0041-0045.

European Parliament and Council of the European Union (2001a), Directive 2001/12/EC of the European Parliament and of the Council of 26 February 2001 Amending Council Directive 91/440/EEC on the Development of the Community's Railways, OJ L 75 of 15 March 2001, pp.0001-0025.

European Parliament and Council of the European Union (2001b), Directive 2001/16/EC of the European Parliament and of the Council of 19 March 2001 on the Interoperability of the Trans-European Conventional Rail System, OJ L 110 of 20 April 2001, pp.0001-0027.

Gobin C. (1996a), *Consultation et concertation sociales à l'échelle de la CEE. Études des positions et stratégies de la Confédération européenne des syndicats (1958-1991)*, Doctoral Thesis, Université Libre de Bruxelles, 2nd edition in two volumes, Vol.1: 1-590 and Vol.2: 591-976.

Gobin C. (1996b), Interview with Eddy Klöcker, Secretary General of the EFA, in Témoignages historiques, Annex XI, pp.161-165, in Gobin C. (ed.), *Consultation et concertation sociales à l'échelle de la CEE. Études des positions et stratégies de la Confédération européenne des syndicats (1958-1991)*, Doctoral Thesis, Université Libre de Bruxelles, 2nd edition in two volumes, Vol.1: 1-590 and Vol.2: 591-976.

Jobert, A (ed.) (2005), "Les nouveaux cadres du dialogue social: l'espace européen et les territories", *Final report for the Commissariat général du plan*, Convention No.2003/10, Paris.

Keller, B. and Bansbach, M. (2000), "The Transport Sector as an Example of Sectoral Social Dialogue in the EU – Recent Developments and Prospects", *Transfer*, Vol.6, No.1, pp.115-124.

Keller, B. and Sörries, B. (1998), "The Sectoral Social Dialogue and European Social Policy: More Fantasy, Fewer Facts", *European Journal of Industrial Relations*, Vol.4, No.3, pp.331-348.

Lyon-Caen, G. (1972), *A la recherche de la convention collective européenne*, Study for the Commission of the European Communities, Brussels.

Nunin, R. (2001), *Il dialogo sociale europeo. Attori, procedure, prospettive*, Giuffrè, Milan.

OSE (2006), "European Sectoral Social Dialogue 1997-2004?", *Discussion Working Paper*, ETUI-REHS, Brussels (forthcoming).

Salesse, Y. (2001), *Réformes et révolution – proposition pour une gauche de gauche*, Agone, Marseille.

Sörries, B. (1999), *Europäisierung der Arbeitsbeziehungen, der soziale Dialog und seine Akteure*, Mehring, Munich.

Weber, T. (2001) "The European Sectoral Social Dialogue" in Compston, H. and Greenwood, J. (eds.), *Social Partnership in the European Union*, Houndsmills, Palgrave, pp.129-153.

List of Interviews

PostEurop (2004), Postal services, Paris, 28 January 2004.

ETF (2004a), Sea transport, Brussels, 26 January 2004.

ETF (2004b), Civil aviation, Brussels, 9 January 2004.

List of Cited Joint Documents

Agriculture

EFA, COPA, Agreement on the harmonization of working hours of permanent agricultural workers in the EC arable farming sector, 22 March 1978

EFA, COPA, Agreement on the harmonization of working hours of permanent agricultural workers in the EC livestock farming sector, 10 June 1980

GEOPA/COPA, EFA/CES, Recommendation framework agreement on the improvement of paid employment in agriculture in the Member States of the European Union, 24 July 1997

GEOPA/COPA, EFFAT, European agreement on vocational training in agriculture, 5 December 2002

Accord relatif à la prévention des troubles musculo-squelettiques, 21 November 2005

Civil Aviation

AEA, ETF, ECA, ERA, AICA, European agreement on the organisation of working time of mobile staff in civil aviation concluded by the Association of European Airlines (AEA), the European Transport Workers' Federation (ETF), the European Cockpit Association (ECA), the European Regions Airline Association (ERA) and the International Air Carrier Association (IACA), 22 March 2000

Railways

CER, ETF, Opinion of the Joint Committee on Railways on the communication from the Commission on the development of the Community's railways, 8 February 1996

CER, ETF, Common position adopted by the joint committee on railways on the White Paper of the European Commission entitled "A strategy for revitalising Community railways", 3 June 1997a

CER, ETF, Common opinion of the joint committee on railways on the effects of the establishment of the freeways, 3 June 1997b

CER, ETF, Joint Opinion on the Organization of Working Time, 3 June 1997c

CER, ETF, Agreement on some aspects of the organisation of working time in the rail transport sector, 30 September 1998

CER, FST, Joint opinion of the Community of European Railways and Federation of European Transport Unions on the "Infrastructure package" as presented by the European Commission, 8 June 1999

Construction

FIEC, EFBWW Joint FIEC-EFBWW Position (Directive 96/71/EC), 23 September 1997

Sea Fisheries

EFA, Europêche, *Déclaration commune des organisations professionnelles de la pêche maritime concernant l'harmonisation sociale dans le progrès des conditions de vie et de travail*, 7 June 1972

Sea Transport

FST, ECSA, European agreement on the organisation of working time of seafarers, 30 September 1998

Textiles

ETUF:TCL, Euratex, Joint opinion on improved access to vocational training for women in the textile and clothing sector, 16 June 1994

Sommet de Lisbonne: contribution des partenaires sociaux du secteur textile-habillement, 1 March 2000

Annex: Joint Committees on Social Problems and *Advisory Committees*

FIRST GENERATION

Sector	**Background to decisions taken** (see complete references below)	**Composition of organisations representing *workers* and employers***	**Working groups**
Agriculture	17/05/1963 (63/326/EEC) (Joint AC) amended 25/07/1974 (74/442/EEC)	56 members including ▪25 GEOPA/COPA ▪25 *EFA* ▪6 others	Training, safety, employment, harmonisation, statistics and forestry
	19/12/1963 (64/19/EEC) AC on the social problems of farmers	23 members ▪5 workers ▪17 farm managers ▪1 rural family	
	1962/1964 Product-based agricultural ACs**	50% producers 25% workers 25% reps. industry + trade + consumers	
	29/07/1964 AC on agricultural structural policy problems	36 members incl. 8 workers	
Road Transport	05/07/1965 (+2) (65/632/EEC) amended 18/01/1985 (85/516/EEC) amended 31/07/1987 (87/447/EEC)	54 members ▪24 from IRU ▪24 from *CTWUEC* ▪6 others	– drafting of a work programme – cab dimensions + ad hoc groups: * vocational training * new technology * working time
Inland Waterways	28/11/1967 (67/745/EEC) (Joint AC) 09/10/1980 (80/991/EEC)	30 members 44 members ▪ 22 UINF, OEB ▪ 22 *CTWUEC*	– vocational training – health and safety – living & working conditions elsewhere than the Rhine (est. 1985)
Sea Fishing	07/06/1968 (68/252/EEC) (Joint AC) amended 25/07/1974 (74/441/EEC) amended 31/07/1987 (87/446/EEC)	Equal representation 54 members: ▪24 Europêche/Cogeca ▪24 *CTWUEC* ▪6 incl.: * 3 employers * 1 *CGT* * 1 *CCOO* * 1 *inter-union*	– vocational training – health & safety – employment & social harmonisation – environment
	25/02/1971 (71/128/EEC)	43 members: incl. 6 *workers* Producers, cooperatives, banks, distributors, consumers	

Railways	24/04/1972 (72/172/EEC) not operational from 1976 to 1982 new status: 19/12/1984 (85/13/EEC)	44 members: ▪22 CER ▪22 *CTWUEC*	– social aspects of the common railway policy – social aspects of the introduction of new technology and high-speed trains – experts groups on working time

* Corresponds to the number of representatives of Community-level professional organisations as well as the various representatives designated by the Commission from organisations other than these.

** There are eight product-based agricultural Advisory Committees, five of which were established in 1962: cereals, pigmeat, eggs and poultry, fruit and vegetables, and wine; and three in 1964: milk and dairy, beef, and rice.

SECOND GENERATION

Sector	**Background to decisions taken** (see complete references below)	**Composition of organisations representing *workers* and employers***	Working groups
Sea Transport	31/07/1987 (87/467/EEC)	42 members: ▪18 ECSA ▪18 *CTWUEC* ▪6 others	– EUROS (European flag and register) – positive measures for sea transport – WG on working time
Civil Aviation	30/07/1990 (90/449/EEC)	54 members ▪24 employers * 13 AEA, 3 ERA, 3 ACE, 2 ACCA & 3 ACI ▪24 *CTWUEC* ▪6 others	– working time – working conditions of cabin crews
Telecommunications	30/07/1990 (90/450/EEC)	50 members ▪22 public & private operators ▪*22 PTTI/Eurofedop* ▪6 *non-affiliates of PTTI (especially CGT)*	– sectoral policies – employment & vocational training developments – health & safety if necessary: * WG on working conditions * WG on worker involvement in the life of the company
Postal Services	27/07/1994 (94/595/EC)	54 members ▪ 27 public & private operators ▪ 27, incl. * 20 *PTTI* * 4 *Eurofedop* * 3 *non-affiliates of PTTI (especially CGT)*	Sectoral policies Working conditions Employment & vocational training Health & safety Worker involvement in the life of the company

* Corresponds to the number of representatives of Community-level professional organisations as well as the various representatives designated by the Commission from organisations other than these.

Source: Compiled by the author on the basis of CEC (1995), CEC (1992) and Gobin (1996a).

FIRST GENERATION

Agriculture	Commission Decision 63/326/EEC of 17 May 1963 setting up a Joint Advisory Committee on Social Questions affecting Paid Agricultural Workers, OJ 80 of 29 May 1963, page 1534. Commission Decision 64/19/EEC of 19 December 1963 amending the Commission Decision of 17 May 1963 setting up a Joint Advisory Committee on Social Questions affecting Paid Agricultural Workers, OJ 2 of 10 January 1964, pp.0027-0028. Commission Decision 74/442/EEC of 25 July 1974 relating to the setting-up of a Joint Committee on Social Problems of Agricultural Workers, OJ L 243 of 5 September 1974, pp.0022-0024.
Road Transport	Commission Decision 65/632/EEC of 5 July 1965 relating to the setting-up of Joint Advisory Committee on Social Questions arising in Road Transport, Commission Decision 85/516/EEC of 18 November 1985 setting up a Joint Committee on Road Transport, OJ L 317 of 28 November 1985, pp.0033-0035. Commission Decision 87/447/EEC of 31 July 1987 amending Commission Decision 85/516/EEC relating to the setting up of a Joint Committee on Road Transport, OJ L 240 of 22 August 1987, pp.0037-0038.
Inland Waterways	Commission Decision 67/745/EEC of 28 November 1967 setting up a Joint Advisory Committee on Social Questions arising in Inland Navigation, OJ 297 of 7 December 1967, pp.0013-0015. Commission Decision 80/991/EEC of 9 October 1980 setting up a Joint Committee on Inland Navigation, OJ L 297 of 6 November 1980, pp.0028-0030.
Sea Fishing	Commission Decision 68/252/EEC of 7 June 1968 setting up a Joint Advisory Committee on Social Questions arising in the Sea Fishing Industry, OJ L 132 of 14 June 1968, pp.0009-0011. Commission Decision 74/441/EEC of 25 July 1974 relating to the setting-up of a Joint Committee on Social Problems in Sea Fishing, OJ L 243 of 5 September 1974, pp.0019-0021. Commission Decision 87/446/EEC of 31 July 1987 amending Decision 74/441/EEC relating to the setting up of a Joint Committee on Social Problems in Sea Fishing, OJ L 240 of 22 August 1987, pp.0035-0036. Commission Decision 71/128/EEC of 25 February 1971, relating to the setting-up of an Advisory Committee on Sea Fishing, OJ L 68 of 22 March 1971, pp.0018-0020.
Railways	Commission Decision 72/172/EEC of 24 April 1972 setting up a Joint Advisory Committee on Social Questions arising in the Railway Industry, OJ L 104 of 3 May 1972, pp.0009. Commission Decision 85/13/EEC of 19 December 1984 relating to the setting up of a Joint Committee on Railways, OJ L 008 of 10 January 1985, pp.0026-0028.

SECOND GENERATION

Sea Transport	Commission Decision 87/467/EEC of 31 July 1987 setting up a Joint Committee on Maritime Transport, OJ L 253 of 4 September 1987, pp.0020-0022.
Civil Aviation	Commission Decision 90/449/EEC of 30 July 1990 setting up a Joint Committee on Civil Aviation, OJ L 230 of 24 August 1990, pp.0022-0024.
Telecommunications	Commission Decision 90/450/EEC of 30 July 1990 setting up a Joint Committee on Telecommunications Services, OJ L 230 of 24 August 1990, pp.0025-0027.
Postal Services	Commission Decision 94/595/EC of 27 July 1994 setting up a Joint Committee on Postal Services, OJ L 225 of 31 August 1994, pp.0031-0033.

CHAPTER 3

A Quantitative Analysis[1]

Philippe POCHET

The development of cross-industry social dialogue has been presented in various books and articles (Dølvik, 1999; Degryse, 2003; Keller and Sörries, 1999a and b; Keller and Bansbach, 2000, Branch, 2005). Scholars have been interested in the actors' strategy (Arcq *et al.*, 2003; Branch and Greenwood, 2001; Braud, 1998; Dølvik and Visser, 2001; Gobin, 1996; Groux *et al.*, 1993; Tyszkiewicz, 1999) or in the results (Degryse, 2000; Falkner, 2003; Keller and Sörries, 1997, Keller, 2005). Traditionally, cross-industry social dialogue is presented as having developed in three phases: a) the emergence from the Single Act to Maastricht; b) the consolidation from Maastricht to 2000; c) the uncertain time from the autonomous joint programme to today (Bureau du plan, 2005).

On the other hand, sectoral social dialogue has attracted less attention until now. This lack of interest is all the more surprising in that most negotiations in the vast majority of Member States (EU-15) actually take place at sectoral level (see, for example, the *Industrial Relations Report* 2004). Only very recently have there been any multi-sector, cross-cutting studies which adopt both a quantitative and a qualitative approach (Benedictus *et al.* 2002; de Boer *et al.*, 2005; Dufresne, 2002; OSE, 2004; CEC, 2004; Nordestgaard and Kirton-Darling, 2004; Pochet and Degryse, 2005; Weber, 2001, special issue of *Transfer*, 2005). All

1 The analysis of agreements between 1978 and 1996 and for the year 2004/2005 at sectoral level was conducted together with Christophe Degryse, and for the period 1997 to 2003 with Anne Dufresne and Christophe Degryse. The analysis for 1997-2003 is contained in chapter 3 of the quantitative and qualitative analysis of a study commissioned by the European Commission (No.VC/2003/0400 – SI2.365647). I subsequently classified the 52 documents issued by the cross-industry social partners (1986 to date) according to the categories we used for the sectoral social dialogue. Special thanks to Dominique Jadot for retrieving the documents and to Renaud Smoes for preparing the tables. This chapter was also part of a research project on new forms of governance Newgov (for more detail see www.newgov.org) coordinated by the European Institute of Florence and funded by the sixth EU research framework programme.

of these studies stressed that the type of documents adopted by the sectoral social partners was undergoing a qualitative change. At the same time the cross-industry social dialogue seems to have entered into a crisis, as the last legally binding agreement was signed in 1999. In the new century, the cross-industry social partners have only signed soft law agreements (e.g. telework, stress, life-long learning).

In other words, it appeared that significant developments were underway which needed to be better understood, analysed and assessed. Such an initiative posed two challenges: one quantitative, since there were no standardised data concerning texts signed after 1997 (when the European Commission published a compendium of earlier texts, 1995 and 1997), and the other qualitative, related to the precise nature of the texts adopted. How should they be described? How should they be classified?

At the Observatoire social européen we have created a database including all the joint documents signed by the social partners at European level covering the 31 official sectoral committees and the cross-industry social dialogue. This article will present the results of a quantitative analysis covering all 385 agreements adopted since 1978 at sectoral level and 52 at cross-industry level. This analysis is based on the reading and classification of all "agreements" signed since 1978 at sectoral level. We then classified the documents issued by the cross-industry social partners according to the categories we used for the sectoral social dialogue. In the course of the work with Anne Dufresne and Christophe Degryse we identified a six-category classification of the joint documents produced by the social dialogue actors (see below).

From this quantitative analysis we can already detect certain overall trends on the emergence of and evolution affecting the sectoral social dialogue and compare the dynamics with the cross-industry social dialogue. The qualitative aspects and a typology of the sectors will be examined in the next chapter.

This article is structured in four main parts. First we classify the texts adopted into six categories: "agreements", "recommendations", "declarations", "rules of procedure", "tools" and "common positions". Then we briefly set out the main stages leading up to the formation of the 31 sectoral committees now in existence and the developments at cross-industry level. The two main parts are part 3 and part 4, which present the findings from our data. The third describes the developments in the sectoral social dialogue, analysing the different dimensions (number of documents, type, topics, and to whom they are addressed). The fourth part follows the same line but at the cross-industry level. Then we draw some conclusions.

I. The Texts Adopted: A Clarification

The official titles of the joint documents vary considerably: common positions, declarations, resolutions, proposals, guidelines, recommendations, codes of conduct, social labels, etc. It is not possible to create meaningful categories on the basis of the official designations. We shall refer to them generically as "joint texts" or "joint documents".

We distinguish between "reciprocal commitments between the social partners, and common positions", i.e. documents intended for the public authorities (first and foremost the Commission, but it also could be the Council or national governments). With regard to "reciprocal commitments", we distinguish between "tools", "declarations", "recommendations" and "agreements". Each is addressed to the social partners but the degree of constraint is different. The last category is "rules of procedure", laying down the rules of the game. These categories allow us to test the hypothesis that the social dialogue is increasingly taking place between the social partners or mainly addressed to the public authorities.

We can also test whether we notice a trend from non-binding to more binding documents or whether the story is more complex. Having all the joint texts from the beginning of the social dialogue process, this gives us a time frame for which we have distinguished two sub-periods. From the beginning to 1998 (when the Commission issued a Communication creating the new sectoral committees and giving them a dual goal of consultation and of negotiating agreements) and 1998 to today. We do not use sub-periods for the cross-industry social dialogue as it is not relevant.

Before analysing the tables, let us spell out the differences in more detail.

a) Agreements: This category corresponds to agreements initiated between the European social partners (pursuant to Article 139), intended for national organisations and with a follow-up procedure determining precise mechanisms and deadlines for implementation. Agreements may or may not be converted into directives.

b) Recommendations: This category comprises texts whose provisions are drawn up by the European social partners, intended for national organisations and for which a follow-up and evaluation procedure is laid down at national and European level. There is deemed to be follow-up if the text of the joint document sets out (reasonably precise) procedures for national implementation and for a European-level evaluation of this follow-up at a given point in time. This is therefore a procedural definition. Follow-up as defined here should not be confused with implementation, which relates to substantive aspects.

c) Declarations: This category corresponds to "declarations of intent" drawn up by the European social partners, intended for national organisations or for themselves, and where no explicit follow-up procedures are set out in the text or where the procedure is vague.

d) Tools (for training and action): This category comprises various sub-categories: studies (only studies carried out jointly by the social partners and not by European and/or national consultants); handbooks; glossaries or databases.

e) Rules of procedure: Rules of procedure are recognition agreements between the social partners.

f) Common positions: This category corresponds to texts addressed to the European institutions. These texts may be produced under very different circumstances. Sometimes the prime purpose of a common position is very obvious but, in other cases, it may be vague due to being watered down by the numerous matters covered.

It should be noted that our categories are not exactly the same as those proposed by the Commission in its Communication (2004) aimed at clarifying the nature of the joint documents adopted by the social partners (see Dufresne in this volume).

II. The Main Institutional Developments at Sectoral and Cross-industry Level

These developments have been presented in detail in the two first chapters of this volume. Here we summarise the main points pertaining to the purpose of this chapter. Originally the bodies serving for the consultation of the European social partners were joint committees, established by the European Commission. A first wave of six joint committees was formed in the sectors covered by the "integrated" common policies: mines (1952), agriculture (1963/1974)[2], road transport (1965), inland waterways (1980), fishing (1974) and railways (1972). Their members were appointed by the Commission, with an equal number of employers and employees. Informal working parties, set up at the request of the social partners, began to appear during the 1980s. They provided for a more pragmatic and flexible form of social dialogue, as well as being more informal. Such working parties were formed in a number of sectors with the Commission's backing: Horeca (1983), commerce (1985), insurance (1987), banking (1990), etc. A second wave of joint committees took shape in the late 1980s and early

---

2 The social dialogue began in 1963 but the committee was not formally established until 1974.

1990s in the following sectors: sea transport (1987), civil aviation (1990), telecommunications (1990) and postal services (1994).

In 1985, the Single Act introduced a provision recognising the social partners and allowing them to hold a dialogue. With the support of the President of the Commission, Jacques Delors, cross-industry social dialogue between ETUC, UNICE and CEEP began.

The 1991 Social Protocol laid down a legal framework which opened up new scope for dialogue at cross-industry level as well as in the various sectors. The entry into force of the Maastricht Treaty (and its Social Protocol) resulted in an obligation on the Commission to consult the social partners prior to the adoption of a legislative proposal, and the possibility for them to sign collective agreements which may either be extended *erga omnes* by means of a Council directive or else be implemented by the social partners themselves at national level.

The cross-industry social partners agreed on three collective agreements transformed into a directive by the Council (parental leave, part-time work, fixed-term contracts). They failed to agree on others, such as works councils or information/consultation at national level. The turning point was the failure in 2001 of the negotiations on temporary agency work, which should have been the last text on atypical employment (after the fixed-term and part-time agreements).

Concerning the sectoral level, following its framework decision of 20 May 1998 (CEC, 1998) the Commission decided on 1 January 1999 to harmonise the system, replacing the two former types of body with sectoral social dialogue committees (SSDCs), "intended to promote dialogue between the social partners at European level". Thus the sectoral social dialogue was put on an institutional footing as an extension of the cross-industry social dialogue initiated at Val Duchesse in 1985.

The number of sectoral social dialogue committees (SSDCs) has grown since the reform: the sectors organised into committees increased from 20 in 1998 to 31 in 2004. By contrast, certain sectors with a tradition of national collective bargaining are not represented, for example metalworking and public services (see chapter 8 in this volume).

As far as the cross-industry social dialogue is concerned, the turning point was represented by the social partners' autonomous work programme (2002-2005) which seeks to increase the degree of autonomy from the Commission. Even though there have been numerous measures, the number of joint documents negotiated with potential binding effects is limited (Degryse, 2005). At the time of writing, a new programme (2006-2010) is under review by ETUC, UNICE and CEEP.

III. A Qualitative Analysis of Sectoral Joint Documents

We will examine the number of documents adopted both globally and per sector. We then disaggregate these data year by year in a table, stating in how many years each sector has signed one or more text(s) and how many sectors have signed one or more text(s) per year. Section 4 analyses the types of texts adopted in relation to the six categories defined below. The next step is to look more closely at the themes covered, based on 11 topic areas: a) Health and safety b) Training c) Employment d) Working time e) Social dialogue f) Enlargement g) Working conditions h) Non-discrimination (including equality between men and women) i) Sustainable development j) Economic and/or sectoral policies k) Social aspects of Community policies. Last of all we shall consider the addressees of these texts.

Our analysis will be based on two periods. The first period covers all documents since the very outset, i.e. beginning with the first joint document in 1978 on working time in agriculture; the second period runs from 1998 onwards, the date when it was decided to establish the new social dialogue committees. Even though these were only set up from 1999 onwards, we have kept 1998 as the starting date because that is when the Commission clearly stated that it expected to see a renewed sectoral social dialogue.

A. Number of Documents

The social dialogue resulted in 385 joint texts during the period under investigation (1978-2005).

Since the very first joint text was signed in the sectoral social dialogue in 1978, the yearly distribution reveals a significant increase in their numbers. Yet the increase is not continuous and there are sharp fluctuations from one year to another (see for example 2002 and 2003). In addition, more documents were signed after 1998 than between 1978 and 1997 (that year alone accounted for 32 joint documents). Finally, the number of documents began to rise in 1996, two years before the formation of the new committees.

Figure 1: Number of Documents per Year (1978-2005) (385 documents)

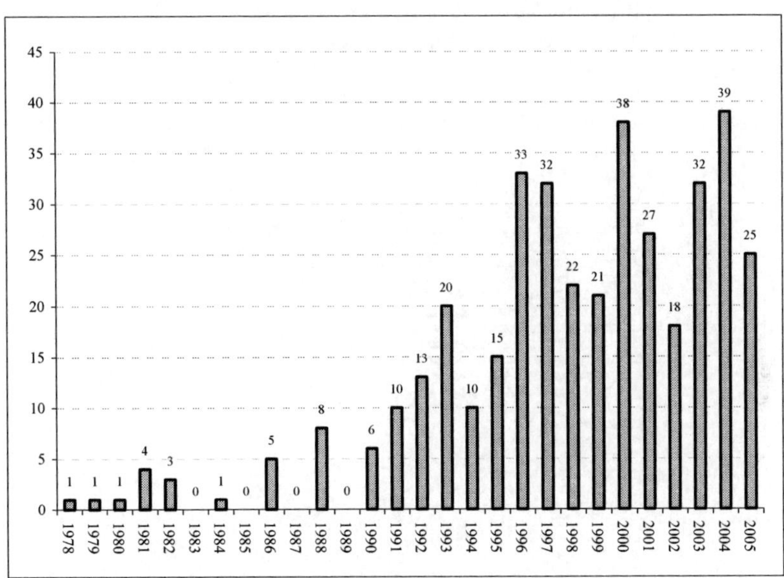

Source: Observatoire social européen, own database.

We should sound a methodological note of caution here: there have been more committees as time has gone by, and it is therefore quite natural to find a growing number of joint documents. Table 2 shows the total number of committees (officially established) by year. The second row shows the number of committees at the time when they signed their first agreement. The difference between the two figures derives from the fact that once a committee is officially recognised we have included agreements signed earlier, when it was not yet official.

Table 1: Establishment of SSDCs and Dates of Signature of First Agreements, by Year

	1952	1965	1967	1969	1972	1974	1978	1982	1983	1985	1986	1987	1988	1990
No. of SSDCs	1	2	3	4	5	7	7	8	9	10		12		15
First text							1				2		4	7

	1991	1992	1993	1994	1995	1996	1997	1998	1999	2000	2001	2002	2003	2004
No. of SSDCs		18	19	21		23		24	27		28		29	31
First text	8	9	11	14	15	19	21	22	23	27	28	29	30	31

The 33 (Figure 1) agreements of 1996 (for 23 committees of which only 19 had already issued a joint text) are therefore more numerous in relative terms than the 27 documents (Figure 1) of 2001 for 28 committees. In the former case, each committee issued 1.5 texts on average; in the latter just one each. The following Figure shows the relative productivity of each sector.

Figure 2: Number of Documents per Sector – 1978-2005 (385 docs)

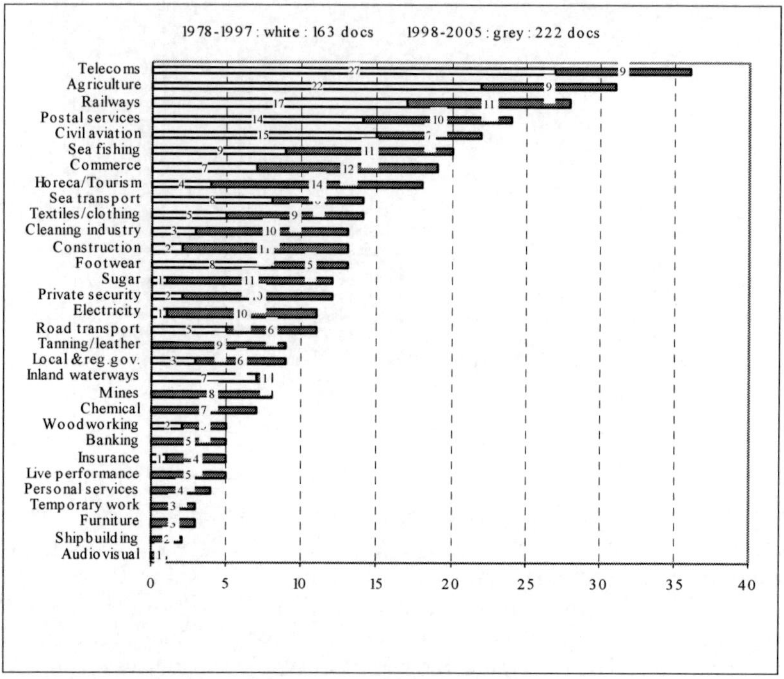

1978-1997 : white : 163 docs 1998-2005 : grey : 222 docs

Source: Observatoire social européen, own database.

There are highly significant differences between one sector and another. Five of them (telecoms, agriculture, railways, postal services and civil aviation) each signed more than 20 joint texts and account for more than a third of all joint documents. Nine sectors, on the other hand, signed five joint documents apiece or fewer: these are recently established committees for the most part. The sectors which were the most prolific before 1998 were no longer so thereafter. After 1998, Horeca, commerce, sea fishing, construction and sugar signed 11 or more documents.

Further detailed examination of the overall figures show in how many years (since 1998) there was one or more document(s) per sector. Only two sectors, sugar and commerce, signed one or more document(s) per year. Private security signed one in six years out of seven. Railways, Horeca/tourism, postal services, sea fishing, telecommunications and sea transport: five years out of seven. Moreover, five sectors signed no joint texts at all in 2003 and 2004: these are agriculture, footwear, personal services, textiles/clothing and temporary work.

One limitation of quantitative analysis is that, by its very nature, it focuses on figures. In actual fact, on the one hand, not all sectors are equally ambitious with regard to the quantity of texts they wish to produce; on the other, the generation of a large number of texts says nothing about the quality of those texts, nor about the internal dynamic at work. Such data alone, therefore, can certainly not be considered indicative of the vitality of dialogue in a sectoral committee. For example, Horeca is the sector which signed the most joint documents, but a careful analysis reveals the weakness of the content of these texts. Thus we must draw a distinction according to the types of document signed. It should also be noted that in other cases, such as textiles/clothing, the absence of any joint texts did not prevent the protagonists in the sector from cooperating intensively when confronted with the end of the multifibre agreements (see chapter 8 in this volume).

B. Types of Document

As stated above, we have defined six types of joint document: agreements, recommendations, declarations, tools, rules of procedure and common positions.

Figure 3: Number of Documents per Type (1978-2005)

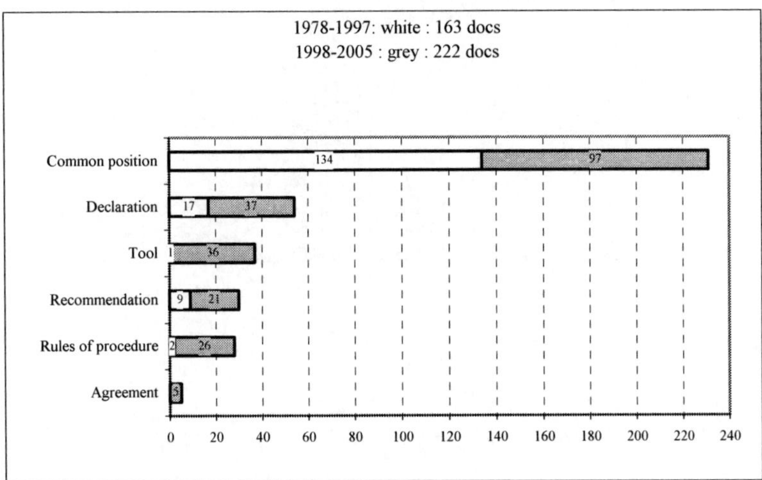

Source: Observatoire social européen, own database.

An analysis of all 385 documents reveals that a large majority of them – 231 (60%) – are common positions. Next come declarations – 54 – and then, in turn, tools (37), recommendations (30) and rules of procedure (28) and lastly agreements (5).

Therefore, if we interpret the social dialogue restrictively as the negotiation of binding agreements, "agreements" constitute fewer than 2% of all texts. Three of these are directly related to the sectoral implementation of the 1993 Working Time Directive in the transport sectors, in the wake of the European directive. The other two were signed in the rail transport sector in 2004 (for a detailed analysis see Hilal in this volume).

A somewhat different view is obtained by scrutinising the texts signed since 1998. 96 of these are common positions, which still constitute the largest category but now cover around 45% of all joint texts. Declarations, tools and recommendations are clearly gaining ground. The question now arising is how this move towards more social dialogue between social partners is distributed across time. The next table presents the results (1998-2005) on an annual basis so as to give a more precise idea.

Figure 4: Number of Documents by Type and by Year (1998-2005)

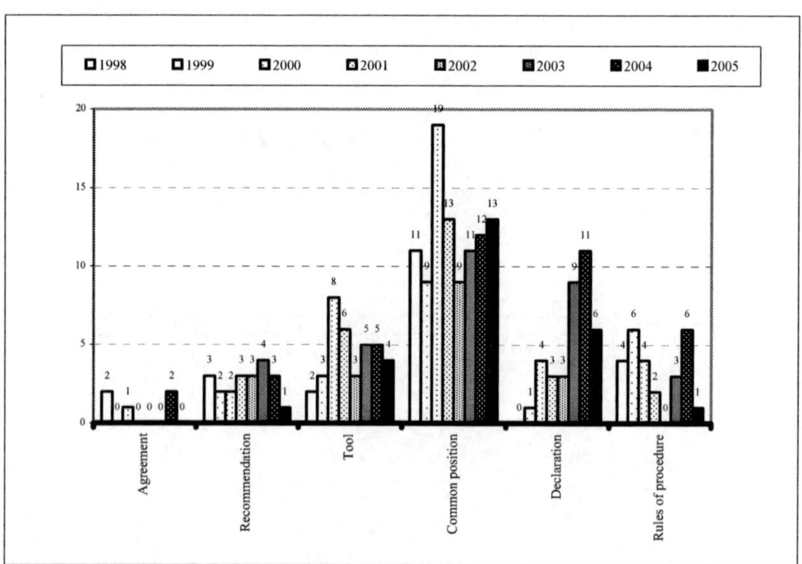

Source: Observatoire social européen, own database.

What is striking about the distribution of documents is that it seems erratic rather than representing a systematic year-on-year trend. There are clear peaks for tools, rules of procedure and declarations. Common positions seem to move within a corridor of between 9 and 13 texts per year except for 19 in 2000; recommendations between 1 and 4.

In 2003, for the first time, there were fewer common positions (11) than the sum of declarations, recommendations and agreements (13), i.e. joint commitments by the social partners. This seemed to indicate a shift from a social dialogue initially more prone to issue common positions addressed to the Community authorities, towards a social dialogue focusing more on internal social partner priorities. But 2005 did not confirm this trend. Of 23 joint texts, 13 were common positions. Only one was a recommendation and the sum of agreements, recommendations and declarations totalled 7. Only the results of the next few years will confirm whether the 2003/2004 results were a meaningful trend or just an exception.

Figure 5: Number of Types per Sector (1978-2005)

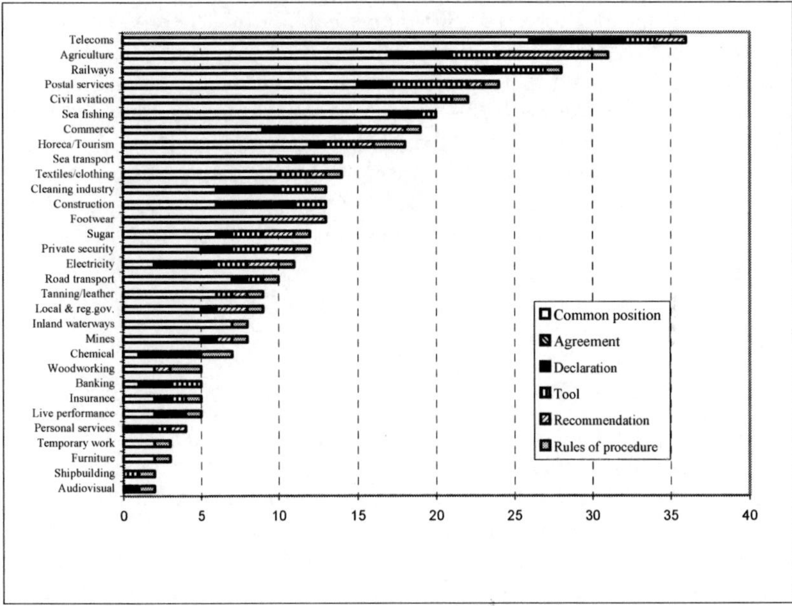

Source: Observatoire social européen, own database.

Between 1978 and 2005, 13 sectors adopted recommendations and three others, agreements. Interestingly, they are not the same ones. One might think that this outcome is mainly due to the implementation of the Working Time Directive, but we should add that the trade union side in the transport sector is reluctant to sign up to "soft" instruments such as recommendations (Noordestgaard and Kirton-Darling 2004). So-called recommendations are often codes of conduct or charters, as in the case of sugar, textiles, footwear, leather, woodworking and private security. Agriculture has adopted several recommendations on working time and has been a pioneer in this field. Three sectors – agriculture, electricity and sugar – have passed recommendations on training and one sector – agriculture – on health and safety issues.

We know extremely little about the effective implementation of recommendations: in many cases follow-up has been minimal and fragmentary (see chapter 10 on implementation in Sweden) and, as in textiles for example, has sometimes been set in motion after a delay of several years. The sugar code of conduct is innovative in that it arranges for precise follow-up of implementation with the publication of a summary document (see chapter 7 in this volume).

This figure also shows that 21 sectors out of 31 at best adopted declarations, a rather meagre achievement in terms of joint commitments.

A detailed sector-by-sector analysis (Benedictus *et al.*, 2002, de Boer *et al.*, 2005 and Pochet *et al.* 2004) makes plain that there is no general dynamic progressing from common positions to tools, declarations, recommendations and then agreements. In other words, an examination of each sector individually reveals no obvious gradual move towards more binding commitments in terms of follow-up. Thus the idea that the trust created between the actors in signing common positions can be translated into more binding agreements is not substantiated here. Meaningful trends in this direction can only be inferred from the sum of all the different sectors.

It is now time to turn our attention to content, and to analyse the topic areas covered by these joint documents.

C. Topic Areas Covered

Many joint documents are confused and deal with a variety of topics without their main objective emerging clearly. For a number of them we had to make a choice, which proved quite difficult in some cases[3]. We could not emphasise too strongly the need for caution when interpreting these results. For this reason we used several fields when constructing our database. Here we shall present the results for the main fields only.

The topic areas have been grouped into 11 categories:

1. Health and safety
2. Training
3. Employment

[3] The same difficulty has been highlighted by other research teams who have analysed these agreements (in particular De Benedictus *et al.*, 2002).

4. Working time
5. Social dialogue (including the 28 sets of "rules of procedure")
6. Enlargement (the texts on enlargement mainly deal with the issue of extending social dialogue to the east European countries)
7. Working conditions (including non-standard forms of work: telework, illegal employment, etc.)
8. Non-discrimination (including equality between men and women)
9. Sustainable development (including environment)
10. Economic and/or sectoral policies (in a sense, "industrial" policy in the broad sense of the term)
11. Social aspects of Community policies (social consequences of sectoral strategies).

For the most part, the topic areas selected correspond to those put forward by the European Commission in its *Industrial Relations Report* for 2000.

The main difference is that we distinguish between "economic and/or sectoral policies" and "social aspects of Community policies" while the Commission had only one common broad category.

Figure 6: Number of Documents by Topic (1978-2005)

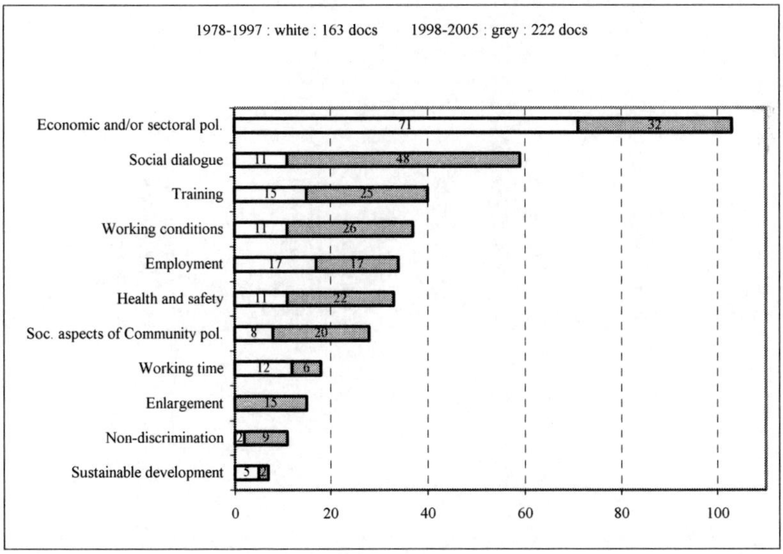

Source: Observatoire social européen, own database.

"Economic and/or sectoral policies", "social dialogue" and "training" are the three largest topic areas judging by the number of texts. The order is different after 1998, with "social dialogue" in the lead followed by economic and/or sectoral policies' and, in third position, "working conditions'. We would however be particularly reluctant to comment in any further detail, since these are also the areas with the most general headings; hence they encompass many documents whose aims are equally general. We would recall in addition that the "social dialogue" category also covers "rules of procedure" between social partners, of which there are 28 sets. The rarest topics are sustainable development, non-discrimination, enlargement and working time. Health/safety comes around the half-way mark as 2005 was very productive, with 5 joint texts on this issue. It is particularly surprising to see non-discrimination, including gender equality, so low down the list. Contrary to expectation, "employment" and "working time" are the only themes to crop up more frequently before 1998 than afterwards, or at least as often.

Let us now move on to the distribution by year and by topic. Here too, there are significant differences for certain years.

Figure 7: Number of Documents by Topic and by Year (1998-2005)

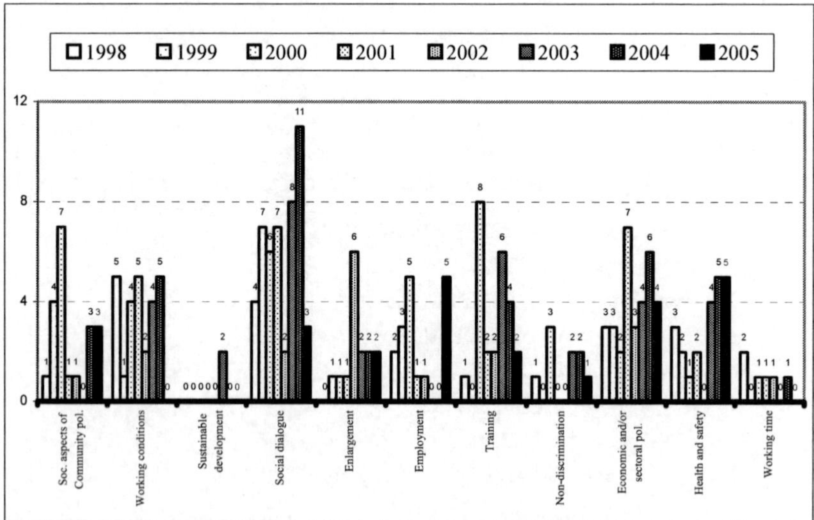

Source: Observatoire social européen, own database.

No very clear trends emerge from a year-on-year analysis of topic areas. The number of texts on economic and/or sectoral policies falls off sharply as from 1997 (there were 11 in that year) but since then they have remained relatively stable at around 3 per year. Seven texts on the social aspects of Community policies were signed in 2000 and none at all in 2003, but 3 again in both 2004 and 2005. One might infer from this that the most general topics intended for the European institutions are on the decline. It should also be noted here that many "common positions" were directly linked to the process of deregulation in utility sectors. Deregulation is virtually complete in many of these sectors. In 1997, 12 out of 32 joint documents came from just two sectors: telecommunications and postal services. "Enlargement" peaked in 2002. More surprisingly, not one text geared directly to employment was signed in either 2004 or 2005 and there was only one each in 2002 and 2003, despite it being a period of economic crisis.

The next table crosses the topic area and the type of document (here we limit ourselves to analysing three types: agreements, recommendations and declarations) in order to ascertain whether some topics go hand in hand with a certain type of document.

Table 2: Occurrence of Topic Areas in Three Types of Joint Document (1998-2005)

	Declarations	Recommendations	Agreements
Social aspects of Community policies	1	0	0
Working conditions	4	10	1
Social dialogue	5	3	0
Enlargement	6	0	0
Employment	0	1	0
Training	10	2	0
Non-discrimination	3	2	0
Economic and/or sectoral policies	3		0
Health and safety	4	1	0
Working time	0	0	4

Working time is the principal topic area as far as Agreements are concerned. This is not surprising because it proved possible to adapt the 1993 Working Time Directive to the transport sector, giving rise to three Agreements. As for Recommendations, working conditions was the topic most frequently addressed. Here too, the outcome would appear logical because most of the documents are codes of conduct. We did in fact define working conditions very broadly, and this tallies with the subjects covered by the various codes of conduct. With respect to Declarations, the main theme is training, followed by enlargement. The "Common positions" deal above all with economic and sectoral policies, followed by the social consequences of Community policies. Once again, this finding was to be expected since these are documents addressed to the Community authorities. As for Tools, health and safety is the main topic area. Even though we should remain cautious and not draw over-hasty conclusions, it does seem that each instrument lends itself to particular topic areas.

D. Addressees

Five categories of addressee have been identified: 1) European social partners, 2) European institutions, 3) national organisations, 4) enterprises and 5) national public authorities. As for the topic areas, we have created two fields in order to take account of the diversity of addressees in many documents.

A large majority of documents are primarily intended for the European institutions, yet this applies basically to the period as a whole. It is no longer the case if we take 1998 as our starting date. Next come national organisations: of the 75 documents, just 13 were addressed to them before 1998, thereby marking a major change in the nature of the social dialogue. Last of all come national public authorities with a fairly high figure, since there are 28 sets of "rules of procedure" which are by definition addressed first and foremost to the national authorities.

Figure 8: Number of Documents per Addressee (1978-2005)

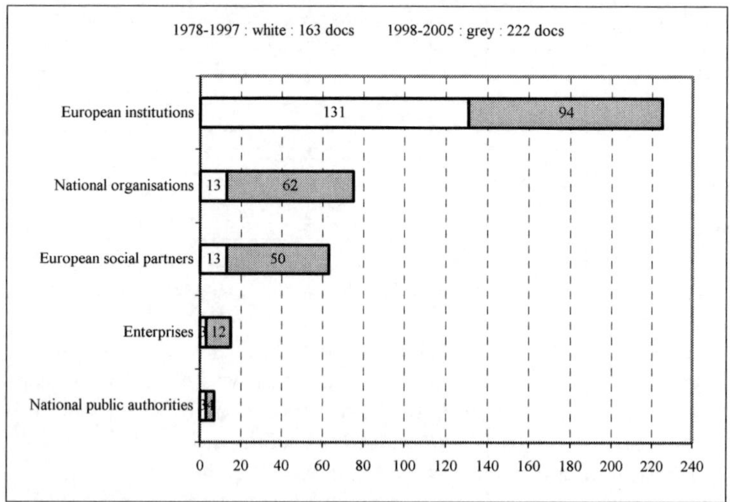

Source: Observatoire social européen, own database.

It is worth noting that 15 joint texts are intended primarily for enterprises, while 20 more have enterprises as a second addressee. The emergence of enterprises as addressees is worth singling out and must be related to two factors: firstly, codes of conduct, which usually have enterprises as one of their addressees and, secondly, the important role played by multinationals in certain sectors (in some cases they are direct members of employers' organisations).

Lastly, national public authorities are also mentioned, especially with respect to training and lifelong learning.

IV. Quantitative Analysis of Cross-industry Joint Documents

In this part we will analyse the outcome of the cross-industry social dialogue, producing the same data as those presented for the sectoral level. Nevertheless, in this case we do not identify two separate periods. We will present the data on the number, the types of document, the topics covered and their addressees.

A. Number of Documents

52 joint documents have been signed by the ETUC, UNICE and CEEP since the start of the Val-Duchesse social dialogue in 1986: roughly a seventh of the number signed at sectoral level over the same period. On average, the cross-industry social partners sign 2.5 joint documents per year.

Just three documents were signed between 1986 and 1990, whereas 14 were adopted during the following four years. 1994 was exceptional in that it was the only year when no documents at all were adopted. Thereafter there was a resumption of activity, albeit with highs and lows: five years with four or more documents signed and six years with two at most.

**Figure 9: Number of Documents per Year (1986-2005)
(52 documents)**

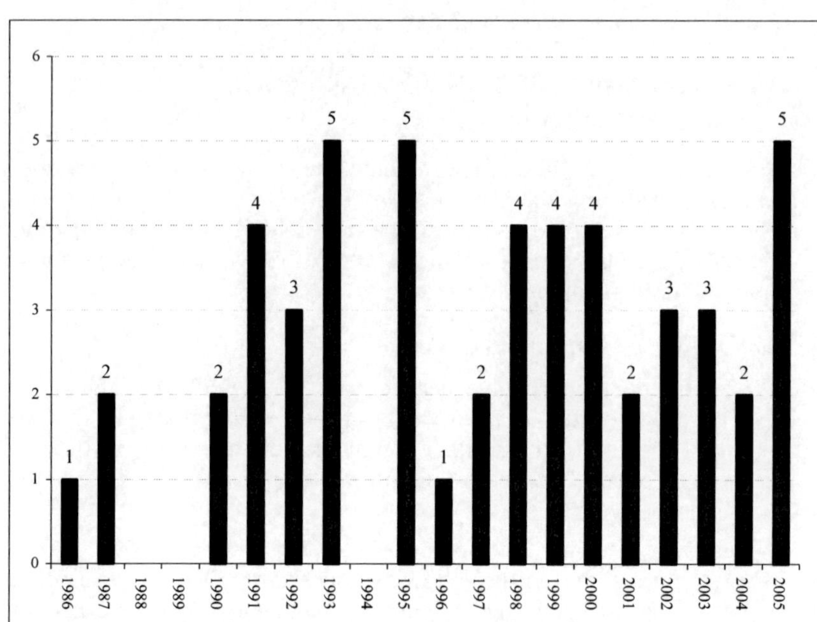

Source: Observatoire social européen, own database.

B. Types of Document

The joint documents are also of a very different type from those adopted in the sectoral social dialogue. The six agreements include three which were subsequently transposed into directives (parental leave, fixed-term employment and part-time work) and two agreements implemented by the social partners themselves: those on telework (2001) and stress (2003). Lastly, the other agreement in this category is the one which became the Maastricht Social Protocol.

There have been hardly any recommendations. The bulk of the activity (at least judging by the number of documents) has revolved around common positions: these constitute 60% of the documents adopted. Similarly, there have been only four tools.

Figure 10: Number of Documents per Type (1986-2005) (52 documents)

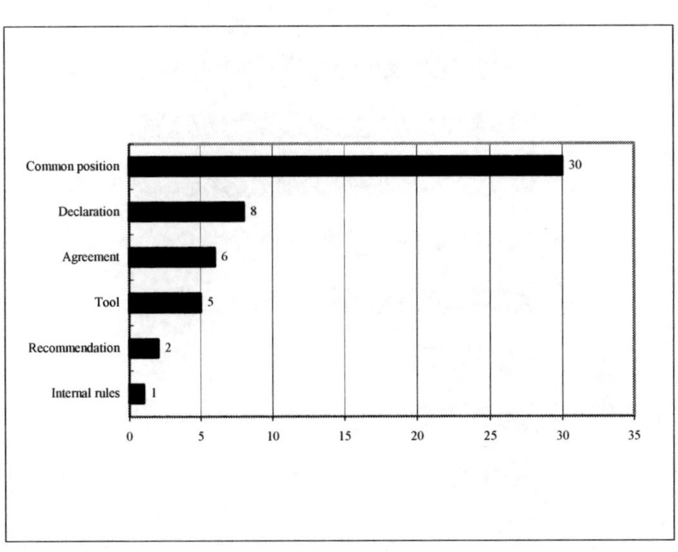

Source: Observatoire social européen, own database.

C. Topic Areas Covered

As indicated in the first part we identify 11 topics: a) Health and safety b) Training c) Employment d) Working time e) Social dialogue f) Enlargement g) Working conditions h) Non-discrimination (including equality between men and women) i) Sustainable development j) Economic and/or sectoral policies k) Social aspects of Community policies.

Topic area frequency of coverage is also different from that in the sectoral dialogue. Employment and training come top of the numerical list. In contrast to the sectoral dialogue, however, there are few joint documents concerning economic policy or the social consequences of integration.

As with the sectoral dialogue, social dialogue itself appears as a major topic in several documents. This shows the importance of defining and even redefining joint activities and the objectives pursued. Nevertheless, the vast majority of the documents with social dialogue as their principal topic area are addressed to the Commission. The cross-industry social partners wish to exert influence over the Commission, which they see as the principal actor/organiser of social dialogue (see below).

Figure 11: Number of Documents per Topic (1986-2005) (52 documents)

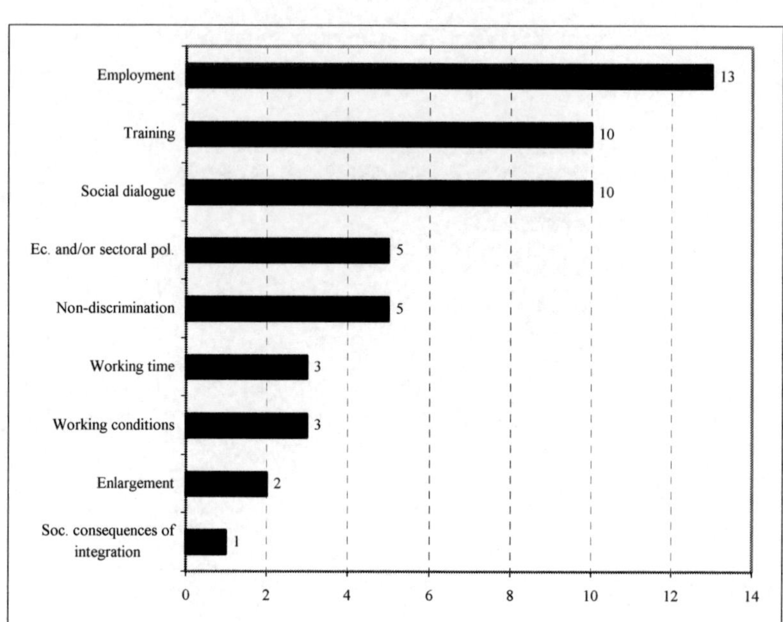

Source: Observatoire social européen, own database.

D. Addressees

An analysis of the addressees of joint documents reveals that, more often than not, they are intended for the European institutions themselves (35 out of 52, a far higher proportion than in the sectoral dialogue). This can be partially explained by the fact that most of the documents dealing with employment matters are addressed to the European institutions, as are some of those concerning training. There are also more documents addressed to the Commission than common positions (30), since the agreements were sent to the Commission with a view to becoming directives (the same applied, in the sectoral dialogue, to the working time agreement and especially the railway agreement).

However, a more careful analysis (see next table) indicates that documents have been addressed to the Commission in almost all fields. This is radically different from the case of the sectoral dialogue, where there was some equivalence between the number of documents addressed to the Commission and the common positions, most of which related to the social consequences of integration or EU sectoral policies. The national social partners come second and the European social partners third. The two missing categories are the national authorities and enterprises: hardly surprising, given that UNICE does not (formally) represent multinational enterprises.

Uncertainty surrounds the question of addressees, as it does for the sectoral dialogue, since often the joint texts are ambiguous and intended for more than one recipient. The situation is sometimes worse in respect of the cross-industry dialogue, since an attentive reading demonstrates that certain texts – above all those adopted in the 1980s, at the start of the process – appear not to have any real addressee. They are more akin to the minutes of a meeting, highlighting points of consensus and taking stock of divergent views. In other words, the substance of the document is less important than the process leading to its signature, served to foster mutual trust in something new: the social dialogue itself.

Figure 12: Number of Documents per Addressee (1986-2005) (52 documents)

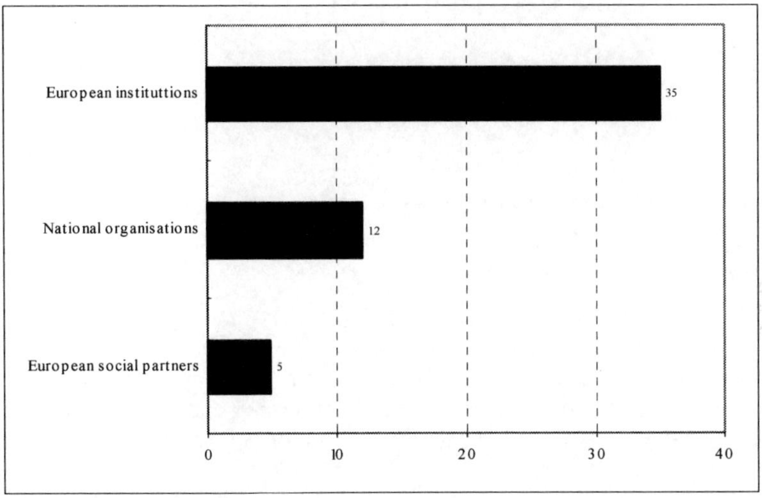

European institutions 35
National organisations 12
European social partners 5
0 10 20 30 40

Source: Observatoire social européen, own database.

The final table shows all 35 joint documents addressed to the Commission, detailing the main topic areas covered.

Figure 13: Number of Documents for the European Institutions Classified by Topic (1986-2005: 35 documents)

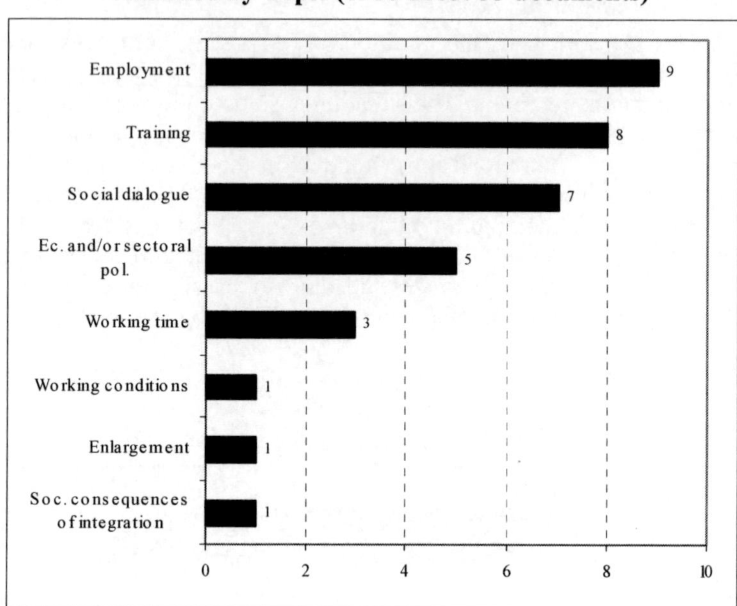

Source: Observatoire social européen, own database.

Concluding Remarks

It could be said, in summary, that the cross-industry social dialogue has three main strands. The first is its involvement in a range of general European policy areas: macroeconomic policy, employment policy, etc.; the aim being to influence the overall European agenda. Didry and Mias (2005) have shown how the earliest joint opinions had a limited yet distinct impact on certain Community texts.

The second strand is the reinforcement of social dialogue. This has happened in two different ways: firstly, the conclusion of agreements for which the Treaty makes provision (subsequently transformed into directives or else implemented by the social partners themselves); secondly, various initiatives aimed at encouraging the Commission to shape the social dialogue. The social partners took similar action when seeking to step up the role of social dialogue in Article I-48 of the constitutional Treaty (Pochet, 2006), which is another illustration of their desire for autonomy and their dependence on the Community authorities.

The third and final strand is the construction of an independent agenda. The 2001 document on the three-year work programme is clearer than any other in this regard; it is nevertheless ambiguous since it overwhelmingly falls in with the EU's priorities, as proclaimed by the Commission. The autonomy is therefore only relative. Training, in our opinion, is a case in point.

Sectoral social dialogue has not developed in a way that mirrors the cross-industry social dialogue. The latter began with non-binding texts, principally in consensual areas and addressed to the Commission. Then there was a move towards "agreements" extended *erga omnes* by means of Council directives, finally ending up with so-called voluntary agreements and more flexible instruments as in the case of lifelong learning (Kerckhofs and André, 2003).

Our quantitative analysis has brought to light a plethora of documents distributed unevenly across the years but growing in number especially from 1996 onwards. The majority of these documents are "common positions" addressed to the European institutions, particularly before 1998.

There is no evidence of a gathering momentum from "tools" towards "agreements". Nor has there always necessarily been a consensual issue at the outset. This is borne out by an analysis of the questionnaires used in our research which makes plain that, whatever the topic area, the conclusion of an initial joint document is consensual by its very nature (for example working time in agriculture). Therefore training, which was so important in the Val Duchesse social dialogue, has not always come first in the sectoral dialogue.

It proved difficult to classify many of the texts, and choices had to be made. However, the aim was not to supply precise statistics but to distinguish between – and highlight – dynamics and trends. One point is clear: fewer than 2% of the texts adopted are agreements with binding effect. The results for 2005, which should be interpreted very cautiously, also indicate that the momentum we noticed over the last few years did not materialise this year. The Commission's attempt to clarify the nature of the documents signed in order to improve their quality and make them more binding has not been a success when we examine the number and quality of the 2005 joint texts.

What we have sought to highlight are the differing tendencies, some more inclined towards consultation – "common positions" – and others more for internal consumption in given sectors – "reciprocal commitments". This duality is confirmed by an analysis of "rules of procedure", which likewise demonstrate divergent degrees of ambition. Some of them mention the possibility of arriving at detailed, binding texts but others avoid this subject.

Topic areas were a particularly sensitive matter. This was undoubtedly the most difficult part of our quantitative work, but the difficulty is also very indicative of the ambiguous nature (to put it mildly) of many joint documents. Without going into detail, divergent tendencies emerge. Nonetheless, our quantitative and qualitative analysis does reveal certain overall trends.

The diversity of situations, issues and dynamics explains why it is so difficult to build a well-structured system of industrial relations at Community level. It nevertheless seems that several sectors have reached a critical point. First and foremost, in view of the overall development of the sectoral social dialogue, those sectors which are performing least well, in whatever category they may be, are confronted with various questions as to the prospects for further dialogue, entailing an analysis of the obstacles and how to overcome them.

However, the same applies to sectors which have made substantial headway in recent years. They all in fact come up against the same problems: how should the texts be followed up? What linkage should there be between the European and national sectoral levels? and between the sectoral and cross-industry dialogue? Thus the aims of the social dialogue have to be clarified.

Our general conclusion, however, is that the cross-industry and the sectoral social dialogue – albeit in largely different ways – are converging towards the production of texts which are not legally binding but are increasingly coming to resemble codes of conduct or optional guidelines: what we have called recommendations. Thus implementation is the task of decentralised stakeholders, perhaps with moral pressure exerted on those who fail in their duty.

References

Arcq, É., Dufresne, A. and Pochet, P. (2003), "The Employers: Hidden Face of European Industrial Relations", *Transfer*, Vol.9, No.2, pp.302-321.

Benedictus, H., de Boer, R., van der Meer, M., Salverda, W., Visser, J. and Zijl, M. (2002), "The European Social Dialogue: Development, Sectoral Variation and Prospects", Report to the Ministry of Social Affairs and Employment, Amsterdam Institute for Advanced Labour Studies, Universiteit van Amsterdam, December 2002.

Branch, A. and Greenwood, J. (2001), "European Employers: Social Partners?", in Compston, H. and Greenwood, J. (eds.), *Social Partnership in the European Union*, Palgrave, Houndmills, pp.41-70.

Branch, A. (2005), "The Evolution of the European Social Dialogue towards Greater Autonomy: Challenges and Potential Benefits", *The International Journal of Comparative Labour Law and Industrial Relations*, No.21, pp.321-346.

Braud, M., assisted by Rehfeldt, U. (1998) "Union européenne – Le Dialogue social: instances, acteurs, enjeux"', *Chronique internationale de l'IRES, Hors série, Les acteurs sociaux nationaux face à la construction européenne*, pp.85-112.

Bureau du plan (2005), L'Europe et le dialogue social, *Recueil de notes*, Groupe de projet Thomas, No.12, Paris, September 2005.

De Boer, R., Benedictus, H. and van der Meer, M. (2005), "Broadening without Intensification: The Added Value of the European Social and Sectoral Dialogue", *European Journal of Industrial Relations*, Vol.11, No.1, pp.51-70.

Degryse, C. (2000) "European Social Dialogue: A Mixed Picture", *ETUI Discussion Working Paper*, No. 2000.01.02, Brussels.

Degryse, C. (2003), "Cross-industry Social Dialogue in 2002: A Testing Year", in Degryse, C. and Pochet, P. (eds.), *Social Developments in the European Union 2002*, European Trade Union Institute, Observatoire social européen and Saltsa, Brussels, pp.177-207.

Degryse, C. (2005), "European Social Dialogue: Modest Achievements in a Climate of Conflict", in Degryse, C. and Pochet, P. (eds.), *Social Developments in the European Union 2004*, ETUI-REHS, Observatoire social européen and Saltsa, Brussels, pp.19-54.

Didry, C. and Mias, A. (2005), *Le Moment Delors. Les syndicats au coeur de l'Europe sociale*, P.I.E.-Peter Lang, Brussels.

Dølvik, J. E. (1999), *An Emerging Island? ETUC, Social Dialogue and the Europeanisation of the Trade Unions in the 1990s*, European Trade Union Institute, Brussels.

Dølvik, J. E. and Visser, J. (2001), "ETUC and European Social Partnership: A Third Turning-Point?" in Compston, H. and Greenwood, J. (eds.), *Social Partnership in the European Union*, Palgrave, Houndmills, pp.11-40.

Dufresne, A. (2002) "La branche, niveau stratégique de la coordination des négociations collectives?", *Chronique Internationale de l'IRES*, No.74, January 2002, pp.59-70.

ETUC, UNICE/UEAPME and CEEP (2001), "Report of the Conference on Social Dialogue in Candidate Countries for Accession to the European Union", Bratislava, 16 and 17 March 2001.

CEC (1995), *Dialogue social: le bilan communautaire en 1995*, Directorate General for Employment, Industrial Relations and Social Affairs, Luxembourg.

CEC (1997), *European Social Dialogue – Main Joint Texts*, CD-ROM, European Commission, Brussels.

CEC (1998), Commission Decision of 20 May 1998 on the Establishment of Sectoral Dialogue Committees Promoting the Dialogue between the Social Partners at European Level, OJ L 225, 12 August 1998, pp.0027-0028.

CEC (2004), *Industrial Relations in Europe – 2004*, Office for Official Publications of the European Communities, Luxembourg.

Falkner, G. (2003), "The Interprofessional Social Dialogue at European Level: Past and Future", in Keller, B. and Platzer, H.-W. (eds.), *Industrial Relations and European Industrial Integration: Trans-and Supranational Developments and Prospects*, Ashgate, Aldershot, pp.11-29.

Groux, G., Mouriaux, R. and Pernot, J.-M. (1993), "L'européanisation du mouvement syndical: la Confédération européenne des Syndicats", *Le Mouvement social*, No.162, January-March 1993, pp.41-67.

Jacobi, O. and Kirton-Darling, J. (2005), "Creating Perspectives, Negotiating Social Europe", *Transfer*, Vol.11, No.3, Autumn 2005, pp.333-341.

Keller, B. (2005), "Europeanisation at Sectoral Level. Empirical Results and Missing Perspectives", *Transfer*, Vol.11, No.3, Autumn 2005, pp.397-407.

Keller, B. and Bansbach, M. (2000) "Social Dialogues: An Interim Report on Recent Results and Prospects", *Industrial Relations Journal*, Vol.31, No.4, pp.231-307.

Keller, B. and Sörries, B. (1997), "The New Social Dialogue: Procedural Structuring, First Results and Perspectives", in Towers, B. and Terry, M. (eds.), *Industrial Relations Journal – European Annual Review 1997*, Blackwell Publishers, Oxford, pp.77-97.

Keller, B. and Sörries, B. (1999a), "The New European Social Dialogue: Old Wine in New Bottles?", *Journal of European Social Policy*, Vol.9, No.2, pp.111-125.

Keller, B. and Sörries, B. (1999b), "Sectoral Social Dialogues: New Opportunities or More Impasses?", *Industrial Relations Journal*, Vol.30, No.4, pp.330-344; reprinted in Towers, B. and Terry, M. (eds.), *Industrial Relations Journal. European annual review* 1998/1999, pp.83-101.

Kerckhofs, P. and André, M. H. (2003), "European Social Dialogue on Lifelong Learning", in Gabaglio, E. and Hoffmann, R. (eds.), *European Trade Union Yearbook 2002*, European Trade Union Institute, Brussels, pp.127-150.

Nordestgaard, M. and J. Kirton-Darling (2004), "Corporate Social Responsibility within the European Sectoral Social Dialogue", mimeo, 29 pages. Abridged version in *Transfer* (2004), Vol.10, No.3, Autumn 2003, pp.433-451.

Pochet, P. (2005a), "Le dialogue social dans le secteur du textile et des vêtements: l'expérience européenne", in Sajhau, J.-P. (ed.), *Promoting Fair Globalization in Textiles and Clothing in a Post-MFA Environment*, Report for discussion at the Tripartite Meeting on Promoting Fair Globalization in Textiles and Clothing in a Post-MFA Environment, International Labour Organisation, Geneva, pp.60-64.

Pochet, P. (2006), "Commentaires structurés du traité constitutionnel. Un nouvel Article I-48", in Burgorgue-Larsen, L., Levade, A. and Picod, F. (dir.), *Traité établissant une Constitution pour l'Europe. Commentaire article par article. Tome 1 – Architecture constitutionnelle*, Bruylant, Brussels (forthcoming).

Pochet, P. and Degryse, C. (2005), "Social Dialogue at UNI-Europa", report presented at the 7th meeting of the UNI-Europa Executive Committee in Berlin, 12 and 13 May 2005.

OSE (2004), "Dialogue social sectoriel 1997-2004", Final report produced for the European Commission, DG Employment and Social Affairs, Brussels, March 2004 (http://europa.eu.int/comm/employment_social/social_dialogue/docs/rapport_final_dss_fr.pdf).

Tyszkiewicz, Z. (1999), "The European Social Dialogue 1985-1998: A Personal View", in Gabaglio, E. and Hoffmann, R. (eds.), *European Trade Union Yearbook 1998*, European Trade Union Institute, Brussels, pp.35-46.

Weber, T. (2001) "The European Sectoral Social Dialogue" in Compston, H. and Greenwood, J. (eds.), *Social Partnership in the European Union*, Houndsmills, Palgrave, pp.129-153.

CHAPTER 4

A Typology

Philippe POCHET, Christophe DEGRYSE and Anne DUFRESNE

Introduction

In chapters 1 and 2 we described the historical evolution of the sectoral and cross-industry social dialogue, taking stock of the overall situation. Chapter 3 completed this initial picture by assessing the quantitative outcomes of the social dialogue; in it we highlighted the differences in momentum between sectors, but also between the sectoral social dialogue as a whole and the cross-industry dialogue. This chapter will round off our quantitative appraisal by examining qualitative aspects in an attempt to establish a general typology of sectoral developments. We shall then take a more in-depth look at certain sectors in the chapters that follow. Here we shall begin by summarising very briefly the dynamics of the sectoral social dialogue (driving forces and impediments), before devising a model which comprises the main variables to be used in our typology. We shall present the typology by singling out a few sectoral characteristics, and shall test its robustness by analysing the themes addressed and the nature of the documents signed.

I. Dynamics of the Sectoral Social Dialogue[1]

A. Driving Forces

It is interesting to note the sharp contrast between the responses from employers' and employees' organisations, with the former essentially wishing to promote the consultative function of social dialogue while the latter aspire to hold negotiations.

1 This section is based on the findings from interviews we conducted for various projects related to the sectoral social dialogue, in particular the study for the European Commission (OSE, 2004) in which we also used a questionnaire sent out to all the players not interviewed. We shall not specify the exact organisations quoted, since the major dividing-line lies between employers and trade union rather than between sectors.

Representatives of Europe's employers identify driving forces which can be classified in five categories:

1) the common policies (CAP, common transport policy, etc.): the subject matter is directly, and manifestly, European, and this is the level at which influence can be exerted on political decision-making (even if it may be done via national authorities);
2) reducing distortions of social competition: this means establishing a level playing field where competition can be kept under control. For example, many employers have reservations about the directive on services in the internal market, since it does not set out the ground rules for competition;
3) the restructuring of industries in decline: "the sector is doomed to a scaling-down of business. The partners are standing shoulder to shoulder so as to safeguard business and employment". It is difficult to distinguish trends in the sector as such from Community policies in the field: "preserving and maintaining the sector's capacity to survive in the context of European legislation (especially in the light of future market pressure)"; "decision-making by the European institutions is becoming increasingly incisive and is determining economic life in the sector, which reduces the capacity of the social partners to put across their interests at national level";
4) the effects of liberalisation, which is increasingly exposing previously national arenas to direct competition (between arenas) and indirect competition (due to outsourcing abroad);
5) promoting greater visibility at Community level: the aim is to raise the sector's profile in order to gain access to European resources (political and material).

Wages, by contrast, are a topic which the employers we interviewed flatly refuse to address at European level.

The responses given by the trade union organisations, for their part, indicate that the following factors could drive forward a negotiation-based social dialogue on social aspects:

1) the nature of the sector, which implies a strong tradition of sectoral bargaining: "a very labour-intensive sector with specific problems (e.g. construction: illegal employment, abuse of workers' status, subcontracting, posting of workers, etc.)". In such cases, some people consider that "the employees are the driving force";
2) shared social policy goals: "objectives in the field of training have made it possible to build trust between the social partners,

which has made it possible to place more sensitive issues on the agenda, such as health and safety";

3) sectoral developments related to EU policy developments.

B. Impediments

How can the weakness of sectoral social dialogue in certain sectors be explained? We note that both sides tend to accuse one another of holding back dialogue for various reasons, given their respective conceptions of what this dialogue should comprise. For instance, the obstacles to dialogue named by employers' federations wanting a primarily consultative dialogue were "the politicisation of discussions", "the trade unions' attempts to extend social dialogue to include subjects that are not part of their remit", and "interference from politics and strike action". The employers' organisations likewise complain of "obligations or pressure to sign agreements" and of "a poor understanding of whether or not issues such as working time ought to be handled at European level". Another obstacle is their "fear that this will entail additional costs for companies". All of which clearly arises out of a vision of social dialogue confined to consultation, and from the ensuing fear of becoming embroiled in bargaining on social matters.

The main impediment to social dialogue from the point of view of trade union federations was "the employers' lack of political will", "the employers' reluctance", or more specifically in some sectors "certain national employers' federations that hold things up". They complain that the employers' organisations "are reluctant to discuss conditions for dialogue" and are "afraid of change and refuse to see the benefits of a more rational organisation of work". More generally, they also take issue with "a total failure to take account of social policy at EU level".

In addition, other more objective limitations – to do with the very nature of the social dialogue, namely sectoral and European – are sometimes singled out:

1) – national differences as concerns the traditions of organisations: "the conviction that national situations are unique and cannot be compared with other countries";
   – national differences regarding negotiating methods and the lack of knowledge about European issues:
   – the distribution of competence between the EU and its Member States, "the principle of subsidiarity and the lack of harmonisation" and "an inherently local sector has been used as a pretext to invoke subsidiarity, to hold things back";
2) the complexity of the sector and its contours: "many different sub-sectors"; "elements of such complexity that they can only be

addressed at national level"; "a different breakdown at national level";

3) the general economic situation: company closures, which are hardly conducive to dialogue and solidarity;
4) a lack of resources (particularly Commission funding), along with problems due to poor organisation of meetings[2].

C. Constructing "European Substance"

The main aim is of course to construct some "European substance" for the social dialogue, based on the factors driving it forward and holding it back, which is after all the very reason for having dialogue, and perhaps bargaining, at European level. This is especially true in that one of the traditional motives for national-level centralised bargaining, be it cross-industry or sectoral – the desire to remove the wage component from inter-company competition – is missing at European level[3].

In certain cases, of course, this European substance is "given" by the very existence of European policies which shape the sector and determine its future. But in many other cases it needs to be constructed. This construct may reflect national priorities, or it may reflect the fact that issues crucial to social dialogue are deliberately being addressed in a European framework. Indeed, to most of our interviewees, the diversity of national situations is a key limiting factor and is further accentuated by enlargement. As in the case of the building of Europe itself, it is easier to react than to construct (negative vs. positive integration). But it also seems that the players' strategies sometimes enable "political entrepreneurs" to develop European-scale activity in sectors where, at first sight, there would not appear to be any transnational implications (e.g. the hairdressing sector).

It is worth mentioning that some players regard themselves more as lobbies seeking to influence European policy (including on a joint basis) than as social partners with a negotiating mandate (see chapter 8). National organisations are not always prepared to consider their European representative as having responsibility for industrial relations matters at sectoral level. Of the other elements which came to our notice, we would single out a fragmentation of interests in various

---

2 Many of our interviewees mentioned very specific language problems (interpretation, translation of documents), which are amplified by enlargement and by the modest command, in some of the new Member States, of the "standard" languages (English, French, German). English is very widely spoken on the employers' side, whereas on the trade union side there is greater linguistic diversity, often a cause of added difficulty.

3 Wage coordination does exist in a few sectors, but it impact has so far been negligible.

associations which are sometimes complementary and sometimes in competition.

Finally, from a micro-sociological point of view, difficult interpersonal relations between trade unions' and employers' representatives were cited as a handicap, of varying magnitude, in setting the agenda. More generally our interviewees, both employers and trade unionists, often explained success and failure in terms of the intrinsic nature of their relationship. That relationship may be characterised by mutual trust and informality ("we deal with that on the phone between ourselves"), time considerations ("she's new, she still has to get organised"), or even transparency of action ("we no longer understand his strategy, he vetoes everything"; "he's a wheeler-dealer, he talks a lot but nothing of substance"). Whereas interpersonal relations between the players are clearly relevant, they are nevertheless difficult to quantify scientifically – especially given the considerable differences in the interests of national members who do not participate in this regular interaction.

The typology which follows led us to attempt to identify ways in which the players in each sector juggle the potential benefits and risks of a European social dialogue for themselves.

II. Typology: Methodological Considerations

Before presenting our typology, we feel it is necessary to underscore one thing: given the huge profusion of highly diverse texts adopted in the 31 sectors covered, no attempt to draw up a typology could fully take account of the range of diversity. The very act of establishing a typology entails establishing categories which make sense and enable us to do more than just taking stock of particular features. But such categories are inevitably somewhat porous. The typology presented below can of course be discussed and debated but, having cross-checked the data, we believe that it gives a reasonably coherent picture of the type of social dialogue and the exchanges arising out of it[4].

Our approach was an inductive one. It appeared to us during the course of our research and interviews, as well as after having classified the joint documents, that there were a number of similarities between different sectors (for example, sectors exposed to the full force of international competition such as textiles; sectors without any obvious European dimension such as hairdressing; sectors closely connected with Community policies such as agriculture; etc.), enabling us to identify and point out their common dynamics.

4 Even though this is not a scientific argument, we would also point out that our typology was presented to sectoral social dialogue players on several occasions and it made sense to them.

It thus emerges that the principal factor shaping European sectoral social dialogue is whether or not Community and/or international policies exist in the sector[5]. Indeed, it is difficult nowadays to find any trace of social dialogue which is totally independent of these policies. This stimulus varies in strength and affects sectors differently depending on whether or not they are afforded protection from international competition (World Trade Organisation, common external tariff, multilateral and bilateral agreements: in short, the EU's key role in external trade policy), and depending on the internal policies pursued by the Community institutions. The effects of this stimulus can be quite significant beyond the national level. It also impact on the players, especially the European ones, representing these sectors, and for them constitutes a fresh set of opportunities and constraints.

Europe's sectoral players are imbued with the national traditions of collective bargaining in the sector they represent, including a greater or lesser degree of conflict and cooperation. Nevertheless, precisely because of the specific nature of this social dialogue (see previous section), the room for manoeuvre possessed by these European players is at the same time broader and narrower than that of national players. It is narrower in the sense that national practices within one and the same sector can be so diverse. They have to manage such huge diversity. It is broader in that they are less constrained by their national industrial relations background (less path dependent). Indeed, a greater or lesser degree of European and international pressure is intermediated via particular strategies more consensual in the case of some social partners than others.

As far as social dialogue outcomes are concerned, we have defined two general categories: firstly "common positions" mainly addressed to the European institutions, and secondly "reciprocal commitments" (agreements, recommendations, declarations and tools), i.e. joint texts mainly binding on the social partners themselves (see chapter 3). Two types of strategy are developed by the players as a result of European pressure: either, acting on the source of pressure itself, trying to influence European policies (a function deriving from that of consultation); or managing change in the sector, whether or not it results primarily from Community policies[6].

---

5 This is the general case although, for reasons which will be explained at the end of this section, in certain sectors there is still no social dialogue even now despite the major impact that Community policies are having on them.

6 Reciprocal commitments can also arise from specific problems in the sector, even though these are very rare at present. For instance, the theme of violence in the commerce sector.

In our typology, our main interest lies in the outputs which we have described as "reciprocal commitments", since these construct an arena for relations between trade unions and employers. It would be worthwhile conducting further research to systematically analyse the "common positions" and their impact on the formulation of Community policy.

The diagram below is a graphical representation of the main interactions occurring.

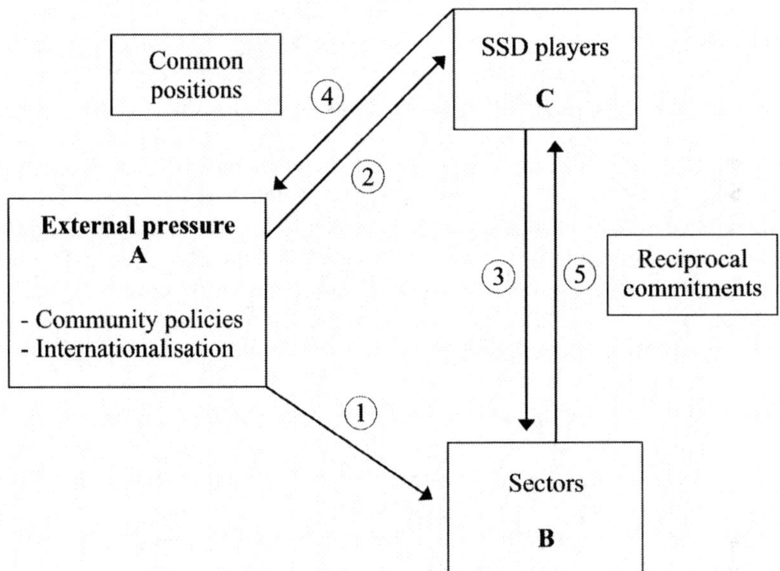

Community policies and the level of internationalisation affect particular sectors (1), as well as the players who have to determine their position and strategy in this new context (2). Moreover, the players are also affected by the nature of the sector at national level and its place in the economic structure (3). They attempt to influence supranational constraints (4) and, more rarely, to jointly carve out an arena for their bilateral relations and a means of handling these constraints (5).

It thus becomes possible to create broad categories of social dialogue according to two main factors: the external environment and the players' strategies. The interaction between these two variables will determine the objectives assigned to the sectoral dialogue. As we shall see, some of the categories we are dealing with are more homogeneous than others. All of the categories defined are subject to different types of pressure from what we have termed the external environment. The greater the pressure, the easier it is to construct a "European object" of social dialogue. When the pressure is more diffuse, the players have a more important role in crystallising that "European object" around which dialogue takes place. In this context, therefore, a sector may change category in the typology when European and/or international pressure intensifies or, on the contrary, abates, or else when the players develop European strategies.

The situation of the players is highly asymmetrical, as we have shown. Streeck has pointed out that the logic underpinning the interests of representatives of capital and labour is fundamentally different in practice (Streeck, 1994). While employers attempt to remove obstacles to the mobility of capital and labour so as to extend markets without any compensatory regulation, employees believe that the supranational level may afford protection against this deregulation and social dumping. The employers' inherent strength at European level therefore derives from the fact that all they need to do is obstruct institutional progress, whereas the trade unions need to construct new European institutions and modes of regulation in order to achieve their objectives. In other words, the employers could make do with negative integration (removing barriers to competition), whereas the trade unions must achieve positive integration and the creation of common rules (see Scharpf, 1999).

Be that as it may, the reality is more complex; otherwise there would be no social dialogue. As suggested by our typology, trade unions have a preference for reciprocal commitments while employers prefer common positions. Nevertheless, in the absence of collective trade union action on a transnational scale (the right to strike does not exist at European level), no pressure can be put on the employers, and to a large extent it is they who determine how ambitious the social dialogue will be.

III. Typology: Six Categories of European Sectoral Social Dialogue

A. European-scale Industrial Relations

This first category is characterised by the predominant role played by the European Union in drawing up common policies. These are for the most part policies where international competition is (potentially) fierce and which are often circumscribed by waiver agreements. Agriculture and fisheries obviously fall under this definition. Transport policy is much less clear-cut, even though it is provided for in the Treaty of Rome, and not until the 1990s was there a policy – above all one of deregulation[7] – which affected all the various sub-sectors (cf. chapter 2 in this volume).

One distinctive feature of the social partners in these sectors is that they are structurally involved in Union policy-making and are consulted about the numerous projects underway. Information is readily available to them and they can influence Community policies in many ways. Their "preference" in terms of social dialogue outputs (at least on the trade union side) is for binding agreements, as was made plain during our interviews and is indirectly borne out by the Nordestgaard and Kirton-Darling survey (2004) on codes of conduct. Indeed, the table showing the different sectors' attitudes towards these new instruments revealed that *all* the sectors in this category responded in the same fashion: they prefer classic instruments in the form of legislation or collective agreements. They were the only ones to express this preference in such strong terms.

The explanation for this may lie in the fact that they are consulted on a regular basis, and hence already fully integrated into the Community decision-making machinery, and that, in their opinion, common positions do not necessarily have very much added value in the long term[8]. Thus the aim of the players in these sectors is to arrive at collective bargaining and binding agreements.

Having said that, the results in terms of attaining these goals differ from one sector to another. In transport, sectoral negotiations on the "working time" directive were a factor which favoured the development of social dialogue (see chapter 2), creating an opportunity to achieve a binding outcome by means of collective bargaining. Only agriculture and the railways (see chapter 5) really seem to be heading tentatively towards European-scale industrial relations, even though the "agreements" signed are manifestly different in nature from national collective agreements.

B. Exposure to Competition and Interconnection across National Borders

What characterises this second category is not integration with Community policies but a high degree of exposure to the various processes of liberalisation, deregulation and competition across Europe. These processes occurred throughout the 1990s: they have had a consid-

7 For example concerning the railways (European Parliament and Council of the European Union, 2001a, 2001b and 2001c).

8 It is interesting to note that these sectors set up joint committees back in the 1960s and 1970s, and in those days generated a large number of "joint opinions", the equivalent of our "common positions" category.

erable impact on the utility sectors (telecommunications, postal services and electricity) and, consequently, on the nature of social dialogue. The opening up of telecommunications to competition back in the late 1980s, the gradual deregulation of postal services since 1997 (European Parliament and Council of the European Union, 1997 and 2002) and the measures aimed at establishing an internal market in electricity (European Parliament and Council of the European Union, 2003) led, first of all, to the adoption of numerous common positions in a bid to take action upstream of Community policies: enforcement of competition rules, effects of liberalisation on employment, organisation of the sector, the social dimension, universal service, etc. This category is the one which has produced the most joint documents: 10 for postal services and 9 for telecommunications (for the period 1998-2005).

Since then, the European social partners have undertaken to carry out a number of joint activities by way of coping, downstream, with the social consequences of liberalisation. To this end they have produced not only a whole host of training and information tools (studies, glossaries, etc.), but also several recommendations or "frameworks of action" (postal services, telecommunications, electricity). We distinguish here between "framework of action" recommendations and codes of conduct in sectors undergoing change (see below). These reciprocal commitments usually cover the following topics: training, employment, non-discrimination and health/safety.

As far as the players are concerned, trade unions are normally well represented in national enterprises and a culture of partnership prevails. Some of the employers initially contested the proposals for European liberalisation on the grounds of the uniqueness of the sector, but subsequently came round to managing the Community processes underway. With privatisation occurring gradually over time, the public and private sector employers' organisations began to see their interests diverge. That situation was short-lived, however, since the problems affecting traditional operators simply shifted to the new enterprises. Exchanges with the trade unions thus relate to aspects of these changes.

The construction sector occupies a place of its own within this category. Unlike the others, it is not a utility sector. Nevertheless, the debates around the "posting of workers" directive (European Parliament and Council of the European Union, 1996), the provision of cross-border services and the exchanging of such services between companies have for the most part generated the same dynamics as those we have highlighted (in particular an exposure of national spaces to European-level competition) and a desire to find joint solutions. The aim here has not however been to manage the transition towards greater competition, but to consolidate achievements already made and stabilise the conditions for competition. The proposal for a directive on services in the internal market (CEC, 2004), however, means thinking ahead to new developments.

C. Keeping Pace with European Developments and Ensuring Industrial Peace

European and international pressure on sectors in this third category is relatively insignificant and relates mainly to the establishment of common national rules. Although these sectors are subject to extensive change, the principal factor here is to keep pace with European developments with a view to maintaining industrial peace. We have grouped together under this heading banking and insurance, two sectors whose activities are particularly similar, and we have added the chemical industry.

The European Union has adopted a number of directives as part of the completion of the internal market (annual accounts of banks and other financial institutions, accounting standards, etc.; REACH in the chemical industry). There have not been any major European implications for industrial relations, even though in recent years these sectors have undergone many mergers and restructuring operations, first at national and then at European level. They are, however, sectors which remain essentially national (e-banking and e-insurance are not yet well developed at transnational level).

As concerns the players, trade union organisations generally have a noticeable presence in businesses in the banking and insurance sectors as well as in the chemical industry; national social dialogue enables the two sides of industry to work on the basis of a trusting relationship and can be regarded as a traditional factor for industrial peace. Given that there are no major European issues at stake, Community-level social dialogue in these sectors appears to mirror the partnership practices established at national level without having discovered a driving force of its own. It is not particularly dynamic, but nor are there any obvious obstacles (for example training is a fairly consensual topic). It appears that on the employers' side there is no desire to move in the direction of binding agreements.

The output of joint texts in these three sectors has been relatively modest (four to five agreements per sector over the period under consideration). European social dialogue is evidently still seeking a momentum that will give it shape. That said, the situation is not static and the banking sector is showing signs of movement in respect of corporate social responsibility – a source of some tension between the different employer organisations in the sector. Furthermore, the introduction of new technology and the intensifying process of concentration could alter the situation.

D. Coping with Change in a Context of Globalisation

Our fourth category is strongly affected by the impact of globalisation. It brings together traditional sectors of activity (textiles/clothing, tanning, footwear, woodworking/furniture, sugar shipbuilding), all of which are experiencing outsourcing overseas and/or enhanced competition from less developed countries, and Asia in particular. Whether or not business will continue on European soil is in most cases (textiles, sugar, footwear, furniture) uncertain in the long term. There is still a European level of regulation, but it is negotiated mainly within – or under pressure from – international bodies such as the World Trade Organisation (WTO).

What is specific about these sectors is that they are highly labour-intensive and have a strong tradition of trade unionism. These traditional industries are in fact experiencing an economic crisis of such proportions that the effects on employment can be attenuated only by introducing global measures backed by all the social partners. Under threat from the disappearance of these industries, the social dialogue is influenced by external factors (internationalisation, outsourcing abroad) and internal criteria (a shared interest in managing change) which have fostered intense activity on the part of the social dialogue committees, especially around codes of conduct. These texts take international conventions of the ILO (International Labour Organisation) as their starting point and then attempt to graft on social rights specific to the EU.

We would also point out that, in these sectors under threat, the code of conduct is a strategy aimed at reaching out to competitors located beyond Europe's borders, in companies and/or countries where the presence of trade unions is weak or even non-existent. It is also a means of gaining access to Europe's political authorities and can slow the pace of trade liberalisation. Sugar is a somewhat different case, in that there are two different products (beet and cane); but environmentally and socially responsible production can help to increase the visibility of the sector among decision-makers. Access to the appropriate decision-makers is in any event crucial in order to alleviate competition.

E. Constructing a European Dimension (and a European Profile)

The fifth category is both relatively immune to international competition and relatively unaffected by Community policies. Unlike the other categories, there are no obvious European issues which would "naturally" favour the construction of a European dimension. The sectors falling into this category are all private service sectors: private security, the cleaning industry, personal services, live performance, temporary work, Horeca and audiovisual.

The features specific to these sectors often include difficult working conditions, non-standard forms of employment (part-time or temporary) and irregular working hours (nights, weekends), which frequently raises questions about a sector's image. Although most of these sectors are seeing a growth in employment (above all private security, temporary work and cleaning), trade union organisations membership is low, especially among peripheral workforce.

There are no overall, indisputable European issues which could account for social dialogue in these sectors but rather partial, indirect and diffuse issues. Thus, certain directives (e.g. on VAT rates in highly labour-intensive services) may indirectly have a substantial impact on industrial relations. In certain sectors, such as live performance, the social partners draw attention to what sets them apart: the directives on non-discrimination between men and women in respect of access to employment, for example, have little relevance to an opera...

The comparatively marginal impact of the European Union, and the fact that these sectors remain largely national and national enterprises are not in direct competition with one another, explain why the European social dimension has to be not so much endured than constructed. (Although in a sector such as the audiovisual industry, the "television without borders" directive has an important European dimension, the overriding purpose of social dialogue is to construct a European *social* agenda.) And this need to construct something renders this category more susceptible than others to the players' strategies and their interpersonal relations. The employers frequently find an element of European interest (e.g. joint training for hairdressers or theatre technicians) and invite the trade unions to share it. The same applies to "best value" in the private security and cleaning industry sectors, and to VAT for Horeca. This may likewise involve codes of conduct (private security and personal services). Training is an important topic in all instances, most notably with a view to improving the image, professionalism and attractiveness of these sectors.

F. Developing an Autonomous Social Dialogue Independent of Cross-industry Dialogue

We considered the commerce and local and regional government sectors to be a separate category since we believe them to be driven by particular forces. They seek to proclaim their uniqueness at all levels. In order to do so, the players have developed an all-round strategy ranging from lobbying the European institutions to conducting internal social dialogue.

As far as commerce is concerned, it is not a matter of resisting international competition but of benefiting from it in order to reduce prices of sale. Moreover, there is tension between representatives of the sector and the European cross-industry organisations, which to a certain extent creates a climate of competition. The joint document (recommendation) on telework, signed in the commerce sector ahead of the cross-industry agreement, constitutes one example.

With respect to local and regional government, one important aspect of social dialogue is to safeguard public services. One example is the 2003 joint declaration on the role of local and regional public services and on the White Paper on services of general interest; another is the common positions on safeguarding jobs in the public sector, quality of employment and social dialogue.

The following table shows in summary form the various key points and dynamics set out above.

Table 1: Correspondence between Social Dialogue Categories and Types of Joint Document Adopted

	Category 1	Category 2	Category 3	Category 4	Category 5	Category 6
External environment: degree of integration with Community policies	Very strong	Average + considerable EU legislative activity	Average + little EU legislative activity	Weak	Weak	Specificity of services *versus* industry
Exposure to international competition	Controlled	Weak	Weak	Strong	Weak	Benefits from international competition (lower prices) or is not sensitive to it
Sectors concerned	***Agriculture*** ***Fishing*** ***Railways*** ***Sea transport*** ***Civil aviation*** ***Road transport*** ***Inland waterways*** ***Mines***	***Telecommunications*** ***Electricity*** ***Postal services*** -------------- ***Construction***	***Banking*** ***Insurance*** ------------ ***Chemicals***	***Textiles/clothing*** ***Tanning*** ***Footwear*** ***Sugar*** ***Woodworking*** ***Furniture*** ***Shipbuilding***	***Private security*** ***Cleaning industry*** ***Personal services*** ***Live performance*** ***Temporary work*** ***Audiovisual*** -------------- ***Horeca***	***Commerce*** ***Local and regional government***

Players' strategies	Trade union preference for legislative measures	National traditions of social partnership (public services)	National social partnership	Survival of the sector; incorporation of (ILO) social standards (specific to Europe *vs.* rest of world)	Employers wish to use the SSD to construct a European dimension in the sector	Emulates cross-industry level
	Close involvement of social partners in implementing, and even in determining, Community policies	Action to influence policy-making and competitive conditions		Access to decision-makers on trade matters	Access to decision-makers concerning unique features of the sector	Participation at all levels of consultation
Goals of European social dialogue	Creation of a European level of industrial relations	Coping with exposure to competition and the interconnection of national spaces	Monitoring European developments (mergers, concentrations, etc) and industrial peace	Managing restructuring and outsourcing abroad	Construction of a dimension directly at EU level (image modernisation)	Development of an autonomous dialogue

IV. Robustness of the Typology: Data Cross-checking Test

In order to test the typology and verify its coherence, we cross-checked two data fields: first the type of document adopted, and second the topic addressed. The ultimate objective was to see whether there was any correlation between the output of joint documents and the themes addressed for each category. In other words, we sought to check whether the aims of social dialogue in each of the six categories defined, resulting from European and international pressure and from the players' strategies, resulted in specific types of output. The results were as follows for the years 1998 to 2005.

During this period, 97 common positions were adopted. They relate in the main to the following topics:

- economic and/or sectoral policies (24%)
- social aspects of Community policies (20%)
- employment (17%)
- other (each equal to or less than 10%): working conditions, health/safety, training, social dialogue, enlargement.

Almost two thirds of all common positions concern economic and/or sectoral policies, employment policies and the different social aspects of Community policies.

Common positions – addressed principally to the European institutions – represent a clear majority of the texts adopted, but are to be found above all in categories of sectors with considerable exposure to Community regulatory activity (e.g. on liberalisation): telecoms, postal services and also railways, as well as in sectors subject to the full force of international competition, such as textiles/clothing, sugar, tanning and leather. The subject matter of all 5 agreements is working time.

These occur in a category of sectors which is integrated into Community policies (transport).

Most of the 21 recommendations deal with the following themes:

- working conditions (48%); social dialogue (19%)
- next come topics such as non-discrimination, training, employment and working time.

These recommendations, significantly, are to be found in all the sectors subject to the full force of international competition (textiles, clothing, leather, footwear, sugar, woodworking), as well as in some of the sectors integrated into, or highly exposed to, Community policies (agriculture, telecoms, postal services, electricity) and some of the sectors which are seeking to enhance their European profile (private security, personal services, commerce).

The 37 declarations essentially cover the following themes:

- enlargement/social dialogue (32%)
- training (27%)
- next come topics such as health/safety (13%) working conditions (11%) and non-discrimination (8%).

Declarations are addressed to national organisations, companies and/or the social partners but without any particular follow-up provisions; they are mainly to be found in sectors which are integrated into, or highly exposed to, Community policies. It is noteworthy that there are hardly any declarations in sectors subject to the full force of international competition, which tend to prefer recommendations with follow-up procedures (see below). Almost two thirds of all declarations deal either with training or with social dialogue in the context of enlargement.

Finally, the 36 tools relate primarily to the following themes:

- training (27%)
- health/safety (27%)
- next come topics such as non-discrimination, working conditions.

Quite logically, the tools are distributed across all categories, but they predominate in the categories of sectors integrated into and/or exposed to Community policies. Nearly two thirds of all tools cover training and health/safety at work.

In terms of overall output, taking all types of document together, two more conclusions we can draw are that, between 1998 and 2005:

- in its consultative role (common positions), sectoral social dialogue has related mainly to Community policies (economic, sectoral and employment) and their social consequences; and
- in its negotiating role (reciprocal commitments), sectoral social dialogue has related mainly to working time, working conditions and training.

The next table summarises the data presented and demonstrates the correlation existing between the categories we have identified and the instruments selected. We remain quite tentative, however, and do not claim to have established any hard-and-fast causal links. It simply would seem that each category has until now shown a preference for certain instruments which correspond to its principal concerns and the priorities of the players concerned.

Table 2: Correspondence between Social Dialogue Categories and Types of Joint Document Adopted

	Category 1	Category 2	Category 3	Category 4	Category 5	Category 6
	- Sectors highly integrated into Community policies - Regular international competition	- Sectors moderately integrated into Community policies, but highly exposed to European legislative activity - Little exposure to international competition	- Sectors moderately integrated into Community policies, but not greatly exposed to European legislative activity - Little exposure to international competition	- Sectors scarcely integrated into Community policies - Considerable exposure to international competition	- Sectors scarcely integrated into Community policies - Little exposure to international competition	- Specific nature of services *versus* industry - Benefits from, or is not sensitive to, international competition (lower prices)
Preferred instruments	- Agreements - Recommendations (quasi-agreements) - Common positions	- Common positions - Recommendations	- Tools - Declarations	- Recommendations/ codes of conduct (international standards) - Common positions	- Recommendations/ ethical codes and quality labels - Common positions	- Array of instruments
Preferred types of theme	- Working time (for agreements) - Economic and/or sectoral policies; social aspects of Community policies	- Economic and/or sectoral policies - Working conditions (in a broad sense)	- Training	- Working conditions - Social dialogue - Social aspects of Community policies	- Strengthening of national social dialogue - Economic and/or sectoral policies	- Social dialogue - Employment

Conclusion

This chapter has highlighted the impediments to the development of sectoral social dialogue, as identified by those engaged in it. Based on the information gathered, we constructed an interactive model revealing the external (European and international) pressures as well as the players' strategies. We postulated an inverse relationship between external pressure and the players' strategies: the greater the pressure, the more obvious the European "substance"; the less pressure there is, the more the players have to create their own European substance.

Our typology has enabled us to shed light on the types of exchanges taking place in each category: those sectors where there are common policies are endeavouring to build a European platform for industrial relations; sectors being forced to interconnect with one another are coping with deregulation/privatisation by opening up space for negotiations where there is already a tradition of partnership. Certain sectors have transposed their social dialogue from national to Community level until such time as they can find some true European substance; sectors in decline are handling jointly the industrial crisis and employment difficulties; and those sectors more concerned about creating a European image are constructing their "substance" with varying degrees of success, some of them striving to use Europe as a means of cleaning up their own act.

These distinctions result in social dialogues with different types of output. The largest number of agreements has been reached in sectors closely connected with European policies. Those sectors which have been deregulated nationally and obliged to compete and interconnect are the ones where there have been most recommendations (not codes of conduct). Sectors such as banking, insurance and to a lesser extent chemicals are in search of European substance. The largest number of codes of conduct has been signed in sectors which are in decline and exposed to the full force of international competition. Sectors seeking visibility and a European quality label are experimenting with codes of conduct not based on ILO standards (e.g. ethics). Lastly, the commerce sector is trying out all the various instruments with a view to giving its specific characteristics a higher profile.

The following chapters will explore the categories of our typology in more detail by analysing particular sectors. The case of the railways (category 1 in our typology) will be considered by Nadia Hilal in chapter 5; that of services and Uni-Europa in chapter 6 by Philippe Pochet and Christophe Degryse (categories 2, 3, 5 and 6); textiles and sugar (category 4) by Philippe Pochet in chapter 7. This will enable us to identify in a more detailed way what is happening in each of these diverse sectors. Finally, an analysis of the absentees (metalworking, public administration and until recently chemicals) will give us a closer insight into the dynamics responsible for holding up the process and getting it moving again (chapter 8).

References

CEC (2004), Proposal for a Directive of the European Parliament and of the Council on Services in the Internal Market, COM (2004) 2 final of 13 January 2004 (http://europa.eu.int/eur-lex/en/com/pdf/2004/com2004_0002en03.pdf).

European Parliament and Council of the European Union (1996), Directive 96/71/EC of the European Parliament and of the Council of 16 December 1996 concerning the Posting of Workers in the Framework of the Provision of Services, OJ L 018 of 21 January 1997, pp.0001-0006.

European Parliament and Council of the European Union (1997), Directive 97/67/EC of the European Parliament and of the Council of 15 December 1997 on Common Rules for the Development of the Internal Market of Community Postal Services and the Improvement of Quality of Service, OJ L 15 of 21 January 1998, pp.0014-0025.

European Parliament and Council of the European Union (2001a), Directive 2001/12/EC of the European Parliament and of the Council of 26 February 2001 Amending Council Directive 91/440/EEC on the Development of the Community's Railways, OJ L 75 of 15 March 2001, pp.0001-0025.

European Parliament and Council of the European Union (2001b), Directive 2001/13/EC of 26 February 2001 Amending Council Directive 95/18/EC on the Licensing of Railway Undertakings, OJ L 75 of 15 March 2001, pp.0026-0028.

European Parliament and Council of the European Union (2001c), Directive 2001/14/EC of 26 February 2001 on the Allocation of Capacity and the Levying of Charges for the Use of Railway Infrastructure and Safety Certification, OJ L 75 of 15 March 2001, pp.0029-0046.

European Parliament and Council of the European Union (2002), Directive 2002/39/EC of the European Parliament and of the Council of 10 June 2002 Amending Directive 97/67/EC with Regard to the Further Opening to Competition of Community Postal Services, OJ L176 of 5 July 2002, pp.0021-0025.

European Parliament and Council of the European Union (2003), Directive 2003/54/EC of the European Parliament and of the Council of 26 June 2003 concerning Common Rules for the Internal Market in Electricity and Repealing Directive 96/92/EC, OJ L 176 of 15 July 2003, pp.0037-0055.

Nordestgaard, M. and Kirton-Darling, J. (2004), "Corporate Social Responsibility within the European Sectoral Social Dialogue", mimeo, 29 pages. Abridged version published in *Transfer* (2004), Vol.10, No.3, Autumn 2003, pp.433-451.

OSE (2004), "Dialogue social sectoriel 1997-2004", Final report produced for the European Commission, DG Employment and Social Affairs, Brussels, March 2004 (http://europa.eu.int/comm/employment_social/social_dialogue/docs/rapport_final_dss_fr.pdf).

Scharpf, F. W. (1999), "The Viability of Advanced Welfare States in the International Economy: Vulnerabilities and Options", *Working Paper*, No.99/9, Max-Planck-Institut für Gesellschaftsforschung, Köln.

Streeck, W. (1994), "European Social Policy after Maastricht: The 'Social Dialogue' and 'Subsidiarity'", *Economic and Industrial Democracy*, Vol.15, No.2, pp.151-177.

PART II

SECTORAL CASE STUDIES

CHAPTER 5

The Case of Rail Freight

Nadia HILAL

According to the European Commission, consultation and involvement of the social partners in the development of Community policies represents "an undeniably important aspect of the European social model" (Durst and Grillo, 2003: 3). Odile Quintin, Deputy Director-General of the Directorate-General for Employment and Social Affairs, stated in 1999 that the Union must become "a vast area for exchanges between different parts of civil society about major social issues" (Quintin and Favarel-Dapas, 1999: 8). From 1985 onwards the process of "European social dialogue" was viewed as a way of involving trade union and employers' organisations in European policy.

The term "social dialogue" covers a number of different processes: simple consultation of the social players by Community institutions; discussions between trade unions and employers culminating in advisory joint opinions; and finally, since 1991, the negotiation processes leading to European agreements. Sectoral collective bargaining is a significant innovation that provides opportunities for the social partners to participate in the production of European standards. In the rail sector a sectoral social dialogue committee (SSDC) was established in 1998 following the Commission's framework decision of 20 May 1998 (CEC, 1998). Negotiations on working time led to the first European agreement.

The sectoral level represented the first stage in efforts to reduce the great diversity of economic circumstances and national social legislation. The Commission expressed the hope that a European interest would more readily emerge if linked with professional interests. This new procedure was to make it possible to move away from the system of cross-industry negotiations which had not been very productive and failed to live up to all the hopes of 1991. Rather than dealing with important general issues, sectoral dialogue aimed to focus more closely on employees' immediate concerns within their own sector.

The SSDCs were inspired by a Community approach that entailed defining specific objectives or precise methods (e.g. negotiations on working time in the rail sector) and establishing a mandatory time-scale (negotiations to be completed within a period of nine months). For all these reasons, European sectoral social dialogue was considered as the process most likely to succeed (according to Siweck, 1999: 243). However, despite the many hopes vested in the SSDCs, their manner of operation has so far been little studied (see Dufresne, 2002; Keller and Bansbach, 2000a). Studies have tended to focus more on cross-industry negotiations (see, for example, Dølvik, 1999; Benedictus *et al.*, 2002).

European officials believed that discussions in the SSDCs – along with studies produced in their working groups, joint opinions on – European social policy, collective agreements and seminars in Brussels would lead to an exchange of experience and learning processes[1] which, over time, would promote areas of convergence both between national trade unions and between European social partners. By bringing together trade union officials, the social dialogue would have a knock-on effect on the grassroots, for these officials would be able to act as channels for relaying European policies to their members (Streeck and Schmitter, 1991: 134-135).

The Joint Committee on Railways notably produced a relatively large number of joint opinions and social agreements. However, we will demonstrate that the process of Community social dialogue fell far short of the hopes of European institutions and social players. What was achievable generally did not meet the expectations of the social partners. The issues discussed, considered of secondary importance, were insufficient to encourage national organisations (trade unions or employers) to really invest in the process at European level. The process also proved counterproductive in a number of significant ways. Not only did social dialogue in the rail sector fail to promote a broad consensus on European transport policy, which was the very reason for its establishment, but it gave rise to a need for other kinds of action seen as much more effective, i.e. lobbying by the railway companies and collective action by the rail unions.

Indeed, the social dialogue process essentially gave the social partners – the Community of European Railways (CER)[2] and the European Transport Workers' Federation (ETF)[3] – an opportunity to oppose the

---

1 Learning processes based on cooperation between elites (see Haas, 1968).

2 This organisation brings together the national railway companies in the European Union (generally one traditional operator such as SNCF in France or Deutsche Bahn in Germany, and in the United Kingdom the numerous private railway companies created in the wake of network privatisation in 1993).

3 This organisation brings together the principal trade union organisations in the transport sector in the European Union. The FST became the European Transport Workers' Federation (ETF) in 1999. The FST was highly representative of the sector, covering over three-quarters of railway workers in the Union.

direction of European transport policy. Firstly we will consider how, from 1986 to 1997, rail unions and railway companies joined forces in criticising the liberalisation of land transport and the introduction of generalised competition to the sector[4]. Then, between 1998 and 2000, once the opening of national railway markets became inevitable, the social partners modified their strategy. The railway companies were the first to change course to focus on adequate preparation for forthcoming liberalisation. This change in strategy created conflict in relations with the trade union organisations, themselves increasingly divided on European policy.

In a second and final section we will show that, while European social dialogue facilitated discussion and exchange between the social partners and allowed them to meet and interact at European level, the reaching of European agreements demonstrated a new priority, that is, putting in place minimum safeguards against the imagined adverse effects – such as social and fiscal dumping – of the arrival of new private entrants on the railway market. Far from being pleased with these agreements, the Commission viewed them as little more than protectionist measures designed to hinder free and unfettered competition in the railway sector.

I. European Social Dialogue Remains Difficult, Despite Agreements

A. Opposition to European Transport Policy: Joint Opinions from 1986 to 1997

Between 1986 and 1997, European trade unions and national railway companies within the Joint Committee on Railways adopted 17 joint opinions on Commission initiatives[5]. These opinions expressed strong opposition on the part of these national organisations to the policy of deregulation[6]. From 1986 to 1997 the trade unions and traditional railway companies in Europe united against the Commission initiatives. Together they condemned "ruinous competition" (Railways, 1996: 2).

---

4 Directive 440 of 1991 represented the first stage in the reorganisation of rail freight. On 15 March 2003 goods transport was opened to competition. In 2005 European discussions focused on the opening of passenger transport in 2008 or 2010. For a detailed presentation of European railway policy, see Hilal (2005: 93-100).

5 See the descriptive table relating to these agreements in Dufresne (chapter 9 in this volume).

6 On the extent of national opposition to liberalisation between 1986 and 1996, see Hilal (2005: 100-144).

1. Conditions not in Place for Opening the Sector to Competition

First of all, the railway companies and trade unions united in condemning the unfair advantages enjoyed by competing modes of transport, particularly the road haulage sector. For them, railway liberalisation was non-negotiable until the conditions for competition between rail and road were harmonised. In February 1988 the Joint Committee thus concluded that there was a need for "wide-ranging harmonisation of intermodal competition rules, for example funding of infrastructure, charging for the use of infrastructure, technical regulations, social regulations, financial and tax conditions" (Railways, 1988a: 1). This was a leitmotiv running through the joint opinions delivered between 1986 and 1997.

The views expressed by the company managements and trade unions joined in condemning the dominance of "all things road" in Europe. Roads and motorways on the continent accounted for two-thirds of national expenditure on transport infrastructure. Both organisations, employers and trade unions, emphasised the fact that rail transport had long suffered at the hands of economic policy that favoured heavy goods vehicles. Motorways construction had taken precedence over railway construction. They highlighted the fact that the rail sector financed its own infrastructure, while the road sector continued to enjoy a traditional advantage (road infrastructure being financed partly by motorists and the State). In contrast to the rail sector, which was itself responsible for maintaining lines, the road haulage sector did not pay its own costs in their entirety. This being the case, both organisations asserted that simply introducing intermodal competition would worsen the decline in the railway market share rather than curbing this trend.

In October 1993 the Joint Committee also supported the idea that rail transport could not compete with road transport as long as the latter continued to practise social dumping. The text agreed underlined that "The Joint Committee on Railways must criticize the working conditions of road transport drivers and the complete absence of any concept of daily and weekly working time in that vocation, given that driving time is only part of working time and no willingness to impose effective controls has yet become apparent" (Railways, 1993a: 3)[7]. The social partners noted that: "Compliance with social legislation alone would

---

[7] For a detailed analysis of working conditions for road transport drivers in Europe, see Hilal (2005).

increase road transport costs by more than 20%" (Railways, 1986: 1-2)[8]. They demanded that practical measures be taken.

The trade unions and companies together stressed the need for internalisation of the external costs of road transport (environmental pollution, use and maintenance of infrastructure, social insurance costs, accidents). At the same time they highlighted the specific nature of the railway sector, showing it as a discrete sector in need of State intervention, above all to put an end to chronic underinvestment.

The FST and the CER therefore called for a European policy that would restore the balance between modes of transport. Both organisations considered the rail/road debate as key. Focusing on this also allowed them to avoid dwelling on internal divisions within the sector. Above all, this approach transformed the social partners' reservations about liberalisation into an argument that was potentially acceptable to the Community authorities: the basis for their protest against the prospect of free competition in the rail sector was to safeguard the very principles of free competition. This was also a sphere in which Commission action might theoretically be possible, since Commission powers to ensure fair competition are extremely broad.

Furthermore, the social partners asserted that, under these circumstances, rail liberalisation amounted to a mere *ersatz* for the release of funds needed for modernisation, which they felt required substantial investment (Railways, 1986: 2). Opening up the European sector to competition would necessitate technical harmonisation and interconnection of networks, the elimination of numerous bottlenecks, the construction of new lines and upgrading of rolling stock, etc. The social partners called for a Community budget to finance joint research.

The companies and trade unions formed a practical alliance based on defending the assets of rail transport, seen as "space and energy saving and non-polluting [...]. It is certainly the safest and most reliable form of transport" (Railways, 1986: 2). In addition, it "offers large advantages to the whole Community" (Railways, 1988b: 2).

2. *Social Aspects Ignored by the Commission*

The trade unions and companies put forward the view that the Commission ignored the main advantages of rail transport for the community at large and underestimated the importance of safety and social issues. Hence the Joint Committee of June 1987 emphasised that the measures

8 "The Joint Committee on Railways appeals to the Commission in order to check as much as possible the observance of social prescriptions in freight traffic by road, vehicle safety [...] this should occur by means of reinforced controls" (Railways, 1988b: 3).

advocated were "artificial, unrealistic and dangerous for safety and for the level of employment" (Railways, 1997: 2). The Commission proposals were considered to be a threat to employment[9] and working conditions (Railways, 1986: 3). The Committee condemned "considerable risks [...] of arriving at a two-tier system of social conditions: on the one hand, employees of the national networks having good social conditions and, on the other, railwaymen taken on by the international groupings on worse conditions [...] It is to be feared that an improvement in the financial situation of the railways will be realized at the expense of their employees" (Railways, 1990: 3 and 6). The Committee pointed out the danger of undermining the professional status of railway employees.

In view of these new risks, the Committee advocated the harmonisation of social regulations at European level, an issue to which the Commission had paid insufficient attention. The Committee defended the need for training and retraining of railway workers to enable them to adjust to the new circumstances. It raised the issues of driver competences and proficiency in other European languages. The social partners recalled that "a single European internal market can only be built with the cooperation of European workers – and not at all by defying them" (Railways, 1990: 6).

The rhetoric used in the Committee conclusions is noticeably much closer to the language of the trade unions than that of the companies. This suggests that the railway companies' strategy at the time was to make use of the trade unions' concerns in order to play for time, rather than to advance genuine arguments against the direction of Commission policy. For evidence of this, one need only consider that certain companies (in Germany, Sweden, the Netherlands and the United Kingdom, for example) had already agreed at national level to go beyond the principles of European Directive 91/440, without this causing a stir in the CER.

3. An "Incoherent" European Railways Policy

The social partners denounced the "caricatural vision" of the Commission (Railways, 1997: 2). They questioned the legitimacy of Community decisions, which they considered to run counter to the development of rail traffic: "The stress laid on the appearance of new entrants is likely to lead to phenomena of cut-price selling of transport services, creaming of prices, which would go against the aim of revitalisation of the railway" (Railways, 1997: 4). The companies and trade unions feared that the most profitable lines would operate to the detriment of the secondary network. They also accused the Commission of applying

---

9 For a detailed assessment of job cuts in the European networks between 1990 and 1998, in some cases affecting more than half the workforce, see Hilal (2005: 134).

the same formula to rail as to road and air transport without taking account of the specificities of rail transport, and of encouraging the "over-simplification" of problems arising. They described Community policy as an "experimental" method with an impact that was at the very least "uncertain and risky" (Railways, 1993b: 1). They believed that the projected reform would be too rapid, the proposed adjustments requiring "a long time" and "time to provide the necessary investment" (Railways, 1986: 2).

The agreement between the companies and trade unions came about as an alliance of fear, with the trade union organisations fearing that employees' working conditions and social benefits would be called into question, and the companies afraid of competition from new entrants and aware of the strong inertia that prevented them from making speedy preparations before the deadline. Both sides needed more time: the trade unions so that they could gather political support in their favour, the companies so that they could introduce internal reforms geared to opening up to competition. Social dialogue offered them an opportunity to act in concert against the Commission, but from extremely standpoints.

The texts produced by the work of the Committee testify to this wish to slow down Commission initiatives on deregulation. Thus the Committee criticised the "vague definition" (Railways, 1993c: 1) of railway companies authorised to operate trains on the networks and condemned an attempt to overstep Directive 91/440 by extending liberalisation beyond the limits set by the Council of Ministers. The text from October 1993 underlined that "it is important not to stray outside the scope of Directive 91/440/EEC; i.e. the scope can be specified but not enlarged" (Railways, 1993c: 1). The strategy pursued by the companies and unions consisted of making this directive the basis for a sufficiently lengthy continuation of the status quo.

This shared attitude of opposition from 1986 to 1997 eventually ran out of steam and subsequently the employers and trade unions adopted positions that were further apart. The trade unions, for their part, considered that the Committee's opinions were little heard. The organisations felt that the social partners had been insufficiently consulted. The FST condemned the non-binding nature of joint opinions. A representative of the FST voiced her discontent in an interview (ETF interview, Brussels, 2001a): "The Commission asks us to consider an issue. We come to an agreement, with difficulty. But at the end of the day, very frequently our joint opinions have no effect. What's the use of negotiating if the Commission doesn't even take them into account?"

The dialogue between the Commission and the railway undertakings proved equally difficult, as confirmed in an interview with an administrative official from DG Tren in 2002:

> The problem is that the CER does not include the new private companies. It is not sufficiently representative […]. The railway companies don't want to make any effort. Nevertheless, their whole mentality, their whole culture has to change. Take the example of rail freight management in the south of France. The situation is extremely serious: there is co-management with the unions […]. The company Usinor has made numerous complaints about the service available. Either SNCF will have to make an effort, or Usinor will set up its own railway company (CEC interview, Brussels, 2002a).

With companies' – genuine or affected – attachment to the status quo on the one hand, and such exaggeration by Commission officials of the nature of the railway companies on the other, there was very little room for discussion.

In this climate of mutual mistrust, it is hardly surprising that the trade unions and companies complained that the Commission attached greater importance to work carried out by its own experts than by the social partners.

As far as the railway companies were concerned, their stated opposition to liberal policies in Europe had not prevented the introduction, several years previously, of reforms paving the way towards competition on the network. In the second half of the 1990s deregulation appeared to have won definitive acceptance, with the creation of RFF in France in 1997, for instance, despite the strict tone adopted by SNCF towards Brussels. On 1 January 1994 in Germany the law on railway restructuring confirmed the merger of Deutsche Bundesbahn with Deutsche Reichsbahn, creating the joint stock company Deutsche Bahn AG (DB AG). The public enterprise became a private company and was progressively split into four divisions which became limited companies in 1998[10], each with its own profit centre to enhance internal efficiency. Privatisation of DB AG was scheduled for the beginning of 2000, with the company gradually opening up to private investment.

From 1997 the employers' view changed: imminent liberalisation was no longer a taboo subject, and the aim of negotiations for the companies was now to prepare for implementation.

The tougher line taken by the trade unions and the softening of the companies' position on opening to competition meant that it became more difficult for the social partners to deliver joint opinions. This shift in the social dialogue was not without impact in the trade union camp,

---

[10] The divisions are freight transport, long-distance passenger transport, short-distance passenger transport and infrastructure.

which, in the face of adversity, soon became divided on the strategy to adopt: whether to continue opposing deregulation, or to try to contain it by means of European social agreements.

B. 1998 to 2000: Social Dialogue Obstructed by Trade Union Divisions

1. Low Level of Trade Union Participation in Negotiations on the Working Time Directive

From 1998 onwards, the trade unions and companies were involved in negotiating the inclusion of the railway sector in the European directive limiting weekly working time to 48 hours. This entailed reaching a European agreement on paid annual leave, night working, rest periods and weekly working hours for railway workers. The sector had been excluded from the framework directive by the Council of Ministers in 1993[11]. This directive laid down minimum rest periods of 11 consecutive hours in any 24-hour period, a break after six hours of work, at least one full day off per week, maximum weekly working time of 48 hours (including overtime), night shifts not exceeding 8 out of 24 hours, and four weeks of paid annual leave.

On 15 July 1997 the European Commission published a White Paper on the sectors excluded from the 1993 Directive, and so sectoral negotiations between the social partners could then begin. With this opportunity for a first European social agreement, why were the trade unions and companies unable to change their view of the European social dialogue and devote more energy to it? Despite efforts by the FST to involve the trade unions in the negotiations, divisions between national organisations remained a dominant feature of this period.

The FST was actively involved in calling for better regulation of working time for railway workers. Aware of the new opportunities created by the dynamics of the Community process, it repeatedly called for the rapid inclusion of transport in European law. Since 1993 the FST had put constant pressure on the Commission for a Community solution, expressing impatience on numerous occasions. In an interview an FST official admitted her amazement at the slowness of decisions establishing sectoral social dialogue committees: "Transport was excluded from the 1993 framework directive on working time, and it was four more years until the European Commissioner for transport decided to publish a White Paper" (ETF interview, Brussels, 2000).

[11] Directive 93/104/EC of 23 November 1993, to be transposed by 23 November 1996 at the latest (Council of the European Union, 1993).

In calling for social regulations on working time in the rail transport sector, the FST attempted to deepen the involvement of national trade union organisations in the workings of the Community. By seeking to create a common European cause, it sought to be instrumental in bringing trade unions together. The establishment of the sectoral social dialogue committee in 1998 gave the FST new scope. It viewed the negotiations as a chance to increase its activities and authority and to become a genuine centre for coordination between national trade unions. The FST acted strategically to involve the national trade union organisations in the negotiations. The organisations, however, took a rather different approach.

The appeal of a European directive limiting working time to 48 hours per week in the railway sector proved insufficient to bring about genuine trade union cooperation. Indeed, virtually all the railway companies already operated shorter weekly working hours than the European standard. In 1997, average working time varied between 35 hours in SNCF and 44 hours in the Portuguese railways.

The northern European trade unions continued with minimal participation in the SSDC, viewing the social issues at stake as of only minor importance. Trade unions from Scandinavia, the Netherlands and Germany, where national social legislation afforded more generous protection than in southern Europe, involved themselves little in the process. This lack of interest was also due to the traditional reticence of these unions about developing European procedures that were concurrent with national competences[12]. These trade unions frequently expressed mistrust of European collective bargaining. According to Jacques Freyssinet, this trade union attitude was one of "acquiescence mixed with concern" (Freyssinet, 1998). The German unions, for example, feared above all that on the basis of European comparisons, their employers would ask for concessions at national level or would use European social standards, invariably lower than national levels, "as an argument in favour of dismantling German social legislation" (Rehfeldt, 1998: 35).

On the grounds of defending their rights within the national railway company, the northern European trade unions were conspicuous by their absence from the SSDCs. This was especially true of Germany between 1994 and 2000, where priority was given to national negotiations on social regulations and the management of railway restructuring after unification. Trade union involvement in the European social dialogue was not, therefore, self-evident in countries with more advantageous social standards than those likely to be established at Community level

---

12 They believed they could obtain more from national negotiations (see Reder and Ulman, 1993: 39; Freyssinet, 1998: 5-23).

(in Germany, France, the Netherlands, Belgium and the Scandinavian countries).

Besides the absence of northern European organisations and the presence of a majority of trade unions hostile to the Community proposals, another more general obstacle emerged. From the beginning, the unions had been extremely pessimistic about achieving effective harmonisation of social legislation through negotiations with the companies. The perceived strong challenges to railway workers' rights at national level did nothing to promote the idea of ambitious Europe-wide harmonisation of social legislation, particularly since agreement had to be achieved between fifteen different national positions. The trade union organisations feared that European negotiations would lead to greater flexibility in working conditions for railway workers. Patrick Hamelin, a researcher at the Institut national de recherche sur les transports et leur sécurité (INRETS, National institute for research into transport and transport safety) sums up this attitude: "There is a paradox in talking about regulation in the context of labour law, since in fact the trend towards deregulation has accelerated over just under ten years in certain sectors, and has become the stated creed of transport policy, and of economic policy generally, to a fairly marked extent in the various European countries" (Hamelin, 1992: 105). Under these circumstances, adopting ambitious social standards at European level "will take several years' work" (Hamelin, 1992: 106).

An example of this trade union pessimism was found in the CGT-Cheminots (CGT Railway Workers' Section), which in 1992 gave its view of European social dialogue: "The social harmonisation that the supporters of Maastricht say they want is not designed to improve collective guarantees for all – purchasing power, working conditions, social protection, reduction in working time, etc. – but represents a minimum standard, that is, below existing levels for the majority of employees"[13]. This view strengthened during this period, and the meagre content of the social negotiations helped to confirm it. Thus in 1999 Bernard Thibault, General Secretary of the CGT, observed: "Let us not be naïve: there are no grounds for obtaining at European level what has been refused at national level"[14]. This feeling was not confined to the CGT: the representative of the CFDT-Cheminots at the European negotiations said of the SSDCs that "we should not imagine that much is happening there" (CFDT interview, Paris, 2000), which reflected the general feeling of the trade unions represented in the SSDC. The fact that there was little at stake in the regulation of weekly working hours seemed to confirm the trade union organisations' reading of the situation.

[13] "L'intérêt des cheminots: non à Maastricht", *La Tribune des Cheminots*, April 2002.

[14] Speech by Bernard Thibault at the *Institut d'études politiques*, Paris, on 11 May 1999.

Nevertheless, the trade unions from the Latin countries, Belgium and Luxembourg became more active in the SSDC, and this allowed them to continue with their previous strategy of opposing the Commission proposals. These unions, which were against reorganisation of the European railways, condemned the European social dialogue for not allowing them to give their views on the political and economic direction taken. A trade union representative of the CGT-Cheminots underlined, "The Commission revels in big words like social dialogue, concertation, consultation of the social partners. But they are just words. We are not allowed to put forward trade union proposals until we consent to the principle of competition. Our objections are brushed aside as "not serious" or "not relevant". The Commission has split the social dialogue into merely a series of technical questions – social issues, interoperability – whereas in fact everything is connected. The FST is not entitled to discuss overarching political issues such as the introduction of competition. Under these circumstances, any dialogue is impossible" (CGT-Cheminots interview, Paris, 2002).

For its part, the Commission expressed incomprehension at the demands of the "French-speaking trade unions". It stressed "the lack of representativeness" of the trade union working groups in the SSDC, where it felt that discussions were far too dominated by the French, Belgian and Luxembourg trade unions and "their political and ideological traditions" (TRANSNET interview, Paris, 2003 and ETF interview, Brussels, 2001b) (i.e. by issues related to public service). An administrative official from DG Transport observed that "Very often, issues to do with harmonising working conditions or safety standards are merely a pretence designed to delay integration of the European railways, a protection against rail modernisation. This is protectionism in disguise. Like the railway companies, the trade unions refuse to reform" (CEC interview, Brussels, 2002a).

The low-level involvement of the railway companies in the European social dialogue committee served to strengthen the initial disinterest of the trade unions. The national companies, which were progressively going back on numerous nationally established social standards, had no interest in encouraging the emergence of binding regulations at Community level. Indeed, the new private companies in the United Kingdom, advocating greater flexibility in management of railway personnel, were completely absent from the SSDC. Their defection only reinforced the low level of participation of UK trade unions, the only organisations present which viewed the development of European social dialogue as truly important (see Freyssinet, 1998: 13), and for which the weekly working limit of 48 hours might be significant (UK railway workers worked particularly long hours compared with the European standard, and in addition, weekend working without days off in lieu was common practice). The railway companies, too, did not want the European social dialogue to frustrate discussions and negotiations at national level[15].

Despite these difficulties between the trade unions and companies, and given that neither organisation felt that there was much was at stake, an agreement was quickly signed, on 30 September 1998. They considered that "the principles of Directive 93/104/EC [were] already integrated into the regulations or texts governing the working conditions of the personnel in the railway undertakings". The FST and CER also managed to agree to maintain the link between social conditions in the railway sector and in the road transport sector: "Whereas, in order to avoid intermodal competition resulting from the application of different rules with regard to health and safety of staff, this agreement will enter into force only the day when similar agreements or a legislative act of the Council shall cover all the transport sectors excluded from Directive 93/104/EC." Rail transport was the first of the "excluded sectors" to reach such an agreement. It was incorporated, unamended, into the text of the framework directive on weekly working time in 2000 (European Parliament and Council of the European Union, 2000).

2. *Diverging Views of Social Partners on the Content of the European Social Dialogue*

Unlike the national trade union organisations, the FST had ambitious demands of the European social dialogue process. It was keen to seek areas of agreement with the railway companies and develop topics for discussion with a view to producing joint opinions. In the SSDCs the social partners autonomously draw up their joint working programme[16]. The FST, for example, expressed strong interest in a European study of the new working conditions in the liberalised rail freight sector and the number of jobs cut. For the FST, one essential step was the establishment of an information network on the development of social conditions in the European railways, including in the countries which were candidates to join the Union. The FST condemned the lack of an in-depth study and of consideration of these issues at European level[17].

An FST official described their perception of the European social dialogue and their dissatisfaction with the new strategy pursued by the railway companies. From 1998 the companies refused to discuss any subjects in the working groups other than those of immediate interest to

---

15 See Champin (2003) on the strategy of the railway companies.

16 They also choose their legal instruments: agreements (Article 139 of the Treaties), codes of conduct, guidelines, recommendations, joint declarations, etc.

17 Yannick Moreau, describing developments in the rail sector, also complains about the lack of information for "a detailed comparison of social systems" (Moreau and Maquart, 1996: 7).

the Commission[18]. The FST lamented the companies' reluctance to discuss subjects not directly connected with the Community agenda. The companies, at the Commission's request, contented themselves with negotiations on weekly working hours and procedures for consulting the social partners. The companies, themselves highly divided on the pace of liberalisation, did not wish to embark on negotiations or discussions on their own initiative or obtain resources for the social dialogue other than what was provided for by the Commission[19]:

> The FST sees railway safety as a priority. We want to participate in study groups on the responsibilities of the different parties in the event of an accident, and particularly to establish training requirements for when trains travel between countries. We need to have uniform requirements for drivers, for those who monitor the goods carried by freight trains, etc. We want to discuss what the profile for a European train driver should contain. These questions are very simple: for example, what conditions will be in place for accommodation of drivers outside their own borders? Introducing competition into the rail sector throws up new questions which are not being answered and which the companies have absolutely no wish to discuss with us (ETF interview, Brussels, 2001c).

The autonomy of the social partners within the rail sector was therefore extremely limited. In evaluating the various SSDCs, Anne Dufresne noticed this tendency, which held true for rail transport: "The European sectoral federations seem to be dependent on the Commission's agenda and [must] essentially serve to validate Community policies" (Dufresne, 2002: 62).

The rail sector also confirmed the analysis made by Berndt Keller and Matthias Bansbach (2000b: 120) which refers to the value of joint opinions and agreements "being more symbolic than practical". From the Commission's point of view, discussions and exchanges between social partners, the "codes of conduct and best practice manuals" that may result, and the need to "take a small step forward together" (ETF interview, Brussels, 2002) represented the essential contribution of the social dialogue. With very different concerns, the FST argued in terms of influence, tangible results and ambitious social agreements. The FST and the Commission clearly worked to different time-scales. The latter saw the fostering and strengthening of relations between social partners

---

18 Discussions between the social partners are organised at the initiative of the Commission, either with the latter using its right of initiative laid down in the Treaties, or on the basis of powers delegated by the Council or European Parliament using the comitology procedure, for example.

19 Within the European social dialogue the social partners are entitled to funds for financing studies. Adhering to the Community agenda means being assured of an operating budget for travel, meetings, etc.

as a long-term process. Odile Quintin mentions "the similarity of problems [that] require, if not joint solutions, then at least joint consideration" (Quintin and Favarel-Dapas, 1999: 8). For their part, the European trade unions focused more on the urgent social consequences of deregulation. They viewed social dialogue as a immediate practical response to problems in the sector: for example, how to prevent job losses, a decline in working conditions and an increase in social dumping at European level.

The FST condemned the reduction of the social dialogue to a bare minimum. It requested that the trade unions be more thoroughly consulted about Commission proposals on rail transport policy. It challenged the split between DG Social Affairs managing the social dialogue and DG Transport dealing with technical and economic issues. The FST continually criticised this division of labour between social issues on the one hand and the economic and "technical" aspects of transport policy on the other. It considered itself excluded from the crucial working groups. The FST insisted that trade unions be admitted to meetings held by DG Transport, which generally contented itself with the opinions of the employers and railway experts. The European Commission, for instance, never asked the trade unions for their opinion on the railway interoperability proposals (Council of the European Union, 1996). The FST highlighted the fact that economic and technical issues have repercussions for the working conditions of railway personnel. It wished to take part in discussions on most of the proposals for cooperation between networks (harmonisation of rolling stock, signalling, creation of circulation slots, etc.).

The lack of trade union consultation described by the FST was confirmed by an administrative official from DG Transport (CEC interview, Brussels, 2002a). When asked about the groups consulted prior to the 2001 White Paper, which set out the broad thrust of European transport policy for the coming years (up to 2010), he stated:

– This time we not only consulted people in the institutions, but had a very broad consultation of economic interest groups in Europe. We received six representations from interest groups every week, and gave them a lot of time. We consulted numerous industrialists such as the managing director of General Motors, for example, who explained that it was impossible for him to send his cars from Sweden to Andalucia by rail [...]. We also thoroughly consulted the shippers.

– Who else?

– User associations, ecologists, railway customers, obviously.

– Representatives of the railway companies?

- Yes, of course, but we're getting to know their tune. We're used to it: apart from asking us for cash we don't have…They think we're made of money […].
- Which other groups were consulted?
- That's about all.
- What about the railway unions, or the FST? Did you meet with them?
- No, that would be up to DG Social Affairs.

The European social dialogue is different from national negotiation procedures, since it takes place in a codified, pre-established, rigid framework designed to ensure that the principle of subsidiarity is respected. Unlike the national framework, it does not allow the inclusion of other issues as an aid to achieving compromise. Richard Balme and Didier Chabanet (2002: 111) note the underlying disagreement between the trade unions and the Commission. They describe European governance as "European liberal corporatism". Similar to national neo-corporatist procedures, the social dialogue encompasses participation of interest groups in public policies, concertation as a means of conferring legitimacy, and efforts for social cohesion based on dialogue. Where it differs, however, is in its sectoral divisions, condemned by the FST, and because it "takes place against a backdrop of values that are no longer solidarity and redistribution, but competitiveness and free trade within and outside Europe" (Balme and Chabanet, 2002: 112)[20].

It is on this latter point, the purpose of European social policy, that there is most disagreement between the trade unions and the Commission. Odile Quintin describes it as "an integral part of the elements that combine to create economic efficiency" (Quintin and Favarel-Dapas, 1999: 5). She maintains that "The social dialogue is considered an essential lever for successful modernisation"; it is "the best way of developing, by consensus, a Community framework which reconciles industry's need for flexibility with the increased safety that workers seek". Social policy is described as "a factor in economic performance, at the heart of the process of adjustment [to globalisation]" (Quintin and Favarel-Dapas, 1999: 8 and 26). The necessity, urgency, methods and means of this adjustment have been challenged by some trade unions. The unions felt that social policy focuses above all on economic objectives and managing "the adaptability of economies" (Quintin and

20 They describe the shift from classic national neo-corporatism (social-democratic and linked to Keynesian policies) to "European sectoral corporatism [which] thus appears incongruous in a context where economic policies tend to be more liberal than Keynesian" and which is more based on a belief in the benefits of the market and in competition.

Favarel-Dapas, 1999: 25-26), dealing insufficiently with the consequences for employment or working conditions.

The advent of the Amsterdam Treaty in 1997 and the European Employment Strategy led to more extensive consultation of the social partners. The Commission called on the trade unions and companies to contribute to the development of new initiatives on employee adaptability and employability. These aimed to promote the modernisation of work organisation and the negotiation of agreements seeking to increase flexibility, enabling enterprises to become productive and competitive, and striking a balance between flexibility and safety. These issues were discussed from 1999 onwards in working groups. The railway companies expected the discussions to bring a change of heart in the trade unions opposing deregulation, but the latter did not find this consultation exercise any more satisfactory. The FST official wondered about the relevance of this process: "How can we calmly discuss improving productivity and flexibility when all over Europe the rail sector is in the throes of major restructuring, and already thousands of jobs have been cut? There's no point" (ETF interview, Brussels, 2002).

3. Social Dialogue and Deepening Divisions between National Trade Unions

The European trade unions viewed European social dialogue as a lever by which they could influence the direction of Community transport policy. Their experience within the SSDCs was of huge disappointment with the actual content of negotiations. This European social vacuum, as the trade unions saw it, confirmed their view that the national level was the most appropriate framework for negotiations. With no plan for, or prospect of, far-reaching European harmonisation, all that the rail unions could do was acknowledge their differences.

In the discussions within the SSDCs, two concepts continued to confront each other, two antagonistic views of what was at stake at European level. These consisted, on the one hand, of the trade unions and companies in northern Europe who defended the liberalisation strategy, and those wishing to promote cooperation between networks while remaining opposed to the introduction of competition, on the other. The different time-scales of national reforms – earlier in northern Europe and much later in the south – proved to be a determining factor. Between 1997 and 2000 this territorial split constituted an impassable dividing-line.

The southern trade unions harboured a great deal of resentment towards the organisations that had accepted the introduction of liberalisation. The German and Dutch trade union strategy was viewed both as undermining national struggles and as a "betrayal" of the cause of

European trade unionism. The unions of southern Europe considered this the weakest link in what should have been a united front of European trade unions that rejected Community policy. The trade unions from the Latin countries likened the position of "the other camp" to a compromise with discredited liberal views, seeing them not as an organisation defending workers' interests but as belonging to the enemy camp.

For their part, the Nordic and German unions regarded the strategies of the southern unions as "irresponsible". From 1999 the German unions, by default in favour of social harmonisation across Europe[21], considered the southern trade unions an obstacle to obtaining a *quid pro quo* on social issues at European level through negotiation. The German unions did not hesitate in condemning their positions, criticising a model of industrial relations that was based on conflict and an approach to managing reform that relied on open hostilities.

The trade unions accepting the principle of liberalisation, for their part, viewed the strategy of the southern unions as selfish "stowaway" behaviour. The unions' rejection of opening up national networks to competition was tantamount to protectionism, while at the same time railway companies such as SNCF, for instance, were trying to acquire lines in the Nordic and German networks. With the southern unions refusing to play by European rules, the Swedish trade unions feared one-way deregulation.

Interviews with representatives of European trade unions show how impossible dialogue was between European organisations and how trade union representatives fell into two opposite camps. A representative of CGT-Cheminots testified to this: "I remember a number of meetings at FST headquarters where, after hours of discussion, we got nowhere. We left without having made an inch of progress. So much so that we even wondered what we were doing there. At some point you just have to recognise that you are speaking a completely different language. Often we admitted that we felt closer to and had more affinity with the directors of SNCF than with the Scandinavian unions: that really capped it all!" (CGT interview, Paris, 2002). In a climate of mutual condemnation, with national unions holding competing positions, each became an obstacle to the other's strategy.

The process of social dialogue helped to deepen these divisions. The Nordic and German unions wished, for instance, to establish working groups on employability, feeling that even an unsatisfactory text was

[21] After 1998 the German trade unions had to renegotiate a national collective agreement. They did not manage to prevent mass redundancies at DB AG or the erosion of social protection. Subsequently they were more active at European level in calling for – even minimal – harmonisation of social provisions.

preferable to no agreement at all. The Nordic unions viewed the southern unions' entrenched positions as obstructing the development of European social legislation.

Acknowledging the extent of the differences between European railway workers seemed to discourage the trade unions. A militant railway worker from the CFDT pointed out that "Working time (weekly or annual, taking into account annual leave and rest periods, rules for entitlement to these, the concept of a working day, the definition of overtime, payment rules etc.), an essential element of the platform of demands, is not dealt with in the same way by an SNCF official or an Italian or Spanish railway worker" (Célié, 1994: 124). Social diversity "means that workers and their organisations set different priorities". He spoke of the diversity of national sets of demands:

> an SNCF official will focus on the application of rules, including on a case-by-case basis, while in the United Kingdom the priority today is having a trade union recognised as a discussion partner. When in France we proposed that adhering to the rules of the P4 – our working time regulation – should be a priority, the Italian driving crew proposed that a rule requiring two-person driving (which still existed only in Italy) be imposed everywhere. In Spain, railway workers have six or eight different P4 regulations […]. If the workers in question are to unite and establish these social regulations, we need to have a common definition of our demands. And in this regard it can't be said that there has been much progress (Célié, 1994: 123).

The issue of the European trade union organisations dragging their feet is a recurring theme. Henri Célié notes that whilst "the employers forge ahead, the trade union movement is bogged down in establishing a common platform of demands". This phenomenon, he says, was not only due "to the extremely bureaucratic nature of the international trade union bodies, but also […] to the illusory idea harboured in each country that its own set of demands must form the basis of the European set of demands, and this is a difficult stumbling-block" (Célié, 1994: 124). The feeling in the northern countries and France that their national system was best and should be applied to the others brought about a stalemate. Each trade union wanted to discuss European harmonisation on the basis of its own national model. Thus a member of the FGTB-Cheminots asserted: "The French think they have the best regulations, the Germans say they have the highest salaries, the Belgians believe their system is better as a compromise between these two models, etc. It is very difficult to avoid taking one's own social system as a blueprint for European model. No one wants to give any ground" (FGTB interview, Brussels, 2002).

The social dialogue helped not only trade unions and companies to close ranks in defending national positions, but also national unions. Countries with a high degree of union fragmentation saw organisations that were such rivals nationally that they never even met, draw closer together at European level. Trade union divisions were perceived as counterproductive and obstructive to the defence of national interests. For example, from 1995 the CGT-Cheminots was involved in European-level discussions via other national organisations, which had withdrawn their veto on the CGT participating in discussions in the FST[22]. This greater unity among trade unions then led to the organisation of preparatory meetings aiming to defend a national position. A trade union official from CGT-Cheminots even maintained that the European social dialogue had helped to promote united action in the rail sector during the national strikes of November and December 1995. The European meetings were considered to have paved the way solidly to unity between the CFDT and the CGT-Cheminots. At its 1997 congress, the FGTE adopted a resolution underlining that "For reasons of credibility and efficiency, we need to strive for unity between the French trade union organisations that are affiliated to the same Internationals as the CFDT; this unity can be created by means of preparatory discussions for European meetings, joint action *vis-à-vis* the government and the employers, and joint training on international issues"[23].

It should be pointed out that the Commission made substantial efforts to foster greater cohesion among the European trade union organisations (CEC interview, Brussels, 2002b). By focusing on procedural rules[24], it accelerated the rapprochement of national positions. In 1998, for instance, the SSDCs provided for a maximum of forty participants[25]. The Commission paid accommodation and travel costs for a maximum of thirty representatives. Meetings took place in Brussels, usually twice yearly. However, in the SSDCs from 1 January 1999[26], one single representative per country could have their costs reimbursed. By reducing the size of delegations to the SSDCs, the Commission was expressing a wish to rationalise the negotiation process by avoiding having an infinite number of discussion partners. This reform therefore forced the national trade unions to pool their demands so that they could attend on a rotating basis and share the seats on the social dialogue committees (see also Balme, 2001).

---

22 In 1995 CGT-Cheminots was admitted as an observer to the FST railways section.

23 Resolution III.3.1, adopted at the Bresse congress (1997: 39).

24 The European Commission set out its vision of the social dialogue in "The European social dialogue, a force for innovation and change" in June 2002 (CEC, 2002).

25 There had to be an equal number of representatives of employers and employees, with twenty representatives each.

26 On 1 January 1999, the European Commission reformed the system: the two previous structures (joint committees and working groups) were replaced by one, the SSDCs. The Commission wished to simplify the rules by reducing the number of members on each committee.

In highlighting the usefulness of European comparisons, Yannick Moreau observes that decisions on reform in one country "in any sector are inspired by those already taken in other countries and sometimes prompt countries to anticipate future decisions: this is what appears to have happened in several countries in the railway sector" (Moreau and Maquart, 1996: 154). This European comparison, far from bringing trade unions together, served to justify each trade union camp digging in its heels. So if the southern trade unions followed the reform in the northern countries with interest, this was not to bring about rapprochement between European unions, but "in order to know what fate awaits us" (Interviews with activists and protesters in Brussels, 2002 and Paris, 2001). The overall result was that they felt a need to take more radical positions. Such was the paradoxical impact of the European social dialogue in the rail sector: the more the trade unions met each other, the more they found their own ideas and fears strengthened.

II. Achievements and Limits of European Social Dialogue

A. Minimal European "Socialisation" through the Social Dialogue

In spite of its limits, the trade union divisions and very little involvement by the railway companies, the European social dialogue has made it possible for a European learning process to develop. In particular, it has given the trade unions valuable European experience. It has provided opportunities for meetings, dialogue, sharing information and encountering different points of view. Through discussions with railway companies from other countries and visits to networks abroad[27], the rail unions have become aware of the vast diversity of working conditions, professional regulations and national legislation.

The process of European social dialogue has allowed the trade unions to reorientate and improve their strategies. Meetings in Brussels initially gave them an opportunity to learn about how the Community works and the rules of the European game. Interviews with trade union officials reveal their surprise at decision-making processes different from the models used in national politics. By attending meetings in Brussels they have come to understand the specific nature of European political authority and the original aspects of its decision-making processes (Quermonne, 2005). A French trade union official confirmed, "I see it as my duty, during trips from Paris to Brussels for meetings with the employers, to explain thoroughly to union activists how it all works,

[27] See, for example, the conclusions of the working group on the use of new technologies in training, May 2000.

who decides what, when and with whom. It's very important. It's a briefing session that I give to newcomers and people from transport sectors who aren't used to working in the European sphere. The issues are highly complex" (CFDT-Transport interview, Paris, 2002).

The social dialogue has provided opportunities for European trade unions to mix with each other regularly. It has allowed them to learn more about the different social systems in Europe. Generally speaking, the idea put forward by Hugues Portelli (1990) that trade unions would gain greater Community expertise through institutional participation in the social dialogue has proven valid. The social dialogue has facilitated greater comparison of industrial relations systems and national policies in the European transport sector. Gradually the trade union organisations in the SSDC have acquired an in-depth knowledge of industrial relations and of the condition of European railway networks and how they operate. Alain Lyon-Caen and Jean-Claude Sciberrasle (1989) describe the European social dialogue as "a mine of information". From this point of view the process has proved invaluable.

Within the SSDCs the trade unions endeavoured to transpose the systems in neighbouring countries to their own frames of reference, aiming to better understand the diversity of the sector. This broader knowledge of Europe is reflected in the trade union press, where more space is now given to articles on "what is happening in our European neighbours". These publications report more systematically than before on the latest developments in the countries of the Union and on the successes (or failures) of the sectoral social dialogue. They give activists a chance to learn about "other people's trade unionism" (*syndicalisme des autres*[28]) and make them realise that the same words do not necessarily refer to the same situation in reality. Such articles endeavour to be highly educational, demonstrating similarities and differences in the views of the European trade union organisations. They represent a response to the unions' tardiness in providing training on European institutional matters and information to activists and members on what is at stake in Europe.

During meetings in Brussels the trade unions have also come to understand the considerable linguistic pitfalls of European negotiations. The language problem is a pivotal one. Interpreting costs for trade union meetings at the FST are substantial and limit the number of meetings. Many representatives of the transport unions are not proficient in a foreign language. As with the European population at large, the northern European countries have an advantage in terms of proficiency in English. In the southern countries (Portugal, Spain, Italy Greece and France), lack of knowledge of English often represents a real handicap.

[28] Expression borrowed from Jean Auger (1980).

In Spain and Portugal, representatives of railway workers have sometimes been replaced by their colleagues in the aviation sector (most flying personnel in Europe have collective agreements guaranteeing them free travel and, in addition, they have to be proficient in English).

No doubt the trade union organisations have benefited from meetings in Brussels and the resources of the social dialogue in learning more about Community instruments and institutions. National trade unions have come to know each other better, as have the unions and railway companies. But this is not the main point. From a political point of view, what dominated the situation between 1997 and 2000 was the lasting difference in approaches and strategies, as long as many unions continued to see rail liberalisation as nothing but a distant possibility.

First of all, from a strategic point of view, prior to 2000 trade unions were not all convinced that the political, economic and social framework in Europe was incontrovertible. When the social dialogue began, European reform of the railways was still at the planning stage and the trade unions still had the feeling – reinforced by certain Member States and companies – that nothing had been decided, that everything was still possible. The national context remained not only the principal reference framework, but also a credible hypothesis for the future. Under these circumstances such organisations did not yet consider their own interests to be Europe-wide. This analysis goes some way towards a satisfactory explanation of the different levels of involvement of the rail unions in the institutional social dialogue process. For some, the common European framework was nothing but a vague, still rather improbable notion, while for others it was already a tangible reality.

Generally speaking, extreme disappointment with the content of the European social dialogue has encouraged the southern trade unions and the FST to engage in other kinds of action to bring influence to bear on European transport policy. Between 1996 and 1998, the FST and the trade unions from the Latin countries progressively organised protest demonstrations[29]. The northern trade unions have supported this strategy from 2000 onwards.

The process of rapprochement between trade unions and their Europeanisation has come about in the context of workers' demonstrations rather than through the European social dialogue. Demonstrations have served to strengthen the European organisation, which became the ETF, and to reinforce its "federal" authority. Since 2000, with national trade unions, north and south, speaking more radically, the ETF has been able

[29] Within the scope of the present article we will confine ourselves to mentioning the process of European collective action. For a more detailed analysis of the 1996 European protests in Strasbourg and Brussels, the Euro-strike of 23 November 1998 and the European days of action from 2000 onwards, see Hilal (2005: 264-394).

to gather a minimum consensus among trade unions, particularly on railway safety issues. This consensus notably made it possible to return to the negotiating table in a context unfavourable to the unions.

B. Since 2000, a Forced Return to Cooperation between the Social Partners

Competition between European networks remained minimal throughout the 1990s. Private railway companies still only existed in a few countries (e.g. Sweden, United Kingdom, Germany). However, since 2000 the economic context has undergone rapid change. The timetable for opening up the railway market has gathered speed: in 2003 the issue of rail deregulation was no longer up for discussion in the Community institutions. The only unknown factor was the pace of reform, with the European Parliament applying strong pressure to achieve the complete opening up of the networks as early as possible. Liberalisation of freight was introduced on 15 March 2003, and of cabotage and passenger transport negotiated for 2006 and 2008. The prospect of European trains running on national networks has become more widespread. With the European timetable speeding up, trade union interests have found a lowest common denominator in their refusal to accept a decline in social conditions.

In 2000 the trade unions saw that they were now in a tight spot, for their national strategies of opposing liberalisation had failed. The example of countries where private trains were already operating gave many trade unions a fright. In Italy, for instance, where deregulation was well advanced, a new private Italo-Swiss company was established in the freight sector and announced its intention not to implement the national collective agreements applying to Italian and Swiss railway staff. In the face of this emergency, the ETF (formerly FST) argued in favour of European agreements which, though inadequate, would help to avoid the worst. The southern trade unions then agreed to review their position and to discuss an agreement with the railway companies in order to limit the social consequences of opening the market.

The return to the negotiating table in 2000 was also due to greater involvement by trade unions from countries where rail had been liberalised (German, Scandinavian and UK unions in particular).

From the point of view of the railway companies, the economic climate is also thought unfavourable for the traditional operators. The SNCF considers its costs to be 30% higher than those of future new private operators in France. In Germany the DB, which was initially in favour of liberalisation, radically changed its tune after it lost numerous market shares at national and regional level.

On 17 October 2003 an agreement was signed between the CER and the ETF on the European train driver's licence and conditions for railway staff working in more than one country. The social partners defined new minimum health standards and levels of competence in order to promote interoperability of staff. Another agreement between the ETF and the CER was signed on 27 January 2004 establishing specific rules for working time, driving time and rest periods for railway personnel working on the railway network of at least two Member States in the course of the same day. In February 2005 a proposal for a European directive on working conditions for railway workers on cross-border services incorporated this text in conformity with Article 139 of the EC Treaty. The European Commissioner for Social Affairs, Vladimir Špidla, welcomed "the proposed directive [which] makes the agreement negotiated (in 2004) by the social partners legally binding throughout the EU" (CEC, 2005a). This directive will, for instance, guarantee greater protection for workers by stipulating a daily rest period of twelve consecutive hours (instead of eleven hours laid down in the directive on working time), breaks of 30 to 45 minutes and 24 "double breaks" (i.e. 48 hours instead of 24 hours over the period of a week). It also limits daily driving time to 9 hours on day shift and 8 hours on night shift, in return for greater flexibility on rest periods away from home (CEC, 2005b).

These two agreements between the social partners increased entry costs for new companies and ensured that they adhered to the social and safety standards applying at national level. Both agreements were signed in the space of a few months, and this speed demonstrated the wish to reach an agreement laying down conditions of market access for new entrants before enlargement of the Union on 1 May 2004. The railway companies in Western countries feared that the entry of new Eastern European states would increase the diversity of interests within the employers' camp. The two main companies, in Germany and France, had put all their weight behind convincing more reluctant companies, particularly in the United Kingdom.

As we can see, the signing of this agreement was largely due to the political situation prevailing in the Community.

In the literature on the European social dialogue, emphasis is laid on the lack of tangible results. This is not true of the railway sector, where numerous joint opinions were delivered between 1986 and 1997. Moreover, two social agreements covering working time and training were signed in the sector, and so from this point of view, the railway sector is exemplary.

However, in a sector where there is substantial social protection at national level, the European social dialogue seems to have had very little added value. This is not only because of the reticence of the employers: for many trade unions, the social dialogue has brought little benefit. It has seemingly failed to live up to two main expectations: establishing an *ambitious* social protection framework to deal with deregulation in order to prevent social dumping resulting from the creation of new private companies; and having real influence on the Community decision-making process in order to limit the scale of network liberalisation. The trade unions' weak position in the SSDCs, their divisions and lack of resources in this context are attributable, in the final analysis, to their weak commitment to Europe.

The fact that Community negotiations only deal with one issue at a time is a genuine handicap. This leads to a segmented view of the sector and makes compromise, and the obtaining of social concessions in return, difficult to achieve[30]. Discussing the issue of working time in isolation, for example, meant ignoring the problem of job cuts, which were huge throughout the decade.

It must be observed that in the face of the historic upheavals in the railway sector, European social regulation through social dialogue remains largely inadequate, and invariably lags behind economic decisions.

This study of the social dialogue in the rail sector demonstrates how this process can lead to the upgrading of other strategies for collective action that are viewed as more effective. Established to foster the development of European industrial relations, it has had unexpected effects. By paying inadequate attention to European harmonisation of social regulations, it has encouraged people to resort to transnational protest action. The aim of this was to enable trade unions to appeal directly to the European Parliament, which is more sensitive than the Commission to the issue of safeguarding social standards and employment, and to European public opinion.

References

Auger, J. (1980), *Syndicalisme des autres, syndicats d'Europe: les Internationales syndicales*, Les Éditions ouvrières, Paris.

Balme, R. (2001), "Dialogue social européen et transformation des négociations collectives", *Politique européenne*, No.4, Spring 2001, pp.119-139.

[30] Catherine Paradeise notes that national social regulations "correspond to specific ways of balancing the interests of social players in different geographical areas". They are the product of social history and "are often accompanied by other social conventions designed precisely for the purpose of circumvention" (such as fraud in road transport) (Paradeise, 1992: 8).

Balme, R. and Chabanet, D. (2002), "Introduction. Action collective et gouvernance de l'Union européenne", in Balme, R., Chabanet, D. and Wright, V. (eds.), *Collective Action in Europe*, Presses de Sciences-Po, Paris, pp.21-120.

Benedictus, H., de Boer, R., van der Meer, M., Salverda, W., Visser, J. and Zijl, M. (2002), "The European Social Dialogue: Development, Sectoral Variation and Prospects", Report to the Ministry of Social Affairs and Employment, Amsterdam Institute for Advanced Labour Studies, Universiteit van Amsterdam, December 2002.

CEC (1998), Commission Decision 98/500/EC of 20 May 1998 on the Establishment of Sectoral Dialogue Committees Promoting the Dialogue between the Social Partners at European Level, OJ L 225 of 12 August 1998, pp.0027-0028.

CEC (2002), Communication from the Commission "The European Social Dialogue, a Force for Innovation and Change" – Proposal for a Council Decision Establishing a Tripartite Social Summit for Growth and Employment, COM (2002) 341 final of 26 June 2002 (http://europa.eu.int/eur-lex/lex/LexUriServ/site/en/com/2002/com2002_0341en01.pdf).

CEC (2005a), "Rail Transport Sector: Vladimír Špidla Puts Forward Proposal on Working Conditions for Railway Staff that Cross Borders", *Press Release*, IP/05/165, Brussels, 11 February 2005.

CEC (2005b), Proposal for a Council Directive on the Agreement between the Community of European Railways (CER) and the European Transport Workers' Federation (ETF) on Certain Aspects of the Working Conditions of Mobile Workers Assigned to Interoperable Cross-border Services, COM (2005) 32 final of 8 February 2005 (http://europa.eu.int/comm/employment_social/news/2005/feb/com_2005_0032_f_en.pdf).

Célié, H. (1994), "Acquis sociaux et concurrence internationale", *Données et arguments, AC !*, Paris, Syllepse.

Champin, H. (2003), "Le dialogue social européen sectoriel: étude de cas du secteur ferroviaire", Observatoire social européen, Brussels, mimeo.

Council of the European Union (1993), Council Directive 93/104/EC of 23 November 1993 concerning Certain Aspects of the Organisation of Working Time, OJ L 307 of 13 December 1993, pp.0018-0024.

Council of the European Union (1996), Council Directive 96/48/EC of 23 July 1996 on the Interoperability of the Trans-European High-speed Rail System, OJ L 235 of 17 September 1996, pp.0006-0024.

Dølvik, J. E. (1999), *An Emerging Island? ETUC, Social Dialogue and the Europeanisation of the Trade Unions in the 1990s*, European Trade Union Institute, Brussels.

Dufresne, A. (2002), "La branche, niveau stratégique dans la coordination des négociations collectives?", *Chronique internationale de l'IRES*, No.74, January 2002, pp.59-70.

Durst, E. and Grillo, P. (2003), "Le social et le ferroviaire à la croisée des chemins", *Rail International*, April 2003.

European Parliament and Council of the European Union (2000), Directive 2000/34/EC of the European Parliament and of the Council of 22 June 2000 Amending Council Directive 93/104/EC concerning Certain Aspects of the Organisation of Working Time to Cover Sectors and Activities Excluded from that Directive, OJ L 195 of 1 August 2000, pp.0041-0045.

Freyssinet, J. (1998), "Dialogue social et construction européenne", *Chronique internationale de l'IRES*, hors série, October 1998, pp.5-23.

Haas, E. B. (1968), *The Uniting of Europe: Political, Social and Economic Forces, 1950-1957*, Stanford University Press, Stanford.

Hamelin, P. (1992), "Réglementation du travail et pratiques: interrogations à propos d'un certain écart", in Hamelin, P., Ribeill, G. and Vauclare, C. (eds.), *Transports 93, Professions en devenir, enjeux et réglementations*, Presses de l'École nationale des ponts et chaussées, Paris, pp.105-114.

Hilal, N. (2005), "La naissance d'une coordination syndicale européenne: les mobilisations sociales dans le secteur des transports ferroviaires et routiers", *Thesis*, Institut d'études politiques, Paris.

Keller, B. and Bansbach, M. (2000a), "The European Social Dialogue: An Interim Report on Recent Results and Prospects", *Industrial Relations Journal*, Vol.31, No.4, October-November 2000, pp.291-306.

Keller, B. and Bansbach, M. (2000b), "The Transport Sector as an Example of Sectoral Social Dialogue in the EU: Recent Developments and Prospects", *Transfer*, Vol.6, No.1, Spring 2000, pp.115-124.

Lyon-Caen, A. and Sciberrasle, J.-Cl. (1989), "Pratiques et perspectives de la négociation collective européenne. Impressions", *Travail et emploi*, No.42, April 1989, pp.22-28.

Moreau, Y. and Maquart, B. (1996), *Entreprises de service public européennes et relations sociales: l'acteur oublié*, ASPE Europe, Paris.

Paradeise, C. (1992), "Avant-Propos", in Hamelin, P., Ribeill, G. and Vauclare, C. (eds.), *Transports 93, Professions en devenir, enjeux et réglementations*, Presses de l'École nationale des Ponts et chaussées, Paris, pp.7-10.

Portelli, H. (1990), "La CES", in Devin, G. (ed.), *Syndicalisme. Dimensions internationales*, La Garenne-Colombes, Erasme, pp.143-156.

Quermonne, J.-L. (2005), *Le système politique de l'Union européenne: des Communautés économiques à l'union politique*, 6th ed., Montchretien, Paris.

Quintin, O. and Favarel-Dapas, B. (1999), *L'Europe sociale, enjeux et réalités*, La Documentation française, Paris.

Reder, M. and Ulman, L. (1993), "Unionism and Unification", in Ulman, L., Eichengreen, B. and Dickens, W.T. (eds.), *Labor and an Integrated Europe*, The Brookings Institution, Washington, pp.13-44.

Rehfeldt, U. (1998), "Le dialogue social sous le primat de l'autonomie collective de branche", *Chronique internationale de l'IRES*, hors série, October 1998, pp.24-35.

Siwek, J.-L. (1999), "Le dialogue social au niveau communautaire: d'où vient-on, où en est-on?", *Revue du Marché commun et de l'Union européenne*, No.427, April 1999, pp.238-251.

Streeck, W. and Schmitter, P. C. (1991), "From National Corporatism to Transnational Pluralism: Organized Interests in the Single European Market", *Politics and Society*, Vol.19, No.2, pp.134-135.

List of Joint Documents – Railways

Common Opinion of the Joint Committee on Railways on the Effects of the Establishment of the Freeways, 3 June 1997.

Opinion of 8 February 1996 of the Joint Committee on Railways on the Communication from the Commission on the Development of the Community's Railways, 8 February 1996.

Opinion on the Commission's White Paper on the Future Development of the Common Transport Policy, 1 October 1993a.

Opinion on the European Commission's Draft Directive on the Allocation of Railway Infrastructure Capacity and the Charging of Infrastructure Fees, 1 October 1993b.

Opinion on the European Commission's Draft Directive on the Licensing of Railway Undertakings, 1 October 1993c.

Opinion on the Communication on a Community Railway Policy, 1 November 1990.

Opinion on the Liberalisation of the Internal Market in 1992; Commission Proposal on the Improvement of the Situation of Railway Undertakings and the Harmonisation of Rules Governing Financial Relations between such Undertakings and States, 1 February 1988a.

Opinion concerning the Development of Combined Transport, 1 December 1988a.

Memorandum concerning the Common Transport Policy, 19 November 1986.

CHAPTER 6

Social Dialogue in UNI-Europa Sectors

Philippe POCHET and Christophe DEGRYSE

Introduction[1]

In the previous chapters we have described the dynamics of the sectoral social dialogue, the quantitative results across all sectors and a typology applied to all the sectors, which enables us to identify six major trends. This chapter will take our analysis one stage further by focusing on the case of UNI-Europa, which in essence represents the service sectors (UNI-Europa is the European regional organisation of Union Network International – UNI). It is a particularly interesting case, in that UNI-Europa encompasses 11 of the 31 sectoral social dialogue committees: insurance, banking, cleaning industry, commerce, private security, personal services, telecoms, postal services, live performance, temporary work and audiovisual. Only three sectors belonging to this organisation have no social dialogue committee: UNI-Graphics, UNI-IBITS (industry, business and information technology services) and UNI-Gaming which represents casino employees.

One clarification is required at the outset. Can UNI-Europa be considered an appropriate level of analysis? Can one analyse the 14 sectors of UNI-Europa, 11 of which have a sectoral social dialogue, taking them to be a coherent set of sectors? We will discuss several arguments pro and contra in the following paragraphs.

First of all, UNI-Europa is the product of a merger of four organisations (EuroFIET and the postal, media and graphical sectors), each of which had its own characteristics and institutional background. Al-

---

1 This study is based on nearly 20 interviews conducted in Brussels and Nyon (Switzerland), covering the 13 sectors referred to in this article. Furthermore, we attended sectoral meetings of the social partners, in Brussels, in the following sectors: cleaning industry, private security, commerce and personal services. In the study we carried out for the European Commission, we also conducted interviews with the employer side in a number of cases. We wish to thank all of our informants for giving us their time and Bernadette Ségd (usual caveats applied).

though the merger occurred relatively recently (2000)[2], the revival of social dialogue in these sectors dates from 1998, with the formation of the new sectoral social dialogue committees (SSDCs) in 1999. Yet the graphical industry still has no social dialogue committee, while the audiovisual sector established one in 2004, i.e. after the merger.

The table below gives more detail about participants in the social dialogue committees[3]:

Sector	Employees	Employers
Audiovisual	UNI-MEI (1999), EFJ, FIA (1952), FIM	EBU, ACT, AER, CEPI, FIAPP
Banking	UNI-Europa (2000)	FBE (1960), ESBG (1963), EACB (1970),
Cleaning industry	UNI-Europa (2000)	EFCI (1988)
Commerce	UNI-Europa (2000)	EuroCommerce (1993)
Insurance	UNI-Europa (2000)	CEA (1953), BIPAR (1937), ACME (1978)
Live performance	EAEA (1999)	Pearle (1991)
Personal services (hairdressing)	UNI-Europa (2000)	CIC Europe (1991)
Postal services	UNI-Europa (2000)	PostEurop (1993)
Private security	UNI-Europa (2000)	CoESS (1989)
Telecommunications	UNI-Europa (2000)	ETNO (1991)
Temporary work	UNI-Europa (2000)	EuroCIETT (1967)

Above all, however, the sectors covered (and those not covered) are extremely disparate, in terms of the workers covered as well as their rate of union membership, the homogeneity/heterogeneity of sectors and their trade union traditions. What could the hairdressing and telecoms sectors have in common? Or the graphical industry and commerce? And so on. Thus there is great diversity within UNI-Europa, just as there was great diversity prior to the merger within EuroFIET. That is indisputable. Moreover, there is no trade union strategy coordinated by a European "headquarters" at the top of a hierarchy; each sector has preserved a high degree of autonomy. Lastly, some sectors are based mainly in Nyon, Switzerland, others are split between Nyon and Brussels, while others still are fully established in Brussels. This specific feature, allied with the fact that UNI-Europa is the European regional organisation of

2 For the sake of simplicity, in the rest of this chapter we shall use the label UNI-Europa for all of the sectors, even those independent prior to the merger.

3 As far as UNI-Europa is concerned, the six informal groups – insurance (1987), banking (1990), cleaning industry (1992), commerce (1992), private security (1993) and personal services (1998) – became SSDCs in 1999, as did the joint committees in telecoms (1999) and postal services (1994). Live performance (1999), temporary work (2000) and audiovisual were set up directly as SSDCs.

UNI, which is international, reflects a particular desire to be more alive to global issues than other federations, or to be less Eurocentric.

All of these elements must be kept in mind when conducting an overall analysis. That is why, when we come to our typology, we shall take account of UNI-Europa as a whole but also of its individual parts. Even though each sector has remained autonomous, it is worth pointing out that regular talks – often more informal than formal – on strategies, decisions and sectoral problems do take place in both Brussels and Nyon. Official documents are adopted too, setting out objectives shared by all sectors, as was the case at the Stockholm regional conference in 2003.

The purpose of this chapter is not to chart the history of each individual sector, but to take stock of the situation and challenges in the sectoral social dialogue. We are therefore primarily interested in recent developments and points of convergence. For a long while the service sector was less affected than others by competition, but that situation is changing rapidly with the freedom of movement for services – even if it is regulated –, the advent of a European financial market, and the opening up of various sectors to competition: telecoms and audiovisual (almost complete), postal services (underway), and live performance, private security and the cleaning industry (in the pipeline).

As we emphasised in our introductory chapter, it is difficult to assess the outcomes of sectoral social dialogue since this is still a new and evolving phenomenon. European social dialogue is different from national collective bargaining and national industrial relations. If these activities are used as a yardstick, the outcomes will inevitably be deemed disappointing (Keller, 2005). Yet without a point of reference, one might run the risk of over-estimating the slightest substantive or procedural innovation and attaching excessive importance to events which, all things considered, are of minor significance.

In order to minimise this problem, we shall assess the social dialogue in UNI-Europa sectors according to the organisation's own stated objectives. These objectives result from compromises between some trade unions wishing to preserve the power of national federations and others wishing to transfer part of that power to the European federation. At its first regional conference, held in Stockholm in 2003, UNI-Europa defined its aim is as follows.

> The objectives of the sectoral social dialogue should be to:
>
> a) promote constructive relations between social partners, including the partners in the EU accession countries;
>
> b) influence, in co-operation with the ETUC, EU policies, particularly on employment, training, integration and equal opportunities, as well as

those policy issues which are considered of decisive importance by the respective UNI sectors;

c) offer a European platform where national trade union concerns can be discussed and solutions promoted;

d) negotiate European framework agreements designed to improve the social model and guard against attempts at social dumping.

The UNI-Europa sectors were requested to:

a) work towards developing formal relations with employers in the European Union and to set up social dialogue committees where they do not exist;

b) promote the acceptance and recognition of trade unions as social partners at all levels;

c) promote discussions and decide priorities in the framework of the social dialogue;

d) negotiate binding sectoral framework agreements and work towards their effective implementation at European, national or enterprise levels, as appropriate.

Having explained our context and methodology. Let us set out the structure of this chapter. Part one puts the social dialogue in the UNI-Europa sectors into perspective by comparing it statistically with the outcomes in all the sectors presented in chapter 3. Part two describes sectoral developments on the basis of the six-category typology presented in chapter 4. Part three, drawing on our interviews, reveals the successes and difficulties of the sectoral social dialogue. We shall not look at each and every sector, but shall attempt to paint an overall picture by taking particular sectors as examples. It would be impossible to be exhaustive, and that is not our aim. Rather, we seek to identify the principal issues at stake in several or, in some cases, all sectors.

We will close with some concluding remarks.

I. Quantitative Analysis: Statistics on Social Dialogue in UNI-Europa Sectors

Our analysis embraces all of the sectors currently belonging to UNI-Europa and having a sectoral committee compared with all existing sectors (31) of the sectoral social dialogue in 2005. The idea is to try to see whether the texts signed indicate anything distinctive about the sectors belonging to UNI-Europa. This quantitative analysis is relevant when we bear in mind the total number of joint documents covered: over 385. A minor inaccuracy and/or the omission of one or other text would not radically alter the overall trends, and what we seek to do here is highlight general trends rather than conducting a detailed analysis based on any minimal divergences.

We have selected two periods: 1978-2005, covering the entire period since the first agreement, and 1998-2005, covering the period since the establishment of the new social dialogue committees. Any agreements previously signed by the sectoral social partners as part of their informal social dialogue are included once they have been recognised. Clearly, our main interest lies in the results achieved since 1998, since the merger process was underway at that time.

Out of the 31 sectors, UNI-Europa sits on 11 committees. To keep things simple, we shall take it that this represents one third of all the committees. From now on, when we refer to the "average", it means a third.

The first table shows that, overall, approximately a third of all documents have been signed by UNI-Europa sectors. This is true both for the period 1978-97 and for 1998-2005. Our first finding, therefore, is that there is nothing specific about UNI-Europa in quantitative terms.

Table 1: Number of Agreements for Each Period

SSD: Number of agreements	UNI-Europa sectors (11)	Other sectors (20)	All sectors (31)
Period 1978-1997	54	109	163
Period 1998-2005	73	149	222
Period 1978-2005	127	258	385

This broad-brush analysis needs to be refined by means of an annual breakdown (see graph below). With the exception of one joint document on training in the commerce sector in 1989, the UNI-Europa sectors began to sign joint texts in 1992, with a peak of 16 documents in both 1996 and 1997, followed by 14 in 1998. Between 1995 and 1998 the UNI-Europa sectors signed an above-average number of joint texts. Since 1999 UNI-Europa has been around the average mark or even below it, particularly in 2002 (only one document signed).

This pattern is of no notable significance in qualitative terms: the number of texts adopted is no indication of the quality of social dialogue. It may also reflect the decision to sign the most significant joint texts. That applies for example to telecoms, which has latterly signed only three joint documents, but all three are regarded as important ones – telework (7 February 2001), enlargement (19 May 2005) and call centres (15 June 2004) –, even though it was the most "productive" sector in the mid-1990s, with no fewer than thirteen documents mainly addressed to the Commission in 1997 and 1998.

Figure 1: Number of Documents per Year (1978-2005)

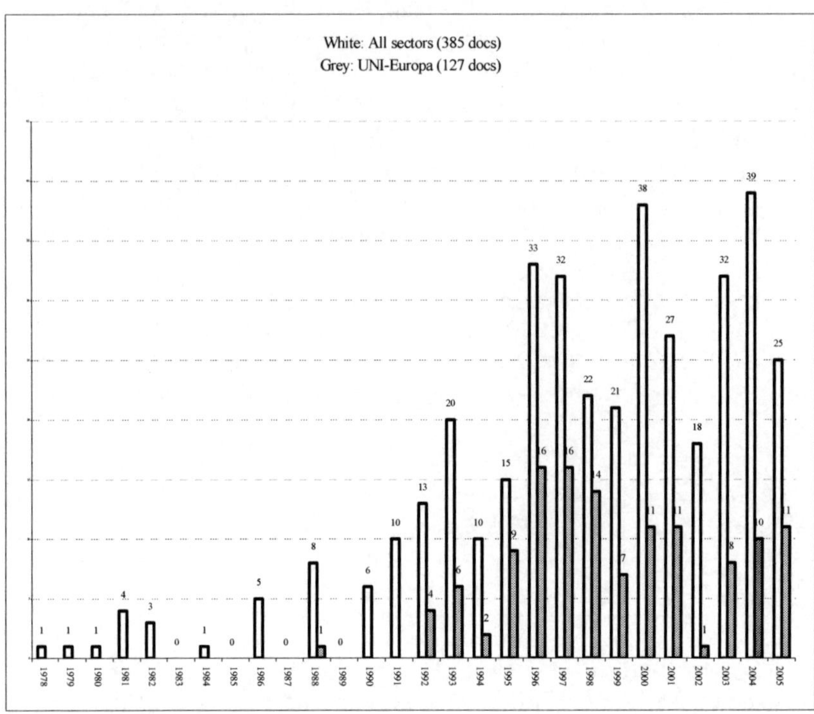

In order to interpret these figures, we must take account of the "productivity" differences from one sector to another, as reflected by the number of joint documents adopted in each sector. This is illustrated by the following graph, in which we also distinguish between the totality of texts and those concluded since 1998, thereby enabling us to see which sectors have been the most productive throughout the entire period and/or since 1998.

Figure 2: Number of Documents per Sector

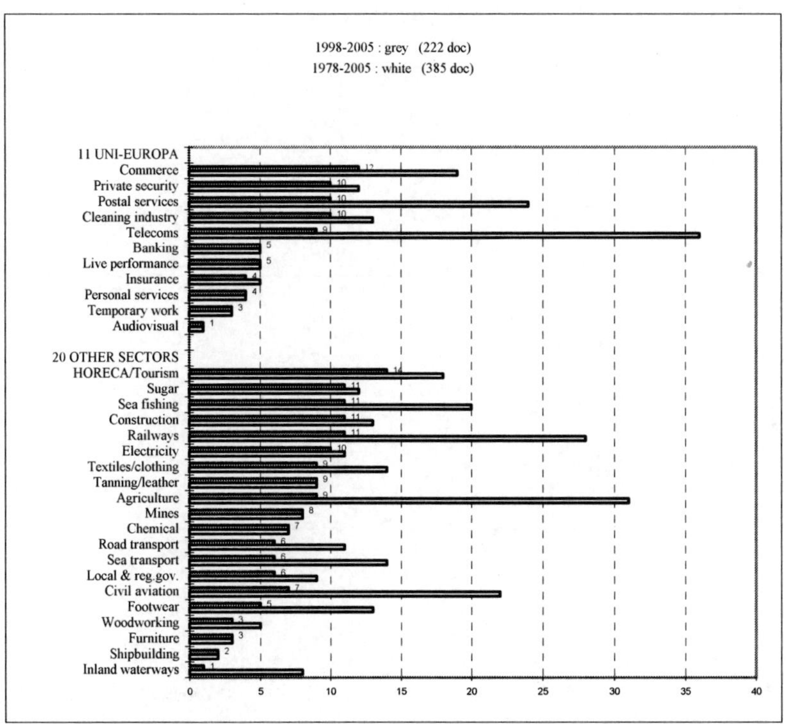

It immediately becomes apparent that telecoms and postal services are the two most productive sectors. The opening up of these two industries to competition and deregulation is what explains the large number of joint documents, the bulk of which are addressed to the European Commission in an attempt to influence its privatisation policies.

Our second finding is that telecommunications has remained the most productive sector since 1998, followed by postal services and commerce. Once again, we would point out that these figures do not tell us anything about the quality of the documents signed, nor about the quality of the social dialogue in general (especially as we must bear in mind that certain sectors created their committees only very recently – audiovisual in 2004). Nevertheless, our interviews and analysis of texts in both commerce and private security do mark these out as very dynamic sectors.

When we examine the types of documents signed over the entire period (see definition in the introduction), we note that the number of "common positions" is lower than average, despite the fact that – as pointed out above – telecoms and postal services have produced a particularly large number of common positions. On the other hand, there are more "tools" and especially "declarations".

Figure 3: Number of Documents per Type (1978-2005)

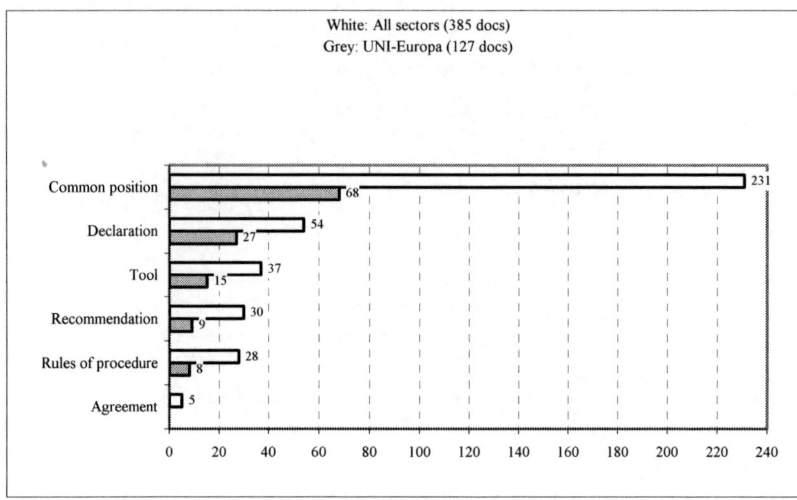

The next graph refers to all the joint documents adopted since 1998. There is evidence of a growing divergence from the average as concerns common positions, which in fact constitute less than a quarter of the total.

Figure 4: Number of Documents per Type (1998-2005)

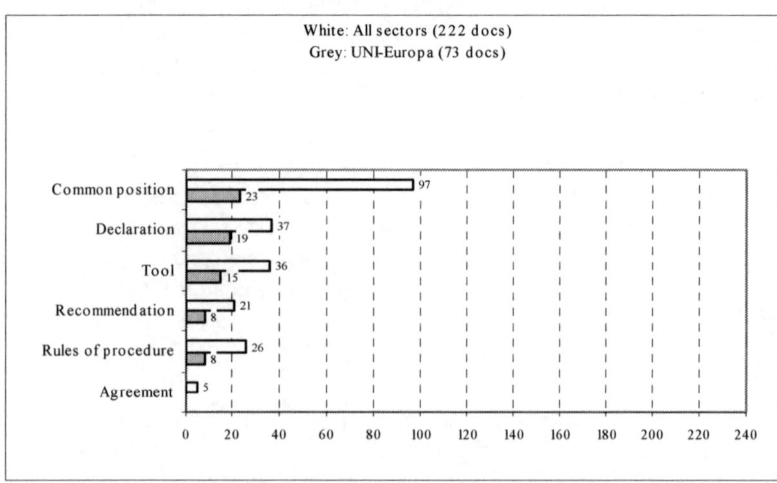

Here, then, is confirmation that on the whole sectoral social dialogue in UNI-Europa sectors is less geared towards Community policies than other social dialogues (apart from telecoms and postal services in the 1990s), and that this is a growing trend. Unlike the majority of players in the sectoral social dialogue, the employers' organisations in banking and insurance have no mandate to negotiate sectoral policies. In these sectors there has been just one common position, in 1998, on a partnership for a new organisation of work.

By contrast, the number of tools, declarations and recommendations is above average. UNI has not signed any binding agreements; those have all been adopted in the transport sector (see chapter 2) and above all the railways (see chapter 5).

The next graph summarises the information provided and indicates the number of documents per sector and per type for all sectors.

Figure 5: Number of Types per Sector (1978-2005)

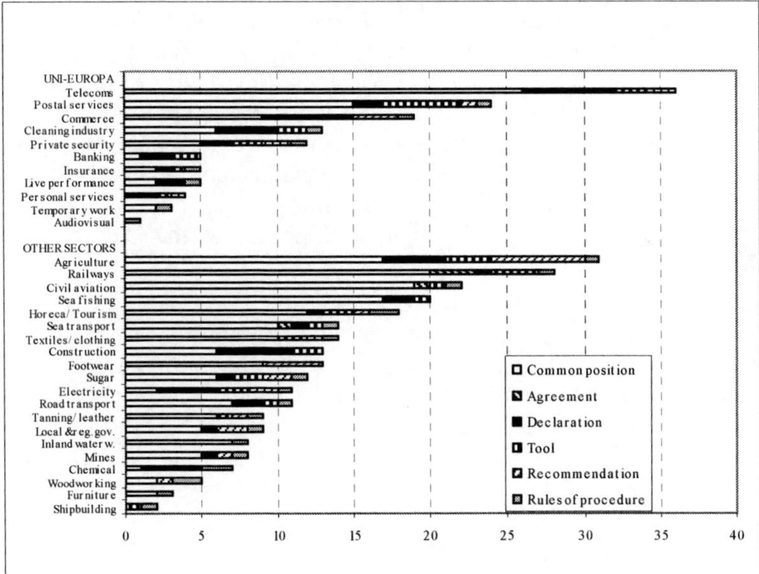

The results of our quantitative analysis tell us that social dialogue in UNI-Europa sectors has in recent years been an exchange between sectoral partners ("reciprocal commitments") rather than aimed at the European Commission. This dialogue has led in the main to joint tools and joint declarations, i.e. low-intensity commitments. Nevertheless, certain declarations or tools can have a significant impact at national level, and social dialogue can do much more than generate texts. UNI-

Europa's objective, as recalled at the Stockholm regional conference, is after all to draw up "binding framework agreements", and the adoption of joint texts with verified and verifiable effects makes a major contribution towards this objective.

Even though there is a predominance of declarations and tools, our comparative analysis also shows that the UNI-Europa sectors are more productive than the other sectors on average when it comes to the number of recommendations. All eight recommendations adopted since 1998 have been produced in five of the 11 sectors: commerce, private security, personal services, postal services and telecoms. As for other sectors, 13 recommendations have been signed in nine sectors: agriculture, woodworking, footwear, local and regional government, electricity, sugar, tanning & leather.

This overall outcome needs to be put into perspective. Indeed, over the past four years (2002-2005) only two of the nine recommendations adopted (less than a quarter) come from UNI-Europa sectors. Caution is of course required here since, according to our definitions, the difference between a recommendation (explicit follow-up) and a declaration (no explicit follow-up) can sometimes be tenuous. For instance, the 1998 postal services recommendation was not followed up at all, since the change from a joint committee to a social dialogue committee necessitated intensive internal discussion, particularly about representation on the trade union side. On the other hand, the telecoms declaration on call centres has no explicit follow-up built into the text, but there is a consensus that it will be followed up during talks at the sectoral social dialogue committee.

We believe that the existence of follow-up and explicit follow-up procedures is a political matter for negotiation between the sectoral partners. In most instances the employers' federations want this to remain as informal as possible, and this element must be taken into account. Even so, there has at the very least been a loss of momentum.

Table 2: "Recommendations" per Sector since 1998

	Other sectors (13 recommendations)									UNI-Europa sectors (8 recommendations)					
1998-2005	Agriculture	Woodworking	Footwear	Local and regional government	Electricity	Horeca	Mines	Sugar	Tanning and leather	Telecommuni-cations	Postal services	Commerce	Private security	Personal services	Total
1998				1				1			1				3
1999												1	1		2
2000			1						1						2
2001										1		1		1	3
2002	1	1			1										3
2003					1			1				1	1		4
2004				1		1	1								3
2005	1														1
Total	2	1	1	2	2	1	1	2	1	1	1	3	2	1	**21**

Let us turn now to the subject matter of the joint documents. As we stated in chapter 3, particular caution is required when analysing these themes because many documents deal with several issues at once, so it is not easy to determine the main theme. Minor quantitative differences are of no real significance, however, and certain overall trends can be detected.

Figure 6: Number of Documents by Theme (1978-2005)

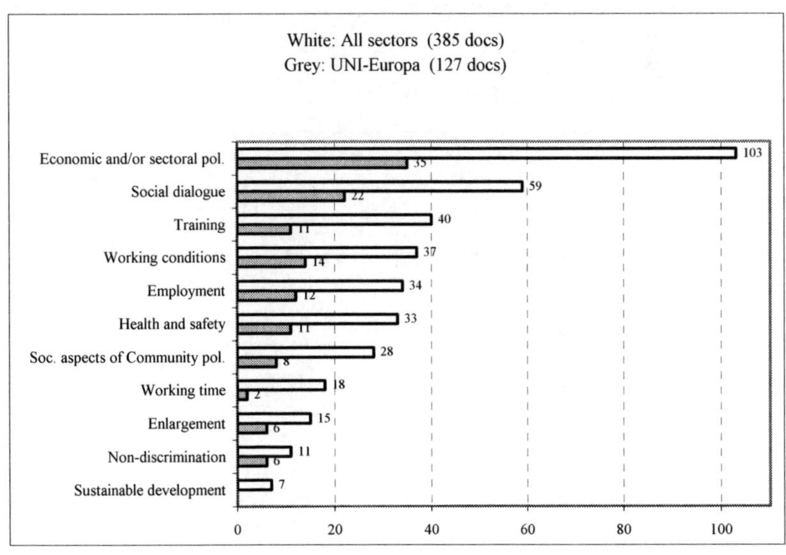

First of all, there is an above-average number of documents relating to social dialogue. This ties in with our previous remarks to the effect that the social dialogue in UNI-Europa sectors is more for internal consumption (reciprocal commitments) than directed towards the European Commission or the EU in general. Conversely, this finding is also borne out by the low number of joint texts adopted concerning social aspects of Community policies (which is the commonest category of documents addressed to the Commission).

Secondly, we note that the "non-discrimination" theme is of key importance, in that 55% of all joint documents on this theme come from UNI-Europa sectors and, more particularly, from commerce: joint statement on combating racism and xenophobia (15 May 2000), agreement on the prevention of racial discrimination (1 October 1997), guidelines supporting age diversity (11 March 2002), and the statement on promoting employment and integration of disabled people (28 May 2004).

Thirdly, and very obviously, working time and, to a lesser extent, training are themes which crop up much less often than in other sectors.

The final aspect of our quantitative analysis is to look at the addressees of joint texts. As shown by the next table, certain characteristic features of UNI-Europa come to the fore here too. More joint documents than average are addressed to the national public authorities (above all in the cleaning industry and private security) and to businesses (commerce, telecoms, cleaning). The national social partners are likewise major addressees. This once again confirms that social dialogue in UNI-Europa sectors is above all else an internal dialogue, aimed less at the European Commission as a regulatory authority.

Figure 7: Number of Documents per Addressee (1978-2005)

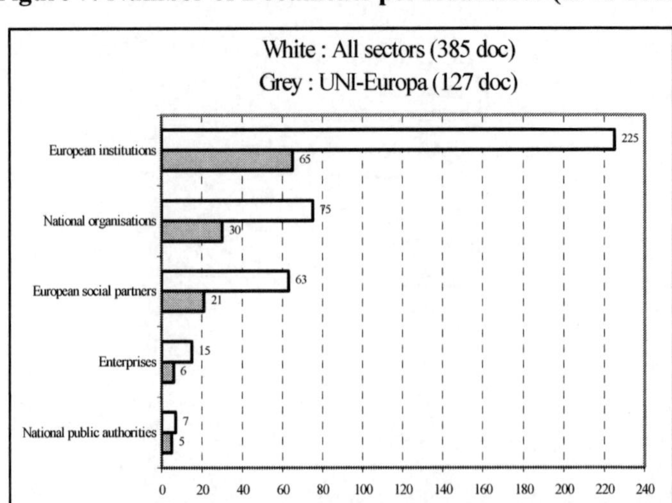

This quantitative analysis has enabled us to illustrate the diversity of sectors in terms of the number and type of joint documents adopted, which was to be expected given the heterogeneity of UNI-Europa sectors. It has also enabled us to highlight some overall trends indicative of a certain "tone" distinguishing social dialogue in UNI-Europa sectors. We move on now to a brief description of the outcomes in accordance with our typology.

II. Typology of Sectors

The twenty or so interviews we conducted with international, European and national UNI officials very largely corroborated the typology previously drawn up in our study for the European Commission, as outlined in chapter 4. Here we take another look at the various categories and summarise the principal developments occurring in the UNI-Europa sectors. As far as other sectors are concerned, we would refer the interested reader to the *Working Paper* published by the ETUI-REHS (Pochet *et al.*, 2006).

For the record, we identified three variables which have a bearing on the nature of sectoral social dialogue:

1) Community policies
2) International factors
3) The players' strategies.

On this basis, we grouped the sectors into the following six categories.

1. Sectors Aspiring to European-scale Industrial Relations

These are agriculture, fisheries and transport, where European Union policies go to the very heart of the sector. The social partners' aim is to achieve collective bargaining and binding agreements. *Common positions* would not necessarily give sufficient added value in this instance, except where the social partners manage to have a bearing on Community policy-making. The outcomes vary. Only *agriculture and the railways* seem to have managed to take the first step towards European-scale industrial relations. No UNI-Europa sectors fall into this category.

2. Sectors Opening up to Competition and Interconnection across National Borders

This second category is notable for its strong exposure to the various processes of liberalisation, deregulation and opening up to competition within the EU (*telecommunications, postal services, electricity*), which has an impact on the dynamics of social dialogue. The opening up of telecommunications to competition back in the late 1980s, the gradual deregulation of postal services since 1997 and the measures aimed at establishing an internal market in electricity led, initially, to the adoption of numerous *common positions* in a bid to influence the Community policies: enforcement of competition rules, effects of liberalisation on employment, organisation of the sector, the social dimension, universal service, etc. This category is the one which has produced the most joint documents: 26 for telecommunications and 15 for postal services.

Since then, the European social partners have undertaken to carry out a number of joint activities in order to cope with the social consequences of liberalisation. To this end they have produced not only a whole host of training and information tools (studies, glossaries, etc.), but also several recommendations or "frameworks of action" (postal services, telecommunications, electricity). This transition towards joint commitments has been easier for telecoms than for postal services, where the change from a joint committee to a social dialogue committee disrupted the former status quo and problems of representation arose between national trade unions. Furthermore, Deutsche Post and the Dutch postal service rapidly developed international strategies.

Enlargement, telework and call centres are the themes recently addressed in telecoms. This sector is set to experience another technological revolution which could lead to significant job losses (see part three). Trade unions are generally well represented in the traditional operators, where there is a culture of partnership.

3. Sectors Keeping up with European Developments

This third category covers banking and insurance, represented by UNI-Finance. Here, European and international pressure is relatively insignificant and relates mainly to the establishment of common national rules. However, after a spell of mergers and acquisitions mainly within national borders, there seems likely to be increasing concentration at European level (and no doubt globally).

The European Union has adopted a number of directives as part of the completion of the internal market (annual accounts of banks and other financial institutions, accounting standards, etc.). The finishing touches are being put to the European financial market (some directives need to be rewritten). One noteworthy feature of social dialogue in this sector is that the employers' mandate is confined to social policy matters. And there have in fact been no significant European developments on the social policy front in recent years, even though these sectors have experienced a number of mergers and restructuring processes at national and, now, European level.

National social dialogue is well developed and enables the partners to work at European level on the basis of trusting relationships at national level. The output of joint texts in both of these sectors has been relatively modest. European social dialogue is evidently still seeking a momentum that will give it shape. These two very closely related sectors affect one another, especially because within UNI they are one and the same sector: finance. That is not necessarily an advantage, however, because negotiations in one of them set a benchmark for the other and limit the room for manoeuvre on both sides. The employers in the two sectors are very different in size and sometimes have divergent interests. The *banking* sector is showing some signs of movement in respect of corporate social responsibility – a source of some tension between the different employer organisations. Enlargement is another important theme which has prompted a flurry of activity. As in the case of commerce, there is a desire to be involved in the full range of cross-industry activities (e.g. the tripartite summit) as a way of putting forward the sector's priorities.

In the *insurance sector*, on the other hand, the latest negotiations on lifelong learning came to nothing (the problems being follow-up, the number of conditions laid down in the text and, more significantly, the fact that the employers refused to consider time spent in training as paid working time). The social partners are seeking a way out of the impasse. They are discussing pensions and corporate social responsibility. The employers involved in social dialogue in insurance are in no hurry at all to achieve joint documents of any great substance. One representative of the sector's employers expressed the view that the main difficulty in progressing the European social dialogue is limited interest on the part of national associations. This indicates an obvious lack of vision concerning what the social dialogue could amount to. The employers complain that the social dialogue committee was not consulted about the European Commission's proposal for a directive on equal treatment for women and men in financial services (CEC, 2003).

4 Sectors Coping with Change in a Context of Globalisation

No UNI-Europa sectors belong to our fourth category, which is strongly affected by the impact of globalisation. It comprises traditional industries (*textiles/clothing, tanning, footwear, woodworking/furniture and sugar*), all of them exposed to outsourcing and/or enhanced competition from less developed countries. Chapter 6 examines the sugar and textile sectors in detail.

5. Sectors Constructing a European Dimension

In our typology, all the sectors falling into this category are service sectors and all belong to UNI: *private security, cleaning industry, personal services, live performance, temporary work and audiovisual* (the exception being HORECA, a somewhat atypical case). These sectors are both relatively immune to international competition and relatively unaffected by Community policies – or at least they were until the proposal of the "services" directive, which could thoroughly disrupt the rules of the game and have far-reaching effects on social dialogue in the future (for a description see Van den Abeele, 2005). Certain service sectors, such as private security, have been confronted, since EU enlargement, with a considerable increase in competition from the new Member States. But be that as it may, unlike other categories, there are no obvious European issues which would "naturally" favour the construction of a European dimension here.

The features specific to these sectors often include difficult working conditions, non-standard forms of employment (part-time or temporary) and irregular working hours (nights, weekends). Image problems can sometimes loom large too. Although most of these sectors are seeing a growth in employment (above all private security, temporary work and cleaning), trade union organisations generally have less of a presence than in more traditional services such as banking and insurance. Competition often derives from undeclared work, which is sometimes well organised in structural terms and sometimes less so.

There are no overall, indisputable European challenges which could account for social dialogue in these sectors but rather partial, indirect and diffuse issues. For instance, certain directives (e.g. on VAT rates in highly labour-intensive services, transport of funds for private security) may indirectly have a substantial impact on industrial relations. Access to public procurement has led to the adoption of texts on "best value" in the private security and cleaning industries, and on VAT for hairdressing. Codes of conduct may also be used for this purpose (private security and personal services).

Given that these sectors have no intrinsic European substance, they have to invent it. For this reason the social dialogue is more dependent here than elsewhere on the players' inventiveness. Much depends on the employers. In certain sectors (private security, cleaning industry, personal services) the employers are dynamic; that is not so much the case in the temporary work, audiovisual and live performance sectors.

Job insecurity is a major issue: it constitutes the hidden face of attempts to professionalise these sectors. Training (e.g. for hairdressers or theatre technicians) is an important theme in all instances, most notably with a view to improving the image, professionalism and attractiveness of these sectors, but also employee mobility.

In *private security*, the employers have pursued a strategy of looking to Europe rather than individual Member States to improve the sector's image. They have constructed a European agenda and attach a key role to their cooperation with the trade unions. This sector has also been restructured, and large Europe-wide groups of companies have emerged. Enlargement has been a particularly sensitive matter. As pointed out by De Marchi (2005: 373), a former UNI official in the sector, "the weakness and/or inexistence of trade union structures in the new Member States is an important issue". The security firms now emerging in the central and Eastern European countries are largely unregulated and poorly organised. In addition, wages are particularly low, arousing fears of social dumping.

Like private security, the *cleaning industry* suffers from an image problem and non-standard working conditions, in the form of work done outside of normal hours (early morning, evening and weekend) as well as flexible contracts. Common positions have been adopted on employment and undeclared work, as have two training tools, one on health/ safety and the other on "selecting best value". One important topic from the employers' point of view is ensuring that public authorities do not systematically select the lowest-price bid but also take account of quality. Particularly sensitive topics for the trade unions include health/safety and enlargement. Just as for private security, there does not seem at first sight to be a European social agenda, so one has to be constructed.

For the time being, the "personal services" sector encompasses only *hairdressing*, which is attempting to promote dialogue in the field of beauty care. Social dialogue in hairdressing is very lively, down-to-earth and pragmatic. One of its main drivers appears to be a desire for a Community-scale profile and professionalism, with a view to giving the sector a quality brand-image. Relations between employer and employee representatives are described as very good and largely conflict-free, albeit a little more difficult this past year, particularly around the subject of workplace health and safety. The purpose of the social dialogue is to reach agreement on certain specific aspects of Community policy, such as the cosmetics directive and REACH (see also chapter 8 in this volume).

The sectoral social dialogue in the *temporary work* sector was formalised at the very time when the cross-industry social partners were tackling the issue, only to fail in their efforts a few months later. Given that the Commission then put forward a draft directive, it was only logical that the sectoral social partners should opt for a strategy of consultation rather than direct negotiations with one another. This led the employers to sideline the social dialogue, although it is now picking up again thanks to a study of the sector being carried out by the Dublin Foundation. The topics under discussion are training and how to integrate difficult individuals.

European social dialogue in the *live performance* sector was only initiated fairly recently, which explains why its output, in terms of agreements, so far remains very limited. This sector is distinctive in that it often consists of initiatives emanating from micro-firms or even individuals – with the exception of major festivals, operas, etc. – which may be largely, or entirely, unstructured. Another specific feature here is the role of public subsidies in supporting cultural events. Representation on the employer side is a problem, and relations have not been of the best in recent years, although a thaw does seem to be setting in. Although European concerns are not always taken on board by the members of employer and employee organisations in this sector, an external dynamic is clearly at work in the social dialogue. These concerns are linked in the main to mobility within the EU and indirectly related issues, such as taxation (e.g. of orchestras staging a European tour). The sector also claims a unique status with regard to certain European directives, such as those on working time, "noise" (concerts) and gender equality, as well as the possible impact of multilateral trade negotiations (GATS) on the sector. The social dialogue agenda in these very specific areas is linked to the European agenda. Its *raison d'être* is to enlighten the Community institutions about the singularity of a sector not really comparable with any other service sector or industry. However, there is also evidence of an internal dynamic which has arisen around the subject of training for theatre technicians and the establishment of a Europe-wide diploma: two themes designed to foster the mobility of workers in the sector.

As for the *audiovisual* sector, the social dialogue was not put on a formal footing until 2004, even though talks began back in 1995. Three plenary meetings have taken place until now, leading to the adoption of a work programme and one joint text. Dialogue is conducted between five employer organisations and four trade union bodies (see Table 1). In addition to UNI-Europa, trade unions representing actors, musicians and journalists also take part. The employers sometimes find it difficult to cooperate and coordinate their views on matters such as public funding for television channels and commercial television stations. This can create tension. UNI-Europa would have preferred two separate social dialogues, one with producers and the other with broadcasters, but the Commission preferred one large sector.

There is no shortage of topics for the social dialogue: public service financing, media concentration, job insecurity, outsourcing, free movement of audiovisual products, changing occupations, technology, training of casual staff, health/safety and stress. Training is a cross-cutting issue affecting all the players. The aim is to take stock of the situation and, on that basis, to encourage the recognition of qualifications with a view to promoting mobility.

As concerns enlargement, the objective is to produce a text underlining the importance of national social dialogue and trade union rights.

There is a shared interest here, in that the employers wish to be independent of governments and of tripartite dialogue. The sticking points include private broadcasters, but also public broadcasters, especially regarding casual staff. For affiliates in search of recognition, the European route can be a useful option (e.g. Slovenia). Public broadcasters are often on the same wavelength as the trade unions when it comes to sectoral issues.

6. *A Sector Striving to Be Independent of the Cross-industry Social Dialogue*

We have placed the *commerce* sector in a category of its own because we consider it to be motivated by quite separate factors. Its intention is to make plain the specifics of services in general and of commerce in particular at all levels, not so much with a view to resisting international competition as to making the most of it so as to bring down prices of sale. Similarly, EU enlargement is a veritable windfall for this sector, due to the increase in sales outlets in the central and Eastern European countries (countries, moreover, which are not very competitive in this area).

Commerce is incontestably the largest sector in terms of its workforce – over 20 million. In order to make its specific voice heard, an all-round strategy has been devised, consisting of lobbying the European institutions as well as holding an internal social dialogue. This dialogue is fostered by the shared interests of major companies and trade unions, especially to combat the labour practices prevalent among "hard discounters". The ultimate hate-figure is the US giant Wal-Mart, but Lidl is regarded as one of the worst offenders in Europe. As pointed out by Jan Furstenborg (2005: 356), head of the commerce sector at UNI-Europa, on the subject of scandals among the low-cost retail giants, "so there is a situation in commerce which is conducive for developing the European social dialogue, a situation where the serious players on the business side should have broad joint interests with unions".

The rules of procedure governing social dialogue in this sector are the lengthiest and most comprehensive of all such documents stored in our database (four pages). By the same token, the social dialogue in commerce is one of the most dynamic. The main internal stimulus has to do with the fact that, in the opinion of the social partners, the sector's specific interests do not receive sufficient attention from the European authorities, which they regard as being more sensitive to the concerns of industry. There is moreover tension between representatives of the sector and the cross-industry European organisations, which provokes a degree of competition.

The strategy deployed by the trade union side is to base the social dialogue on fundamental rights. These are then broken down into several areas: prevention of racial discrimination, combating racism and xenophobia, violence at work and supporting age diversity. The next topics to be addressed will be gender equality and social exclusion/inclusion.

Looking ahead to future negotiations, technological innovations (such as shops without checkouts and self-scanning by customers) could pave the way towards important negotiations aimed at improving training and wages for the remaining workforce.

III. Qualitative Developments and Cross-cutting Aspects

Having surveyed the main quantitative trends and examined developments in individual sectors, let us now turn our attention to cross-cutting aspects of the social dialogue. Our analysis will be based on the interviews we conducted. We shall begin with the players' own assessment of the social dialogue, before outlining the resultant ideal model. After that we shall examine in turn the role of the employers, the Commission and national trade unions, as well as the way in which the texts adopted are followed up and implemented. Lastly we shall look ahead to the themes of the future.

The importance of social dialogue was emphasised by all the players we interviewed, including those who were critical of its outcomes, or else of what they deemed to be the absence of any significant outcomes. Similarly, those sectors without an official social dialogue (graphical industry and IBITS) hoped to establish one and believed that it would in particular lend structure to their internal debates[4]. Social dialogue also requires a considerable investment in human terms, bearing in mind the limited number of staff available. Generally speaking, two positive aspects are highlighted. Firstly, the very creation of a sectoral dialogue body (11 sectors have managed it): according to our informants, that would not have been thought possible ten years ago. Despite their weaknesses, SSDCs mean that meetings and debates can be organised around European issues. Secondly, these bodies can help in conveying messages from sectoral trade unions to the European institutions – not always successfully, it is true.

---

4 These two sectors are very different, and the reasons for their lack of dialogue are equally different: the absence of an employers' mandate for IBITS, and the unwillingness of certain national delegations (especially in Germany) for the graphical industry. This has not prevented the graphical industry from being very dynamic (collective bargaining committee; demonstrations by members in the Quebecor case).

The players consider this to be a long-term process and investment which takes time to bear fruit. But they point out at the same time that the outcomes have to make sense to their members.

The ideal general model put forward by many of those we consulted comprises the following elements[5]:

a) identifying with national trade unions the internal priorities to be raised at European Union level
b) negotiating with the employers in the hope of concluding substantive voluntary agreements
c) these agreements should be put to good use by the national sectoral partners.

Various problems have been singled out in connection with this ideal model. They relate first of all to the employers and their limited interest in social dialogue. Next come problems and questions related to the Commission and its supporting role, as well as the involvement of national trade unions both in identifying priorities and in implementing the outcomes of European social dialogue. Lastly there are problems to do with the follow-up – or rather the lack of any systematic follow-up – of recommendations and declarations, and national-level implementation.

A. Employers

The employers play a crucial role in developing social dialogue. Many of our informants believe that they take an interest in the social dialogue only so as to gain recognition of their status but do not wish to go any further. For this reason it is often difficult to achieve anything substantial, especially in sectors where the employers are split between several organisations (banking, insurance, audiovisual) or are unwilling to cooperate.

In addition, our attention was sometimes drawn to a lack of representative status, in the sense that not all countries or not all employers are represented (e.g. insurance, live performance). In sectors with traditional operators, new businesses may not be represented at all. For instance, ETNO represents traditional telecoms operators but not mobile phone companies (although that might change) or some of the newcomers. Some of our informants also pointed to the competition between traditional operators but also the complex relationships linking them together, none of which facilitates the emergence of common positions. In the words of Colclough (2005: 395), "the internal struggles in ETNO will therefore naturally influence the willingness of member companies

[5] This stylised model emerges equally from interviews in other sectors.

to support, implement or even initiate common goals". Finally, when traditional operators and private operators do come together, as in the audiovisual sector, it does not make for an easy consensus on the objectives of the sector and of Community policies.

If neither side is in a position of strength and no external pressure is exerted, the usual approach is to seek a consensus. This is easier when it suits the employers' own interests (giving the sector a higher profile or making it more attractive, worker mobility, major technological change, impact on Community legislation, etc.). However, the picture as explained to us is more complex than that, and some national employers' delegations and multinational groups are indeed convinced of the value of European sectoral dialogue.

Coordination of transnational action (in accordance with the different countries' traditions) is not really on the cards. The demonstrations in favour of Quebecor by graphical industry workers in 13 countries would appear to be an exception in a sector without a properly structured social dialogue. According to our interviewees, any such action is unthinkable in their sector, at least for the time being (with the possible exception of postal services). Two main reasons are given: the lack of any demand from national trade unions to that effect, and the consensual nature of the social dialogue which steers clear of public demonstrations and open crisis. On the other hand, the European social dialogue can help in settling national or regional disputes in certain sectors.

B. European Commission

Opinions about the Commission's role differ quite widely. Many commentators believe that it prefers to remain neutral and is not proactive enough in bringing the employers to the negotiating table. Some even suggest that it should make negotiations compulsory. Others would like to see additional Commission involvement, but confined to the provision of effective technical support. It was also pointed out that organisational arrangements were sometimes chaotic (uncertainty about meeting dates, interpretation, etc.). Funding problems were raised and, in particular, the co-financing of studies by the social partners: this harks back to the shortage of resources in certain sectors (most notably postal services). On the other hand, the Commission provides vital back-up in establishing structures in the new Member States. Lastly, the point was also made that the Commission puts the social dialogue players under great pressure to improve their coordination and become more efficient, but it is not always very well organised itself, particularly as concerns coordination between the Directorate General for Employment and the other DGs (Competition, Internal Market, etc.).

C. *Involvement of National Trade Unions*

In order for there to be strong national involvement, the players must have a strategic and far-sighted approach to the importance of transnational bargaining, because national trade unions can rarely make any immediate gains. Attendance at social dialogue meetings is normally good but can on occasion be patchy. Trade unions from the new EU Member States are (very) gradually beginning to attend more frequently, although many of them still experience difficulties when travel expenses are not paid in advance and when deciding how to allocate very limited human resources.

Generally speaking, a distinction also needs to be drawn between attendance at meetings and active participation. This information ties in with our own experience: at the sectoral social dialogue meetings (UNI-Europa and others) which we attended in order to present the study undertaken for the Commission, we were struck by the lack of active participation on the part of many delegates. Several sectors emphasise how difficult it is to agree on strong joint demands. Only the Graphical and Finance (banking and insurance) sectors have collective bargaining committees. They are the exception to the rule. One of the reasons for this might be that the "inflation plus productivity" formula used as a bargaining tool in other sectoral federations does not really apply in services. In addition, there seems to be no real demand on the part of national members.

The development of European social dialogue also requires the involvement of strong trade unions in their home countries so as to convince the employers to participate. Transnational bargaining, as envisaged in the Commission's communication on the social agenda, does not seem to be on the cards, since there is no demand coming from national trade unions. This obstacle could be removed if a small number of countries decided to go it alone.

Relations are built around an annual work programme, more rarely a two-year programme. It would not necessarily be appropriate to have a multiannual programme, as happens at cross-industry level, since that might entail entering into commitments at the wrong point in time and cause a lack of flexibility.

While the aim of the trade union movement is to create a system of industrial relations in Europe, not enough work has been done to raise specifically European issues. Such issues could heighten the synergy between the different players and promote a degree of coherence in putting forward shared objectives. The interplay between the cross-industry and sectoral dialogues is certainly not a strong point. Whereas telework has been the subject of agreements in both the commerce and telecoms sectors (one of them predating the cross-industry agreement on the same theme), the issue of stress at work has been dealt with at cross-industry level but not really taken up at sectoral level – except in the case of the cleaning industry and private security where the responsible official in Brussels was also a member of the ETUC delegation. Colleagues in some sectors even admit to not having read the cross-industry agreement on stress at work.

In terms of strategy, some players prefer to participate fully in a Europe in the making, whereas others link their participation to global challenges (trade union membership, global agreements, the emergence of China and India). Even though these two approaches are not incompatible – far from it – it seems to us that the right balance has not (yet) been struck.

D. Follow-up and Implementation

As we saw in chapter 4, a distinction must be drawn between follow-up and implementation. Follow-up mainly consists in monitoring the progress of a European joint document at national level: e.g. what developments arise from it, as the case may be. It is procedural – for instance the organising of a seminar – and mainly relates to information. Implementation is substantive and consists of active steps taken to transpose European rules at national level.

National-level follow-up and implementation are at the very heart of sectoral social dialogue. They were a priority for the private security and cleaning industries in 2005. The commerce sector has initiated a review of five joint texts. Telecoms has carried out a survey on telework. The monitoring of certificates is also very much a live issue in the hairdressing sector. Generally speaking, however, the texts adopted are followed up in a weak and patchy fashion. Round-table talks are held, of course, and sometimes documents are issued summarising the feedback received, but not systematically and not in such a way as to provide much telling information about actual implementation.

This finding is not specific to UNI-Europa; it applies across the board in the sectoral and cross-industry dialogue. The lack of effective follow-up is not least attributable to limited staff numbers and to the inadequacy of external support (e.g. from research centres). Thus there is little reliable information available about national-level implementation of the texts adopted at European level. Collective bargaining committees can sometimes serve as a follow-up platform (e.g. on the lifelong learning declaration in the banking sector).

In certain instances, participants in the European social dialogue have been able to use its outcomes in their national collective bargaining. This is the case in Italy for hairdressing and for training in the commerce sector; similarly in Sweden for lifelong learning in banking.

Other examples do exist, but they appear to be exceptions rather than the general rule – that much is clear from the partial evidence, but no detailed study has been carried out in this field. In cases such as the code of conduct in commerce and telework in telecoms, multinational companies play a particularly important role. But not all of them respond to questionnaires.

This poses a major problem. If European texts are implemented nationally on a voluntary basis (in the sense of "optional"), there is a significant risk that they will be used in a positive and dynamic manner only by those trade unions which are already the strongest at national level, leaving the others behind. If this happens, there can be no guarantee of achieving common basic rules applying to the majority of workers in a sector.

We would nevertheless point out that another strategy is unfolding, especially with regard to the new Member States and their wish to guarantee trade union rights (in commerce, audiovisual, etc.). Here, through the documents signed or the trust established between partners, sectoral social dialogue can contribute towards the creation and/or recognition of local-level trade unions. Such action strengthens the weak links in the trade union movement, especially in the new and future Member States. And nor is this confined to the trade union side: it can also help the employers to become more representative (e.g. in the live performance sector), thereby helping to promote national sectoral social dialogue.

IV. Looking Ahead

In this section, still on the basis of the interviews conducted, we shall examine the factors liable to strengthen or revive sectoral dialogue. Indeed, as we have shown in earlier chapters, if the social dialogue is to develop, talks need to be prompted by shared threats or problems. We shall look in turn at the "services" directive, enlargement, technological change, demographic trends and restructuring.

The "services" directive. UNI-Europa, the number-one service sector trade union organisation, could not possibly remain indifferent to the proposal and has been particularly active in this field. The directive has been discussed with employers in the cleaning industry, private security and audiovisual sectors. The employers in the live performance sector have not wanted to broach this subject. Talks have been held in commerce, but those employers are very much in favour of liberalising services. The directive has not been discussed formally in the temporary work sector, where the employers are in favour of including agency work in the directive but the trade unions are steadfastly against. UNI-Europa and the lottery companies have adopted a common position calling for gambling to be removed from the "services" directive[6]. Last of all, an agreement has almost been reached in the audiovisual sector. For the record, a waiver is planned for postal services and an exemption for finance and telecoms. This directive will have a major impact on affiliates to IBITS, a sector where there is no social dialogue.

The trade unions' main criticism of the initial proposal for a directive related to the much-discussed country of origin principle (COP), whereby a service provider operating in a country other than his own would still be subject to the legislation – including on industrial relations – in force in his country of origin. Thus the COP would have had a significant impact on the conduct of the social partners. The UNI-Europa executive's stance on the COP was to accept this principle only on condition that there was adequate harmonisation of social policy standards between countries. However, in its report adopted at first reading in February 2006, the European Parliament removed the COP from the text and replaced it with the "freedom to provide services". The Commission then put forward a new version of the directive in early April 2006, taking over most of the Parliament's amendments. At the time of writing these lines, the final negotiations had yet to take place in the Council of the European Union. It is therefore too soon to assess the potential impact of this draft directive on social dialogue in the services sector. At the very least, the draft has highlighted the need for a well-focused debate on the concept of fair competition between EU countries and branches of industry.

Technological change. The technological revolution is continuing, and sectors such as telecoms and commerce are likely to surge forward in the next few years. Huge job losses could occur, especially as the qualifications required will be quite different from those of today's workers. How to cope with these upheavals is a very real issue and opens the door to the possibility of negotiations.

Demographic change (qualifications and training). Demographic change is not a topic normally discussed by trade unions, but employers in various sectors are concerned about the potential consequences of demographic trends on their sector's capacity to attract well-trained young people, since there will be fewer entrants to the labour market in future. It is therefore likely that several sectors will discuss how to make the sector and its working conditions more attractive (private security, industrial cleaning, but also banking and telecoms).

---

6 It should be pointed out that the gaming industry has mixed views on the matter: the RGA (Remote Gambling Association) and the EBA (European Betting Association) are both in favour of the gaming sector being included in the "services" directive.

Restructuring. A Communication adopted by the Commission on 31 March 2005 states that "As regards employment and training issues, it will involve the European sectoral social dialogue committees where appropriate" (CEC, 2005: 9). The Commission also envisages setting up high-level groups involving all stakeholders, and will open a new phase of negotiations on restructuring and European Works Councils. It plans to present this initiative in detail to the different sectoral social dialogue committees. This is a very sensitive matter for the employers. A study by the McKinsey Global Institute (2005) reveals the considerable potential of outsourcing for the services sector.

Conclusions

In this chapter we have examined the general and specific changes underway in the social dialogue in UNI-Europa sectors. It emerges from both our quantitative and our qualitative analyses that the sectoral social dialogue covered by UNI-Europa, taken as a whole, lies close to the European average. But it must be pointed out at the same time that the European sectoral social dialogue in its entirety is rather weak. The outcomes of this dialogue have until now been relatively limited in terms of the quality of the texts adopted and also their follow-up, despite some improvement in recent years. The social dialogue has brought about common structures and has had an influence on European policies, albeit to varying degrees from one sector to another. It has fostered relations between the players and even led to reciprocal commitments. Yet UNI-Europa is notable for the comparatively low number of common positions adopted in service sectors (with the exception of telecoms and postal services in the 1990s), which some might explain in terms of their remoteness from day-to-day European policy-making (let us not forget that part of the organisation's staff is still based in Nyon (Switzerland).

Our analysis of the individual sectors confirms that the rationale behind talks with the employers varies. What each sector needs to do now is find the most appropriate discussion topics. Relations with the employers are good in the vast majority of cases, and a degree of mutual trust has been built up. But that is not enough to ensure the adoption of texts which are more precise and entail greater commitment, or even binding and verifiable texts – especially since ways of putting pressure on the employers are limited. Quebecor is an exceptional case rather than a first step leading to wider national mobilisation.

National members ask themselves what is the added value of European-level social dialogue. They do of course become involved at transnational level, but not wholeheartedly, since there is little evidence of short-terms gains and the long-term gains seem uncertain. Herein lies the contradiction between the ideal model envisaged by the players and the reality of social dialogue on the ground. Therefore, in the absence of a clear structure at European level, and unless the key players decide to invest in this level of regulation, the dichotomy between an ideal social dialogue and what happens in practice will remain.

Various new and emerging themes could give fresh impetus to the sectoral social dialogue and help to shape it. On the negative side, at least initially, enlargement constitutes a huge challenge for certain sectors. It is a structural matter: bodies need to be established on both the trade union and employer sides. Some aspects of health and safety and vocational training (certification) are likewise major issues at European level. Technological and demographic change may act as catalysts. But one crucial issue for the UNI-Europa trade unions is the "services" directive, because it raises fundamental questions about the notion of fair competition between countries and within sectors. By taking a cross-cutting approach, the services directive should demonstrate the need for a similar horizontal approach from the trade unions, i.e. coordination between sectors and with the cross-industry level. The directive constitutes a unifying force in that it encompasses diverse sectors all very aware of their own specific characteristics and history. Nevertheless, these windows of opportunity will close unless the players take some key decisions on strategy.

References

CEC (2003), Proposal for a Council Directive Implementing the Principle of Equal Treatment between Women and Men in the Access to and Supply of Goods and Services, COM (2003) 657 final of 5 November 2003 (http://europa.eu.int/eur-lex/en/com/pdf/2003/com2003_0657en01.pdf).

CEC (2005), Communication from the Commission "Restructuring and Employment. Anticipating and Accompanying Restructuring in order to Develop Employment: The Role of the European Union", COM (2005) 120 final of 31 March 2005 (http://ec.europa.eu/comm/employment_social/news/2005/apr/com_restruct_en.pdf).

Colclough, C. (2005), "The Sectoral Social Dialogue – Telecommunications", *Transfer*, Vol.11, No.3, Autumn 2005, pp.391-396.

Furstenborg, J. (2005), "Social Dialogue in Retail and Commerce", *Transfer*, Vol.3, No.05, pp.353-358.

De Marchi, S. (2005), "European Social Dialogue in the Private Security Service Sector", *Transfer*, Vol.11, No.3, Autumn 2005, pp.369-373.

Jobert, A. (ed.) (2005), "Les nouveaux cadres du dialogue social: l'espace européen et les territories", Final report for the Commissariat général du plan, Paris.

McKinsey Global Institute (2005), *The Emerging Global Labour Market*, June 2005.

Van den Abeele, É. (2005), "The Draft Services Directive: A Visionary Instrument Enhancing Competitiveness or a Trojan Horse Threatening the European Social Model?", in Degryse, C. and Pochet, P. (eds.), *Social Developments in the European Union 2004*, ETUI-REHS, Observatoire social européen and Saltsa, Brussels, pp.109-147.

CHAPTER 7

Textiles and Sugar

European Social Dialogue under Pressure from International Rules

Philippe POCHET

Introduction

The textile and clothing sector accounts for 4% of manufacturing output and 7% of jobs in Europe. Following EU enlargement to 25 countries (EU-25), there are more than 2.7 million people working in this sector (an increase of a third as compared with the EU-15). It consists mainly of small and medium-sized enterprises (177,000 in the EU-15).

Restructuring has been a permanent feature of the European textile sector since the 1970s. Innovation has brought a considerable rise in productivity, with the least competitive firms either closing down or having to outsource their production in order to survive. This phenomenon gathered pace during the 1990s: 636,000 jobs were lost in the Europe of Fifteen between 1995 and 2003. Output fell by 4.4% and employment by 7.1% in 2003 (EU-25). More than 165,000 jobs disappeared in the EU-25 in the year 2004 alone. Even before the huge influx of Chinese products, experts estimated that the sector is likely to lose half of its current workforce by 2020.

The sugar sector is a good deal smaller. The sugar industry in the enlarged EU employs approximately 60,000 people in 234 factories. Indirect employment is thought to affect some 500,000 people (planters and subcontractors). These figures, dating from July 2004, are however already out of date due to the restructuring process which is already well underway in the central and Eastern European countries. The pace of restructuring is accelerating due to the drastic reduction in EU support for sugar prices decided in 2005.

At first sight the two sectors have nothing in common, except that they are both experiencing a profound change in the rules of competition, resulting from decisions of the World Trade Organization (WTO).

The purpose of this chapter is to compare and decode the strategies of the players in two sectors confronted by the same global threats. In order to survive in Europe, both industries must adopt fresh strategies: specialisation for textiles and adaptation to industrial change for sugar.

According to our typology (see chapter 4), both sectors belong to group three, "sectors engaged in restructuring". For this reason the social partners in these sectors are particularly attentive to Community initiatives. The EU is becoming increasingly alive to this issue. The European Commission adopted a Communication on restructuring in 2004. It is worth citing the passage relating to the social dialogue *in extenso* because it indicates how the Commission intends to proceed, which will shape the debate in the years ahead.

> In recent years the Commission has set up high-level groups, which are informal temporary bodies bringing together all stakeholders in order to compare their points of view on each sector's difficulties and opportunities and achieve a common vision. A number of sectors have also seen rapid and far-reaching changes, in some cases with a severe impact in certain regions with insufficient diversity in available jobs and workforce skills. In view of this experience and the risks involved, the Commission intends to ensure more attentive follow-up in the sectors likely to experience significant changes in the short term. It will concentrate on analysing the development of competitiveness, environmental threats and opportunities, consequences at regional level, and measures likely to be taken at Community level to anticipate and accompany change. As regards employment and training issues, it will involve the European sectoral social dialogue committees where appropriate. These arrangements will be set out in a communication being prepared on the sectoral dimension of industrial policy. In 2005 the Commission will concentrate its efforts on developments in the textile and shipbuilding sectors, as well as the car industry (CEC, 2005a: 8).

The agreement reached by the European Council in December 2005 on the new financial perspectives provides for a special fund to assist with restructuring.

Although restructuring was without doubt the main issue for both sectors in 2005, this chapter will examine the distinctive events and strategies of the past ten years. It will highlight the achievements and limits of the social dialogue in terms of producing joint texts but also as a common strategy for influencing the Commission and European policy-making.

This comparison has been facilitated by contacts and contracts between the Observatoire social européen and each of these sectors. Anne Dufresne and Philippe Pochet undertook some research for the European textiles trade union on a wage standard (wage snake), which was discussed internally and then officially approved in a slightly modified form by the European Trade Union Federation of Textiles, Clothing and

Leather (ETUF:TCL). Contact was maintained in the form of a study carried out for the French Ministry of Social Affairs on Europeanisation in the sector (Dufresne, 2000) and a study on social dialogue for the ILO (Pochet, 2005). Contact with the sugar sector took the form of an investigation on access to the structural funds in the context of the sugar reform (Degryse and Pochet, 2006). We had an opportunity in this case to present our findings to internal bodies within each of the social partners.

The structure of this contribution is as follows. We shall examine the two sectors in turn according to the same model. First of all we shall briefly describe the players and the aims of the social dialogue. Section two in each case will review the documents adopted so far, the topics covered and the addressees. The third section will be devoted to codes: the code of conduct for textiles (1997) and the code of conduct on corporate social responsibility for sugar (2003) as exemplary tools for cooperation. Finally we shall look at the strategies designed to exert influence on Community policy, especially in the management of restructuring. To conclude, we shall compare the different strategies and the results achieved.

I. Textiles

A. Development of the European Social Dialogue: A Few Key Facts

1. The Players

The two main players in the social dialogue are the European Trade Union Federation of Textiles, Clothing and Leather for the employees and the European Apparel and Textile Organisation (Euratex) for the employers.

The European Trade Union Federation of Textiles, Clothing and Leather was officially founded on 24 March 1975 in Brussels under the name European Trade Union Committee of Textiles, Clothing and Leather. The ETUF:TCL brings together 70 free and democratic trade union federations stemming from 40 European countries (mainly in the European Union, the European Economic Area, accession countries and EU candidate countries, but also from the Balkans and a number of other Eastern European countries). The ETUF:TCL represents more than one million workers. It is affiliated to the European Trade Union Confederation (ETUC).

Membership of Euratex consists of 35 national sectoral organisations representing sectoral or sub-sectoral organisations. Euratex has national members in all the Member States apart from Luxembourg, Cyprus,

Malta and Hungary. Turkey is likewise a member. Euratex does not have a mandate to negotiate on wages and working conditions at European level, since its members consider that these matters must remain under national responsibility.

Even though membership extends to most of the new EU Member States, enlargement represents a major challenge for this sector, as for others. The tradition of sectoral social dialogue is less well established, or indeed totally absent, in many of the Eastern European countries. What is more, their national organisations are relatively weak and divided (see the study on representativeness by UCL-IST, 2004 and chapter 11).

2. *The Social Dialogue Committee*

Sectoral social dialogue in the textile sector came about in accordance with the overall institutional dynamic described in the first chapter of this book. The ETUF:TCL and Euratex decided in 1992 to set up an informal working group. In 1999, following the Commission's Communication aimed at putting the sectoral social dialogue committees on a more formal footing (CEC, 1998a and 1998b), the textile/clothing sector was among the first to call for the establishment of such a committee.

Until the end of 2005, the textile/clothing sector was the only major manufacturing industry still not fully subject to the rules of the General Agreement on Tariffs and Trade (GATT). It was organised around a system of quotas, applied since 1962 by all major importing countries including the European Union. The system was extended in 1974 to cover commodities other than cotton and became the Multifibre Arrangement (MFA). At the end of the Uruguay Round the sector was authorised to maintain quotas for a maximum of ten years, with 1 January 2005 as a cut-off date. From its very inception, therefore, the committee had to operate in this context of changing international rules.

The committee's aims are described in its rules of procedure. These are to:

– deliver opinions to the Commission on initiatives with regard to social policy and on developments in European policy having social implications in the European textile and clothing sector;

– promote the social dialogue [...] in order to contribute to the development of employment and competitiveness in this sector[1].

---

1 Rules of procedure for the sectoral dialogue committee in the textile and clothing sector, 29 March 1999 (http://europa.eu.int/comm/employment_social/social_dialogue/docs/153_19990329_textile_en.pdf).

On closer inspection it is possible to distinguish five main areas of activity, namely to:

– exert influence on international trade negotiations at which the Commission negotiates on behalf of the Union;

– have a say in sectoral industrial policy;

– influence general European decisions which impact on the sector internally;

– monitor in a dynamic and proactive fashion the restructuring underway in the sector as it relates to the process of innovation and liberalisation;

– develop common basic social regulations for companies working within and outside of the EU.

This is done by means of three types of instrument:

a) the drafting of joint texts (common positions) addressed to the European institutions. Their intention is to influence European policy-making;

b) the drafting of joint recommendations or declarations which are equally binding on both of the social partners. For the record (see Introduction and chapter 3), recommendations contain a follow-up clause whereas declarations are commitments without any formal follow-up set out in the text.

These first two instruments have led to the signing of nine texts so far (see below), but there are in addition other joint activities which can have major consequences. We shall call these "joint actions".

c) joint actions consist of studies and research projects commissioned by both sides together, participation as social partners in official groups set up by the European authorities, and common appraisals of joint texts either on the ground or for the institutions.

Full market liberalisation in 2005 did not come as a surprise but had been negotiated and accepted ten years earlier. In this context of obligations laid down and accepted by the players, the European Commission attempted to put in place preventive policies designed to boost the sector's competitiveness as a means of anticipating change. These policies revolve around innovation and research and development, respect for intellectual property rights, regional aspects and trade policy. Nonetheless, the effects of full market opening proved to be more of a shock than had been expected.

After the boom in Chinese exports, a Memorandum of Understanding was signed in Shanghai on 10 June 2005, whereby the EU and Beijing made arrangements for the growth in certain categories of Chinese exports to be restricted during a three-year adjustment period.

Without calling into question full trade liberalisation, this agreement should give the European industry more time in the case of certain products to adjust to changes in the competitive environment following trade liberalisation.

B. Outcome of the Sectoral Social Dialogue

Thus the social dialogue simultaneously produces jointly adopted texts and joint actions. We shall first examine all the texts adopted and assess their outcomes. Then, in order to illustrate some joint actions, we shall describe the 2004-2005 work programme and point out different facets of the social dialogue. We shall not take stock here of internal coordination activities such as the wage coordination introduced by the ETUF:TCL, initially on an autonomous basis and then in close association with the European Metalworkers' Federation (EMF) through the Eucoba project.

1. Joint Texts

It is only logical to begin by looking at the written output of the social dialogue, since these joint documents demonstrate the organisations' priorities and degree of commitment. The succession of texts also reveals the extent of what is possible and what has been achieved by adopting a common approach.

The table 1 below lists the fourteen texts adopted hitherto, indicating the type of document, its main theme and its addressees, as well as whether or not provision is made for any formal follow-up.

Table 1: Texts Adopted, Theme, Type of Document and Addressees

Date	Title	Theme	Type	Addressees	Follow-up
01/12/2002	Public procurement awarding guide for the Clothing-textile sector	Economic and/or sectoral policies	Tool	National authorities	
8/06/2001	Procédure de fixation du calendrier des réunions du Comité du dialogue sectoriel textile-habillement	Social dialogue	Common position	European institutions	
1/08/2000	Equal opportunities: Vade mecum. Best practices in the textile and clothing industry	Gender equality	Tool	National organisations	Yes
5/06/2000	Programme d'action sociale	Social aspects of Community policies	Common position	European institutions	

1/03/2000	Lisbon Summit: contribution of the social partners in the "textile and clothing" sector	Employment	Common position	European institutions	
20/12/1999	Joint declaration on the sectoral dimension of the observatory on industrial change	Social aspects of Community policies	Common position	European institutions	
21/05/1999	Suivi du dialogue social sectoriel textile-habillement et chaussures	Employment	Common position	European institutions	
29/03/1999	Rules of procedure for the sectoral dialogue committee in the textile and clothing sector	Social dialogue	Rules of procedure	European social partners	
13/07/1998	Lettre à MM. Santer et Flynn sur la Communication de la Commission sur le travail non declaré	Working conditions	Common position	European institutions	
10/07/1997	A charter by the social partners in the European textile and clothing sector. Code of conduct	Working conditions	Recommendation	National organisations	Yes
10/07/1997	Déclaration conjointe sur l'emploi textile et habillement en Europe	Employment	Common position	European institutions	
13/12/1996	Avis conjoint au sujet de la communication de la Commission sur le dialogue social	Social dialogue	Common position	European institutions	
28/03/1996	Déclaration commune en vue du Conseil Industrie du 28 mars 1996	Economic and/or sectoral policies	Common position	European institutions	
16/06/1994	Joint opinion on improved access to vocational training for women in the textile and clothing sector	Training	Common position	European institutions	

Source: Database of European sectoral agreements, Observatoire social européen.

This table tells us several things. First of all, the texts adopted cover a wide variety of fields. Secondly, most of them are addressed to the European Commission. Mostly they deal with matters related to employment or training. It is worth noting that there is not one joint text relating to restructuring in its own right. Lastly, there are few reciprocal commitments between the sectoral partners for implementation by the national social partners. Only two contain a follow-up clause.

As stated above, Euratex has no mandate to negotiate on working conditions and wages, which considerably limits the scope for agreements in social policy fields. The sole exception was the adoption in 1997 of a code of conduct reproducing the principal basic conventions of the International Labour Organization (ILO). We shall analyse these in more detail in the next section.

For the sake of completeness we should mention two "tools": good practice guides on equal opportunities and on public procurement. These may be used on a decentralised basis and could have a significant effect in respect of employment and quality of work, but no assessment of the impact of such instruments has yet been made.

Not one new text has been adopted since 2002. Our interviewees told us that the strategy pursued has been to maximise the effects of existing documents and to face up to new challenges, one of which is undoubtedly enlargement. Yet the biggest challenge is of course the end of quotas and the major restructuring plans afoot in the sector, especially as a result of competition from China. The players therefore need to turn their attention to other types of activity, which we have referred to as joint actions and examples of which can be found in the work programme (see below). Participation in the High Level Group on the future of the textile and clothing sector, set up by the Commission is certainly the most symbolic of these activities.

Whilst it is appropriate to underscore the achievements of the social dialogue, there are other areas where no agreements at all have been reached. For instance, compulsory indication of origin ensuring full traceability of the production process, and actions for alternative funding of social charges without cutting down benefits (ETUF:TCL, 2005).

2. *Annual Work Programme: An Illustration of the Wide Range of Activities*

We shall now scrutinise the work programme for 2004-2005 in an effort to grasp all the complexities of the sectoral social dialogue. This will give us a good picture of the various strands of the sectoral dialogue process, which we shall return to in more detail later.

The first three points relate to the impact of globalisation and ways of adapting to change. These are: monitoring the state of affairs regarding textiles/clothing in the context of the World Trade Organization (WTO) negotiations; following up the European Commission's Communication on the restructuring of the textile/clothing sector, which proposes measures to boost competitiveness in the sector as well as acting on the discussions and proposals emanating from the High Level Group (see below); and finally, as concerns enlargement, plans to hold a socio-economic forum in Bulgaria.

The next point relates to public procurement and builds on the PROMPTEX initiative (a guide drawn up for the social partners to aid those involved in public procurement awarding procedures to take into account criteria other than price alone) by holding roving seminars to help disseminate the guide.[2]

With regard to the code of conduct (see below), the aim is to press on with efforts to have the textile/clothing code applied in Turkey. Talks are to be held about implementation and verification of the code. The intention is that a joint drafting group (Euratex/ETUF:TCL) will be set up to examine ways of putting the code into practice, based on experience in Turkey and elsewhere. Following on from that, a more general debate will take place about how to improve the visibility and linkage of sectoral social dialogues at European and national level. This question of links is on the agenda in a number of sectoral committees and was addressed by the European Commission in its most recent Communication on the future of the social dialogue (CEC, 2004a).

On the subject of corporate social responsibility, the work programme states that progress made in European-level discussions will be monitored.

As concerns vocational training, it will be a matter of acting on the recommendations of the High Level Group (media pool, observatories, job classification – see below).

The 2005 programme basically takes up where the 2004 programme left off, but with two important innovations. One is the holding of a seminar on anticipating industrial change, aimed at identifying good practices for managing change and its social consequences. Another seminar will deal with European Works Councils, assessing their outcomes and analysing good practices in the textile sector but also in other industries; it will in addition address the issue of enlargement.

Clearly, therefore, the fact that no texts have been adopted since 2002 does not mean that nothing has been happening. Strictly speaking, however, these joint activities cannot be defined as national-level industrial relations and collective bargaining.

---

[2] It is interesting to note that this guide is shown as an instance of good practice on the website of the Commission's DG Enterprise (http://europa.eu.int/comm/enterprise/textile/ind_policy.htm#procurement).

C. The 1997 Code of Conduct: An Exemplary Tool

The textile/clothing code of conduct[3] constitutes a key element of the social dialogue between Euratex and the ETUF:TCL. The code was adopted in 1997, and should be viewed in relation to similar codes in the leather and tanning sector (10 July 2000) and the footwear sector (updated on 17 November 2000) (Dufresne, 2000). It is a relatively short document which refers to six fundamental ILO Conventions, states how the code is to be circulated and promoted, and finally makes provision for follow-up and assessment.

The code of conduct is reproduced in its entirety in the Box below.

The Textile/Clothing Code of Conduct

Preamble
The European Apparel and Textile Organisation (EURATEX) and the European Trade Union Federation of Textiles, Clothing and Leather (ETUF:TCL), convened within the social sectoral dialogue at European level, re-affirm their earnest allegiance to the respect of human rights (*).
Social partners at European level hope for fair and open world-wide trade.
These partners agreed to work towards a European textile and clothing industry that is productive, internationally competitive and based on the respect of both workers and employers.
Article 1 – Code of Conduct
EURATEX and the ETUF:TCL call on their members (**) to encourage actively the companies and workers of the European textile and clothing industry to comply with the following ILO Conventions:
1) The ban on forced labour (Conventions 29 and 105): Forced labour, slave labour and prison labour is banned.
2) Freedom of association and the right to negotiate (Conventions 87 and 98): The right for workers to form and join a trade union, as well as the right for employers to organise, are recognized. Employers and workers may negotiate freely and independently.
3) The ban on child labour (Convention 138): Child labour is forbidden. Children under 15 or younger than the age of completion of compulsory schooling in the countries concerned are not admitted to work.
4) Non-discrimination of employment (Convention 111): Workers are employed on the basis of their ability to work and not on the basis of their race, individual characteristic, creed, political opinion or social origin.
Article 2 – Circulation and promotion
a) EURATEX and the ETUF:TCL commit to promote and circulate this present Charter in the relevant languages and at all levels by December 31, 1997 at the latest.
b) EURATEX and the ETUF:TCL call on their respective member organisations to adopt this Charter and to encourage its progressive implementation at the companies' level.

3 A charter by the social partners in the European textile and clothing sector, Code of conduct, Brussels, 10 July 1997 (http://europa.eu.int/comm/employment_social/social_dialogue/docs/137_19970711_textile_en.pdf).

Article 3 – Follow-up and assessment a) EURATEX and the ETUF:TCL agree to follow up, in the framework of the Social Sectoral Dialogue at European level, the progressive accomplishment of the implementation of this Charter. b) To this effect, EURATEX and the ETUF will conduct a yearly evaluation of the Charter's implementation, the first evaluation will take place no later than 10th July 1998. The results of such an evaluation will be reported in the framework of the Social Sectoral Dialogue. EURATEX and the ETUF could ask the Commission and Member States to supply the necessary assistance in order to carry out this evaluation. c) EURATEX and the ETUF:TCL may, in the framework of the Social Sectoral Dialogue at European level, decide jointly and freely to start any other initiative in pursuit of the implementation of this Charter. * http://europa.eu.int/comm/employment_social/soc-dial/news/1#1 ** As they are notably defined in the Universal Declaration on Human Rights.

Three aspects are of particular interest to us here: how the content has evolved, dissemination of the code and monitoring.

As to how the code has evolved, an attempt was made to update/ extend it in 2001-2002. Some of the organisations belonging to Euratex had reservations about certain points proposed by the trade union side, above all concerning supervision and possible sanctions. Subsequently, all energies were devoted to full market liberalisation in 2005. Implementation of the code was simultaneously pilot-tested in Turkey and in central and Eastern Europe. The issue of the code of conduct returned to the agenda in 2005, with the aim of harmonising the different codes and improving follow-up. The new codes, in particular that of leather and tanning dating from 2000, take account of other ILO standards on matters such as reasonable working hours, decent working conditions and the payment of a decent remuneration. As far as monitoring is concerned, this code stipulates that "the implementation of the results of the code have to be controlled in an independent fashion, guaranteeing the credibility of the control to all interested parties"[4].

The new work programme likewise made provision for holding talks about implementation and verification by setting up a joint drafting group on implementation methods, which would take account of experiences in Turkey and elsewhere.

Disseminating the code and monitoring its application were crucial issues. The code was gradually incorporated into collective agreements in fourteen of the EU-15 Member States (not Portugal), which made it legally binding: firstly in Finland in 1997, then Germany Belgium and

4 Code of Conduct in the Leather and Tanning sector, Brussels, 10 July 2000 (http:// europa.eu.int/comm/employment_social/social_dialogue/docs/109_20000710_leather _en.pdf).

Italy in 1998, Spain in 1999, and so on. It was therefore an ongoing process, with some countries taking longer than others to incorporate the code into national law. The code has also been translated into all the EU-15 languages and very widely circulated among companies. In the run-up to EU enlargement, the social partners decided to broaden the dissemination of their code of conduct to include the new Member States and Turkey. In 2000, for instance, 40,000 copies were circulated in the eleven EU languages, 10,000 in the CEEC languages and 10,000 in Turkish.

There are considerable differences between the EU Member States and the accession countries, above all in respect of working time and working conditions. The process is a gradual one, also comprising "capacity-building" actions (to be financed by the European Commission due to the weakness of organisations in those countries).

These dissemination activities are to be conducted in association with the ILO, whereby the ILO and the European Commission's Employment and Social Affairs Directorate have signed an agreement related to two pilot projects. A pilot project for the textile sector in Turkey aims to demonstrate that there is a link between productivity and the quality of production on the one hand, and industrial relations and social dialogue on the other. The second project deals with working and employment conditions in the ten accession countries joining the European Union, and in three other candidate countries (Bulgaria, Romania and Turkey). These pilots have fed into deliberations about a new version of the code of conduct (see above).

Even though the code has been successfully disseminated, it is not yet possible to assess precisely what impact it has actually had on the ground. More than anything else, the code sets out a framework and serves as a reference document to be drawn on when specific problems arise. It should not therefore be read in an overly narrow or legalistic fashion, but should be seen as a means of progressively strengthening mutual trust and the capacity to jointly handle particular problems, especially as concerns trade union rights. According to our interviewees in Brussels, the code has helped them resolve a dozen or so difficult cases related to trade union representation, merely by threatening to address the issue in the context of the social dialogue.

Nevertheless, the fact still remains that this code, which could be dubbed "first generation", is very weak in terms of both follow-up and content when compared with more recent codes signed in other sectors (Nordestgaard and Kirton Darling, 2004). As we shall see, the code of conduct in the sugar sector is much more substantial and makes provision for annual follow-up.

D. The High Level Group: Involvement in Strategic Decision-making

The High Level Group was formed in the wake of the Commission's 2003 Communication on the future of the textiles and clothing sector in the enlarged European Union (CEC, 2003) and the European Parliament's resolution of 29 January 2004 (European Parliament, 2004). It comprises all the main decision-makers: the three Commissioners concerned, representatives of the four Member States with a significant textile industry, one MEP, representatives from industry and trade union organisations, retailers and importers etc. The Group met on more than 50 occasions in just a few months (March-June 2004).

The conclusions of the High Level Group, reiterated following the agreement with China in June 2005, urged all parties to:

1) support innovation, such as the new Strategic RTD Objective on "ICT for networked businesses", collaboration schemes with the Innovation Relay Centres and the National Patent and Trademark Offices;

2) encourage research, for instance for technical textiles with high added value content, to develop new markets in construction, protective clothing and medical uses;

3) implement an Action Plan on market access, which identifies the main barriers to access to third country markets in the textile and clothing sector and ways of addressing them;

4) step up protection of intellectual property rights, in particular by creating a new Helpdesk to provide assistance, in particular to SMEs;

5) support education and training, such as actions under the Leonardo da Vinci programme to develop common European qualification standards;

6) strengthen dialogue with Europe's Mediterranean partners.

The Group addressed itself to various issues such as competitiveness, intellectual property rights, regional aspects, innovation, research and development, and trade policy. As far as the social dialogue is concerned, the main topics were education, training and employment. The High Level Group stressed the need for a European lifelong learning strategy for the sector and the need to ensure a better match between training supply and demand. It proposed establishing national and European "observatories" on training and employment, developing common qualification standards, strengthening social dialogue at all levels, setting up "reconversion and reclassification units", and lastly using resources from the structural funds and from the regional policy budget. All these matters are now on the agenda of the sectoral social dialogue (see below).

One outcome of the work of the High Level Group was to give the social dialogue a higher profile within the Commission. In its Communication on the Group's work, the Commission recognises the importance of social dialogue as a driving force behind successful economic and social reforms. It considers that the European social dialogue in the textile and clothing sector plays a major role in addressing key challenges of the sector, such as enhancing skills and qualifications, modernising work organisation, promoting equal opportunities and developing active ageing policies. The Commission believes that social dialogue and social partnerships are also a fundamental element of efficient and responsible restructuring. In this context, negotiations between the social partners are the most suitable way forward on questions related to modernisation and management of change. This document therefore spells out as plainly as can be the role of social dialogue in adjusting responsibly to change.

As far as education and vocational training is concerned, the Commission can agree with the High Level Group's analysis of a need for a Europe-wide lifelong training strategy for the sector and to ensure a better match between supply and demand for training. At EU level, the Leonardo da Vinci programme and "Article 6" measures under the ESF provide the framework for funding sectoral projects with European added value and innovative actions in the area of employment and adaptation to industrial change (CEC, 2004b: 5-6).

The experience of the High Level Group is without doubt more symptomatic than anything else of the social partners' capacity to be involved along with other players in defining European public policy. Their participation was facilitated by the deep crisis in the sector, which necessitated a broad consensus on appropriate measures for coping with it. Yet this experience also has its limits, given it took place within a framework predetermined elsewhere in which the trade unions had no say at all.

II. Sugar

A. Development of the European Social Dialogue: A Few Key Facts

1. The Players

The players in the social dialogue are the European Federation of Trade Unions in the Food, Agriculture and Tourism sectors and allied branches (EFFAT) for the trade unions and the European Committee of Sugar Manufacturers (CEFS) for the employers.

On the trade union side, the interests of workers in the sugar industry are represented by the European Federation of Trade Unions in the Food, Agriculture and Tourism sectors and allied branches (EFFAT). This body was formed on 11 December 2000 as a result of a merger between the ECF-IUF (the European Committee of Food, Catering and Allied Workers' Unions within the IUF) and the European Federation of Agricultural Workers' Trade Unions (EFA). It comprises 128 national trade unions set up in 37 European countries representing some 2,600,000 members and covering workers in agriculture, agri-foodstuffs, catering and tourism.

On the employers' side, the European Committee of Sugar Manufacturers (CEFS) (1954) represents the interests of all industrial sugar producers in the European Union of 25 (excluding the non-sugar-producing countries Cyprus, Estonia, Luxembourg and Malta). Factories are concentrated in just a few large producer countries, especially France, Germany and Poland. Other countries have only a few plants each.

2. *The Social Dialogue Committee*

The social dialogue committee was founded in 1997. Sugar is the only sector apart from commerce in which at least one joint text was signed every year between 1997 and 2004. None was signed in 2005, however. This is one of the smallest sectors in the sectoral social dialogue and the workforce is declining steadily. The number of refineries in the EU-15 fell from 360 to 150 in 30 years (1968-1998), and there were just 134 left in the EU-15 in 2002-2003, on the eve of enlargement. Enlargement added another hundred or so factories. It likewise had significant effects in terms of the restructuring of production in the new Member States, above all Poland. Sugar is not so much a sector as a set of companies. The country by country distribution of sugar factories in 2005 was as follows.

Country	Sugar Factories	Country	Sugar Factories
France	42	Lithuania	4
Poland	42	Portugal	4
Germany	26	Slovakia	4
Italy	19	Austria	3
Spain	12	Denmark	3
Czech Republic	12	Finland	3
Belgium	6	Sweden	3
The Netherlands	6	Ireland	2
United Kingdom	6	Latvia	2
Greece	5	Slovenia	1
Hungary	5		

The main issues affecting regulation of the sector arise at international level, as a result of competition from sugar cane (considerably less expensive than beet). As in the case of textiles, the opening up of trade would produce one principal beneficiary: in the case of sugar it would be Brazil.

The World Trade Organization (WTO) established a panel to examine the Community sugar regime on 23 December 2003, at the request of Brazil, Australia and Thailand. These countries took particular exception to:

- the EU's right to re-export, with subsidies, an amount equivalent to the refined sugar produced from raw sugar coming from the ACP countries (1.6 million tonnes). In their opinion these re-exports go beyond the EU's undertaking to reduce export subsidies, made under the agricultural agreement concluded as part of the Uruguay Round;
- the EU's right to export C sugar (off-quota sugar) at world market prices, since manufacturers already receive a subsidy in the form of revenue from quota sugar ("cross-subsidies").

The report by the WTO panel, published on 15 October 2004, upheld these charges. The European Union immediately appealed against this decision, which was upheld by the WTO in 2005. The Commission therefore decided to undertake a thorough reform of the sugar market and to drastically cut its support for prices (by around 38%). This proposal was approved in a slightly milder form by the Agriculture Council in November 2005.

It can therefore be said, perhaps a little crudely, that the principal concern is to cope as best as possible with the extensive changes in the sector over as long as possible a period of time, so as to mitigate the economic and social consequences. Social dialogue has been one way of doing this.

Access to European decision-makers, particularly DG Trade, is vital under these circumstances. Social dialogue is also a means of adopting common positions addressed to the European institutions.

Under the committee's rules of procedure[5], social dialogue within the sugar sector relates to:

- information and exchanges of views on all questions connected with European legislation and Community policy that have economic or social repercussions for the sugar sector (common or-

[5] Agreement between the CEFS and the ECF-IUF, Brussels, 12 November 1997 (http://europa.eu.int/comm/employment_social/social_dialogue/docs/120_19971112_sugar_en.pdf).

ganization of the market, international agreements, food laws, the environment, social questions, etc.);
- work carried out together, for example with regard to health and safety vocational training, within the framework of the Community's major vocational training programmes;
- the possibility of drawing up joint statements on subjects of common interest;
- the possibility to intervene jointly, if necessary, in the frame of the Social Protocol.

B. Outcomes of the Sectoral Social Dialogue

A particularly large number of joint documents has been adopted. One noteworthy feature of the common agenda taking shape is the fact that employers in the sector demonstrate an ongoing interest in building a social dialogue and trusting relationships.

Table 2: Texts Adopted, Theme, Type of Document and Addressees

Date	Title	Theme	Type	Addressees	Follow-Up
4/06/2004	Joint website www.eurosugar.org	Social dialogue	Tool	European social partners	
2/04/2004	Commission Green Paper on preferential rules of origin	Economic and/or sectoral policies	Common position	European institutions	
7/02/2003	Corporate social responsibility in the European sugar industry. Code of conduct	Working conditions	Recommendation	Enterprises	Yes
5/11/2002	Joint declaration by the European social partners in the sugar industry	Enlargement	Declaration	European social partners	
14/12/2001	Social responsibility and the social model in the sugar industry. Joint declaration	Working conditions	Common position	European institutions	
14/11/2001	Joint position paper. Generalised System of Preferences. Clear and coherent rules of origin seen as essential in return for the opening-up of frontiers	Economic and/or sectoral policies	Common position	European institutions	

20/02/2001	Joint declaration of the social partners in the European sugar industry. Revised proposal for a regulation on "everything but arms" in favour of the least developed countries	Economic and/or sectoral policies	Common position	European institutions	
13/11/2000	Joint labour-management declaration on apprenticeship	Training	Common position	European institutions	
23/11/1999	Common organization of the market in sugar and its importance for employment	Economic and/or sectoral policies	Common position	European institutions	
1/01/1999	Active/interactive safety in the sugar factory. An exemplary vocational training tool available in all European sugar factories	Health and safety	Tool	National organisations	
1/12/1998	Apprenticeship in the sugar sector. Joint recommendation	Training	Recommendation	National organisations	Yes
12/11/1997	Agreement between the CEFS and the ECF-IUF	Social dialogue	Rules of procedure	European social partners	

Half of the ten joint documents are common positions. The sugar sector is in fact under increasing threat from the turn which trade negotiations are taking. Rules of origin are another very important aspect, since they determine the conditions of entry onto the European market on a case-by-case basis. According to one employers' representative, the most significant text to have emerged from the social dialogue is the one on "Everything but arms" (2001). It enabled market opening to be confined to the least advanced countries (by means of rules of origin), as had initially been sought by the former European Commissioner for foreign trade, Pascal Lamy.

The activities of the sectoral committee are not limited to adopting common positions on this matter; it also organises joint conferences such as the one on the reform of the sugar regulation, held in June 2005 and attended not only by the social partners but also by beet growers and key players at the Commission and the European Parliament.

Our correspondents informed us that the health/safety training tools have been widely used at national level.

Joint action by the social partners to defend sugar factories and employment in Europe is therefore backed by a broad array of instruments. In other words, these instruments result from exchanges between trade unions and employers which enable them to speak with one voice to the European institutions. From a trade union point of view, the code of conduct is undoubtedly the most valuable of them all.

C. Joint Code of Conduct on Corporate Social Responsibility

The social dialogue led in 2003 to the drafting and adoption of an innovative sectoral code of conduct, whose follow-up procedures are among the most stringent of all the texts analysed (see in particular Nordestgaard and Kirton-Darling, 2004). We quote from it at length below and examine its principal provisions.

Joint Code of Conduct on Corporate Social Responsibility, 2003 (excerpts)

Minimum standards

The Members of the CEFS undertake to comply with the minimum standards set out below and, as appropriate, to promote these standards beyond the area of activities for which the CEFS has a mandate. These voluntary standards of a general scope are usually much lower than the standards actually applicable in the Union. The respect of these standards shall not constitute a valid reason for reducing pre-existing higher standards, on the contrary.

1. HUMAN RIGHTS

The European Sugar Industry complies with the principles and rights at work as defined by the ILO and in the UN Universal Declaration of Human Rights and the European legislation.

The European Sugar Industry:

a) respects the freedom of association and thus the right for all workers to establish trade unions and to affiliate, including for workers representatives the right of access to the enterprise (ILO convention 87).

b) recognizes the effective right to collective bargaining as well as the right for worker representatives to get facilities as appropriate in order to carry out their functions promptly and efficiently. (ILO conventions 98 and 135).

c) confirms the fact that exercising these rights won't cause any personal of professional damage to the workers and their representatives.

d) will not operate with any form of forced or compulsory labour (ILO Convention 29).

e) is opposed to child labour (Convention 182) and meets ILO convention 138 in relation to the minimum age for admission to employment.

f) Is against all discrimination, be it based on ethnic or national origin, religion, sex, sexual orientation, affiliation to trade union, age or political affiliation and undertakes in particular to guarantee and promote equal opportunities and equal treatment for men and women (ILO conventions 100 and 111 – EU directives n° 76/207/EEC of 9.2.1976, n° 2000/43/EC of 29.06.2000 and n° 2000/78/EC of 27.11.2000).

2. EDUCATION, VOCATIONAL AND LIFE LONG TRAINING
The European Sugar Industry endeavours to invest in its employees by providing them with the best possible skills and abilities in order to develop their individual potential to the maximum.
Education and training constitute an integral part of the social dialogue in the companies. Proposals and initiatives by the employees and their representatives are welcome and will be implemented in accordance with national habits.
recommends to sugar companies, whenever economically and socially feasible, to make a significant effort to offer more young people training periods and places as apprentices in order to improve their skills on the labour market.

3. HEALTH AND SAFETY
The European Sugar Industry pays special attention to health and safety.
In cooperation with the Employees and their representatives, the Sugar Industry will care for a healthy and safe working environment based on secure facts and practices regarding work protection; all preventive measures on health and safety are considered as a priority. The sugar industry does not only pay special attention to the European legislations on health and safety, but in most cases, il goes beyond the legislations.
Specific training programmes, safety procedures and policies, tailor-made for the sugar industry and taking into account the specific hazards linked to the manufacturing process, are implemented in all sugar factories and pay special attention to prevention.

4. RELATIONSHIP BETWEEN THE SOCIAL PARTNERS
The social partners represented by the CEFS and the EFFAT consider that a constructive social dialogue with the employees representatives and trade unions at all levels is an important element for a successful functioning of enterprises. Informing and consulting the employees representatives promotes confidence and cooperation between employees and employers.
At national level, the representation of employees and collective bargaining apply in accordance with the legislation and often go beyond.
In connection with the enlargement of the European Union, the social partners express the wish that, with the complementary assistance and support of the public authorities, a genuinely constructive and responsible dialogue

5. FAIR PAY
The present pay levels in the sugar industry meet or exceed the minimum rates provided for by branch or industry collective agreements and/or legal provisions. When no agreement or pay scale exists, wages are enough to ensure that workers and their families have a decent standard of living as defined by the Universal Declaration of Human Rights and the ILO Tripartite Declaration.
In order to avoid any discrimination, the sugar industry also recognizes the right for employees in similar conditions to get equal pay for equal work (ILO Convention 100, EU Treaty 141, Directive 2000/78/EC).

6. WORKING CONDITIONS
[…]

7. RESTRUCTURING
At European level, within the framework of the European social dialogue, regular information, exchanges of views and, if necessary, joint action can be organised in relation to all issues, including those related to the Community policy and the Community legislations where they have economic and social effects for the sugar sector.
This dialogue meets or exceeds the national and European legislation on information and consultation.

Since an open dialogue between management and employees is a pre-requisite for a climate of mutual respect and confidence, employees and their representatives will be regularly kept aware of the situation of the enterprise as well as informed and consulted on planned restructuring measures in due time.
In case of restructuring, as well as in the event of investments having a social impact as provided by the present Code of Conduct, the sugar industry acts in a socially responsible way. Steps are taken to improve the employability of employees.
8. BUSINESS RELATIONS AND CHOICE OF SUPPLIERS
The European Sugar Industry expects a socially responsible behaviour from it suppliers. Suppliers are generally chosen on a professional business basis, but for major suppliers this also includes a consideration of their corporate social responsibility according to the provisions of this Code of Conduct. The European Sugar Industry will thus contribute to circulate the concept of corporate social responsibility at global level and see if it can make a concrete contribution to the fight of child labour.
In the general context of business ethics, the European Sugar Industry undertakes to comply with the OECD guidelines for multinational companies, or, beyond the CEFS area of activities, to promote them as far as possible.

What is original about this document is that it covers a broad array of themes and, in particular, encompasses subcontractors (point 8). Moreover, it is subject to annual monitoring. The follow-up report contains three parts: a summary of what has happened over the year and the views of the social partners, follow-up actions as such and new examples of good practice. Once again, it is difficult to gauge the impact of such a code. It seems to have been widely circulated, and a translation into Polish is now available. Both the trade unions and the employers are satisfied. Yet, once again, the code's importance would seem to lie mainly in providing a stable platform on which the two sides can continue their talks and, where necessary, solve one-off problems in individual companies. It likewise offers an opportunity to highlight good practices in the new Member States which, although they may be unexceptional in the eyes of the old EU countries, constitute social progress locally in the CEECs.

D. Ways of Influencing the New Sugar Regulation

Following the WTO panel's ruling against the EU, the Commissioner responsible for agriculture insisted on the need for an early, sizeable cut in sugar prices. When invited by the social partners to their joint conference in June 2005, she maintained that this rather radical reform was indispensable.

The Member States had mixed views, since to some extent the reform spares the most productive countries (France, Belgium and Germany) to the detriment of the more outlying industries/plantations which are also less productive. A decision was taken at the Agriculture Council of 22 November 2005, and the reform is now underway. The main concession made was to lengthen the implementation period.

Many sugar factories are family-run SMEs and do not have the critical mass to survive; neither do they have the wherewithal to develop internationally (by investing in sugar cane). They must therefore choose between grouping together, switching over to bioethanol or closing down.

The reform resulted from a political decision. For the Commission, reforming the sugar sector appears to have been a means of demonstrating its good will to cane-exporting countries amidst the overall and highly complex stand-off over the liberalisation of trade in agricultural produce. Given that the overall context was non-negotiable, economic flanking measures (creation of a specific fund to facilitate closures) and social support measures (retraining and dismissal, access to the structural funds in addition to the specific fund) became the key issues.

The sectoral social partners devised a threefold strategy under these circumstances:

a) allying themselves with beet growers, certain Member States and the European Parliament in an attempt to attenuate the reform;
b) gaining early access to information on Community sources of funding;
c) seeking recognition as a sector requiring careful monitoring by the Commission.

The already existing partnership helped to reinforce this strategy by presenting a united front. All three goals were achieved.

The reform was made a little less radical. An interactive Practical Guide to access to the structural funds for the European sugar industry has been produced[6]. But what is undoubtedly more important for the future is that joint moves have been made to ensure that the sugar sector is placed under close scrutiny and enjoys greater attention from the Commission. Whereas this status was awarded directly to the textile/clothing sector, as we saw in the Introduction, the sugar social partners had to appeal to the Commission. Their request was granted fairly easily, the result being the formation of a monitoring group comprising representatives from DG Agriculture, Regio, Employment and Industry (see below). An interactive guide to access to the structural funds for companies affected by the reform was also commissioned in this context.

6 This guide was written by Christophe Degryse and Philippe Pochet, Observatoire social européen asbl (http://www.eurosugar.org/en/guide.html).

The sectoral social dialogue has eased the reforms, as we have seen, but the real test will come when companies are forced to close down and dismiss their workforce.

Conclusion

This chapter has illustrated the different facets of social dialogue in the textile/clothing and sugar sectors. The social dialogue of course consists of producing joint documents but also of undertaking joint actions. The impact of the latter is even harder to assess than that of the former. Social dialogue in both sectors has enabled the social partners, and above all the trade unions, to have an input into the process of restructuring the sector which is determined at international and European level. Although it would be wrong to overestimate the results achieved so far and to ignore the sometimes highly divergent interests between different countries and different players, the existence of a well-structured social dialogue has nevertheless facilitated access to political decision-makers and made it possible to undertake joint activities.

The two sides of industry do not share the same interests. For the employers, trade union backing lends weight to their lobbying work and justifies it as being of value to the entire sector. For the trade unions, there is the possibility of bringing influence to bear on those Directorates General of the Commission which are unreceptive to trade unions and social problems. They are thus able to highlight the social consequences of decisions taken.

In the case of textiles, the adoption and dissemination of the code of conduct has fostered a climate of trust, which has itself helped in finding solutions to critical situations with regard to trade union rights in certain companies or subsidiaries of large multinational groups. Nevertheless, in comparison with the new generation of codes of conduct such as the one adopted in the sugar sector, the textiles/clothing code is extremely limited in terms of its content and the verification of its implementation. The sugar code also covers principal subcontractors. In both cases, the codes are being circulated in languages other than those initially intended. However, even in the case of sugar, where an annual implementation report is scheduled and carried out, it is hard to identify any instances where the code has had a tangible impact.

The large-scale restructuring which is underway and likely to gather pace will make it possible to gauge the capacity of the sectoral social partners to find acceptable solutions. Until now their strategies have been identical on one point: exerting influence over the Community agenda. But their views differ considerably when it comes to managing the restructuring process. In the case of textiles, the first seminar on this topic did not take place until 2005 even though the sector has been in the throes of restructuring for the past fifteen years. Hence this has always been a delicate issue for the employers and a minefield for the social dialogue. The sugar sector, and the employers' side in particular, on the other hand, has always taken a much more pragmatic approach. They commissioned a study resulting in an interactive tool (produced by the Observatoire social européen) on access to the structural funds, which should be of assistance to companies being restructured.

Innovation is an important issue in both sectors. The textile sector consists of a large number of SMEs which lack the requisite critical mass and industrial specialisation. This will have a major impact on restructuring in the future. In this context, training is at the heart of the debate, with a view to upskilling the workforce in conjunction with a strategy of industrial specialisation. There seems to be no other way forward for textiles in Europe. As for sugar, adaptation to industrial change could well be even more radical because it involves a change of activity. The only possible alternative appears to be producing bioethanol, as well as reducing pollution and also energy dependence.

As in other sectors, the textile/clothing social dialogue is at a crossroads. We shall soon see whether or not it is capable of moving into a new phase, namely more effective verification of the implementation of agreements signed. Sugar, for its part, is heading in a different direction, namely joint management of restructuring, which might perhaps spread to other sectors if it proves successful.

The chapter on the employers (see chapter 9 in this volume) makes plain that the scope of the European social dialogue depends first and foremost on the willingness of the employers. Those in the textile sector have given their European federation only a minimalist mandate. A comparison of the two sectors confirms the relevance of a sector's intrinsic characteristics and their effect on the organisation and interests of the employers' side. The sugar employers have been able to sustain a strategy of European partnership because, with the exception of a handful of multinationals, their interests lie in Europe. Major textile groups, on the other hand, have gone further down the road of internationalisation and, rather than pursuing a Eurocentric strategy, prefer an approach which will guarantee a minimum degree of competitiveness.

References

CEC (1998a), Commission Decision 98/500/EC of 20 May 1998 on the Establishment of Sectoral Dialogue Committees Promoting the Dialogue between the Social Partners at European Level, OJ L 225 of, 12 August 1998, pp.0027-0028 (http://europa.eu.int/comm/employment_social/social_dialogue/docs/decision98_500_en.pdf).

CEC (1998b), Communication from the Commission "Adapting and Promoting the Social Dialogue at Community Level", COM (1998) 322 final of 20 May 1998.

CEC (2002), Communication from the Commission "The European Social Dialogue, a Force for Innovation and Change", COM (2002) 341 final of 26 June 2002 (http://europa.eu.int/comm/employment_social/news/2002/jul/socdial_en.pdf).

CEC (2003), Communication from the Commission to the Council, the European Parliament, the European Economic and Social Committee and the Committee of the Regions "The Future of the Textiles and Clothing Sector in the Enlarged European Union", COM (2003) 649 final of 29 October 2003 (http://europa.eu.int/eur-lex/lex/LexUriServ/site/en/com/2003/com2003_0649en01.pdf).

CEC (2004a), Communication from the Commission "Partnership for Change in an Enlarged Europe – Enhancing the Contribution of European Social Dialogue", COM (2004) 557 final of 12 August 2004 (http://europe.eu.int/comm/employment_social/news/2004/aug/com_final_en.pdf).

CEC (2004b), Communication from the Commission to the Council, the European Parliament, the European Economic and Social Committee and the Committee of the Regions "Textiles and Clothing After 2005 – Recommendations of the High Level Group for Textiles and Clothing", COM (2004) 668 final of 13 October 2004 (http://europa.eu.int/comm/enterprise/textile/documents/com2004_668en.pdf).

CEC (2005a), Communication from the Commission "Restructuring and Employment. Anticipating and Accompanying Restructuring in Order to Develop Employment: The Role of the European Union", COM (2005) 120 final of 31 March 2005 (http://europa.eu.int/comm/employment_social/news/2005/apr/com_restruct_en.pdf)

CEC (2005b), "European Textiles and Clothing in a Quota Free Environment", High Level Group Report and First Recommendations, The Challenge of 2005, June 2005 (http://europa.eu.int/comm/enterprise/textile/documents/hlg_report_30_06_04.pdf).

Degryse, C. and Pochet, P. (2006), Access to the European Structural Funds. Practical Guide & Directions for Use for the European Sugar Industry Developed with the Social Partners of the Sectoral Social Dialogue Committee CEFS-EFFAT, Brussels, January 2006 (http://www.eurosugar.org/en/guide.html).

Dufresne, A. (2000), "L'état des négociations collectives au plan européen dans les secteurs du textile et de l'habillement", in Ministère de l'Emploi et de la Solidarité (ed.), *La négociation collective en 1999*, Tome III: Les dossiers, Dossier No.1: La négociation collective dans les pays de l'Union européenne, Éditions législatives et Ministère de l'Emploi et de la Solidarité, Paris, pp.45-73.

European Parliament (2004), "The Future of the Textiles and Clothing Sector in the Enlarged European Union", European Parliament Resolution B5-0046/2003, 29 January 2004.

ETUF:TCL (2005), Action Programme, 4th Congress 2005, Sofia.

Nordestgaard, M. and Kirton-Darling, J. (2004), "Corporate Social Responsibility within the European Sectoral Social Dialogue", *Transfer*, Vol.10, No.3, Autumn 2004, pp.433-451.

Pochet, P. (2005), "Le dialogue social dans le secteur du textile et des vêtements: l'expérience européenne", in Sajhau, J.-P. (ed.), *Promoting Fair Globalization in Textiles and Clothing in a Post-MFA Environment*, Report submitted for discussion at the Tripartite Meeting on Promoting Fair Globalization in Textiles and Clothing in a post-MFA Environment, International Labour Organization, Geneva, pp.60-64.

UCL-IST (2004), "Monographs on the Situation of Social Partners in the Candidate Countries: Textile Sector", Research project conducted on behalf of the Employment and Social Affairs DG of the European Commission, Université catholique de Louvain, Institut des sciences du travail, March 2004 (http://www.trav.ucl.ac.be/recherche/relations%20industrielles/rapports%202003/rapport%20final%20du%20textile2finalversionpapier2.pdf).

CHAPTER 8

Metalworking, Chemicals and the Public Sector

A Thaw Sets In

Anne DUFRESNE, Christophe DEGRYSE and Philippe POCHET[1]

The metalworking, chemical and public service sectors have one thing in common: they could be described as the main pioneering sectors in the various Member States. In certain circumstances they may become the driving force behind sectoral and national collective wage bargaining. It is interesting to note, therefore, that in all three sectors, which are vital for the national economy and its industrial relations, European social dialogue began only recently, and haltingly[2].

The main obstacle to the development of sectoral social dialogue in these key sectors was the reluctance, even hostility, shown by the relevant European employers' federations. There is now a general improvement in the situation, for various reasons which we shall go into below. In all three sectors, a social dialogue has finally been established. We shall take a look at the factors behind these "new dialogues". Did they result from trade union or employer strategies? Were they set up thanks to the European Commission? Were they triggered by recent industrial policy developments?

There are a number of hypotheses in the relevant literature as to the factors which encourage social dialogue. Leisink has suggested that the key factors are those "that may push (a significant degree of economic integration of product markets) or pull (socio-economic policies of the Commission) employers and trade unions towards social dialogue at European level" (Leisink, 2002: 107). More specifically, others have emphasised the fear felt by employers that the European industry federa-

---

1 The metalworking sector was examined by Anne Dufresne, the chemical industry by Christophe Degryse and central public administration by Philippe Pochet.

2 The SSD, however, is particularly strong in the private-sector service industries (telecommunications, banking, private security etc.) (see chapter 6).

tions might form a joint strategy to coordinate their collective bargaining efforts[3]. In Hoffmann's words (1998: 145-146), "the aspiration is that trade unions will be, as they were (sometimes) at national level, the 'midwives of the birth of the European employers federations at sectoral level'" (Marginson, 2005: 523). We shall test out these two hypotheses on the three sectors under examination.

Since these three sectors are clearly very different, we have not tried to create at the outset a common framework for analysing developments within them. This chapter is the result of an ongoing dialogue: each of the authors has been able to check during discussions whether an aspect highlighted for a particular sector has been equally important for the others. Conclusions shall then be drawn to see what general lessons can be learnt from the way in which social dialogue has been set up in these three sectors from which it was, until recently, absent.

I. Metalworking Industry

Metalworking is one of the oldest industrial sectors in Europe. It is a key sector due to, among other things, the large number of people it employs. It is made up mainly of large companies and multinationals, and has undergone much restructuring over the last ten years.

Our aim is to explain why, at Community level, social dialogue was initiated very recently, and only in a semi-official form, even though there is widespread coordination of collective bargaining in the sector. One initial explanation could be that employers in the metalworking sector, which has a long tradition of strong trade unions, have had (maybe due to union strength) serious misgivings about the concept. They prevented the setting up of a sectoral social dialogue committee, as they feared that events would snowball and ultimately lead to collective-bargaining type negotiations. The employers are aware of the well-established power of the French and German unions in the sector, where IG-Metall, which for a long time was the largest trade union in the world, does not hesitate to bring its strength to bear during negotiations. They fear the power[4] of a "French IG-Metall", which could combine these two strong cultures. A second explanation could be that "EU policy measures have not had a great impact on the metal sector" (de Boer *et al.*, 2005: 64). It was, in truth, only when international developments impacted on certain sub-sectors (such as the end of the ECSC

[3] See Dufresne (2002a) and Marginson (2005) which examine in parallel the industry level, as a strategic level for coordinating collective bargaining and for sectoral social dialogue.

[4] "The strength of a union derives from its actions and its power. It is expressed in the ability to build strong institutional contacts, but is based on an underlying (potential) capacity to move from words to actions" (Pernot, 2005: 263).

Treaty affecting the steel sector or unfair competition hitting the shipbuilding sector) that the organisations representing these sub-sectors called for sectoral social dialogue committees (SSDCs) to be established.

In the following sections we shall examine how the strategies of the trade unions and employers' organisations have changed on this point. We shall then attempt to highlight the way in which this particular sector has moved towards social dialogue, by means of a "meccano"-type assembly of sub-sectoral social dialogues.

A. How Have Strategies Evolved?

1. Two Parallel Trade Union Strategies: Coordination of Collective Bargaining and a Proliferation of Sub-sectoral Social Dialogues

The European Metalworkers' Federation (EMF), the second largest European industry federation after UNI-Europa (representing private-sector service industries, see chapter 6), has more than six million members from 65 affiliated trade unions in 33 countries. It was officially set up, in June 1971, as an organisation entirely independent of the international federation, with its own statutes and bodies. The role it plays as a model for European industry federations in industrial sectors at European level is similar to that played by national negotiators from the sector in many countries. EMF (and particularly IG Metall, its largest member) has a unique influence on European trade union strategy and policies[5]. This is partly for historical reasons, since in this sector "the European Coal and Steel Community (ECSC) meant that industry federations became more involved in European affairs" (Freyssinet, 1998: 20).

As well as its political bodies, EMF has three consultative committees, whose remits reflect the areas currently dealt with by the organisation: the Industrial Policy Committee[6], the Company Policy Committee, dealing with European Works Councils (EWCs), and the Collective Bargaining Policy Committee. Interestingly, there is no special committee on social dialogue.

---

5 Since the private-sector service unions merged to form UNI-Europa, in 2000, there has been a leadership contest between these organisations.

6 In the area of industrial policy, to react to growing liberalisation in the sector, EMF, via its Committee, called for the setting up of tripartite (union, employers, Commission) bodies in the various sub-sectors, of the type which existed under the ECSC. In 1997, although a high level group was set up for the automotive industry, the employers rejected the idea in the other sub-sectors.

EMF's strategy has always been to advocate a strengthening of social dialogue, which it sees as a major part of any European social policy. We should, however, clarify what EMF means when it speaks of social dialogue. At the 2002 meeting of the Collective Bargaining Policy Committee[7], the then EMF Deputy General Secretary, Bart Samyn, pointed to "the current confusion between collective bargaining and social dialogue". He stressed the fact that "collective bargaining may take place outside of a social dialogue committee". Since 1993, the federation has developed a strategy of coordinating national collective bargaining on pay, then on working time and on training. The metalworking sector has been a pioneer in this area[8]. EMF coordinating activities have always been held up as an example, both for cross-industry strategies (the Doorn group[9], ETUC) and for most of the European industry federations which have begun discussions on this subject[10].

The EMF approach has been as follows. Coordination begins within the federation. This allows progress to be made outside the context of social dialogue, i.e. despite the absence of any representative from the employers, who are totally against the idea of negotiating pay at this level (see below). One could even suggest that in this pioneer sector, it was initial resistance from the employers which stimulated the development of this union strategy. "Coordination was taken up after it became clear that joint negotiations were impossible" (Dufour and Hege, 1999: 109). Coordination began, then, as a "default" principle, although EMF added that it would "preferably" take place with the social partners on the other side of the table. The purpose is two-fold: firstly, to develop fruitful coordination, which is useful in itself (as it enables the adoption of general principles on wages, working time, and training); and secondly, in the longer term, to put pressure on national and European employer representatives. This strategy does not seem to have been the direct cause of moves towards social dialogue in other areas. "For the moment", according to one of our informants, "coordination of collective bargaining and social dialogue are two separate proc-

---

7 Meeting of the Collective Bargaining Policy Committee (Prague, 28-29 October 2002), which the author attended.

8 EMF has developed a coordination system which specifies that each union must attain a minimum wage increase corresponding to inflation + a "balanced share" of productivity gains. The initial objective of this strategy (launched by IG Metall) was to prevent wage and social dumping in the European Union.

9 The Doorn group was set up by the Belgian, Dutch, German and Luxembourg unions, which have, since 1997, been attempting cross-border coordination of collective bargaining.

10 For an overview of the various coordination processes, see Dufresne (2002b).

esses. They are handled by different people within the organisation" (interview with EMF, 2005).

As well as pioneering this strategy, EMF has now added, in parallel, another type of coordinated strategy leading towards social dialogue. At its Copenhagen Congress, in June 1999, it decided, firstly, to adopt new statutes setting out a specific procedure for obtaining a mandate from its affiliates (EMF, 1999). Most importantly, however, it decided to begin dialogue gradually in certain pilot sub-sectors: the automotive industry, shipbuilding and steel. This strategy would prove so effective, especially for the latter two sectors (see below), that the then EMF General Secretary, Reinhard Kuhlmann, declared to the next Congress, in June 2003: "We have achieved a real breakthrough in our cooperation with certain employers' organisations in the metal industry in Europe (the employers' organisation for the steel sector, EUROFER, and the Committee of Shipbuilders' Associations, CESA). [...] This is just a beginning, not an end-result" (EMF, 2003c).

In the political resolution drafted by this same Congress, EMF explains that "generally speaking, employers' associations with a mandate to negotiate and industry bodies must be considered as partners in negotiations and the implementation of decisions in social dialogue [...] In addition, the EMF will underscore its own autonomy in shaping the social dialogue *vis-à-vis* the EU institutions" (EMF, 2003a: 11). According to EMF, sectoral dialogue should therefore "help ensure that the social partners' independent power of negotiation in collective bargaining is strengthened" (EMF, 2003a: 11) along the lines of the German or Scandinavian model. EMF's aim for its forthcoming Congress (2007) is now to include the whole of the European metalworking industry and its major sectors in a structured social dialogue. Let us now examine how the employers' response to this strategy has evolved.

2. *The Employers: From Obstruction to Acceptance of a "Semi-institutional" Dialogue?*

At Community level there are two employers' organisations for the metalworking industry: ORGALIME, dealing with economic issues, and CEEMET (Council of European Employers of the Metal, Engineering and Technology-Based Industries), responsible for social issues, which replaced WEM (Western European Metal Trades Employers Organisation) in 2004. ORGALIME is a long-standing organisation (1954) which acts as coordinator for the three economic sectors it covers: the mechanical, iron & steel, and electrical & electronic sectors. WEM (renamed CEEMET) was set up in 1962 as a joint initiative of the French organisation UIMM (Union des industries métallurgiques et minières) and the German Gesamtmetall. It was set up as a central organisation in charge of social issues, bringing together fifteen national organisations responsible for industrial relations in the national metalworking industries.

For a long time WEM was categorically against the setting up of an institutionalised social dialogue on a sectoral level. Its hostility to this sort of process was expressed as an official position in a series of statements. At the beginning of the 1990s, it felt that its main role should be solely to inform its members of social policy developments within the European Union, "unless there are specific problems and certain other criteria are met" (ETUI, 1993: 17)[11]. Only as of 2003 did it agree to meet more frequently with EMF, although these contacts have still been subject to the following pre-conditions, set by the employers[12]:

> the subjects discussed are of specific or major interest for our industry and will add value for our national organisations and the companies that they represent;
>
> they specifically exclude any type of negotiations or collective bargaining and avoid imposing any additional obligations on member companies;
>
> the principal objective of these discussions is to exchange information and reach a better mutual understanding by, for example, organising joint seminars and, possibly, by arriving at some kind of non-binding guidelines or recommendations (WEM, 2003a: 1).

Interestingly, the only new element in these 2003 pre-conditions is the reference to possible non-binding guidelines. WEM feels that "the organisation of seminars, the exchange of experiences and the adoption of recommendations [...] are often more appropriate tools than negotiated European agreements, particularly as [in its view] there is already sufficient social legislation at European and national level (WEM, 2003b: 1).

In 2003, then, despite all these restrictions, WEM departed slightly from its hardline position. It was taking account not only of the new institutional context brought about by the European Commission decision of 1998, which set up "new" social dialogue committees in most sectors (see chapter 2), but also and above all of the above-mentioned EMF strategy of starting a dialogue in certain sub-sectors. According to

---

11 Three conditions were set:
- both parties should agree that a meeting would be useful;
- there should be an agreed agenda;
- the sole purpose of the meetings should be to promote exchanges of information and a better mutual understanding, not to negotiate or conclude collective agreements. (ETUI, 1993: note 5 page 17).

12 A comparison of the pre-conditions for social dialogue set by the employers at the beginning of the 1990s (see note below) and in 2003 shows how persistent their obstructive attitude has been.

an EMF representative, "it was this strategy, rather than the pressure exerted by the coordination of collective bargaining on the trade union side, that led CEEMET (the successor to WEM) to enter into formal dialogue with EMF" (EMF interview, 2005).

In 2003, WEM issued two official statements on social dialogue: one about sectoral and the other about cross-industry dialogue. It wished to "ensure that the division of competences at European level properly reflects the position that generally exists at the national level and provide for an appropriate coordination procedure between the various actors on the employers' side at the European level" (WEM, 2003a: 2). Thus on the pretext of wishing for better coordination between the various levels and desiring not to weaken the position of European employers by a proliferation of sectoral and sub-sectoral positions, WEM stated that it did not want the sub-sector associations to deal with social issues. As the central organisation responsible for these issues, it preferred to keep full and sole responsibility for any future social dialogue with EMF, in order to keep tighter control over its obstructive stance. Moreover, since its ideological views on sectoral social dialogue were in line with those of UNICE, it delegated this same responsibility for social dialogue to the cross-industry organisation[13], which would take the same approach (for more details on UNICE, see Branch and Greenwood, 2001). The employers' obstructive stance can be seen as a set of Russian dolls: the sectoral federation prevents sub-sectoral federations from moving towards dialogue, while shifting responsibility for this to the cross-industry level.

Still giving as a pretext the need to avoid fragmentation of the employers' approach in the sector, WEM was concerned that the Commission or EMF might ask the sub-sector employers' organisations to enter into dialogue on social issues. This is exactly what happened in 2003. Two sub-sectors in particular, the shipbuilding and steel sectors, tried, with varying degrees of success, to enter into social dialogue (see below). CEEMET reacted very quickly, wishing to control the process. It decided to sign an internal code of conduct on European sectoral social dialogue with the sub-sectoral employers' federations, stating that these should concentrate solely on industrial policy issues, and should leave to CEEMET the responsibility for social issues and formal relations with EMF. Finally, as we shall see, what was going on in the sub-sectors led WEM to make more concessions than originally planned.

---

13 WEM was already taking this stance in a statement made in 1990, where it explained that it would rather leave it up to UNICE to take decisions on social issues, in order to avoid the employers' position being weakened by a multiplicity of sectoral positions (Platzer, 1991: 127).

B. Domino Effect: From Shipbuilding... to Metalworking

Berndt Keller has suggested that institutionalised sub-sectoral dialogues could provide a promising and more realistic alternative to sectoral SD, since the parties involved have very similar interests, which are therefore easier to represent than in broader sectors (Keller, 2001). Two sub-sectors of the metalworking industry – shipbuilding and steel – are good examples of this.

EMF's strategy of moving into social dialogue via pilot sectors (steel, shipbuilding) did work relatively well, but another important factor behind the setting up of SSDCs in these sub-sectors came from the European Commission. For some time the Commission had wished to promote dialogue in the "strategic" metalworking industry, and it had implicitly backed union strategy by being lenient, even a little lax, in enforcing the criteria for representation on the employers' side[14]. Over the years, the employers' organisations for the various sub-sectors were therefore more or less invited to "dialogue" (see table 1). For the moment, then, dialogue in the automotive, machine tools and motor trade & repairs sectors[15] is restricted to rather informal discussions, whereas the steel sector has made a joint request for an SSDC, which is currently being set up. The shipbuilding sector, however, has already set up an SSDC, and even the "metal" sector very recently created a supposedly equivalent structure: a "high-level standing committee". We shall now look in more detail at how these recent dialogues, or requests for dialogue, have come about[16].

14 In the case of shipbuilding, for example, the Commission accepted the first joint request for an SSDC, even though there was no representative European employers' organisation.

15 In its report on European industrial relations, the Commission states its view that it is not possible to create SSDCs for small sectors, such as the motor trade and repairs sector. An EMF representative, at the Collective Bargaining Policy Committee meeting, said that: "we do not agree to the Commission accepting a request for an SSDC from the metalworking sector, for example, but not from the motor trade and repairs sector. We will not tolerate this discrimination between sectors" (28-29 October 2002).

16 We shall not deal here with the still informal social dialogues in the automotive, machine tools and motor trade & repairs sectors.

Table 1: The Various Stages of Social Dialogue in Sub-sectors of the Metalworking Sector

Stages of Sub-sector Social Dialogue	Workers	Employers	1st meetings/SSDCs
Recent SD			
Metal	EMF	CEEMET since 2004 (WEM)	2003/February 2006*
Shipbuilding	EMF	CESA	2001 / Sept. 2003
SD requested			
Steel (ECSC)	EMF	Eurofer	2000/November 2004
Informal SD			
Automotive[17]	EMF	EAMA, CLEPA	1985
Machine tools	EMF	CECIMO	1984
Motor trade and repairs	EMF	CECRA	n.d.

* "High-level standing committee" rather than Social Dialogue Committee (SSDC).

In the *steel sector*[18], dialogue with the European Steel Industry Federation (Eurofer) dates back to the European Coal and Steel Community (ECSC) Treaty. This institutional framework, set up to supervise the mining and steel industries, created a decision-making process which itself involved the employers' and trade union organisations. On 23 July 2002, the ECSC Treaty expired after 50 years in force (for further details, see chapter 2). EMF drew positive conclusions from the experience: "The ECSC showed that socially responsible restructuring is possible, and that a competitive European steel industry is partly the result of ongoing sectoral social dialogue" (EMF, 2003b: 50). When the Treaty expired, the activities of the Advisory Committee were transferred to a working group of the European Economic and Social Committee (EESC), entitled the "Consultative Commission on Industrial Change"[19]. This new body has made it possible to continue the consultation and dialogue process for the sector, and to extend the benefits of the experience accumulated under the ECSC to other sectors of industry undergoing restructuring.

17 Without going into more detail on this sub-sector, we note that EMF and the European Council for Motor Trades and Repairs (CECRA) have worked closely on the new draft regulation for a motor vehicle block exemption, and have laid the foundations for future cooperation.

18 Most of the information contained in the next two paragraphs comes from EMF documents (EMF, 2003a and 2003b).

19 This legacy of the ECSC treaty was set up following the Commission communication on the "future of structured dialogue after the expiry of the ECSC Treaty" (CEC, 2000a), and, above all, in the wake up of a campaign organised by EMF, EMCEF and the ETUC to lobby the Commission, Council and the European Parliament to obtain improvements to the Commission recommendations.

As well as the establishment, after the demise the Advisory Committee, of these follow-up mechanisms geared to a structured social dialogue, an SSDC was set up to continue the work of the Joint Committee on steel, which was also due to be disbanded in 2002. EMF and Eurofer proposed, on 12 December 2000, that it should be transformed into an SSDC. In November 2001, a short-term work programme was adopted at the plenary session of the Joint Committee. On this basis, the two organisations began to prepare their joint request to the Commission for the setting up of an SSDC. A first meeting took place in November 2004, on the topics to be dealt with in the committee: health and safety, and vocational training.

Even further forward in this process, the *shipbuilding* sub-sector was the first within the metalworking industry to set up a regular, institutionalised social dialogue. This sub-sector had, since the beginning of the 1970s, suffered restructuring with massive job-losses[20]. The initial spurs to a "dialogue" were the unfair competitive practices of South Korea, distortions of the market and the gradual phasing out of aid to maintain the competitiveness of the industry. This was the backdrop to a first European Day of Action in November 1999, organised by EMF and supported by the employers' organisation, the Community of European Shipyards Associations (CESA). More than 220,000 workers demonstrated in twelve countries, to call for industrial policy to include the protection of jobs (Schulten, 2000: 94). EMF then sought to cooperate with employers at national level, and this cooperation spread to Community level through joint actions. In this context, a first joint declaration was signed by EMF and CESA. Since then, the two organisations have remained in close contact and have informed each other of their respective activities. The second event to bring them together was the joint conference on the shipbuilding industry held on 7 November 2000 at the European Parliament[21]. As a result of these joint efforts, following years of Council discussions, a temporary mechanism was finally agreed on in June 2002, to defend certain segments of the sector's market which had been directly affected by unfair competition.

Following protracted negotiations, the Social Dialogue Committee was set up on 17 September 2003. A work programme was drawn up for 2004-2005, containing four main points: a study of the sector, an initia-

[20] The workforce in the 25 EU Member States decreased from some 461,000 to 100,000 between 1975 and 2003 (CEC, 2003a: 25), cited in Kollewe (2005: 384).

[21] EMF and CESA then strengthened their cooperation with a view to the Council meeting of European Industry Ministers on 5 December 2000, which was to take a decision on whether to prolong aid to the shipbuilding sector.

tive in the area of vocational training[22], a "tool box" based on experiences with industrial change and restructuring[23], and finally the image of the sector (a topic proposed by the employers and accepted by EMF). Ad-hoc groups were formed to discuss these issues.

The "metal" sector was still outside the official framework of SSDCs. Contacts (regular meetings between members of the secretariats and of the Executive Committee) were instituted, and led to the establishment of an official working group entitled "education and training", whose first meeting took place in November 2001[24]. The idea was to make progress on benchmarking and to carry out lobbying of the Commission on training. At the EMF Congress in June 2003, Reinhard Kuhlmann, the then General Secretary, explained that "cooperation between WEM and EMF will be intensified and stabilised: a joint analysis and practical proposals will be presented on the image of the metalworking and electronics industry as well as new possibilities in the area of vocational and continuing training. The first joint conference (30 September and 1 October 2003) will address the lack of skilled labour in the sector" (EMF, 2003c).

Following this first case of informal cooperation on vocational and continuing training, social dialogue in the metalworking sector has progressed. Although there is still no official dialogue, the opposition of the employers' federations has diminished. Within CEEMET there are now differing views. Some members (in particular the French members) would like to be able to submit a joint request to the Commission for an official dialogue, whereas others (especially the British) are totally against this idea. These differences of view have made it impossible to submit a request for an SSDC, but a semi-institutional dialogue has been set up. This new dialogue takes the same form as dialogues set up by the Commission (mandate, common structure, plenary meetings, work programme), except that CEEMET categorically refuses to allow the Commission to be formally involved. The employers are aiming for a sort of "opting out" situation, i.e. they would like to observe the pro-

22 The employers required the final report of this working group to be drafted by an outside party: Cedefop.

23 As part of this, the EMCC (European Monitoring Centre for Change) is producing national reports for EMF on the various ways of ensuring a socially responsible type of restructuring.

24 This group was set up on the basis of the EMF paper adopted in Oslo. The employers attached a number of conditions to the establishment of this joint group. They required there to be the same number of representatives from each country and asked for the degree of representativeness of the committee to be looked into. This was, however, a transitional committee meeting only on an occasional basis. It was not made up of negotiators and its sole purpose was to collect various examples of training systems in the various countries. (EMF, 2002).

gress made in this new committee, before assessing whether it is preferable to continue with it or to establish an SSDC. The aim of the EMF is still, in the long term, to set up the SSDC they have been hankering after for so long. "It is the employers who are wanting to begin a social dialogue, which puts us in a favourable position […] They want to make progress on certain issues, and to heighten their profile as partners […] EMF, then, is no longer in the situation where it is asking for dialogue but being rejected. There has been a reversal of roles" (EMF interview, 2005).

The nature of this process, excluding the Commission, gives rise to the question of funding. EMF had initially proposed that CEEMET should finance it, since it was CEEMET which was rejecting logistical and financial aid from the Commission. Finally a compromise was worked out: plenary meetings would be held at the Economic and Social Committee, as guests of Group 3 (EESC members other than trade union and employers' representatives). This "high-level standing committee" would begin its work in February 2006. The work programme agreed on at the first meeting, held on 30 January 2006, contains the following topics: health and safety, corporate social responsibility (proposed by EMF), restructuring, mobility and vocational training.

One EMF representative said in 2002 that "if the metal sector opens up a bit, things will change. As the first domino in a series of subsectors, if it were to fall, it would lead the other sub-sectors of the metalworking industry to follow suit" (EMF interview, 2002). According to this view, the prospect of the metal sector meeting to discuss issues in January 2006 has opened up a whole range of new possibilities. Some key sectors, such as the automotive industry and its subcontractors, as well as the ICT sector, the aeronautical and aerospace industries, and the defence industry, none of which have yet anything like a social dialogue, could draw on experiences in the steel, shipbuilding and metalworking sectors. Further developments are awaited…

II. Chemical Industry

The European chemical industry is the largest industrial sector in Europe[25]. This sector, however, was very late in setting up an official European social dialogue. It was only in December 2002 that a first joint declaration was signed between the social partners – the European Mine, Chemical and Energy Workers Federation (EMCEF) for the workers, and for the employers the European Chemical Employers Group (ECEG). Since then, progress has been rapid. In 2004 the Sectoral

25 The European chemical industry employs two million workers directly, is the second largest industrial sector within the EU and the largest world market.

Social Dialogue Committee for the chemical industry was set up. The main topics dealt with at European level in this sector, over the last few months, have been the REACH proposal (CEC, 2003b), life-long education and training and the Responsible Care programme[26]. Since 2006, some EMCEF members have been trying to add the issue of health and safety (occupational diseases and accidents at work) to the agenda. Before analysing these developments, we should point out that at national level the chemical sector, unlike the metal sector, has no real tradition of sectoral social dialogue. The sector is made up of a wide range of very different companies: petrochemicals, plastics processing, pharmaceuticals, fertilisers, paint manufacturing, etc. This means that there is a tendency to focus on the company level, rather than the sectoral level, where there could be a "lack of solidarity". We shall identify two main types of factors which explain the slow emergence of a social dialogue in this sector: firstly the fact that the European organisations were slow to structure themselves appropriately, and, secondly, certain developments in the area of industrial policy. Like the ETUC and some European industry federations, EMCEF set up an internal collective bargaining committee. It gave two reasons for doing so. Enlargement of the European Union, firstly, and secondly the introduction of the euro, meant that it was important to create tools which could be used to compare the provisions included in national collective agreements (this would also help with national negotiations). So according to EMCEF, the main role of this collective bargaining committee is to provide information to members on agreements in the various countries, and to help national organisations coordinate their policies and strategies. EMCEF felt that this sort of coordination should prevent employers using the differences between national collective agreements as an argument to set agreements against each other or to weaken their provisions. As things stand, however, our view is that the establishment of this collective bargaining committee has not been an important factor in the development of social dialogue in the sector.

A. Creating the Appropriate European Structures

EMCEF, representing the European chemical industry unions, is a member of the ETUC and has around 120 affiliated trade unions. It came into being in 1996, when the European Mineworkers Federation (EMF) merged with the European Federation of Chemical, Energy and General Workers Unions (EFCGWU). Some sub-sectors of these two

---

[26] Responsible Care is a voluntary initiative, coordinated by CEFIC (European Chemical Industry Council), the objective of which is to improve the sector's performance in the areas of occupational and environmental safety, thus protecting workers, people living close to industrial plants, consumers and the environment.

federations, such as electricity, and, even more, mining, have a long history of European social dialogue[27]. The 1996 merger gave rise, therefore, to an organisation which was new, but whose members were already used to working together. The trade unions were already thinking of setting up a social dialogue in the chemical sector at the end of the 1980s. The prospect of a European single market had led EFCGWU to reflect on the social impact of greater integration of the industries making up this sector. Later, EMCEF would attempt, internally, to clarify which areas should be covered by a European social dialogue. A series of topics would emerge, but it was clear from the outset that "collective bargaining on wages, salaries and working conditions was not understood to be an issue in the social dialogue" (Reibsch, 2005: 366). This probably explains the comments on the collective bargaining committee referred to above.

Originally, the main problem faced by EMCEF was that it had no real formal partner on the employers' side with whom to enter into a social "dialogue". The European Chemical Industry Council (CEFIC) had no mandate to discuss and negotiate with the European trade union confederations. "Agreements or any kind of joint initiatives seemed to be impossible and were refused by CEFIC" (Reibsch, 2005: 364). The employers' industry federations had been set up to defend the interests of their members *vis-à-vis* European Commission initiatives; social issues were outside their remit. During the 1990s, while EMCEF was becoming increasingly worried by developments in the sector (mergers, acquisitions, restructuring), this obstacle to social dialogue remained, at least at European level, since CEFIC refused to see itself as a social partner. The only progress made was the establishment, as of 1994, of European Works Councils in a large number of chemical companies[28].

The first, gradual, signs of an end to the deadlock came instead from certain national organisations. Various initiatives were launched by groups of countries, including the tripartite grouping of employers and unions from Italy, Spain and France. This group launched projects to analyse the impact of economic change on employment and qualifications. Other, similar, projects were launched, in particular, by the United Kingdom and Germany. EMCEF would try to use these bilateral or multilateral initiatives to approach the national employers' confedera-

27 In the electricity sector, a dialogue was set up in 1996 to address the consequences of restructuring and job losses linked to liberalisation. The mining sector was involved in an incipient social dialogue in 1952, with the establishment of the ECSC, and, in particular, of the joint committee for the harmonisation of working conditions (see chapter 2).

28 There are more "European Works Council" agreements in the sectors covered by EMCEF than in those of any other European industry federation.

tions directly, rather than risking renewed rebuffs from CEFIC. It was thanks to the tripartite group, therefore, that a first conference was organised in Milan in 2000. Invitations were sent out to all the employers' and trade union organisations of the EU Member States.

B. Industrial Policy Developments

At the end of the 1990s, external factors intervened: as well as completion of the internal market, enlargement of the European Union to take in the countries of Central and Eastern Europe became a real possibility. Industrial policy issues, moreover, seemed to become an increasing priority at Community level. In particular, the Commission's Green Paper on PVC (CEC, 2000b) led three industrial associations in the PVC sector (ECVM, ECPI, ESPA)[29] to sign a first joint text with EMCEF in October 2000. The aim of this document was to create a Forum for social dialogue within the PVC industry, which would look at the key factors for the future of the industry, and their potential effects on workers. The social partners identified a number of areas for cooperation[30]. Events surrounding the PVC Green Paper seemed to show the European trade union organisation that there were ways of bringing the employers' organisations round to the idea of a European social dialogue. What was needed, in the view of EMCEF, was to include industrial policy themes close to the heart of the employers, and to make sure that the objectives, roles and binding nature of the social dialogue were clearly defined.

CEFIC, under pressure from these various factors, decided to establish, in January 2002, the European Chemical Employers Group (ECEG). This can be seen as the "social wing" of CEFIC. It is responsible for social issues and relations with trade union organisations in the sector. It represents around 10,000 European companies. In December 2002, for the first time, a conference was held in Paris by the two organisations, which then became the official social partners for the chemical industry: EMCEF and ECEG. On 4 December 2002, a joint statement was adopted, in which the two organisations decided "to initiate an ongoing sectoral social dialogue within the European chemical industry, in order both to create a climate favourable to competitiveness and employment in the sector, and also to develop the social di-

[29] European Council of Vinyl Manufacturers, European Council for Plasticisers and Intermediates, and European Stabiliser Producers Association.

[30] Development of the industry in a European context, improvement of health and safety standards, environmental standards, transfer of best practice to candidate countries, worker qualifications, European Works Councils, exchanges of information and consultations on industrial developments in the chemical sector.

mension of Europe"[31]. Further conferences followed, in Madrid in 2003 and Helsinki in 2004. In parallel, the list of topics to be discussed during the dialogue grew longer: qualification issues have remained important (in some European countries there is a lack of skilled labour), but the REACH project, which has sounded warning bells with the European-level social partners[32], is a particular priority, as well as questions relating to health and safety, and the Responsible Care programme[33].

REACH can be seen as one of the main factors to have triggered the European social dialogue. The chemical industry, through CEFIC, had been lobbying the European institutions in many ways for many years, but the REACH proposal, for the first time, introduced a social dimension to industrial policy. The proposal should make it possible to reduce the number of occupational diseases caused by exposure to dangerous substances. According to one of our interviewees, with REACH "social dialogue became an attractive prospect for CEFIC, as it allowed it to expand its lobbying objectives. The social dialogue was clearly being played on, but EMCEF was able to seize the opportunity to put across its own priorities" (CSC interview, 2006). We should however stress that there were sometimes very lively discussions on REACH, and on what position the European trade unions should adopt on the proposal, between the ETUC and EMCEF, as well as within EMCEF itself. At any rate, from this time onwards, social dialogue in the chemical industry began to gather pace, leading to the inaugural meeting of the SSDC (see list of joint documents in the bibliography).

Rules of procedure were adopted at the inaugural meeting of the Sectoral Social Dialogue Committee. According to these, the main objectives of the Committee are to develop a common understanding of the issues facing the chemical industry, and to focus both on social matters affecting the sector and on commercial and company-related matters, environmental and health and safety issues, investor confidence and the dissemination of a scientific and technical culture in Europe. Social issues are not to be taken in isolation from questions of industrial strategy. This approach could support the analysis made by the informant referred to above, who claimed that the sector's employers only accepted the social dialogue in so far as it could be made to serve industrial strategy ends.

The rules of procedure, moreover, contain significant restrictions. They state that the SSDC will not interfere with any national negotia-

31 ECEG/EMCEF joint statement 2002, Paris, 4 December 2002.

32 Joint statement of ECEG, CEFIC and EMCEF on the New European Chemicals Policy (REACH), 27 November 2003.

33 A Memorandum of Understanding on the Responsible Care programme was signed by ECEG, EMCEF and CEFIC on 21 May 2003.

tions on social issues within the sector. The dialogue will therefore focus on subjects not traditionally covered by national collective agreements; it will not create an extra level of discussion for traditional collective bargaining, and neither will it act as an appeal body for the national social partners. Social dialogue in the chemical sector, therefore, will be used only to exchange information and experiences, to provide coordinated information to members, and to reach agreement on joint declarations, official positions or recommendations. It is explicitly stated that no direct obligations may be imposed on companies or workers in the sector. This is in fact one of the most restrictive sets of rules of procedure that we came across in the 31 sectors we analysed.

Following the first SSDC meeting, a work programme was adopted for 2005-2006, in which the REACH draft regulation plays a prominent role. In June 2005, the adoption of another common position on the proposal emphasised the importance of REACH in the development of social dialogue in this sector. Finally, in November 2005, the social partners announced their contribution to the framework of action for the life-long development of competences and qualifications[34]. This framework, adopted at cross-industry level, gave rise to the formation of a working group in the chemical sector to analyse the issues of qualifications and training, and to facilitate the spreading of information and exchanges of good practice in this area. It was also decided to launch a survey on life-long education, training and learning, and to discuss its results in the SSDC. This shared interest in training and learning stems from fears within the sector that it is soon to face a shortage of highly skilled manpower.

Finally, as mentioned earlier, a number of EMCEF member organisations (Femca CISL, CSC Énergie-Chimie etc.) attempted, in 2006, to introduce a new theme into the sectoral social dialogue: occupational diseases. Although the chemical industry prides itself on its low rate of occupational disease, the trade unions believe that this low rate is due to the non-inclusion in the figures of subcontracting industries and downstream sectors using chemical substances (civil engineering and construction, hairdressing, SMEs etc.). The attempt was made to add this point to the agenda as a result of one paradox and two forthcoming opportunities. The paradox is that while emphasis is being placed on the mobility of workers (2006 is the "European Year of Workers' Mobility"), there has still been no harmonisation or even convergence of the national compensation schemes for occupational diseases. Each EU Member State has its own list of occupational diseases. There is a

---

[34] "ECEG/EMCEF contribution to the third follow-up report of the Framework of action for the lifelong development of competences and qualifications", November 2005.

European list, but it is non-binding. This has meant that there are significant divergences in the national records of diseases, as well as in the criteria for recognition, the methods used to declare a disease, and, of course, the compensation rates[35]. The first opportunity is the forthcoming updating, in 2006 and 2007, of the Commission recommendation on the European list of occupational diseases[36]; the second is implementation of REACH. The section of REACH on registration of chemical substances provides for a new risk assessment of these substances. Indirectly, then, this legislation should provide better arguments to support the official recognition of occupational diseases. At the time of writing, however, it is not yet possible to assess the likelihood of this topic being put on the agenda of the SSDC.

Our conclusion is that the European chemical industry was slow to establish a sectoral social dialogue for two main reasons. The first was that CEFIC and the European employers' organisations in the industry had no mandate to discuss social issues with the trade union organisation EMCEF; the second that they were slow to realise the increasing importance of developments in Europe.

III. Central Public Administration

There are a number of reasons for analysing European social dialogue in this sector and considering where it may go from here. Firstly, this is a sector where national trade unions are still very influential, compared to the private sector at least. Comparative studies have shown this to be true throughout Europe (Visser, 2006). These national unions are strong, and have maintained high levels of membership, or are even increasing their membership in some EU countries. Public administration, moreover, is by definition a protected sector, which does not suffer overmuch from the direct effects of globalisation and the opening up of borders, although it may be indirectly affected when governments decide to reduce public spending, to introduce wage moderation or to redeploy certain functions by means of outsourcing or privatisation. This status as a protected sector has meant that the civil service, or, more generally, the public sector, can in certain circumstances become the driving force behind sectoral and national wage bargaining – like the metalworking and chemical sectors.

---

35 The situation of the Italian miners who worked in France, Germany and/or Belgium is a good example of this paradoxical situation: free movement of workers but a lack of harmonisation of the national compensation schemes for occupational diseases, with all the difficulties this lack of consistency entails.

36 Commission Recommendation of 19 September 2003 concerning the European schedule of occupational diseases, OJ L 238 of 25 September 2003, pp.0028-0034.

There are, however, a number of factors which make it more difficult to develop sectoral dialogue. The first problem is how to define the exact scope of the sector. In other words, where can the line be drawn with the private sector (a line which is blurred because of the many private/public partnerships, for example), or with other levels of a decentralised civil service, such as regional and local government? There are also differing national definitions of what is meant by the public administration. We shall not look in more detail at these issues, which have generated lengthy comparative studies. We shall merely bear the problem in mind and stress the fact that the social partners in the sector tend, for the moment, to use a restrictive definition, i.e. their discussions concern those who work for central ministries.

Another difficulty for the social dialogue is the question of how are organised the negotiations with an employer which represents the public authorities (the State). In some countries, such as Italy, collective bargaining is run more or less as for the private sector, but in others, the terms of contracts may be set unilaterally by the State. Between these two extremes, there are many shades of grey, for instance informal or formal consultation of the trade unions or partial negotiations (UCL-IST, 2004; Kirton-Darling, 2004).

Finally, a distinction is usually drawn between "career" civil services (basically where civil servants have tenure), and "professional" ones where workers have contracts similar to those in the private sector, although, in reality, increasing use is made of hybrid forms. Current and future enlargement is not a problem for this sector, since there are, of course, public administrations in each of the new Member States. The new structure of these administrations, moreover, is closer to the system in Germany or France (career civil service) than to that in Italy or the United Kingdom (professional civil service).

Social dialogue began in the early 1990s and has not progressed easily. We shall now examine the factors driving it on and those holding it back.

A. The Problem of Representativeness

The main problem which this sector has had to resolve is that of representation, i.e. which parties should participate in the dialogue? This question held up initial progress in the 1990s. The first attempts to set up a structured dialogue took place in 1994. These were informal meetings between the European Federation of Public Service Unions (EPSU), affiliated to the European Trade Union Confederation (ETUC), and the Directors General of the public administrations. Various meetings took place between 1994 and 1998. The Commission's 1998 communication (CEC, 1998a and 1998b) revived cooperation, and in 1999 it was decided to create an informal social dialogue. Between 1997 and 2000 three round tables were organised, covering topics such as mobility, modernisation and flexibility. The Belgian presidency (2001) sought to extend trade union representation and to involve other organisations (CESI and Eurofedop) in the sectoral dialogue. A number of trade unions involved in national negotiations (such as the Belgian liberal union or the union representing those German career civil servants not represented by the ETUC) had set up the European Confederation of Independent Trade Unions (CESI), which wished to be recognised as a full cross-industry partner. At the sectoral level, Eurofedop represents in some sectors the Christian trade unions affiliated to the World Confederation of Labour (WCL).

These events triggered a conflict of representation and precedence between the three trade union organisations, which made all progress in sectoral dialogue impossible. Significantly, the question of representation became far more pressing when the Commission decided to introduce new social dialogue committees. In the running-in years of these committees, a number of conflicts on the union side needed to be settled in various sectors[37]. These divisions between trade unions were mainly a problem for the public sector, where three organisations – EPSU, CESI and Eurofedop – coexist. Of the three, the largest is EPSU, which belongs to the ETUC and represents 8 million public service workers and 1,217 affiliated unions. It also organises social dialogue in the electricity sector with EMCEF (see below), for the local and regional public services and in the social services and health sectors (hospitals).

Following the Belgian attempt to put all three partners on the same footing, EPSU decided no longer to participate in meetings where it was treated as equal to participants from Eurofedop and CESI. It decided to wait for publication of the results of the Commission study on representativeness (UCL-IST, 2004). This study resolved the situation. It showed that EPSU was by far the most representative organisation, but also that there was a problem with certain countries, especially Germany, Luxembourg and Austria. CESI is very strong in Germany and Luxembourg, where it has more members than EPSU. In Austria, the Christian section of the ÖGB – one trade union with two sections – is affiliated to Eurofedop. Following the study and after pressure from the European Commission to find a solution, EPSU and CESI signed a memorandum,

---

37 The problem is different for the employers, where there are several co-existent organisations representing precise interests (see chapter 9). On the union side, the ETUC and its federations see themselves as the only recognised worker representatives in sectoral and cross-industry social dialogue. Multiple interests are represented within one organisation, rather than by various organisations representing the various union sympathies (Social Democratic, Communist and Christian).

containing a technical solution satisfactory to both parties. EPSU and Eurofedop, however, although close to signing an agreement, were not able to finalise it formally. Eurofedop's position is becoming increasingly weaker with the creation of a new unitary international organisation. Increasingly, moreover, the Christian unions, including for example the Belgian Christian trade union, have chosen to belong to both organisations and have joined EPSU.

The solution found was based on the system used in the sectoral dialogue for local and regional government, which has a similar problem with trade union representation. EPSU has overall responsibility for the delegation, but for each country the most representative union acts as the official representative. The agreement between EPSU and CESI, then, means that the German and Luxembourg delegations are headed up by unions belonging to CESI. Two members of the CESI secretariat are also members of the trade union delegation (on an equal footing with EPSU). In the absence of a formal agreement with Eurofedop, the same system was used at the December 2005 meeting, which issued a joint statement (see below), and at which the Austrian and Hungarian members of Eurofedop were part of the united trade union delegation.

On the employers' side, two organisations have a legitimate claim to participate in social dialogue (CEEP and EPAN). The public administrations in five countries (Denmark, Finland, Sweden, Italy and the United Kingdom) are affiliated to the European Centre of Enterprises with Public Participation and of Enterprises of General Economic Interest (CEEP). This is a recognised cross-industry social partner but is searching for a (new) role. It has redefined itself as the organisation representing local public services such as hospitals (Arcq and Pochet, 2002; Degryse and Pochet, 2004).

However, the official partner in the dialogue should really be the informal European network of Directors General responsible for Public Administration (EPAN). This network exchanges information and (good) practices in four areas of cooperation: innovative public services, human resource management, e-government and better regulation. EPAN's action programme for 2006-2007 (Luxembourg Presidency, 2005) states the following: "The constitution, in spring 2005, of a common and pluralist delegation of trade union organisations that are representative of public employees at European level, has enabled social dialogue to take a step forward. The Ministers responsible for Public Administration, meeting in Luxembourg on 8 June 2005, give the Directors General the mission to examine how the social dialogue can be developed and improved, and how the employers and the employees can be consulted on issues and topics of their concern" (EPAN, 2005: 9).

Developments on the trade union side have led the public authorities to consider their own objectives. There have been, as a result, two internal surveys as to the possible aims of social dialogue. The survey asked, for example, whether the national administration was ready to move from an informal to a formal social dialogue. If so, would this be done according to the provisions of the Treaty, or in a less binding fashion? Was EPAN the right body for this? Which topics should be dealt with? And so on. It would seem that the employers have yet to determine the very purpose of social dialogue.

B. The Driving Forces behind Social Dialogue

We can identify three main driving forces or factors promoting social dialogue.

Public administration, firstly, is affected by the outcomes of the cross-industry dialogue. The agreement on parental leave, for example, persuaded some national players in the central administrations that they should organise themselves properly at European level in order to participate in negotiations whose outcomes affect their situation.

The second factor was a tendency to compete with the local public authorities, which set up a formal committee in 2004. This is a motivational factor which we have come across several times. One of the reasons, for example, for UNICE deciding to join the social dialogue in 1995/96 was its fear of sectoral developments (Arcq *et al.*, 2003, Branch and Greenwood, 2001; Marginson, 2005; see also above the cases of the chemical and especially the metalworking sectors).

Finally, the third factor was linked to the desire of participants in the dialogue to be present in the advisory bodies, in order to influence the European political and social agenda. Some groups, for example, considered joining CEEP as a way of being recognised directly and of having access to all the European consultative processes and forums (Mangenot and Polet, 2004)[38].

We should note, too, that in the case of public administration, the European Commission also has an ambiguous status, since it is an employer at European level and as such has a place on the EPAN delegation.

C. Initial Results

At the time of writing, resumption of the dialogue between the trade union delegation and EPAN has so far led them, in December 2005, to adopt a declaration on equality and diversity, along the lines of the

---

[38] This phenomenon also occurs in other sectors, such as commerce, where groups wish to transcend their purely sectoral interests and influence a general political agenda.

declaration on the same topic made by the local and regional government sector. This joint text has a number of objectives:

1) to show that the former hindrances to dialogue have been overcome and that there is now one sole "trade union delegation";

2) to provide some points of agreement on this question;

3) to place what is being done in the context of the UK presidency and future EU action;

4) to provide some ideas for a future work programme.

There has been, therefore, some progress in the field of sectoral social dialogue, but it is still hesitant. It has been made possible thanks to the solution found to the problem of trade union representation. The first steps are above all procedural in nature, and show the wish to create a climate of mutual trust, in order to move towards the setting up of a formal committee. Some on the employers' side are still against the idea of such a committee, because they wish, firstly, to avoid giving further power to the national unions, and also since they fear that a formal dialogue will ultimately give rise to binding agreements.

General Conclusions

The chemical and metalworking industries were slow to enter into a European sectoral social dialogue, largely because of the strategies of the organisations involved. In both cases, it took a long time for the trade union side to convince the employers to structure themselves as social partners, partly because the employers' representatives lacked a mandate. For public administration, however, the first impediment was the issue of competing trade union organisations. Once this question of representativeness had been resolved, the question of how the employers were to structure themselves and what strategies they should follow arose as in the other sectors.

One hypothesis is that wage coordination has an impact on social dialogue. This, however, does not seem to apply to these three sectors. Indeed, EMF's coordination of collective wage bargaining took place in parallel to the social dialogue and does not seem to have influenced it. Wage coordination in the chemical and public administration sectors does not seem to be a plausible explanation for the breaking of the deadlock.

By contrast, the first hypothesis mentioned in the Introduction (the impact of industrial policy developments, or, in the case of public administration, of more general issues) does seem to be borne out here. If we wish to understand how these sectors finally progressed towards social dialogue, we should look at the specific issues on which industry wished to lobby: the REACH proposal for the chemical sector and the "silica" directive for the metalworking sector. Since the Commission's initiatives in these sectors had a social impact, it became worthwhile for European employers to expand their lobbying strategies. The difference, nevertheless, is that employers in the chemical industry were more in favour of joint action on REACH. EMCEF and EMF were then able to seize the opportunity to push forward their own institutional priorities. This finally led to the establishment of the Sectoral Social Dialogue Committee. In the case of public administration, it was the outcomes of cross-industry dialogue (especially the parental leave directive, which emerged from negotiations between the cross-industry social partners) which convinced some employers of the urgent need to improve the way they organised their activities at sectoral level, in order to influence the outcomes of the cross-industry dialogue. But this has not been enough to convince the public administration representatives to structure themselves as full-blown social partners at sectoral level.

Another factor, however, must also be borne in mind here: the emergence of sub-sectoral social dialogues (encouraged by the European industry federations) which helped trigger the setting up of committees. In other words, although relatively little is said in the relevant literature about competition between sectoral employers' groupings, it clearly played an important role in the three cases we analysed.

In the cases of metalworking and chemicals, European trade union strategy – assisted to a greater or lesser extent by the European Commission's DG for employment – consisted of working with associations of European employers in their respective sub-sectors (the PVC associations for the chemical sector; shipbuilding and steel for metalworking) in order to get the ball rolling on industrial policy issues. EMCEF also tried to "bypass" the deadlock at European level by working with certain national employers' confederations. The same was true of the public service unions. They were able to open up dialogue at the level of local and regional government, and this then pointed the way forward for national administrations. In order to avoid being overtaken by their own members in the area of social dialogue, the central employers' federations responsible for social issues –, CEEMET, ECEG and EPAN respectively – were "forced" into a dialogue.

Despite the removal of some of the obstacles, these social dialogues are still subject to many restrictions. EMCEF, for example, may not intervene in national negotiations on social issues, it may not create a further level of discussion in the negotiation of collective agreements, and nor may it constitute an appeal body for the national social partners. Legal instruments which would impose direct obligations on companies or workers are also explicitly ruled out. This is due to fears, probably more prevalent in this than in other sectors with less influential trade unions, of becoming caught up in a process leading to European-level collective bargaining. Although all these three sectors, with a strong tradition of national bargaining, seem to have entered the arena of European sectoral dialogue, their involvement has been low-key, and employers have shown considerable hesitancy.

References

Arcq, É. and Pochet, P. (2002), "UNICE and CEEP in 2001: Changes in Prospect?", in Gabaglio, E. and Hoffmann, R. (eds.), *European Trade Union Yearbook 2001*, European Trade Union Institute, Brussels, pp.205-222.

Arcq, É., Dufresne, A. and Pochet, P. (2003), "The Employers: Hidden Face of European Industrial Relations", *Transfer*, Vol.9, No.2, pp.302-321.

Branch, A. and Greenwood, J. (2001), "European Employers: Social Partners?", in Crompston, H. and Greenwood, J. (eds.), *Social Partnership in the European Union*, Palgrave, New York, pp.41-70.

CEC (1998a), Communication from the Commission "Adapting and Promoting the Social Dialogue at Community Level", COM (98) 322 of 20 May 1998 (http://europa.eu.int/comm/employment_social/social_dialogue/docs/com322_en.pdf).

CEC (1998b), Commission Decision 98/500/EC of 20 May 1998 on the establishment of Sectoral Dialogue Committees Promoting the Dialogue between the Social Partners at European Level, OJ L 225 of 12 August 1998, pp.0027-0028.

CEC (2000a), Communication from the Commission to the Council, the European Parliament, the Economic and Social Committee, the ECSC Consultative Committee and the Committee of the Regions "The Future of Structured Dialogue After the Expiry of the ECSC Treaty", COM (2000) 588 final of 27 September 2000 (http://europa.eu.int/eur-lex/lex/LexUriServ/site/en/com/2000/com2000_0588en01.pdf).

CEC (2000b), Green Paper – Environmental Issues of PVC, COM (2000) 469 final of 26 July 2000 (http://europe.eu.int/eur-lex/lex/LexUriServ/site/en/com/2000/com2000_0469en01.pdf).

CEC (2003a), Communication from the Commission "LeaderSHIP 2015. Defining the Future of the European Shipbuilding and Repair Industry – Competitiveness through Excellence", COM (2003) 717 final of 21 November 2003 (http://europa.eu.int/comm/enterprise/maritime/shipbuilding_market/doc/leadership_en.pdf).

CEC (2003b), Proposal for a Regulation of the European Parliament and of the Council concerning the Registration, Evaluation, Authorisation and Restriction of Chemicals (REACH), Establishing a European Chemicals Agency and Amending Directive 1999/45/EC and Regulation (EC) {on Persistent Organic Pollutants} and Proposal for a Directive of the European Parliament and of the Council Amending Council Directive 67/548/EEC in Order to Adapt it to Regulation (EC) of the European Parliament and of the Council concerning the Registration, Evaluation, Authorisation and Restriction of Chemicals, COM (2003) 644 final of 29 October 2003 (http://europa.eu.int/eur-lex/en/com/pdf/2003/act0644en03/1.pdf).

De Boer, R., Benedictus, H. and van der Meer, M. (2005), "Broadening without Intensification: The Added Value of the European Social and Sectoral Dialogue", *European Journal of Industrial Relations*, Vol.11, No.1, pp.51-70.

Degryse, C. and Pochet, P. (2004), "UNICE/UEAPME and CEEP in 2003", in Jørgensen, H., Bærentsen, M. and Monks, J. (eds.), *European Trade Union Yearbook 2003-2004*, European Trade Union Institute, Brussels, pp.235-254.

Dufour, C. and Hege, A. (1999), "Quelle coordination syndicale des négociations en Europe?", *Chronique Internationale de l'IRES*, No.60, pp.108-117.

Dufresne, A. (2002a), "La branche, niveau stratégique de la coordination des négociations collectives?", *Chronique Internationale de l'IRES*, No.74, January 2002, pp.59-70.

Dufresne, A. (2002b), "Wage Co-ordination in Europe: Roots and Routes", in Pochet, P. (ed.), *Wage Policy in the Eurozone*, P.I.E.-Peter Lang, Brussels, pp.79-109.

EPAN (2005), Mid-term Programme 2006-2007 for Cooperation between the Directors General Responsible for Public Administration in the EU Member States, June 2005 (http://www.eu2005.lu/fr/actualites/documents_travail/2005/06/08fpprogram/midtermfp.pdf).

ETUI (1993), Les *comités syndicaux européens et le dialogue social: expériences au niveau des secteurs et dans les multinationales*, European Trade Union Institute, September 1993, Brussels.

EMF (1999), 1st Congress of the European Metalworkers' Federation, Copenhagen, 17-18 June 1999.

EMF (2003a), EMF Political Resolution "Our Future in Europe: Continuing to Develop the European Social Model, and Consolidating the Trade Unions' Bargaining Mandate", Adopted by the 2nd Congress of the EMF, Prague, 13-14 June 2003.

EMF (2003b), *Secretariat's Report on Activities 1999-2003*, Presented at the 2nd Congress of the EMF, Prague, 13-14 June 2003.

EMF (2003c), EMF Newsletter, Consulted Online at http://www.emf-fem.org.

Freyssinet, J. (1998), "Dialogue social et construction européenne", *Chronique Internationale de l'IRES, Les acteurs sociaux nationaux face à la construction européenne*, Special Edition, October 1998, pp.5-23.

Hoffmann, R. (1998), "Book Review of Jacobi, O. and Pochet, P. (eds.), *A Common Currency Area – a Fragmented Area for Wages*", *Transfer*, Vol.4, No.1, pp.144-146.

Keller, B. (2001), *Europäische Arbeits- und Sozialpoliti*k. 2., völlig überarbeitete und stark erweiterte Auflage, Oldenbourg Verlag, Munich.

Kirton-Darling, J. (ed.) (2004), *Représentativité des syndicats du secteur public en Europe, administrations nationales et collectivités territoriales*, European Federation of Public Service Unions, European Trade Union Institute, Brussels.

Kollewe, K. (2005), "The Sub-sectoral Social Dialogue in the European Shipbuilding Industry", *Transfer*, Vol.11, No.3, Autumn 2005, pp.383-389.

Le Queux, S. and Fajertag, G. (2001), "Towards Europeanization of Collective Bargaining?: Insights from the European Chemical Industry", *European Journal of Industrial Relations*, Vol.7, No.2, July 2001, pp.117-136.

Leisink, P. (2002), "The European Sectoral Social Dialogue and the Graphical Industry", *European Journal of Industrial Relations*, Vol.8, No.1, pp.101-117.

Luxembourg Presidency (2005), "A New Space for Public Administrations and Services of General Interest in an Enlarged Union", Study Intended for the Ministers Responsible for Public Administration of the Member States of the EU in Collaboration and Carried Out under the Responsibility of the European Institute of Public Administration, Maastricht (http://www.mju.gov.si/fileadmin/mju.gov.si/pageuploads/mju_dokumenti/pdf/ETUDE_un_nouvel_espace_pour_les_adm.pub_EN.pdf).

Mangenot, M. and Polet, R. (2004), *European Social Dialogue and the Civil Services. Europeanisation by the Back Door?*, European Institute of Public Administration, Maastricht.

Marginson, P. (2005), "Industrial Relations at European Sector Level: The Weak Link?", *Economic and Industrial Democracy*, Vol.26, No.4, November 2005, pp.511-540.

Pernot, J.-M.(2005), *Syndicats: lendemains de crise?*, Gallimard, Paris.

Platzer, H. W. (1991), *Gewerkschaftspolitik ohne Grenzen? Die transnationale Zusammenarbeit der Gewerkschaften in Europa der 90er Jahr*e, Dietz, Bonn.

Reibsch, R. (2005), "Social Dialogues in the EMCEF Industries", *Transfer*, Vol.11, No.3, Autumn 2005, pp.363-367.

Schulten, T. (1999b), "Franco-German Cooperation Agreement between Chemical Workers' Unions", 28 May 1999 (http://www.eiro.eurofound.eu.int/1999/05/inbrief/de9905201n.html).

Schulten, T. (2000), "The European Metalworkers' Federation on the Way to a Europeanisation of Trade Unions and Industrial Relations", *Transfer*, Vol.6, No.1, pp.93-102.

UCL-IST (2004), "Représentativité institutionnelle des partenaires sociaux dans les 'services publics centraux'", Université catholique de Louvain and Institut des sciences du travail, July 2004 (http://www.trav.ucl.ac.be/recherche/dg5.html).

Visser, J. (2006), "Union Membership Statistics in 24 Countries", *Monthly Labor Review*, Vol.129, No.1, January 2006, pp.38-49 (http://www.bls.gov/opub/mlr/2006/01/art3full.pdf).

WEM (2003a), "Position on Social Dialogue at European Sector Level", Brussels, May 2003.

WEM (2003b), "Position on Social Dialogue between UNICE and ETUC", Brussels, May 2003.

Interviews with Policy Officers

EMF (2002), Evia (Greece), September 2002.

EMF (2005), Brussels, November 2005.

CSC (2006), Brussels, January 2006.

EPSU (2003), Brussels, April 2003.

EPSU (2005), Brussels, December 2005.

PART III

CHALLENGES

CHAPTER 9

Sectoral Employer Strategies in the EU

Lobbying by Partners?

Anne DUFRESNE

The aim of this chapter is to examine the specific features of a little-understood social player: sectoral employers' organisations at European level. We shall, in particular, question how representative they are, and what strategies result from this in the context of social dialogue.

Given the central part played by employers at European level – especially following the establishment of the Single Market (1985) – one might expect to find a consistent academic literature on employer representation at EU level. But scientific analysis of this subject turns out to be extremely scanty when compared with that related to the Europeanisation of trade unions (Hoffmann *et al.*, 2002). There is a scarcity of empirical discussion, and a general lack of interest in this field of research. We must however distinguish between the different types and levels of European employers' groupings:

UNICE (Union of Industrial and Employers' Confederations of Europe), a cross-industry representative body relating directly to the European institutions[1];

numerous sectoral organisations which seem to be "concerned with their own interests" (Pernot, 2001: 90); and finally,

specialised groupings such as the European Round Table of Industrialists (ERT) (see Apeldoorn, 2000; Lietart, 2002) which have a purely lobbying function and exert ideological pressure on these institutions[2].

---

1 On the structure and operation of UNICE, see for example Tyszkiewicz, 1991; Arcq, 1993; Arcq and Pochet, 1998, 2000 and 2002; Matyja 1999; Branch and Greenwood, 2001.

2 On the subject of lobbying Cowles (1994, 1995 and 1998) shows the ways in which multinational firms manipulate UNICE, while Coen (1997 and 1998) concentrates on their role and their interaction with the European institutions. Finally, Greenwood, the main author on this issue (1997, 2000, 2002a and 2002b), is also the only one to write about the specific features of sectoral lobbies (1995).

For the purposes of this volume, we have decided to look at the second category of organisations, which up to now have been studied even less than the others. Known as European sectoral federations of employers (ESFEs) in Community jargon, we shall refer to them simply as "European federations" in what follows.

Part I will be devoted to the complexity of employers' representation at European level. We will first consider the diverse forms of organisation of European federations (I.A) before seeing how they fit into the multi-layered architecture of employers' institutions, by analysing the relations they do or do not maintain "upstream" with UNICE – which itself is reluctant to become involved in cross-industry social dialogue (I.B)

This initial analysis of European federations will enable us, in Part II, to raise the difficult question of their representativeness on the basis of precise criteria formulated by the European Commission. By way of response, we shall first of all adopt a "bottom-up" approach at the level of Member States, analysing various possible configurations of the very diverse membership of the federations – which may be employers' federations, commercial associations, or even representative multinational undertakings within the sector (II.A); then a "top-down" approach at EU level, studying the formal and actual capacity of European secretariats to negotiate and/or be consulted (II.B). Finally, the degree of representativeness of each of the European federations, however slight, will influence the strategy adopted in their respective social dialogues: we shall examine this in the following section.

Part III will enable us to illustrate and qualify what may be too general an approach at sectoral level by means of case studies. We have chosen a sample of three sectors – construction, transport and textiles/clothing – to highlight the diversity of the strategies implemented by European federations in their social dialogue. Each federation in fact has its own form of organisation, reflecting its history and the characteristic features of the sector concerned. Interviews conducted mainly with the General Secretaries of the different organisations will help to illustrate the high degree of differentiation among the three strategies presented.

I. The Complex Nature of European Employers' Representation

The fact that European employers' organisations have been so little studied until now is partly explained by the difficulty of obtaining an overall picture. Their diversity is an empirical fact. In this study we shall try to obtain a better understanding of the part this diversity plays in the exercise of their representative function. In describing the way in which

European employers are structured as a player, we shall also situate the sectoral players – of whom there are many, representing highly sector-specific interests – within the multi-layered institutional architecture.

A. A Multiplicity of Organisations

At EU level, the large number of European federations presents the image of a very diversified organisational structure within the business world. Moreover, the fragmentation of employers' representation (59 ESFEs)[3] merely reflects the configuration found in the majority of countries. Indeed, "grassroots members of employers' organisations, i.e. companies, insist on their heterogeneity, and manifest it by specialising their representative functions among multiple organisations with limited responsibilities. Multiple membership on the part of companies is the rule" (Bunel, 1997; Traxler, 2001 in Dufour, 2001: 13). At EU level, we find that nine out of 40 sectors have more than one organisation (between two and five ESFEs) to represent them (for details, see Table 1 below).

[3] This fragmentation of employers' organisations contrasts with the increasingly marked tendency towards concentration among European industry federations (EIFs) on the trade union side. There are today only 12 EIFs, and further re-groupings cannot be ruled out.

Table 1: ESFEs Constituted (or not) in Sectoral Social Dialogue Committees in Alphabetical Order of Sectors (as at 31 December 2005)*

Sector	**ESFEs (date established)**
ESFEs constituted in sectoral social dialogue committees	
Agriculture	COPA/COGECA (1962) = COPA (1958) + COGECA (1959)
Audiovisual	EBU (1950), ACT (1989), AER (1992), CEPI (1989), FIAPF (1933)
Banking	FBE (1960), ESBG (1963), EACB (1970)
Chemical industry	ECEG (2002)
Civil aviation	ACI-Europe (1991), CANSO (1998), ERA (1980), IACA (1989), AEA (1973)
Cleaning industry	EFCI (1988)
Commerce	EuroCommerce (1993) = FEWITA + CECD + GEDIS
Construction	FIEC (1905)
Electricity	EURELECTRIC (1999)
Footwear	CEC (1991)
Furniture	UEA (1950)
Horeca/Tourism	HOTREC (1979)
Inland waterways	EBU (2001), ESO (1964)
Insurance	CEA (1953), BIPAR (1937), ACME (1979)
Live performance	PEARLE (1991)
Local and regional government	CEMR (1951)
Mines	APEP (1983) *EURACOAL (2003) = CECSO (1953)+ CEPCEO (1958)* Euromines (1995)
Personal services (hairdressing)	CIC Europe (1991)
Postal services	POSTEUROP (1993)
Private security	CoESS (1989)
Railways	CER (1991) = CER (1988)
Road transport	IRU (1948)
Sea fishing	Europêche / COGECA (1962)
Sea transport	ECSA (1990) = ECSA (1965)
Shipbuilding	CESA (2001) = (1937)
Sugar	CEFS (1954)
Tanning and leather	COTANCE (1957)
Telecommunications	ETNO (1992)
Temporary work	Euro-CIETT (1967)
Textiles/clothing	EURATEX (1996) = Comitextil (textile) + ECLA (clothing) + ELTAC
Woodworking	CEI-Bois (1952)
Total: 31 sectors	**46 ESFEs**

ESFEs not constituted in sectoral social dialogue committees	
Automobile	CEEMET (2004) = WEM (1962) ACEA (1991) CLEPA (1949)
Food	CIAA (1982)
Gas	Eurogas (1990)
Graphics	INTERGRAF (1984)= IBFMP (1930) = IMPA (1946)
Hospital	HOPE (1966)
Media, journalism	EBU (1993) = EBU (1950) + OIRT ENPA (1961)
Steel	Eurofer (1976)
Tobacco	GITES (1987) CECCM (1988)
Water	Eureau (1975)
Total: 9 sectors	**13 ESFEs**
40 sectors	**59 ESFEs**

* A list of abbreviations will be found at the end of the chapter.

Source: Table based on dates extracted from document (CEC, 1995) listing committees in place in 1995, updated by systematic visits to European federation websites (16 August 2005). Mergers between organisations are indicated (e.g. COPA/COGECA = COPA + COGECA), as are changes of name (e.g. CEEMET (2004) = WEM (1962)).

This multiplicity of employers' organisations is partly explained by the need to defend employers' interests in what are sometimes very specific sub-sectors. Grouping takes place around particular interests arising from the sale of a product or service. Yet despite the large number of organisations, there is little overlap or competition among organisations representing the same industry: the way the sub-sectors are distributed among the different organisations shows a surprising degree of clarity. For example, in civil aviation, which is very fragmented, there are clear boundaries among the six organisations involved: IACA represents charter companies, ERA regional airlines, AEA European airlines, ACI-Europe the airport authorities, and finally CANSO the flight crew. All these organisations have to work together when involved in dialogue/negotiations with the trade unions. This shows that the European federations have a high degree of monopoly representation, without overlap or competition, since this is often constituted by the leading organisation within the sector (Dubbins, 2002).

Nevertheless, we also find in some cases a long, dynamic process of redefinition (merging or restructuring) of the sector and the organisations that represent it. For example, in the textile and clothing industry, it was not until 1994 that Euratex came to represent the whole sector. Until then, it was divided among ECLA (European Clothing Association) for clothing, Comitextil for textiles, and ELTAC (European Largest Textile and Clothing Companies) for the large companies in both sub-sectors (CEC, 1995: 90). The sector representative explained that this merger was largely brought about by the European Commission's desire to deal with both these sub-sectors in a single social dialogue (Euratex interview, 2000). Similarly, the commerce sector underwent a major redefinition in 1993. It had always been divided into three sub-sectors: retail, wholesale and international, each represented by one organisation. In January 1993, the Dutch, Belgian, UK and French members of the wholesale organisation FEWITA left it to form ECWITA, while the remaining members of FEWITA and the two other organisations, for retailing and international trade, merged to form EuroCommerce (Dubbins, 2002: 129). This federation was then recognised as the sole representative organisation for retailing at European level (CEC, 1995: 9).

B. The Sector: The Missing Link in the Architecture of European Employer Institutions

We have just shown what complex players the European sectoral employers' organisations are by their very nature. We will now see how much more complex is their involvement in the employers' representational system, because of a lack of interaction between the sectoral and cross-industry layers at EU level. Although difficult to grasp, the structure of European employers' representation differs both from European trade union representation and from the various national employers' systems[4].

---

[4] Available sources for comparative analysis of national organisations are limited: Schmitter and Streeck, 1981 and 1999; Streeck, 1989; Van Waarden, 1991; Sadowski and Jacobi, 1991. More recently, Franz Traxler has compared industrial relations in twenty OECD countries during the period beginning in 1970 (Traxler *et al.*, 2001), concentrating specifically on the role of employers' organisations as employers (see below).

Diagram: Employer Representation at European Level

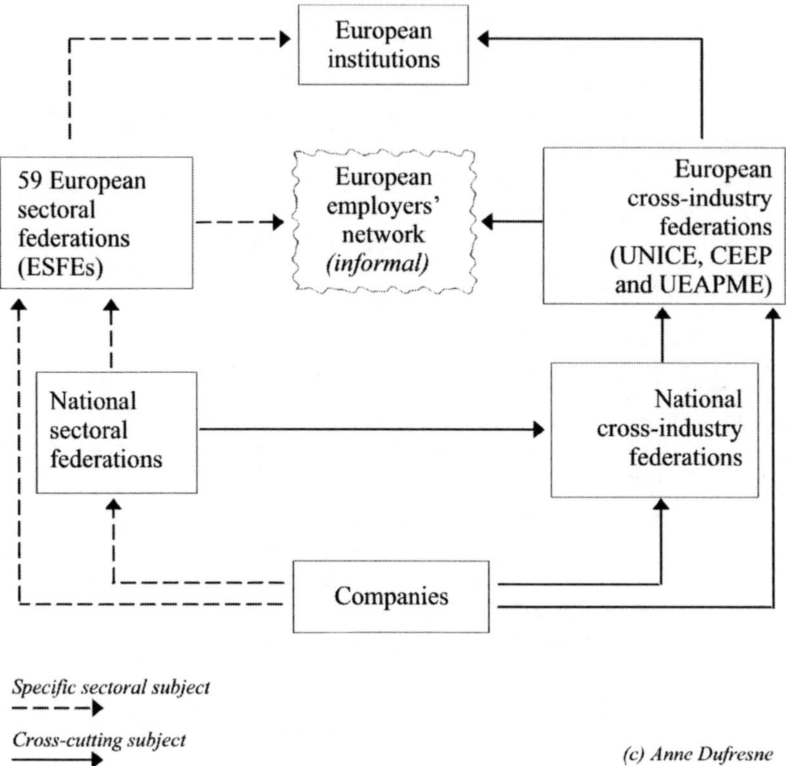

At cross-industry level, only two official players are fully recognised as social partners by the European Commission: UNICE (Union of Industrial and Employers' Confederations of Europe) and CEEP (European Centre of Enterprises with Public Participation and of Enterprises of General Economic Interest). [UEAPME (European Association of Craft, Small and Medium-sized Enterprises) has a special status[5]].

As for the cross-industry social dialogue, UNICE coordinates the CEEP cross-industry employers' delegation, alongside its own delegation,

5 Following the initiation of legal proceedings, UEAPME, because it was excluded from negotiations on collective agreements (see Moreau, 1999), concluded an agreement with UNICE in 1998. This agreement determines a form of collaboration in the framework of preparatory meetings between the two organisations with a view to reaching common positions to be defended in social dialogue meetings.

which includes members of UEAPME. It is worth noting that CEEP has often adopted positions which are more flexible than those of UNICE, and a more open attitude towards signing European collective agreements (Arcq and Pochet, 2000; Pochet and Arcq, 2001). The public services federation was also given an overall negotiating mandate on questions relating to atypical contracts, whereas the UNICE mandate had to be renewed for each negotiation. Indeed, in the event of an agreement, all the UNICE bodies have a given mandate and have to be consulted afresh to check that the result achieved conforms to the initial mandate. UNICE in fact is particularly reluctant with regard to collective agreements being extended *erga omnes*, which could be the outcome of the social dialogue, especially following the adoption of the European Social Protocol in 1991. UNICE believes that "there is no justification for forcing the pace of social harmony in Europe", and in this connection invokes the principles of subsidiarity and proportionality. Based on the diversity of national industrial relations systems and their shared tendency towards decentralisation, UNICE states that "one must not yield to temptations to intervene in systems from a European level" (Degryse, 2000: 78).

Besides this fundamental political reluctance towards cross-industry negotiation, there are difficulties arising from the institution's organisation: a lack of sectoral representation within the UNICE structure (Arcq *et al.*, 2003). "Employers have never had a strategy for institutional grouping" (UNICE interview, 2002). In fact, the European federations are not members of UNICE. The latter has opted for a network form of architecture, with two kinds of members: national cross-industry federations, and national and international firms (not European federations)[6] (see diagram). This non-affiliation of federations at cross-industry level rules them out from having any direct influence on cross-cutting questions. For example, according to a representative of the textile employers: "The role of Euratex (the European federation for the textile industry) in relation to the Commission is totally detached from social matters because Euratex does not even belong to UNICE" (Euratex interview, 2004).

There is nevertheless an informal structure called the "European Employers' Network", which organises several meetings a year between the UNICE secretariat and those of the many European federations on

6 Note here the profound lack of symmetry between employers' and trade union structures: since the reform of 1991, ETUC has accepted European industry federations (EIFs), and not members of European Works Councils, as full members alongside national confederations.

questions of social policy[7]. These regular discussion forums, which bring together those sectors interested in the theme under discussion, are designed to enable European federations to become more rapidly informed about activities of the European Commission (concerning the cross-industry social dialogue, amongst other things) and to enable UNICE to be relatively coherent in the positions it adopts on issues of social policy. In terms of coherence, this approach is aimed at monitoring the sectoral federations coordinated by the network, so as to avoid some of them making excessive "concessions" to the trade unions. This cross-industry level strategy might therefore constitute a major obstacle to strengthening the social dialogue. Moreover, according to comments made by representatives of European sectors about the network, these informal meetings appear to lack consistency: "Admittedly we have an exchange of information with UNICE, but it is a long way from the grass roots" (Euratex interview, 2004). "UNICE is an organisation with a purely horizontal strategy. It ignores the European federations, at the risk of creating inconsistencies when talking to the European institutions" (FIEC interview, 2000).

Another consequence of the non-affiliation of European federations to UNICE is that national sectoral federations have to go through their cross-industry federation which *is* affiliated to UNICE in order to have any influence at EU level (see diagram). "We are not structured. Internally, we have no influence. If we were members of UNICE, I think we would be forced to have more resources. We would carry more weight [...]. In order to influence the European employment strategy, for example, the Belgian organisation has to go through the FEB (Fédération des entreprises de Belgique), not through UNICE. Which is a pity!" (Euratex interview, 2004). This tortuous route to exerting any influence on cross-cutting subjects hampers good representation. However, some European federations have more direct access and a greater weight in general decisions, especially in concertation procedures. The biggest ones, such as those in the commerce sector (EuroCommerce) or agriculture (GEOPA/COPA) have always been part of the employers' delegation on the various tripartite concertation committees for as long as they have been in existence[8], and in the three sets of negotiations in the framework of the cross-industry dialogue leading to the first three agreements (see chapter 1). These federations may be considered as

7 Only in the field of health and safety are UNICE working groups, exceptionally, open to interested European federations, thus giving rise to informal cooperation.

8 Although the concertation committees have changed – the "Standing Committee on Employment", set up as early as December 1970, being replaced by a "Tripartite Concertation Committee for Growth and Employment" in December 2001 – the social partners have remained the same: UNICE, CEEP, UEAPME, COPA and EuroCommerce for the employers and ETUC, EUROCADRES and CEC for the workers.

being "on the fringes of the cross-industry dialogue". EuroCommerce in particular is seeking to have a competitive position in the cross-industry social dialogue.

Thus, having analysed the specific link between the cross-industry level (UNICE) and the sectoral level (European federations) of EU employers' organisations, we shall now examine the set of relations that exist, in purely sectoral terms, between the EU level (the European secretariats) and the national level (their members) [see diagram], raising the fundamental question of how representative they are.

II. Representativeness Called into Question

In November 1993, when the Maastricht Treaty came into force, and the Commission began thinking about the practical implementation of the Agreement on Social Policy (see chapter 1), some organisations, such as UEAPME or EuroCommerce, which had been excluded from the procedure, made the question of representativeness an essential political issue[9]. An initial communication from the Commission (CEC, 1993) at the time defined three criteria of representativeness to determine whether social partner organisations had access to the consultation process established by Article 3 of the Social Policy Agreement (see Box 1). The difficulties caused by recognising one representative organisation in each sector – especially in the commerce sector – then encouraged the Commission to demand criteria of representativeness virtually identical to the 1993 ones, specifically at industry level. These were spelt out in Article 1 of the decision setting up the Sectoral Social Dialogue Committees (SSDCs) in 1998. The differences between the two texts are shown in italics in the box below.

---

9 At the request of the Commission, the Institut des sciences du travail (IST) at Louvain-la-Neuve coordinated studies attesting to the representativeness of the social partners (in 1992 for the cross-industry level and 1996 for the cross-industry and sectoral levels).

Box 1: Criteria of Representativeness

To be sufficiently representative at European level, European employers' and workers' organisations must:
1) be cross-industry, or relate to specific sectors or categories, and be organised at European level;
2)
   a. consist of organisations which are themselves an integral and recognised part of Member States' social partner structures;
   b. have the capacity to negotiate agreements, and
   c. be representative in [all / *several*] Member States, as far as possible;
3) have adequate structures to ensure their effective participation [in the consultation process / *in the work of the Committees*].

Source: (CEC, 1993: 4); (CEC, 1998)
NB: The text underlined does not appear in Article 1 of the 1998 decision, and the text in italics replaces the text in square brackets.

We shall comment on each of these criteria in order to gain a better understanding of the limits to the representativeness of the European federations, according to the European Commission's definition. We shall group together points 2a) and 2c) which both address the nature of the national members of federations (II.A), then points 2b) and 3) which deal with the formal capacity of Euro-organisations to negotiate or be consulted (II.B).

A. The Nature of National Members of European Federations

Point 2a) poses the following question: are the organisations which are members of European federations an integral and recognised part of Member States' social partner structures? It is a difficult question, since depending on different national traditions, recognition of the legitimacy of a social partner organisation to negotiate collective agreements or participate in formulating social policy differs widely. To clarify matters, we come back to the definitions proposed in Franz Traxler's interesting analysis of the leading national employers' organisations in Europe (Traxler, 2000). Traxler identified the various factors that make the study of employer interests so complex, while drawing the necessary distinction between "trade associations" and "employers' associations". The former are principally concerned with the interests of their members on the products market, while the latter incorporate "labour market" interests and correspond to those organisations that "are themselves part of social partner structures". Lastly, some so-called mixed organisations combine both functions.

In the three sectors considered here – construction, transport, textiles/clothing – the majority of organisations recognised as "active" members of European federations are indeed "employers' associations" – whether or not they happen to be at the same time "trade associations" (according to Franz Traxler's definitions). There are about thirty of them for each sector (cf. Table 2). On the other hand, there are two other categories of members which appear very frequently (except in the case of construction) as so-called "associate members": these are, firstly, the trade associations in the particular sector (or sub-sectors of it) and, secondly, individual companies (multinational firms) which are direct members of the European federations without going through a national organisation. "Multinational firms which are active on the European market are over-represented in national bodies, and even more so in European bodies, partly because they have the necessary financial resources to become involved at EU level. SMEs cannot afford to do so" (Euratex interview, 2000).

Table 2: Comparison of the Types of Members of the Three ESFEs Studied

Sector	**Construction**	**Road Transport**	**Textiles**
ESFE	***FIEC***	***IRU***	***Euratex***
– *Active members:* Employers' federations	34	27	34
– Associate members: Trade associations	0	n/a[10]	18
Companies	0	n/a	10

Source: table drawn up on the basis of visits to the websites of the various ESFEs (16 August 2005) – n/a: not available.

In more general terms, Greenwood (2002b) presents a panorama of all the European federations according to the nature of their members. This more or less confirms the results obtained from our sample. He distinguishes three types: "pure" European federations, which include only the corresponding national employers' federations, others which include as members the major companies in the sector (mixed), and still others, a minority, which have only companies as members. In the first category, which corresponds to the construction sector, "firms' opinions are expressed via their regional federation, and then go up to the national level. And the sum of national opinions forms the European opinion" (FIEC interview, 2004). This is an example of a "pure" European federation, the most representative type. In the second category – where members are both national organisations and companies, corresponding to the two other sectors taken as examples – the advantage of

[10] It is interesting to note that, despite numerous e-mail exchanges with IRU, we were unable to obtain these figures: only information appearing on their website is considered to be public. The detailed list of their 179 members is unobtainable.

the mixed structure is that it avoids being overtaken by direct lobbying on the part of major companies while benefiting from their resources, status and expertise (Greenwood, 2002b). Finally there are organisations whose members are only individual companies. They are found in industries where there is only a small number of large firms, such as automobiles (ACEA) or telecommunications (ETNO). These will not be discussed in detail here.

In addition to this initial fault-line, national members subscribe to differing cultural traditions. Point 2c) of the criteria of representativeness requires that members should "be representative in several Member States, as far as possible". We have found that this is consistently the case for the three sectors studied in the former Europe of fifteen Member States. The European federations are therefore faced with the difficulty of dealing with a large number of sometimes divergent national interests. As for the organisations in the new Member States, as a result of enlargement their status as observers often changed to that of active member at the time of their accession to the EU, with a transition period for the payment of annual membership dues (see chapter 11). Although, admittedly, organisations from practically all countries are members, their respective weight nonetheless varies according to their size, and also their political determination. For example, in IRU (road transport) "according to the Articles of Association, all countries have the same weight in the decision-making process. Each organisation has eight votes per section (goods transport and passenger transport sections). Hence in principle, the Luxembourg and German associations have the same rights, even although in practice the German position clearly carries more weight in the final decision when adopting a position, for example. [...]. It is nevertheless worth noting that at EU level a small country may have more influence than a large one if it is very active politically" (IRU interview, 2003).

Finally, we were able to establish the way in which national employers' associations, trade associations and large multinational firms sit side by side within the European federations. Criterion 2a) "consist of organisations which are themselves an integral and recognised part of Member States' social partner structures" may be considered as being fulfilled, even though only the first (and possibly the third) category of members listed respects it. The geographical criterion 2c) seems to be fully respected. A better appreciation of the extent to which the criteria of representativeness are respected can be obtained by reading Box 2, which details the structures of the three European federations used in our sample.

Box 2: Structure of the Three European Federations Studied

FIEC (the European Construction Industry Federation), a legal entity in French law, was founded in 1905 and is the oldest of all the European federations. It was for a long time a branch of the international body (EIC, European International Contractors) before establishing itself as a true European secretariat. It is 100% financed by members' contributions, and is thus not in any way subsidised by the European Commission. Its activities extend to 27 countries (24 from the EU and EFTA, plus Romania, Bulgaria and Turkey). It comprises 34 national member federations representing firms of all sizes (from one-person SMEs through to very large firms), covering all building and civil engineering specialities, practising all kinds of working methods (whether operating as general contractors or as sub-contractors). It is important to note that these are all employers' associations, except in the case of Greece. No trade association or individual company is thus directly involved.

Euratex (the European Apparel and Textile Organisation) was founded in 1996 as a result of the merger of its two founding entities: ECLA (European Clothing Association) and ELTAC (European Largest Textile and Clothing Companies), with Comitextil. The federation has three categories of members: 10 European sub-sectoral associations, 34 national industry associations drawn from 24 countries (19 EU, 2 EFTA, Tunisia, Morocco and Turkey), in addition to 18 associate members and corresponding members representing firms ranging from one-person SMEs to very large companies, including 10 multinationals.

IRU (the International Road Union) was founded in 1948 with the aim of promoting international transport. It is on the one hand a worldwide organisation based in Geneva with a General Assembly, but it is also a European organisation with a Brussels Liaison Committee which remains autonomous on purely EU matters. Originally the network of national member associations of IRU was set up to participate in the operation of the TIR administrative system[11]. It was only later that the organisations became involved in other activities: technical advice regarding vehicles, and in some cases even negotiating with trade unions. IRU today consists of 179 members drawn from 69 countries, including private haulage firms, combined transport undertakings, but most importantly its active members, i.e. the 27 national goods transport associations drawn from 26 EU countries (excluding Malta). The trend, nonetheless, is to develop this latter category of members, since "the purpose of an organisation made up of entrepreneurs is to develop in this direction" (IRU interview, 2003). In some countries (France, Scandinavia, etc.) specific organisations have been set up additionally to represent employers, while in the UK "the employer aspect of IRU membership remains very limited" (IRU interview, 2003).

[11] IRU is a guarantor of this system and its *carnets*, which enable lorries that have been sealed by the Customs Office of departure to cross frontiers without any further monitoring of their cargoes until they reach their destination. This system, moreover, produces a good basis of funding for IRU, in addition to its annual membership subscriptions.

B. The Capacity of European Federations to Negotiate and Be Consulted

The capacity of European organisations, in terms of their consultation structures and their capacity to negotiate agreements, are two major aspects of their representativeness, and amount in reality to their capacity to become involved in the process of social dialogue in its two essential functions: consultation and negotiation.

1. Consultation Structures ...

As far as consultation is concerned, coming back to the criteria of representativeness demanded by the European Commission, point 3) is concerned precisely with the structure of the organisations being adequate "to ensure their effective participation in the consultation process / *in the work of the Committees*" (cf. Box 1). This structure, i.e. the European secretariats of the European federations, generally fulfils two functions, one external, the other internal, each of which contributes to the effectiveness of consultation. Their "external" role is to represent the sector in discussions with the European institutions, starting with the first phase of consultation, to ensure that it is properly followed up and carried through, and to propose initiatives, which might range from a specific, one-off action to the organising of seminars or conferences. This role is on the whole fully accepted by the majority of European federations, since it directly serves their industry-specific interests. The "internal" role of the secretariat is to ensure coordination and proper functioning of the federation's own structures: its governing bodies (General Assembly, Presidential Committee, Management Committee, Executive Committee, etc.) and its political bodies (committees, subcommittees, working groups or groups of experts).

Scanning through the names of these political bodies gives some indication of the themes on which the European federations are most likely to be consulted. We find that the "Social Affairs" committee, when it exists, is generally[12] considered much less important (in terms of staffing and resources) than technical and economic committees. For example, "social affairs represent about 15% of the subjects tackled by IRU" (IRU interview, 2003). More generally, out of 46 federations constituted in Sectoral Social Dialogue Committees (SSDCs), only 22 have a committee of this kind – twelve entitled "Social Affairs", three "Social Dialogue", while seven are sufficiently well-developed to

[12] One exception is the European federation of the "banking" sector, whose sole function is to negotiate on social matters.

include sub-committees, as is the case for the three examples studied in this chapter[13].

Table 3: Comparison of Political Committees in the Three Federations Studied

Sector	Construction	Textiles	Road Transport
ESFE	***FIEC***	***Euratex***	***IRU***
Sub-committees Social Affairs	1. Social: Training Health and safety Economic and social aspects of employment	Social dialogue Training CSR	Social affairs Training Road safety
Other committees	2. Economic: Public procurement and competition, Taxation, Company mergers, infrastructure and finance 3. Technical	Commercial and industrial policy Internal market Research and development, Environment, Legal affairs	

Source: List of websites of European federations (compiled 18 August 2005).

Reading the above table, we note that in all three sectors, there is a "Social Affairs" sub-committee devoted to vocational training, while the subject of safety appears in the case of construction (Health and Safety Committee) and transport (Road Safety). Finally, in two out of the three sectors, restructuring/outsourcing involves specific sub-committees, which may be called "Economic and social aspects of employment" (construction) or "Corporate Social Responsibility – CSR" (textiles). The most powerful of the European federations, IRU, also has a Social Affairs sub-committee, which is useful for concertation on the European Employment Strategy (EES) amongst other things. In these various committees, national experts hold discussions within their own fields, and may reach conclusions which are sufficiently general in scope to be subsequently adopted in the form of resolutions by the governing bodies and then disseminated at their own initiative or following consultation.

But the link between the national and EU levels operates, on the whole, very badly in the European federations, where decisions made at the level of the European secretariat are only rarely endorsed by the

13 Other sectors which have specific social affairs sub-committees are: commerce, fishing (training, social harmonisation and employment, health and safety, enlargement), banking (CSR, demographics, and EEC) and local and regional government (employment and social policies).

membership as a whole. Consultation may thus be limited to the European secretariat working as a restricted group, a structure which is capable of producing advisory opinions to the European institutions, without necessarily passing on the views of all the national associations. In this respect consultation differs from negotiation, which does require a specific mandate from the national members.

2. ... But no Negotiating Mandate?

Thus the capacity to negotiate agreements (mentioned in point 2b) of the Criteria of representativeness) comes down, amongst other things, to a negotiating mandate being granted by the various national member organisations. In fact their heterogeneous nature, and their heterogeneous culture (as previously described, see II.A) make it difficult for them to delegate power to a European secretariat. European federations are thus often "hostile to the very principle of negotiation, for which, besides, they have no mandate (from their members)" (Freyssinet, 1998: 19).

We have found that the formal rules concerning a negotiating mandate for the social dialogue vary greatly among the organisations in the three sectors we have chosen as examples. In FIEC, the mandate is not awarded systematically, but is granted by members voting unanimously after presentation and discussion of the issues at stake[14]. In Euratex, on the other hand, the rules remain informal: the democratic principle of voting, even unanimously, is not accepted by some recalcitrant members. This means that Euratex has been able to make progress in establishing the social dialogue only by being fairly tough with its own members. For the road transport sector (IRU), the experience of negotiating a binding agreement on working time (see below) led to an evolution in its rules and its mandate as a result of forced interaction between the national associations and the European secretariat: "We [the secretariat] felt the lack of purpose among the employers when we were negotiating on working time at EU level. Right at the start, some associations said, 'It's in the rules of IRU, we're not allowed to negotiate!'" (IRU interview, 2003). Then, following difficult negotiations among the national employers' representatives, which led to failure, it was finally decided to grant a mandate by a two-thirds majority in any future negotiation.

The difficulty in establishing rules for granting a mandate in fact reflect the "wait and see" attitude of the majority of members of European

14 Decisions which are internal to the organisation are taken by a simple majority, members having more or fewer votes depending on the size of the country calculated as GDP per head of population (The same applies to the level of annual contributions).

federations, and the difficulty for the European secretariats of trying to interest them in European issues. The European federations therefore have great difficulty in imposing a mode of operation from the EU level. "It's really hard to get my colleagues interested in the European level [on social questions]. Firms are preoccupied with the national level, and there's no real interest in what's being achieved in Europe" (Euratex interview, 2004).

Thus we have found that consultation structures exist, but no permanent negotiating mandate. Negotiation means being willing to meet the other side, to enter into talks, in other words to discuss subjects of common interest in good faith. Certainly this willingness to give a mandate to negotiate remains weak among national employers' organisations so long as the trade unions have no direct or indirect means of forcing them to open negotiations. Negotiation differs from consultation in the need for a "bottom-up" link between the national and the EU level. Negotiation, unlike consultation, has to have not just a formal capacity (the presence of a European structure) but an actual capacity (i.e. the joint political willingness of members to delegate powers to the supranational level), something which is currently lacking. The two functions of the social dialogue therefore reveal different characteristics of the employers' organisations as a player: whereas the consultation function justifies their existence as a social partner on the EU stage, the negotiating function highlights their lack of representativeness as a partner in discussions (and in particular the difficulty over their political mandate).

We therefore note that the two functions of the social dialogue – consultation and negotiation – are unequally exercised. For this reason, when Greenwood (2002b: 117) considers that "*the evolution of the sectoral social dialogue will undoubtedly have an impact on the dynamics of ESFEs in the coming years*", we must emphasise the specifically consultative nature of this dialogue. So we find a twofold movement taking place. While, admittedly, the institutional development of the social dialogue process is compelling the sectoral employers to get their act together, conversely it is the consultative nature of the player that has defined and continues to define the nature of the dialogue. This is the reason why the foregoing analysis of the complex nature of these European federations gives us a better understanding of the nature of their respective dialogues.

III. Diversified Strategies in the Social Dialogue: Case Studies of Three European Sectoral Federations

The preceding sections have enabled us to see that national associations generally have little propensity to grant mandates on social matters to their European federations, which for the most part therefore have no authority to engage in any bargaining activity. We may therefore state as a hypothesis that European employers' organisations intervene in social issues (in the proper sense of the term) essentially in order to acquire legitimacy as a "social partner" to be consulted at EU level. The words of a representative of one of the European federations illustrate this hypothesis of a social dialogue whose essential usefulness is to legitimise a "good social partner":

> The social dialogue, in my opinion, should exist, it should continue… If we don't manage to find areas where it can produce results, in the long run we shall no longer be regarded as a "good social partner" by the Commission. […] For the time being, the important thing is to prove that we are able and willing (IRU interview, 2003).

This attitude may lead to the European federations being confused with other, so-called "traditional", non-representative lobbying groups. Besides, since the 1990s, the question of European employers' representation had for the most part been addressed in terms of lobbying[15] the EU institutions. This extension of employer representation into lobbying is explained in terms of the political block applied by employers who, as often as not, refuse to become institutionalised as a social protagonist at EU level, preferring to constitute themselves as a lobby. Here we shall concentrate, for each of the three sectors mentioned, not on their principal activity, traditional-style lobbying, but on that aspect of employer activity that puts European employers' organisations in the position of "social partners" in the context of the social dialogue. We shall see to what extent the social partner is often in fact a lobbying partner. The term "partner" is a fairly derisory one here, given that the chief characteristic of the situation being described is the refusal of employers' organisations to tackle social aspects as such.

Although this refusal on the part of the employers is the general rule, we shall nevertheless distinguish between two scenarios in terms of the strategies adopted. First of all, when a major political issue is clearly identified at EU level, the European federation is compelled to review its blocking strategy, particularly when it is forced to negotiate under pressure from the European Commission (as in the case of road transport). In other cases (straightforward negotiation at the behest of the

---

[15] On lobbying and European integration, see Gobin and Smets (1998).

partners or at the request of the trade unions), there is nothing to be lost by responding with a flat refusal, unless of course the federation has an interest as a lobbying partner.

For this reason, it is interesting to observe the differences in the strategies deployed in the three sectors included in our sample. All three are recognised by the European Commission as "sectoral social partners" in the framework of the social dialogue (CEC, 1993), yet we shall see how each of these three organisations assumes this role to a differing extent, depending on their approach to the social dialogue.

A. The European Construction Industry Federation (FIEC): Pragmatism Based on Parity

FIEC (the European Construction Industry Federation) maintains a direct link with the Heads of Unit in DG Industry within the framework of "traditional-style" lobbying. But what is of particular interest to us here is that since March 1990, i.e. well before the social dialogue became institutionalised, it has been involved in a sectoral social dialogue, independently of the Commission, with its opposite number on the trade union side, the EFBWW (European Federation of Building and Woodworkers) (see Cremers, 2005). Both organisations "have always attached autonomous importance to dialogue, which is not limited to being a "conveyor belt' for the dialogue referred to in the Social Protocol" (FIEC and EFBWW, 1996: 1). Some years later, they notably formulated joint recommendations which enabled them to "change the majority in the Council thanks to targeted lobbying in homeopathic doses" ending up with the Posting of Workers Directive[16] (European Parliament and Council of the European Union, 1996). This major joint success strengthened their confidence in one another. "To start with, in FIEC, we didn't have much of a social dialogue culture, and we were quite reluctant … even to meet with trade unionists … that was pushing it. Then, things developed. Working together shows that barriers can be broken down, and for me that is the greatest progress we have made in the dialogue" (FIEC interview, 2004). That is the reason why, when the two federations found themselves officially involved in a sectoral social dialogue committee, in 1998, at the request of the European Commission, nothing changed in terms of the qualitative nature of their exchanges. The federations continued to grant the European Commission

16 Starting with their first joint position on posting of workers, adopted as long ago as November 1993, the two partners then signed a declaration on the application of the Directive, in September 1997 (Construction: 1997). The follow-up to the Directive was therefore carried out via the SSD. The new proposed Directive on services presented by the Commission in January 2004 served to re-launch joint activities on the posting of workers.

only a minor role, refusing among other things to draw up Rules of Procedure for their Committee, because they considered this "superfluous".

To quote the identical word used by the General Secretaries of both sides, Mr Cremers (EFBWW) and Mr Paetzold (FIEC), the reason why the sectoral dialogue has been able to become established in this way is because it is "pragmatic" (EFBWW interview, 1999 and FIEC interview, 2000). They deal with problems that are specific to the sector and of interest to both sides. The present three working groups are not very different from the ones they started with: health and safety, employment, and training. "We think there are enough things we can do together to avoid wasting time. We set aside issues where we have no common interests" (FIEC interview, 2004). In fact, both trade unions and employers work on the same subjects, even though their motivation is different. On undeclared work, for example, while the unions' aim is to re-regulate, the employers want to reduce their charges. Similarly on posting of workers, whereas one side wants to harmonise social systems, the other wants to avoid being charged twice. This pragmatism based on parity nevertheless has its limits. Strong differences sometimes make themselves felt, and the employers continue to reject any more advanced form of structuring on certain topics, which might be envisaged in the context of the social dialogue[17], especially wages. "The last topic we will negotiate about at European level will be wages. In my view, it will happen one day. But we are still at the stage of getting to know one another" (FIEC interview, 2004).

B. Euratex: Fear of the "Snowball Effect"

In this sector in decline[18], the threat hanging over the entire industry and the resulting need for a sectoral policy strategy have encouraged both traditional-style lobbying and an acceleration of the sectoral dialogue, both to emphasise the specific features of the sector and to maintain the ILO minimum social standards (see chapter 7), as well as gaining access to the commercial decision-makers.

As far as traditional-style lobbying is concerned, Euratex is a discussion partner for DGs Trade, Industry, Research and Development on the economic situation within the sector. "Numerous meetings have taken place outside the social dialogue, and Euratex is an ideal partner when it comes to drafting European directives" (Euratex interview, 2004). There

17 The third Directive on "work at height" appears "superfluous" to FIEC, whereas EFBWW considers it to be necessary and is therefore working on an exchange of information on the subject.

18 The textile industry alone lost over 500,000 jobs in the space of five years (1995-2000).

is however no point in trying to distinguish between the two types of lobbying, traditional and indirect (i.e. via the social dialogue), which are both linked. "Lobbying is something constant, in my opinion; there are always meetings taking place. Sometimes we get our point across, and every now and then we adopt joint positions and realise that we are the stronger for it" (Euratex interview, 2004). In more general terms, the Euratex strategy is to be there "when something affects the sector" at any level: both within the European Commission and within national governments.

ETUF-TCL and Euratex have continuously produced texts, with initiatives taken since the establishment of the SSDC extending the themes tackled in the former informal groups set up from 1992 onwards. Among the joint positions adopted over ten years (1994-2005), three relate to employment, three to industrial policies and their social aspects, and one each to working conditions and to training. According to Euratex, "the area of training is seen as innocuous, something that can be discussed at a European level. We can even envisage the possibility of a European framework agreement" (Euratex interview, 2000). As for reciprocal commitments, they have signed a code of conduct (recommendation) and two guides (tools).

Although they produce joint texts, the decision by ETUF-TCL to discuss a reference standard on rates of pay internally caused some consternation within Euratex, which had no intention whatsoever of getting involved in that area[19]. "Even though the data are available, a number of our members absolutely refuse to have these issues discussed at European level" (Euratex interview, 2000). The Euratex representatives, commenting on this, both mention the exclusion of wages: "Addressing issues that are specific to the sector, such as equal opportunities or multi-tasking, for example, would be to get caught up in something that could snowball in the direction of wages" (Euratex interview, 2000). According to the former Social Affairs Coordinator of Euratex (1999-2001), "subjects are chosen freely by the partners, and we cannot address the notion of wages because that is a matter for the national level" (Euratex interview, 2004). The sector representative adds, "Unlike the trade unions, Euratex doesn't regard social matters as its final aim. For us, it's about competitiveness, business flair, economic affairs … that's what interests us" (Euratex interview, 2004).

---

19 The "joint" database was therefore transformed in 1999 into an ETUF-TCL working group on European coordination. It proposed the EMF model known as "Eucob@" as an annual reporting system.

C. The International Road Union (IRU): A Lobby First and Foremost

In this sector, which is expanding rapidly within the EU and experiencing fierce competition, we have been able to identify a blocking factor which affects the internal dynamics of the social dialogue: the large number of legislative proposals, which are absorbing all the energy of the social partners[20]. We shall describe, firstly, the process of negotiating the revision of the European Working Time Directive of 1993[21] from the employers' point of view. This will enable us to highlight the strategy of the "employer partner" when compelled to negotiate. Then we shall see to what extent IRU lends itself, as a lobby, to the European Commission's consultation game, and how it coordinates the parallel lobbying taking place at national level.

The European Commission considered the revision of the Working Time Directive to be particularly necessary in the road transport sector because it represents the largest transport sector in terms of employment. It therefore invited the social partners to begin negotiations with the aim of reaching an agreement that could be transformed into a Directive by a decision of Council. Although IRU was particularly reluctant to negotiate, explaining that it would prefer to see the current regulatory system (Regulation 38/20) properly applied[22], rather than adding a new one, pressure from the Commission won it over, and negotiations began in July 1997. After numerous rounds of negotiation, and agreements on general shared principles, negotiations finally broke down in September 1998. There are essentially two reasons for this failure:

– The difficulty of coming up with shared definitions and concepts concerning working time (night working, rest periods, waiting time, etc.) which were acceptable to both sides, and more fundamentally a difference in basic viewpoint: whereas the trade unions saw the Working Time Directive as an opportunity to regulate working conditions, the employers hoped to use it to regulate competition (see Champin, 2003).

– In addition to this ideological blockage, there was a second one linked to the difficulty of delegating national employers' sovereignty: some member organisations actually felt that better results could be achieved by a Commission proposal approved by Council, and therefore withheld their mandate.

---

20 Further blocking factors are linked to the way the players themselves are structured: the economic fragmentation of the employers' representatives (see chapter 11) coupled with a low level of trade union membership in the sector.

21 On the implementation of the Working Time Directive, see chapter 2 in this volume.

22 It concerned a minimum rest period and a maximum driving period per day.

Following the breakdown of negotiations in 1998, the Commission was used as a scapegoat by both sides, who complained of a lack of time to reach a result. ETF accused the Commission of favouring IRU, and vice versa. Then in November of that year the European executive tabled a proposal including the points of agreement achieved during the negotiations. Since then, although the social partners have certainly not made any new negotiating proposal, IRU has nonetheless decided to change its internal operating rules in advance by approving qualified majority voting for its negotiating mandate (see below).

This detailed description of the negotiating process shows that it is always difficult to distinguish between the road hauliers' activities as a lobby outside the dialogue and as an employers' organisation. Even during the period of negotiation, IRU was playing both parts simultaneously. "There are two possibilities: lobbying on the one hand, and social dialogue on the other; you always tend to take the route that promises more in terms of the results you want to achieve" (IRU interview, 2003). Before and after the actual period of negotiation, IRU has continued to defend its own position as a lobbying group. Historically of course, IRU was set up in the first place as an influence group for the road transport sector. It was able to do this all the more easily because its funding came largely from its management of the TIR administrative system (see Box 2), thus making it independent of its members.

Although this lobbying takes place with the EU institutions in the broad sense – Parliament, Economic and Social Committee, Council – it often focuses on the Commission, and in particular on the Directorate-General responsible for transport (DG TREN), which oversees the specific rules on industrial policies, while DG Employment and Social Affairs is only in charge of matters when social considerations are the main factor in the adoption of a Directive – which is rarely the case. Relations between IRU and DG TREN are thus much more consistent than with DG Employment. "Often there is no official consultation: we know the people in DG TREN so well, and they know us so well, that we phone one another up, and they might say to us, 'We need to talk. I'm busy working on such and such and we'd like to have an industry opinion …'". In practice then, there is a great deal of convergence between the objectives pursued by IRU and by DG TREN.

Besides this fairly active lobbying at EU level, to get its position across, IRU also operates through its members who lobby their respective governments in order to gain a majority in the Council. We note that national employers' associations in the sector have strong links with their respective ministries (Lehmkuhl, 1999) and often prefer active lobbying at national level which then goes up to the Council of Ministers of Transport, rather than signing social agreements with their European counterparts. IRU then coordinates its members' lobbying activities in order to reach a common position between the European voice and the many national voices addressing the Council, while at the same time exerting influence on the European institutions.

Concluding Observations

We have thus been able to show how, for the majority of sectors, sectoral employers' representation, in terms of its structural and strategic choices, produces an actor playing many parts and difficult to pin down. The European federations, detached as they are from UNICE, do not exert much influence over the general direction of the cross-industry dialogue (with the possible exception of EuroCommerce), and their representativeness remains dubious both because of the heterogeneous nature of their membership (sometimes dominated by multinational companies) and because of their lack of real negotiating capacity (the federations' internal arrangements for decision-making and adopting positions). On the other hand, their capacity to be consulted, which is better developed, enables them above all to defend the economic interests of their industry with the appropriate institutions.

This general analysis has been illustrated and qualified by case studies, which reflect the differing levels of involvement of the three European federations in their respective SSDCs. While Euratex remains cautious, fearing the "snowball effect", and IRU is even more resistant to dialogue, FIEC may be seen as a fine exception: an employers' association which practises "pragmatism based on parity". It is important to emphasise that the level of organisation and commitment of the various European federations in a social dialogue is the result of their own political choice, not a lack of resources as some might claim. We may draw a comparison with their trade union counterparts: the superiority of the employers relative to the trade unions at European level is due to the fact that they need only block any advances in institutional terms, whereas to assert their interests the trade unions have to construct new European institutions and forms of regulation.

All of this leads us to a further observation: if the European federations, generally speaking, do not really engage in dialogue on social matters, or have difficulty in negotiating, what is their interest in developing social dialogue activities? The raison d'être of the dialogue from the employers' point of view may be partly explained, as in the case of the cross-industry level, as a strategy to gain time, given the pressure of legislation (the "shadow of the law"[23]); but it is also, more specifically for the sectoral level, to do with how the European federations function

[23] The resultant binding agreements apply particularly to the transport sectors (see the latest agreement signed in the railway sector in 2004).

as a social partner, in a way which is close to that of a lobbying partner with the Commission. We can thus identify, in addition to "traditional-style" lobbying, another form of employer lobbying of the EU institutions: lobbying by partners (or partner lobbying). These must be clearly distinguished:

– "Traditional" (or individual) lobbying takes place when the European federation, acting on its own, advises the Commission directly of its position on a proposal affecting it directly or indirectly. In this situation the federation functions purely as a pressure group and intervenes, more or less successfully, in the preparation of draft Community legislation (directives and regulations) in defence of particular interests, and not as a general-purpose employers' association.

– "Partner" lobbying takes place when the federation, as a social partner, draws up a "joint" position with the trade union federation. In this situation we would define the Sectoral Social Dialogue Committee as a "second chamber" of partner lobbying. It enables employers to practise an indirect form of lobbying, inasmuch as the European Parliament is absent from the process, and the "dialogue" with the European industry federation on the trade union side is more a means of obtaining a new entry point to EU decision-making on industrial and commercial strategies than a real social partnership. Often, in order to achieve strategic results for employers in the sector, a European federation will accept a skewed "political trade-off", with minimum compensation in terms of the reciprocal commitments on social issues (training, employment, etc.) claimed by the European industry federations. For this reason, it might be interesting to carry out further research on the parallel timetable of reciprocal commitments and joint positions in each of the sectors studied, in order to gain a deeper insight into the complex strategy of these little-understood players.

References

Apeldoorn, B. (2000), "Transnational Class Agency and European Governance: The Case of the European Round Table of Industrialists", *New Political Economy*, July 2000, Vol.5, No.2, pp.157-181.

Arcq, É. (1993), "L'UNICE et la politique sociale européenne", *Courrier hebdomadaire du Crisp*, No.1400, Centre de recherche et d'information socio-politiques, Brussels.

Arcq, É. and Pochet, P. (1998), "UNICE in 1997", in Gabaglio, E. and Hoffmann, R. (eds.), *European Trade Union Yearbook 1997*, European Trade Union Institute, Brussels, pp.135-146.

Arcq, É. and Pochet, P. (2000), "UNICE and CEEP in 1999: Social Policy Perspectives", in Gabaglio, E. and Hoffmann, R. (eds.), *European Trade Union Yearbook 1999*, European Trade Union Institute, Brussels, pp.173-190.

Arcq, É. and Pochet, P. (2002), "UNICE and CEEP in 2001: Changes in Prospect?", in Gabaglio, E. and Hoffmann, R. (eds.), *European Trade Union Yearbook 2001*, European Trade Union Institute, Brussels, pp.205-222.

Arcq, É.., Dufresne, A. and Pochet, P. (2003), "The Employers: The Hidden Face of European Industrial Relations", *Transfer*, Vol.9, No.2, Summer 2003, pp.302-321.

Balanyá, B., Doherty, A., Hoedeman, O., Ma'anit, A. and Wesselius, E. (2000), *Europe Inc. Liaisons dangereuses entre institutions et milieux d'affaires européens*, Agone, Marseille.

Béthoux, E. and Jobert, A. (2004), "Regards sur les relations professionnelles nord-américaines et européennes: évolutions et perspectives", Note critique, *Sociologie du Travail*, Vol.46, No.2, April-June 2004, pp.261-270.

Branch, A. and Greenwood, J. (2001), "European Employers: Social Partners?", in Crompston, H. and Greenwood, J. (eds.), *Social Partnership in the European Union*, Palgrave, New York, pp.41-70.

Bunel, J. (1997), "Représentation patronale et représentativité des organisations patronales", *Travail et Emploi*, No.70, pp.3-20.

CEC (1993), Communication concerning the Application of the Agreement on Social Policy Presented by the Commission to the Council and to the European Parliament, COM (93) 600 final of 14 December 1993.

CEC (1995), *Dialogue social: le bilan communautaire en 1995*, Directorate General for Employment, Industrial Relations and Social Affairs, Luxembourg.

CEC (1996), Commission Communication concerning the Development of the Social Dialogue at Community Level, COM (96) 448 final of 18 September 1996.

CEC (1997), Communication from the Commission to the Council, the European Parliament, the Economic and Social Committee and the Committee of the Regions "The Competitiveness of the Construction Industry", COM (1997) 539 final of 4 November 1997.

CEC (1998), Communication from the Commission on Adapting and Promoting the Social Dialogue at Community Level, COM (98) 322 final of 20 May 1998.

Champin, H. (2003), "Le dialogue social européen sectoriel: étude du cas du secteur ferroviaire", Observatoire social européen, Brussels, mimeo.

Coen, D. (1997), "The Evolution of the Large Firm as a Political Actor in the European Union", *Journal of European Public Policy*, Vol.4, No.1, March 1997, pp.91-108.

Coen, D. (1998), "The European Business Interest and the Nation State: Large-firm Lobbying in the European Union and Member States", *Journal of Public Policy*, Vol.18, No.1, pp.75-100.

Cowles, M. G. (1994), *The Politics of Big Business in the European Community: Setting the Agenda for a New Europe*, The American University, Washington, Ph.D.

Cowles, M. G. (1995), "Setting the Agenda for a New Europe: The ERT and EC 1992", *Journal of Common Market Studies*, Vol.33, No.4, pp.501-526.

Cowles, M. G. (1998), "The Changing Architecture of Big Business", in Greenwood, J. and Aspinwall, M. (eds.), *Collective Action in the European*

Union: Interests and the New Politics of Associability, Routledge, London, pp.108-125.

Cremers, J. (2005) "Social Dialogue in the European Construction Industry", *Transfer*, Vol.11, No.3, pp.359-362.

Degryse, C. (2000), *Comprendre l'Europe sociale – Le rôle des syndicats*, Editions Vie ouvrière, Brussels.

Dubbins, S. (2002), "Towards Euro-Corporatism? A Study of Relations between Trade Unions and Employers' Organisation at the European Sectoral Level", *Thesis*, March 2002.

Dufour, C. (2001), "Représentations patronales: des organisations à responsabilités limitées", *Chronique Internationale de l'IRES*, No.72, September 2001, pp.5-22.

European Parliament and Council of the European Union (1996), Directive 96/71/EC of the European Parliament and of the Council of 16 December 1996 concerning the Posting of Workers in the Framework of the Provision of Services, OJ L 018 of 21 January 1997, pp.0001-0006.

FIEC and EFBWW (1996), Joint Response to the Commission on the Commission Communication concerning the Development of the Social Dialogue at Community Level, COM (96) 448 final of 18 September 1996.

Freyssinet J. (1998), "Dialogue social et construction européenne", *Chronique Internationale de l'IRES, Les acteurs sociaux nationaux face à la construction européenne*, special edition, October 1998, pp.5-23.

Gobin, C. and Smets, I. (1998), "Introduction: le lobbyisme en question", in Claeys, P.-H. (ed.), *Lobbyisme, pluralisme et intégration européenne*, P.I.E.-Peter Lang, Brussels, pp.13-33.

Greenwood, J. (1995) (ed.), *European Casebook on Business Alliances*, Hemel Hempstead, Prentice Hall.

Greenwood, J. (1997), *Representing Interests in the EU*, Macmillan, London.

Greenwood, J. (2000), "EU Interest Groups and their Members: When is Membership a 'Collective Action Problem'", in Balme, R., Chabanet, D. and Wright, V. (eds.), *Collective Action in Europe*, Presses de Sciences Po, Paris, pp.227-254.

Greenwood, J. (2002a), *The Effectiveness of EU Business Associations*, Palgrave, New York.

Greenwood, J. (2002b), *Inside the EU Business Associations*, Palgrave, New York.

Hoffmann, J., Hoffmann, R., Kirton-Darling, J. and Rampeltshammer, L. (2002), *The Europeanisation of Industrial Relations in a Global Perspective: A Literature Review*, European Foundation for the Improvement of Living and Working Conditions, Dublin (http://www.fr.eurofound.eu.int/ publications/files/EF02102EN.pdf).

Lehmkuhl, D. (1999), *The Importance of Small Differences. The Impact of European Integration on Road Haulage Associations in Germany and the Netherlands*, Thela Thesis, The Hague.

Lietart, M. (2002), *The Institutionalisation of Corporate Lobbying in Brussels*, Master in Global Political Economy, University of Sussex, September 2002.

Matyja, M. (1999), *Der Einfluss der Vereinigung der Industrie- und Arbeitgeberverbände Europas (UNICE) auf den Entscheidungsprozess der Europäischen Union*, Peter Lang, Bern.

Moreau M.-A. (1999), "Sur la représentativité des partenaires sociaux européens", *Droit social*, No.1, January 1999, pp.53-63.

Pernot, J.-M. (2001), "Patrons et patronat, dimensions européennes", *Chronique internationale de l'IRES*, No.72, September 2001, pp.89-103 (http://www.ires-fr.org/files/publicat/chronique/c72/c728.pdf).

Pochet, P. and Arcq, É. (1999), "UNICE in 1998", in Gabaglio, E. and Hoffmann, R. (eds.), *European Trade Union Yearbook 1998*, European Trade Union Institute, Brussels, pp.179-195.

Pochet, P. and Arcq, É. (2001), "UNICE and CEEP in 2000", in Gabaglio, E. and Hoffmann, R. (eds.), *European Trade Union Yearbook 2000*, European Trade Union Institute, Brussels, pp.173-189.

Sadowski, D. and Jacobi, O. (1991), *Employers' Associations in Europe: Policy and Organisation*, Nomos Verlagsgesellschaft, Baden-Baden.

Schmitter, P. C. and Streeck, W. (1981), "The Organisation of Business Interests", *Discussion Paper* IIM/ LMP 81-13, Wissenschaftszentrum, Berlin.

Schmitter, P. C. and Streeck, W. (1999), "The Organization of Business Interests. Studying The Associative Action of Business in Advanced Industrial Societies", *MPIfG Discussion Paper*, No.99/1, Max-Planck-Institut für Gesellschatsforschung, Cologne (http://www.mpi-fg-koeln.mpg.de/pu/mpifg_dp/dp99-1.pdf).

Streeck, W. (1989), "Interest Heterogeneity and Organizing Capacity: Two Class Logics of Collective Action?", *WZB Discussion Papers* FS I89-4, 41, Wissenschaftszentrum Berlin.

Traxler, F. (2000), "Employers and Employer Organisations in Europe: Membership Strength, Density and Representativeness", *Industrial Relations Journal*, Vol.31, No.4, pp.308-316.

Traxler, F., Blaschke, S. and Kittel, B. (2001), *National Labour Relations in Internationalized Markets: A Comparative Study of Institutions, Change and Performance*, Oxford University Press, Oxford.

Tyszkiewicz, Z. (1991), "UNICE: The Voice of European Business and Industry in Brussels – A Programmatic Self-Presentation", in Sadowski, D. and Jacobi, O. (eds.), *Employers' Associations in Europe: Policy and Organisation*, Nomos Verlagsgesellschaft, Baden-Baden, pp.85-101.

Van Waarden, F. (1991), "Two Logics of Collective Action? Business Associations as Distinct from Trade Unions: The Problems of Associations as Organisations", in Sadowski, D. and Jacobi, D. (eds.), *Employers' Associations in Europe: Policy and Organisation*, Nomos Verlagsgesellschaft, Baden-Baden, pp.51-84.

Interviews with the General Secretaries and/or the Social Dialogue Coordinators of European Employers' (and Workers'*) Federations

Euratex (2000), Brussels, 28 March 2000.

Euratex (2004), Brussels, 30 January 2004.

EFBWW* (1999), Brussels, 15 December 1999.

FIEC (2000), Brussels, 15 November 2000.
FIEC (2002), Brussels, 3 December 2002.
FIEC (2004), Brussels, 18 December 2004.
ETUF-TCL* (2003), Brussels, 9 April 2003.
IRU (2003), Brussels, 17 January 2003.
UNICE (2002), Brussels, 14 October 2002.

List of Abbreviations

ACEA	European Automobile Manufacturers Association
ACI-Europe	Airports Council International-Europe
ACME	Association of European Cooperative and Mutual Insurers
ACT	Association of Commercial Television in Europe
AEA	Association of European Airlines
AER	Association of European Radios
APEP	European Association of Potash Producers
BIPAR	European Federation of Insurance Intermediaries
CAACE	European Community Shipowners' Associations
CANSO	Civil Air Navigation Services Organisation
CCRE	Council of European Municipalities and Regions
CEA	European Federation of National Insurance Associations
CECCM	Confederation of European Community Cigarette Manufacturers
CECD	European Confederation for Retail Trade
CECSO	European Solid Fuels' Association
CEEMET	Council of European Employers of the Metal, Engineering and Technology-Based Industries.
CEFIC	European Chemical Industry Council
CEFS	European Committee of Sugar Manufacturers
CEI-Bois	European Confederation of woodworking industries
CEPCEO	Association of the Coal Producers of the European Community
CEPI	European Coordination of Independent Producers
CER	Community of European Railways
CER	Community of European Railway and Infrastructure Companies
CESA	Committee of European Union Shipbuilders Associations
CIAA	Confederation of the Food and Drink Industries of the EU
CIC-Europe	The International Hairdressing Union
CLEPA	European Association of Automotive Suppliers
CoESS	Confederation of European Security Services
COGECA	General Confederation of Agricultural Co-operatives in the European Union
Comitextil	Co-Ordination Committee for the Textile Industry in the EU
COPA	Committee of Professional Agricultural Organisations
COTANCE	Confederation of National Associations of Tanners and Dressers of the European Community
EBU	European Broadcasting Union
EBU	The European Barge Union
ECEG	European chemical employers' group

ECFI	European Confederation of the Footwear Industry
ECLA	European Clothing Association
ECSA	European Community Shipowners' Associations
ELTAC	European Largest Textile and Clothing Companies
ENPA	European Newspaper Publishers' Association
ERA	European Regions Airline Association
ESBG	European Savings Bank Group
ESO	European Skippers' Organisation (ESO)
ETNO	The European Telecommunications Network Operators' Association
Euracoal	European Association for Coal and Lignite
EURATEX	European textile and clothing industry
Eureau	European Union of National Associations of Water Suppliers and Waste Services
Eurelectric	Union of the Electricity Industry
Euro-CIETT	International Confederation of Private Employment Agencies
EuroCommerce	Retail, Wholesale and International Trade Representation to the EU
Eurofer	European Confederation of Iron and Steel Industries
Eurogas	The European Union of the National Gas Industry
Euromines	European Association of Mining Industries
Europêche/COGECA	Association of national organizations of fishing enterprises in the EU/General Confederation of Agricultural Co-operatives in the European Union
FBE	European Banking Federation
FENI	European Federation of Cleaning Industries (EFCI)
FEWITA	Federation of European Wholesale and International Trade Associations
FIAPF	International Federation of Film Producers Associations
FIEC	European Construction Industry Federation
GEBC	European Association of Co-operative Banks
GEDIS	European Multiple Retailers' Association
GITES	Groupement des industries européennes du tabac
HOPE	European Hospital and Healthcare Federation
Hotrec	Hotels, Restaurants & Cafés in Europe Confederation of National Associations of Hotels, Restaurants, Cafés
IACA	International Air Carrier Association
IBFMP	International Bureau of the Federations of Master Printers
IMPA	International Master Printers Association
Intergraf	International confederation for printing and allied industries
IRU	International Road transport Union
OIRT	International Radio and Television Organisation
Pearle	European League of Employers' Associations in the Performing Arts sector
PostEurop	Association of European Public Postal Operators
UEA	European furniture industry
WEM	The employers' organisation of the metal trades in Europe

CHAPTER 10

Implementation of the Sectoral Social Dialogue in Sweden

Sofia MURHEM

Introduction

The sectoral social dialogue is an important feature of the European Social Model. The outcomes of the sectoral social dialogue are described and analysed in this volume. One major aspect, however, remains to be studied: namely, how sectoral social dialogue outcomes are implemented. Over the years, the sectoral social dialogue has resulted in a number of joint texts, reflecting the ideas, but also the efforts, of the social partners in Europe. Implementation is the final challenge for the sectoral social dialogue, transforming paperwork into conditions affecting the daily lives of employees.

Here, Sweden is chosen as a case study on implementation. There are several reasons for choosing Sweden. Firstly, Sweden is the most highly organised country in the European Union, when it comes to both trade unions and employers' federations. More than 80% of all Swedish employees are trade union members, and membership rates in employers' organisations are equally high. In addition, Swedish trade unions and employers' federations are comparatively well funded, due to the high membership rates. Secondly, Sweden has a long tradition of cooperation between trade unions and employers' federations, which further increases the propensity for successful implementation. Admittedly, the golden days of cooperation in the 1950s and 1960s are over, but the overall tendency towards cooperation rather than confrontation remains intact to a large extent. Thirdly, well over 90% of Swedish employees are covered by collective agreements, making implementation via collective agreements reasonably easy. All in all, these conditions may serve to prepare the ground for productive implementation of the sectoral social dialogue.

I. Data, Method and Point of Departure

Using the OSE database of sectoral social dialogue texts as a point of departure, semi-structured interviews were arranged with representatives of Swedish trade unions covered by joint texts. The trade union representatives were asked whether implementation of the text had been an issue, and if so, how the process of implementing joint texts had worked, what the effects were, and if they were not implemented, what reasons there were for the failure to implement. Their experience of the procedure and how they experienced the sectoral social dialogue itself was also up for discussion. Interviews, like all sources, need to be treated with care. People may forget, they may have an agenda of their own when responding, they might want to be politically correct or they might want to rationalise previous actions. All such things may affect the findings. How best to solve that kind of problem depends on the purpose of the interviews. In this instance, the aim of the interviews was to examine the opinions of the interviewees on certain issues. As a means of respondent validation, aimed at correcting possible factual misunderstandings and errors, but not the analysis itself, the study was presented to respondents and trade unionists[1].

Only agreements signed after Sweden acceded to the European Union were included in the study. In all, there were 25 sectors covering 72 texts, between 1995 and 2004. However, of those 25 sectors, the sugar sector should be excluded, as Sweden does not take part in the dialogue[2]. Hence, seven joint texts need to be excluded. Since 2004, Swedish trade unions have no longer taken part in the social dialogue in the tanning and leather sector, due to the existence of very few workers in that sector in Sweden. The sector is, however, included in this study.

The joints texts can, in turn, be divided into six categories: agreements, recommendations, common positions, declarations, tools and rules of procedure, according to the terminology developed by Pochet *et al.* (for details, see elsewhere in this volume). Of those, agreements and recommendations (divided into codes of conduct and frameworks of action) are the categories which can directly include means of implementation. Common positions are addressed to European institutions and are thus by nature unlikely to be implemented nationally. Declarations lack explicit procedures for follow-up, but may nevertheless be implemented nationally. Tools, in the case of manuals, may be used and/or implemented nationally. Rules of procedure are recognition

1 For further discussion on respondent validation, see for instance Bryman (2002: 259).

2 Partly for organisational reasons, as the Swedish trade union organising sugar workers is not part of the relevant industry federation, and partly due to the fact that there are, today, very few sugar workers in Sweden.

agreements and are therefore not to be implemented nationally. Thus, those joint texts falling into the "common positions" and "rules of procedure" categories are not aimed at national implementation. This means that about one fifth of the texts are more or less impossible to implement nationally and not intended for such a purpose. A list of the joint texts included in this study can be found in Annex.

Twelve trade unions, two of which merged on 1st January 2006, were involved. Ten trade unions were affiliates of the Swedish Trade Union Confederation and two were affiliates of the Swedish Confederation of Professional Employees.

In the following, I will use the neo-institutionalist approach. The institutions decide and restrict the possibilities for action of organisations and individuals. By acting from and interacting with institutions, actors may change and develop the institutions[3]. Actors are assumed to be (limited) rational beings responding to and interacting with political and economic changes (North, 1993: 37-63). Today's conditions depend on the historical development of social and economic variables (van der Laan and Ruesga, 1998: 18). Problem-solving traditions evolve, and through those traditions continuity occurs. A path dependency will determine the solutions chosen. These traditions are part of the social concept of the labour market, a social concept that rules out certain ways of solving problems as socially unacceptable.

II. Swedish Industrial Relations – An Overview

The social partners play an important role in Swedish political life. Unionisation has been extremely high for a long time, and, indeed, is still very high. In the early 21st century, union density in Sweden is still above 80%. One of the reasons for this high unionisation is that Sweden retains the Ghent system[4]. This means that, in contrast to other countries, workers who become unemployed tend not to leave the union. There are other contributing factors as well. As in the other Nordic countries, white-collar workers and academics are highly unionised and the public sector is extensive. In addition, Swedish unions are strong, both on a central level and on a local level (Kjellberg, 2001: 31). According to Swedish labour law, trade unions are in most cases legal

3 A discussion on the development of both formal and informal institutions is found in North (1993): see especially pp.16-27.

4 This means that the trade unions administer the unemployment insurance funds. The system was named after Ghent, Belgium, and Belgium still retains the system. The Ghent system was introduced in Sweden in the 1930s, and earlier in the other Nordic countries. Sweden, Denmark and Finland still maintain the Ghent system, while Norway has abandoned it. As a result, unionisation has decreased in Norway, while it is still very high in Sweden, Denmark and Finland.

entities, and not employees themselves. Hence, the trade unions' position is strong and, in fact, all employee representation is via the trade unions.

Swedish trade union organisation is industry-based, i.e. all employees in an industry or branch belong to the same trade union irrespective of their particular occupations. However, there is a division between blue-collar, white-collar and professional employees. To begin with, most industries had their own trade unions, but there have been several mergers over the years, creating larger and larger trade unions. In 2006, the Swedish Trade Union Confederation, (*Landsorganisationen, LO*), founded in 1898, has fifteen affiliates. The latest merger, between *Metall*, the Swedish Metalworkers Union, and *Industrifacket*, the Industrial Workers' Union, created a new union, *IF Metall*, as from 1st January 2006. The largest LO unions are *Kommunal*, the Swedish Municipal Workers' Union (586,000 members), *IF Metall* (469,000 members), *SEKO*, the Union for Service and Communications Employees (161,000 members), *Handels*, the Swedish Union of Commercial Employees (168,000 members) and *Byggnads*, the Swedish Building Workers' Union (130,000 members). White-collar workers became unionised at a later stage than blue-collar workers, a fact that has been attributed to a lingering notion of white-collar worker solidarity with the employer. A main organisation, *DACO* (*De anställdas centralorganisation*, the Employees' Organisation), for private sector white-collar employees was founded in 1931, while the white-collar employees in the public sector formed their own organisation, *Tjänstemännens Centralorganisation – TCO* (Swedish Confederation of Professional Employees), in 1937. The two organisations merged in 1944 under the name of *TCO* (Elvander, 1966: 30-31). In 1947, a central organisation for professional employees, *Sveriges Akademikers Centralorganisation – SACO* (Swedish Confederation of Professional Associations), was founded (Elvander, 1966: 49).

The degree of organisation in the employers' associations is just as high. Swedish employers are better organised than their peers in the other Nordic countries. The reason is probably that the Swedish economy is dominated by large corporations, but also the fact that the trade unions have caused an organisational interaction between employers and employees. Like the trade unions, the employers' associations are also industry-based[5].

Many issues that in other countries are covered by law are decided on in Sweden by collective agreement. For instance, there are no statu-

5 For an overview of the history of the Swedish employers' federation, see De Geer (1992) and for the history of the Swedish trade unions, see Kjellberg (2001).

tory minimum wages in Sweden; instead these are agreed on in the collective agreement. The law recognises collective agreements as written agreements between an employers' association or employer and a trade union concerning employment conditions for the employees or the relationship between the employer and the employees[6]. That means it includes both collective agreements, i.e. agreements between employers' organisations and trade unions, and substitute agreements, i.e. agreements between an individual employer, who is not a member of an employers' association, and the trade union. A collective or substitute agreement signed in a workplace is valid for all employees in that particular workplace, not only trade union members. An agreement has to be signed if at least one employee so demands, but there is no extension to other companies.

There are, surprisingly enough, no statistics on collective agreements in Sweden, but a 1995 estimate holds that about 95% of the Swedish workforce is covered, 72% under direct agreements and the rest under substitute agreements. However, the figure is rather uncertain (Kjellberg, 2000: 204 ff). It is, nevertheless, likely that the coverage of collective agreements is about 90%.

Swedish trade unions and employers' federations began to cooperate in the early 1900s, but cooperation did not really take off until the 1930s. Industrial disputes were abundant in the 1930s. The government threatened the social partners with legislation, should they not come to an agreement and bring an end to the industrial conflict. The result was the *Saltsjöbaden* Agreement in 1938. LO and the Swedish Employers' Confederation (*Svenska Arbetsgivareföreningen, SAF*[7]), founded in 1902, agreed to cooperate without government intervention. Under the Saltsjöbaden Agreement, many issues were solved through voluntary agreements instead of issuing laws (Murhem and Ottosson, 2000). The Saltsjöbaden Agreement was the foundation-stone of the Swedish model of social dialogue and cooperation between the social partners. The reasons for the Saltsjöbaden Agreement should be interpreted as rational actions rather than any kind of idealistic motives. LO wanted to improve wages, which could be achieved through a strong trade union confederation at a central level, with expertise available. Agreements were considered victories for the trade union movement. The notion of economic growth as a prerequisite for wage increases was generally accepted within the trade union movement after World War II. The Saltsjöbaden Agreement was beneficial for the employers as well. It prevented legislation, but did still improve predictability and prevented companies

6 23 § SFS 1976: 580.

7 In 2001, SAF merged with *Industriförbundet*, the Federation of Swedish Industries, and formed *Svenskt Näringsliv*, the Confederation of Swedish Enterprises.

competing over a scarce labour force by bidding higher. In addition, strikes and conflicts were costly, and for that reason industrial peace was favourable for SAF[8].

In 1948, the new Labour Market Board (*Arbetsmarknadsstyrelsen, AMS*) was inaugurated. On the board were representatives of LO, SAF and the AMS' employees. In 1957 the social democrats fully accepted the Swedish model which had developed, a model characterised by collective wage bargaining, central negotiations, full employment and a wage policy based on solidarity. The solidarity-based wage policy meant that all companies, irrespective of their profitability, paid the same wages for the same work done, which in turn caused unprofitable businesses to close down and brought about restructuring between branches. The AMS worked with retraining programmes for those who became unemployed because of the solidarity-based wage policy or otherwise had difficulty fitting into the labour market (Rothstein, 1992: 175-178; Murhem and Ottosson, 2000: 43).

From the 1960s onwards, there was an increasing demand for legislation instead of mutual agreements on employment protection. The employment protection legislation subsequently introduced meant an end to the Saltsjöbaden spirit of the previous decades, an end brought about mainly by political action (Nycander, 2002). Thus, cooperation diminished, but it would be wrong to conclude that it disappeared.

Decreases in economic growth and productivity in the early 1970s caused wage negotiations to become increasingly difficult. When some groups gained wage increases, others demanded compensation, which in turn caused inflation. Politics was aimed at maintaining full employment, which raised expectations of wage increases. Therefore, the centralised bargaining system became increasingly decentralised during the 1980s (Magnusson, 1997)[9].

The 1990s brought increasing global competition, international interdependence and European economic integration. Hence the importance of competitive wage increases, making the Swedish export industry competitive, which was crucial for the employers. In 1996, the government demanded new bargaining models which would make it possible to achieve wage levels that were internationally competitive.

---

8 For a discussion of the development of the Swedish model, see Magnusson (1997: 448-449). Swenson (2002: 113-120) discusses the interaction between employers' organisations and trade unions in shaping industrial relations systems.

9 For a discussion on the transformation of the Swedish bargaining system, see Elvander (1997). Kjellberg (2000) has pointed out that the Swedish highly centralised bargaining system was profitable for the employers at that time, than from any ideals on a model of industrial relations and that the reasons for decentralisation also were mainly economic, as well as the return to centralisation in 1997.

The new Industrial Agreement, *Industriavtalet*, of 1997 meant the beginning of new close cooperation on a sectoral level. The Industrial Agreement represented a common view on economic and industrial policy. It was a new way of negotiating and mediating, and a return towards centralisation, albeit at branch level. Like the Saltsjöbaden Agreement, the Industrial Agreement stipulates that the social partners take responsibility for the labour market without the need for government interference[10]. In addition, Bruun has argued that by the end of the 1990s, the employers' associations and trade unions held a more united view on such important issues as labour law (Bruun, 2003). We might conclude, then, that the foundations for successful implementation, in the sense of effective cooperation between the social partners and a common view on many issues, are indeed found in Sweden during the period of study, i.e. since Sweden became an EU member in 1995.

III. Implementation of the Sectoral Social Dialogue

The number of joint texts studied here differs widely between the different sectors. Several sectors have just one common text, namely Banking, Civil Aviation, Cleaning, Live Performance, Local and Regional Government, Postal Services, Railways, Road Transport, Temporary Work and Woodworking. The sector with the most joint texts is the Commerce sector, which has nine texts, followed by Horeca and Tourism with six, Agriculture, Electricity, Tanning & Leather and Telecommunications with four each, Construction, Mines, Private Security and Textile & Clothing with three each, and Sea Fishing with two.

Two agreements and one common position have been implemented by means of a European Union Commission directive. These are the Civil Aviation sector's Agreement on the organisation of working time of mobile workers and the Sea Transport sector's Agreement on the organisation of working time of seafarers and, finally, the Road Transport sector's Joint Opinion in support of a legislative initiative concerning drivers from third countries. They are therefore excluded from this study.

Swedish trade unions are in general very dedicated to their international work. Prior to Sweden's EU membership, international affairs of the trade unions were mostly in the shape of aid directed towards non-European countries, for instance coordinated through the LO-TCO Secretariat of International Trade Union Development Cooperation. Since 1995, when Sweden joined the EU, European work has been increasingly prominent. In addition, Nordic cooperation has been more

---

10 Elvander has written several articles on the Industrial Agreement and stresses the similarities with the Saltsjöbaden Agreement. See for instance Elvander (2002).

and more important, not in itself, but as a means of coordinating European Union efforts. While the trade unions claim they still spend the same amount of money on non-European work, European work has been upgraded. This means that the total amount of money Swedish trade unions spend on international affairs has increased. Due to reorganisation of the international work done by many trade unions, it is almost impossible to quantify the amount of money and time spent on international affairs. Instead of, as was the practice about ten or fifteen years ago, having just one department for international affairs, many trade unionists today have international, mostly European, issues as part of their job. Swedish trade unions describe themselves as dedicated to the commitments made[11]. This, one might conclude, makes for an appropriate environment, added to the three factors mentioned in the introduction – i.e. a high degree of organisation, long traditions of social dialogue and high coverage of collective agreements – for implementing the joint texts of the sectoral social dialogue.

When the Swedish trade unions were asked whether they have implemented the joint texts of the sectoral social dialogue, all but one answered no. The Financial Sector Union of Sweden, inspired by the 2002 European Joint Declaration on lifelong learning, has developed a new national agreement on competence development/training and lifelong learning, together with their Swedish counterpart, the Bank Employers' Association. The national agreement, "Agreement on competence development", aims at tackling these issues afresh for the trade unions' local branches, shop stewards and members. The trade union expresses satisfaction, as do the employers, with the way the sectoral social dialogue is progressing. The trade union's experiences in Banking are totally different from those in the Insurance sector, which they also represent. In Insurance, they express dissatisfaction, a dissatisfaction stemming from what they consider the employers' lack of interest in dialogue. The result, as felt by the trade union, is that there is little prospect for any fruitful discussion or outcome in Insurance[12].

The new Swedish national agreement in Banking contains a mutual acknowledgement of the importance of lifelong learning. The social partners agree on maintaining a national social dialogue on the subject. Local plans for lifelong learning and competence development will be drawn up. Further, the agreement contains principles for the recognition of qualifications and principles for vocational training[13]. In addition to this successful voluntary implementation, the three joint texts have, as

11 For a discussion on the international work of the Swedish trade union movement, see Misgeld (1997) and Murhem (2003).

12 Interview with representative of the Financial Sector Union of Sweden.

13 Agreement on competence development 2005.

stated above, been implemented by means of European Union directives.

Does this mean that apart from one single declaration, and three European Unions directives, the impact of the sectoral social dialogue is non-existent? To say that is certainly to over-simplify the discussion. One major problem is how to interpret the word "implementation". Because when the trade unions say no, it should not be inferred that they do not care about the texts, or that they just put them in a drawer and forgot all about them. In fact, when questioned about the implementation referred to in the texts, it turns out that they actually do implement obligations they were not fulfilling already. However, if they already have an ongoing process, then they do not adopt new ways of working with the issue. If the Swedish traditional way of working with these issues is political, and the social partners are satisfied enough with the way that process is working, they do not pursue new ways in that case either. But still they do not consider that they are implementing the text. Below, we give an example of how Swedish trade unions work with sectoral social dialogue joint texts. It may serve as a means of analysing what, exactly, Swedish trade unions do mean by implementation.

A. Implementation or Not – An Example

One example is the Agreement on disabled people signed by the Uni-Europa Commerce sector and EuroCommerce. The implementation method set out is that the European social partners will "call on their affiliated employers' organisations and trade unions to:

- convene round table discussions to provide European social partners with feedback on best practice approaches;
- collect and disseminate good practices on support for the employment and integration of disabled people in working life;
- include the promotion of the integration of disabled people into social dialogue;
- present this statement to European Works Councils, where they exist, and encourage a discussion;
- monitor the developments related to this statement on a continuous basis"[14].

The trade union and the employers' organisation already fulfil the first of these obligations as part of an ongoing process. The second and third obligations are in Sweden mainly a political responsibility, which is exercised through an active labour market policy and executed by the Swedish National Labour Market Board and Samhall, a state-owned

---

14 Interview with representative of the Commercial Employees' Union.

stock-company which provides jobs for disabled people[15]. For this reason, the social partners feel that there are other efficient channels for achieving these two goals, outside of the social dialogue. This does not mean that they do not address the issues, but rather that they do so at a workplace level. The central level, they feel, is outside the social dialogue in this particular instance and thus not their responsibility, while the workplace level is. With reference to obligation four, the trade union discusses disabled people on their courses for European Works Council representatives. However, they do not consider this as directly emanating from this text, and in any case, not something that will affect the outcome for disabled people or the procedure for working with the disabled. The fifth, about continuous monitoring, is something they were already doing, well before the joint text was signed[16].

Literally, the trade union has implemented the text, as well as the obligations they did not already fulfil before the joint text was drawn up. When asked, however, they state that they have not implemented the text. Obviously, the trade unions mean something more than the mechanical procedure of implementation. It is thus important to discriminate between implementing in the sense of strictly adhering to the steps laid down in the texts and adhering to them in such a way as to make an impact. Because if we stick to the very strict definition of "adhering", then the Swedish trade union will fall into that category and thus be classified, contrary to its own admission, as implementing the sectoral social dialogue. And this, in spite of the fact that they do not consider implementation of the sectoral social dialogue to have any impact. Thus, the dialogue will, in spite of its apparent implementation, remain the paper tiger referred to at the beginning of this chapter. It will not affect employees.

B. Problems with Implementation

The definition used here is that implementation means to put a joint text into effect. Effect is to be understood as a result or outcome. This definition corresponds to the trade union definition, i.e. the emphasis is on whether the text has had an impact or not.

The problems with implementation differ between the different categories of joints texts, referred to at the beginning of this chapter. One major problem here, as shown in the example given, is, obviously, the fact that many of the texts are on issues that Swedish trade unions and employers have worked on together for a long time. In many cases, such

---

15 Whether the actual outcome of these organisations is a success or not is much debated, but not the issue here.

16 Interview with representative of the Commercial Employees' Union.

as recommendations on fighting racism, against child labour etc., the trade unions and employers share a common view, and thus the need for implementation according to the joint texts is negligible[17]. Such texts are included in the categories covering agreements, recommendations, declarations and tools. There are examples of collective agreements having been more outspoken on issues such as racism and xenophobia, coinciding in time with the joint texts on the same issues. But the trade unions claim that the new, or more precise, clauses are the result of the national social dialogue and not affected by the European level[18].

Also, many of the measures contained in those texts are below the Swedish standards. If, for instance, the texts deal with health and safety regulations, and the levels suggested are below what is stated in the relevant Swedish collective agreement, the text will, naturally, not be implemented. This is the case for instance in Mining, but also in other sectors, mainly those dealing with hazardous chemicals and such like[19]. If implementation does not mean an improvement, but rather no change or a change for the worse, then the need, or indeed the willingness, to implement such measures is virtually non-existent. This reflects the favourable position of Swedish employees compared to those in many other countries[20]. Swedish trade unions are well aware that they cannot pursue goals that would improve the situation for their members, if such standards are higher than what is feasible in many other countries. A Swedish trade unionist claims that "If we were to demand Swedish minimum levels, then we would get nothing!"[21].

Other texts are such that they are meant to be used for adopting a common stand on certain issues towards, for instance, the European Union, rather than to be implemented as such. This applies mainly to the "common positions" category. Such texts include the Mining sector's Joint Declaration concerning the draft European directive on waste management and its Joint Declaration concerning the draft European directive on emissions trading, as well as the Horeca and Tourism sector's Joint Declaration on the effects of VAT[22].

---

17 Interviews with, among others, representatives of the Building Workers' Union, the Metalworkers' Union, the Union for Service and Communications Employees and the Swedish Forest and Wood Trade Union.

18 Interview with representative of the Union for Service and Communications Employees.

19 Interview with representative of the Metalworkers' Union.

20 Interview with representative of the Swedish Forest and Wood Trade Union.

21 Interview with representative of the Union for Service and Communications Employees.

22 Interviews with representatives of the Metalworkers' Union, the Hotel and Restaurant Workers' Union and the Salaried Employees' Union HTF.

Another complication, visible in the above example, is that some issues are such that in Sweden they are, usually, dealt with at another level[23]. This can occur in all categories apart from common positions, as these are addressed to the European institutions. The path dependence of Swedish actors is apparently strong, and new ways of tackling issues get very little attention or approval. This means that irrespective of the texts, if the Swedish actors consider that one or more of the obligations to be implemented are issues that should be dealt with at other levels than the social dialogue, those obligations will be neglected.

The fact that Swedish levels of, for instance, further education are above the suggested levels, may of course be temporary. After a while, it is possible that European levels will improve and thus, more need for Swedish implementation will arise. The Swedish Building Workers' Union claims that a current project being undertaken in both the safety and health and the vocational training working groups in the Construction sector, on required hours of training for certain work groups, may well result in levels above the present Swedish ones, at least for one category of workers[24].

The behaviour of the Swedish trade unions should not be interpreted as meaning that they do not care about implementing joint texts arising out of the sectoral social dialogue. Rather, the outspoken "no", when asked if they have implemented, means that they place great value on implementation. The important thing for the Swedish trade unions is to achieve a positive effect for their members. Sweden's trade unions do after all work with the statements, but leave out what they reckon they have already achieved in one way or the other.

C. Sectoral Social Dialogue – More Than Just Joint Texts

Most of our informants are, at least to an extent, satisfied with the sectoral social dialogue, even though they do not think that the joint texts make any real improvements to their members' working conditions. This can partly be explained by the fact that their goal is not primarily the joint texts as such, but rather to enforce trade union rights or otherwise promote working conditions in order to avoid social dumping. As one trade unionist put it, it is important to improve working conditions and wages in competing countries, in order to "raise the floor"[25].

The sectoral social dialogue is thus mainly part of an overall strategy to establish industrial relations and social dialogue of a Swedish kind in

---

23 Interview with representative of the Commercial Employees' Union.

24 Interview with representative of the Building Workers' Union.

25 Interview with representative of the Industrial Union.

other countries. An example is when the European-level discussions on corporate social responsibility cause Swedish employers to pay more heed to these issues in respect of their foreign subcontractors[26]. The texts are mainly seen as instruments to enforce dialogue, and the actual content is less important, as long as it fits with the normative ideas on how trade unions and employers' organisations should interact. This goes for all international work, not only the sectoral social dialogue, but also work at other European levels, and internationally as well.

Another important feature of the European sectoral social dialogue, valued by the trade unions, is that it enables a common stand to be taken at European level on important issues. It facilitates European-level dialogue and makes it easier for employers and employees to be heard. Swedish trade unionists want to take part in and contribute to this[27].

Some do find the situation in many European countries problematic. They reckon that implementation is rare in many other countries, especially the newer Member States, where trade unions and employers' organisations are totally absent, or have few members. One informant claimed that texts remain "fine words on paper" since implementation is so very difficult in many European countries[28]. They experience frustration and dissatisfaction with the process, due to the lack of implementation. Evidently, the results differ between sectors[29]. Other informants find that the focus on the new Member States has worked well in their sector[30].

Apart from the above, the trade unions experience other problems with the sectoral social dialogue as well. The difficulties differ from one sector to another. Trade unions taking part in two or more sectoral social dialogues may have very diverse experiences in the different sectors. One example is the above-mentioned difference between Banking and Insurance, were one sectoral social dialogue (Banking) is positive and constructive, while the other (Insurance) is unproductive and fruitless. Some problems stem from reasons specific to the national actors, for instance when the Swedish employers do not take part in the dialogue, thus possibly making future texts more difficult to implement. An example here is Construction, where the Swedish employers are absent, causing the Swedish trade union concern about future implementation[31].

26 Interview with representative of the Industrial Union.

27 Interview with representatives of the Swedish Forest and Wood Trade Union and the Industrial Union.

28 Interview with representative of the Transport Workers' Union.

29 Interview with representative of the Union for Service and Communications Employees.

30 Interview with representative of the Metalworkers' Union.

31 Interview with representative of the Building Workers' Union.

Similarly, problems could be caused by the way the sectors are set up, and who the members of the sectoral dialogue are. For instance, in Telecommunications, the employers' organisation represents mainly the former monopolies. The Swedish trade unions thus find it difficult to disseminate the results of the social dialogue to companies not encompassed by the dialogue, but actually working in the same sector[32]. Other problems are the result of inherent procedural difficulties, such as when an informant complains of the slow process, but adds that this goes for the entire European Union, not just the sectoral social dialogue.

There is also some awkwardness related to dissimilar perceptions of the intrinsic reasons for the conditions discussed within the social dialogue. Here, perceptions may differ both between employers and trade unions and also between countries. The differences of opinion between the groups of actors are likely to result from divergences in outlooks, traditions and objectives for the dialogue, while discrepancies between countries may be the consequence of different national path dependencies. Such differences of opinion may affect both the scale and scope of the joint texts finally agreed upon. For instance, many Swedish trade unions mentioned that they feel trade unions from Southern Europe tend to be more confrontational in their orientation, while the Swedish trade unionists perceive themselves as more cooperative. Hence Swedish trade unions want joint texts to contain achievable goals, while others might want them to reflect something to strive for. The importance of the national outlook is emphasised by the fact that many trade unions cooperate closely and successfully with their Nordic peers. In several instances, such as Mining, Telecommunications and Commerce, European-level work is coordinated with the other Nordic countries as a means of ensuring added influence. The cooperation between the Nordic trade unions has a long tradition, but has been enforced since Sweden and Finland joined the European Union in 1995. Denmark is a long-time member, while Norway voted no in its 1994 referendum. While the Nordic level in itself can be judged to have lost in importance since 1995, the general impact of the Nordic level is greater, since it is used for coordination of European-level work[33].

Some informants suggest a more diversified sectoral social dialogue, with more varied outcomes than joint texts. One alternative to the joint texts, suggested so as to improve the impact of the social dialogue, is campaigns all over Europe to achieve a common goal. For instance, the

32 Interview with representative of the Union for Service and Communications Employees.

33 For a discussion on Nordic trade union cooperation and European work, see Colclough (2003) on telecommunications, and Blomqvist and Murhem (2003) on the metal industry.

Swedish Commercial Employees' Union advocates a European day on security issues, focusing on retail robberies[34]. This would refocus the sectoral social dialogue and be a way of emphasising the importance of an actual outcome of the dialogue.

Our informants take great care to point out that they will resist any attempt to use the sectoral social dialogue for bargaining with a view to concluding collective agreements at that level. Collective agreements should, they state explicitly, remain an issue for the national level. Indeed, the Swedish trade union movement is clear on that. Bargaining must remain national, and joint texts agreed upon in other instances, such as European Works Councils or European-level sectoral social dialogue, should be not be written in such a manner that they resemble collective agreements. Some of the reasons given are that wages should in principle be set nationally, that European collective agreements would reduce wages in Sweden and that it would be problematic to establish a European bargaining system, as the national systems are so very different[35]. In addition, Sweden's employers are completely against any transfer of collective bargaining to the European level[36].

Concluding Remarks

The answer to the question posed at the beginning of this chapter – whether or not the joint texts produced by the sectoral social dialogue have been implemented in Sweden – would, if the trade unions were to answer the question, be overwhelmingly negative. An important exception, apart from the three joint texts implemented by means of European Union directives, is the new agreement on lifelong learning and further training, signed in Banking. The Financial Sector Union of Sweden and the Bank Employers' Association, motivated by the 2002 European Joint Declaration on lifelong learning, have signed a new national agreement. This national agreement is expected to have a real impact on members and on trade union officials, helping the actors to get to grip with the issues. The trade union officials are satisfied with the outcome, i.e. the new national agreement, as well as with the dialogue itself.

The negative results of the implementation process deserve closer study, and perhaps also a reinterpretation. When studying the procedure more carefully, we might discuss whether the trade unions' view of non-existing implementation is really appropriate, since some of the implementation measures have actually been adopted. For instance, we saw that the joint text in the Commerce sector on how to improve the em-

[34] Interview with representative of the Commercial Employees' Union.

[35] Interview with representative of the Industrial Union, see also Murhem (2003).

[36] Interview with representative of the Industrial Union.

ployment of disabled people had one implementation point on presenting the statement to European Works Councils and encouraging discussion. This point had, admittedly, been executed. Hence, we could argue that implementation points related to dissemination of the statements have actually been carried out. After all, Swedish trade unions take their commitments seriously in general, and those of the sectoral social dialogue are no exception. In fact, the joint texts are studied, and points for dissemination are disseminated, while points that are measurable are discussed and compared with existing Swedish standards etc. In that sense, the implementation process could be said to be well under way and, moreover, actually achieved, at least in some instances.

However, if by implementation we mean an impact, the negative answer holds true. The trade unions deny that the sectoral social dialogue has had any impact on Swedish working conditions and industrial relations. In that respect, there has been no implementation of the sectoral social dialogue joint texts. It is important to use a definition of implementation which corresponds to the definition the trade unions themselves use. Their definition is evident from their interpretation of the question on implementation, namely whether the text has had an impact or not, rather than a mechanical procedure of checking off points under the heading of implementation in the joint texts. The discussion of sectoral social dialogue outcomes must be relevant to the actors involved. Consequently, the definition used here is that implementation means putting a joint text into effect. Effect is understood as a result or outcome.

There are three sets of reasons as to why the joint texts have not been implemented. Each of the three sets may be divided into several different types. *The first set of reasons* refers to the text itself. The texts are not of a type to be easily implemented. This includes common positions, declarations and tools. The first kind of texts in this category are ones that do not contain objectives intended to be implemented, but rather reflect common positions, such as joint statements on corporate social responsibility. While such joint texts may be valuable in their own right, they are very difficult to implement. In addition, not only may the objective of the text be difficult to implement, but also the way the text is written. Many joint texts are imprecise and in fact rather vague. The vagueness is often due to differences of opinion between the partners to the agreement, making a precise document impossible to achieve. A vague joint text can be achieved, but causes dissatisfaction. Too abstract a text makes implementation difficult, or makes the impact of implementation negligible. The second kind is texts whose objectives can hardly be implemented by a trade union or even by the social partners together, but instead are goals to lobby for, such as Joint Declarations in favour of reduced VAT. Such goals are also notoriously difficult to attain, and reflect something to strive for rather than something to achieve, at least within the short term.

The second set of reasons refers not to the text, but to the objectives. The objectives cannot be implemented, because they have already been achieved in Sweden or otherwise are in the process of being achieved. Such texts include agreements and recommendations. An example of the first type is Joint Declarations on lifelong learning, if the objectives are already in place within that sector in Sweden. While the first set of reasons were difficult, partly due to texts being imprecise, these texts are problematical when their objectives are precise, but below Swedish standards. The second type may be exemplified by joint statements on combating violence or child labour. In most cases Swedish employers and trade unions have a mutual view on such issues, resulting from previous discussions. Means of implementation such as embarking on round-table discussions are therefore obsolete.

The third set of reasons is related to the setting-up of the dialogue and its members. If the Swedish employers' organisation is absent or not representative of the entire sector, then implementation is made harder. Both these cases are evident, if unusual, in sectoral social dialogue. For instance, in Construction, the Swedish employers' organisation is absent, and in Telecommunications, the employers' federation chosen at European level consists mostly of the former national monopolies, leaving many employers outside the sectoral social dialogue.

While it is not fruitful to discuss implementation in the case of the first set of reasons, the second one may well soon offer scope for implementation. Even if levels today in Sweden are comparatively high, there is nothing to say that they will remain above the average European Union levels in the future. One illustration is the above-mentioned Swedish Building Workers' Union, which in its social dialogue is discussing a text most likely to demand more training than is presently the case in Sweden. In that case, the absence of Swedish employers from the sectoral social dialogue might complicate the implementation process further. The third set of reasons may also change, if the set-up of the social dialogue is modified, for example if the employers decide to take part in it.

The clear "no" from the trade unions to the question on implementation could easily be understood as a failure for the sectoral social dialogue. After all, one of the arguments advanced at the beginning of this study was that implementation meant that joint texts could affect the daily lives of employees. Obviously, that has not been the case in Sweden, at least not in most cases. From that perspective, the sectoral social dialogue is a failure in Sweden. However, such a judgement is definitely too harsh, in that we have texts that are not meant to be directly implemented. In addition, the idea of having a good and solid meeting arena may be no bad thing either. For many countries, this may be one of the very few forums where the social partners can discuss issues of common interest. Several informants point out the importance of sectoral dialogue as a meeting ground. They see the value of this, not only for trade unions from countries where such forums are rare or absent nationally, but also for themselves and the trade union movement as a whole, to improve dialogue and the impact of the social partners and their opinions, both nationally and on a European level.

Apart from the question of whether or not it has been a failure, there are certainly more aspects worth discussing with regard to the implementation of the sectoral social dialogue in Sweden. There is a resilient normative element in the opinions of the Swedish trade union movement, as also shown in other studies (see for instance Huzzard and Docherty, 2005). The sectoral social dialogue is not seen mainly as a bench-marking process, a way of learning best practices from other countries, but rather as a way of spreading the Swedish pattern of industrial relations, which one informant expressed as enforcing "normal industrial relations". The international imposition of trade unions and trade union values may be more of a motive for taking part in the dialogue than the likelihood of improving the national situation. Hence, the willingness to adapt may be weaker than in other countries. Of course, the fact that you are (probably) the strongest and most influential trade union movement in the world, considering the size of your country, makes it easier to think that other countries could chalk up the same achievements if they replicated your operational methods.

There is also a strong component of path dependence in the make-up of Swedish trade unions. The Swedish model is still, in spite of the fact that some observers announced its demise in the mid-1970s, still affluent[37]. Even if many of the building-blocks of the model, such as central, national, bargaining and the corporatist tradition, have disappeared, there is still a strong tradition of cooperation is. This is visible not least in the Industrial Agreement. In times of trouble, the Swedish trade unions and employers turned to the Saltsjöbaden Agreement and re-used it, only brought up-to-date. The path dependence reinforces the Swedish

37 For a discussion of the Swedish model and its disappearances, see for instance Visser (1996: 176-200). Visser (1996) points out that the Swedish model as he sees it existed from the 1940s until the 1970s, but has since eroded. Its main characteristics, the high degree of corporatism in combination with high productivity and high wages, declined in the 1970s and the role of the State altered. By demanding labour legislation, the trade unions led the drift away from the Swedish model in the 1970s. In the 1980s and 1990s, the opposite seems to have been true. The employers requested decentralised bargaining and thereby continued the drift away from the Swedish model.

trade unions' belief in their way of working (admittedly not a bad way to gain influence) (Murhem, 2003). Maybe one should not make too much of the specifically Swedish element in this. We have seen over the years that, in spite of the predictions of converging industrial relations models, most countries still retain their own national pattern[38]. The Swedish social dialogue is functioning satisfyingly for both parties in many cases. It is not likely that they would try something new in a different tradition, even if it would appear as best practice somewhere else.

Evidently, there are some problems with using Sweden as an example for studying the implementation of the sectoral social dialogue. The long Swedish tradition of cooperation and the powerful position of Swedish trade unions mean that the position of employees in Sweden is rather fortunate compared to many other countries. Trade unions have been able to achieve good working conditions for their members. The high degree of unionisation means that the trade unions are well funded, making lobbying possible and affordable and campaigns for social issues both feasible and well supported among the public. In many instances, well-established procedures, both political and between the social partners, exist for dealing with issues such as health and safety at work. Social inclusion, which is a topic for many of the joint texts, has been high on the Swedish political agenda for many years. All the factors mentioned at the beginning may not have created the perfect conditions for implementation. Instead, they may have minimised the need for national implementation. A country with less influential trade unions may thus be more suitable for studies on implementation. Too good a national social dialogue may cause texts to be redundant in the national setting. The result could be totally different in a different setting, in another country, or it could be the same for totally different reasons. A country with poor national social dialogue and where trade unions find it difficult to attract attention to their demands may also achieve only small-scale or negligible implementation.

In spite of this, our study of the implementation process in Sweden does shed light on important aspects of the process, namely the importance of the national setting, path dependence and country-specific traditions in shaping the process. Additionally, the goals the actors have when taking part in the social dialogue are important not only in the process and its outcome, but also in the actors' assessment of the sectoral social dialogue. This should be borne in mind when extending the

---

38 See Thelen (2001) for a recent discussion on the remaining national patterns. Crouch (1996) proclaims greater differences than before in industrial relations between, on the one hand, neo-corporatist countries with strong central trade unions such as Scandinavia and Finland, and on the other countries with weaker trade unions.

analysis of implementation of the sectoral social dialogue to other European countries.

List of Interviews

Interviews were conducted during autumn 2005 and winter 2006 with representatives of the following Swedish trade unions:

LO affiliates	Byggnads, the Building Workers' Union Elektrikerförbundet, the Electricians' Union Fastighets, the Building Maintenance Workers' Union Handels, the Commercial Employees' Union Hotell- och Restaurang, the Hotel and Restaurant Workers' Union Industrifacket, the Industrial Union Kommunal, The Municipal Workers' Union Metall, the Metalworkers' Union SEKO, the Union for Service and Communications Employees Skogs- och Träfacket, the Swedish Forest and Wood Trade Union Transport, the Transport Workers' Union
TCO affiliates	HTF, the Salaried Employees' Union HTF Finansförbundet, the Financial Sector Union of Sweden

Note: In January 2006, Metall, the Metalworkers' Union and Industrifacket, the Industrial Union, merged to form IF Metall.

References

BAO and Finansförbundet (2005), Agreement on Competence Development, Stockholm.

Blomqvist, P. and Murhem, S. (eds.) (2003), "Fackliga strategier för att möta globalisering och regionalisering inom metallindustrin. En jämförande studie av fyra nordiska länder", *Working Life Research in Europe*, No.3: 2003, The National Institute for Working Life, Stockholm.

Bruun, N. (2003), "Aktuella trender i arbetsrätten, in von Otter, C. (ed.) Ute och inne i svenskt arbetsliv. Forskare analyserar och spekulerar om trender i framtidens arbete", *Arbetsliv i omvandling*, No.2003: 8, The National Institute for Working Life, Stockholm.

Bryman, A. (2002), *Samhällsvetenskapliga metoder*, Liber Ekonomi, Malmö.

Colclough, C. (ed.) (2003), "Liberaliseringens og globaliseringens konsekvenser for de faglige strategier i den nordiske telekommunikationsbranche – en komparativ analyse af de faglige organisationers udfordringer og udvikling i Danmark, Norge, Sverige og Finland", *Working Life Research in Europe*, No.4: 2003, The National Institute for Working Life, Stockholm.

Crouch, C. (1996), "Revised Diversity: From the Neo-liberal Decade to Beyond Maastricht", in Van Ruijsseveldt, J. and Visser, J. (eds.), *Industrial Relations in Europe. Traditions and Transitions*, SAGE, London, pp.358-376.

De Geer, H. (1992), *Arbetsgivarna: SAF i tio decennier*, SAFs förlag, Stockholm.

Elvander, N. (1966), *Intresseorganisationer i dagens Sverige*, CWK Gleerup Bokförlag, Lund.

Elvander, N. (1997), "The Swedish Bargaining System in the Melting Pot", in Elvander, N. and Holmlund, B. (eds.), *The Swedish Bargaining System in the Melting Pot. Institutions, Norms and Outcomes in the 1990s*, The National Institute for Working Life, Solna.

Elvander, N. (2002), "The New Swedish Regime of Collective Bargaining and Conflict Resolution: A Comparative Perspective", *European Journal of Industrial Relations*, Vol.8, No.2, pp.197-216.

Huzzard, T. and Docherty, P. (2005), "Between Global and Local: Eight European Works Councils in Retrospect and Prospect", *Economic and Industrial Democracy*, Vol.26, November 2005, pp.541-568.

Kjellberg, A. (2000), "Arbetsgivarstrategier i Sverige under 100 år", in Strøby Jensen, C. (ed.), *Arbejdsgivere i Norden. En sociologisk analyse af arbejdsgiver-organiseringen i Norge, Sverige, Finland og Danmark*, Nordiska Ministerrådet Nord, Köpenhamn, 2000: 25.

Kjellberg, A. (2001), *Fackliga organisationer och medlemmar i dagens Sverige*, Arkiv Förlag, Lund.

van der Laan, L. and Ruesga, S. (1998), *Institutions and Regional Labour Markets in Europe*, Ashgate, Aldershot.

Magnusson, L. (1997), *Sveriges ekonomiska historia*, Prisma, Stockholm.

Misgeld, K. (1997), *Den fackliga europavägen: LO, det internationella samarbetet och Europas enande 1945-1991*, Atlas, Stockholm.

Murhem, S. and Ottosson, J. (2000), "The Changing Foundations of Swedish Model Labour Market Policies, in Prigge, R., Buchegger, R. and Magnusson, L. (eds.), *Strategien regionaler Beschäftigungsförderung. Schweden, Österreich und Deutschland im Vergleich. 2000*, Campus Verlag, Frankfurt/New York.

Murhem, S. (2003), *Turning to Europe. A New Swedish Industrial Relations Regime in the 1990s*, Acta Universitatis Upsaliensis, Uppsala.

North, D. (1993), *Institutionerna, tillväxterna och välståndet*, SNS förlag, Stockholm.

Nycander, S. (2002), *Makten över arbetsmarknaden. Ett perspektiv på Sveriges 1990-tal*, SNS förlag, Stockholm.

Rothstein, B. (1992), *Den korporativa staten*, Norstedts, Stockholm.

Swenson, P. (2002), *Capitalist against Markets. The Making of Labor Markets and Welfare States in the United States and Sweden*, Oxford University Press, Oxford.

Thelen, K. (2001), "Varieties of Labor Politics in the Developed Democracies", in Hall, P. A. and Soskice, D. (eds.), *Varieties of Capitalism: The Institutional Foundations of Comparative Advantage*, Oxford University Press, Oxford, pp.71-103.

Visser, J. (1996), "Corporatism beyond Repair? Industrial Relations in Sweden", in Van Ruijsseveldt, J. and Visser, J. (eds.), *Industrial Relations in Europe. Traditions and Transitions*, Sage Publications, London.

Annex

Agriculture	Recommendation framework agreement on the improvement of paid employment
	White paper on vocational training
	Guide to health and safety at work
	Agreement on elimination of restriction on access to labour markets in the European Union
Banking	Joint declaration on lifelong learning
Civil aviation	Agreement on organisation of working time of mobile workers
Cleaning	Common positions on employment, undeclared work and enlargement
Commerce	Joint statement on combating violence
	Joint statement on combating child labour
	Joint declaration against racism
	Joint agreement on fundamental rights and principles at work
	Joint statement on combating racism and xenophobia
	Joint agreement on teleworking
	Joint agreement on guidelines for age diversity
	Joint statement on corporate social responsibility
Construction	Joint declaration on employment
	Guide to best practices for coordination in the field of health and safety.
	Joint declaration concerning the posting of workers
Electricity	Joint declaration on the implications of the internal electricity market
	Joint declaration on the social implications of the restructuring of the electricity market in the candidate countries
	Joint declaration on telework
	Joint declaration on equal opportunities/diversity
Footwear	Code against child labour
	Updated
	Common position in relation to the new European social agenda
	Code of conduct
	Co-signed by footwear distribution
Horeca and tourism	Joint declaration on the promotion of employment in the hotel and restaurant sector
	Joint declaration on the effects of VAT
	Joint declaration in favour of reduced VAT
	Common position on the Commission communication on tourism
	Comments on corporate social responsibility
Live performance	Joint declaration on lifelong learning
Local and regional government	Joint declaration on equal opportunities

Mines	Joint declaration on social policy aspects of the new rules for aid to the coal industry
	Joint declaration concerning draft European directive on waste management
	Joint declaration concerning draft European directive on emissions trading
	Joint declaration on lifelong learning
Personal services/ Hairdressing	Code of conduct Guidelines for European hairdressers
Postal services	Agreement promoting employment in the postal sector
	Joint opinions
Private security	Joint declaration on mutual recognition and social dialogue
	Joint declaration on harmonisation of legislation
	Code of conduct and ethics
Railways	Memorandum ensuring social partners' involvement in technical specifications for interoperability
Road transport	Joint opinion in support of legislative initiative concerning third country drivers
Sea fishing	Social clause to be inserted in protocols to fisheries agreements between EU and third countries
	Joint opinion on Commission on future common fisheries policy
Sea transport	Agreement on organisation of working time of seafarers
	A number of joint declarations, opinions and common positions
Sugar	Joint recommendation Apprenticeships in the sugar sector
	Declaration on less advanced countries
	Common position on rules of origin
	Joint declaration on the impact of enlargement
	Code of conduct (Corporate social responsibility)
Tanning and leather	Joint declaration on training requirements concerning modernisation of work organisation
	Code of conduct
	Joint draft for Lisbon
	Joint draft for Barcelona
Telecommunications	Joint committee including work programme
	Guidelines for telework
	Joint declaration for Lisbon
	Joint statement on telework
Temporary work	Joint declaration on aims of the directive on private-sector temporary employment agencies
Textile and clothing	Code of conduct
	Joint declaration on the establishment of a European monitoring unit for industrial change
	Joint contribution on the Commission's social agenda
Woodworking	Code of conduct

CHAPTER 11

The Challenges of Enlargement

Évelyne LÉONARD, Delphine ROCHET
and Isabelle VANDENBUSSCHE

Introduction

Formally, sectoral social dialogue at European level has existed since the creation of the first joint committee for mines in 1952 (see chapter 2 in this volume). However it has progressively changed, notably with the setting up of the current sectoral social dialogue committees since 1999. In the context of the Lisbon Agenda, the European Commission considers that social dialogue is a key element in the implementation of the Lisbon objectives and, particularly, for social cohesion (CEC, 2004). It promotes the development of social dialogue in all Member States and in the candidate countries and insists on sector-level bargaining, which is considered the most efficient for their socio-economic development. In this framework, enlargement of the EU to include Eastern and Central European countries generates at least two types of challenge for sector-level industrial relations.

The first challenge concerns the relevance and feasibility of sectoral industrial relations as a key level of bargaining within the new Member States and the candidate countries. In the former EU-15 countries, the sector constitutes an important and solid bargaining level in almost all instances. By contrast, the new Member States and candidate countries have very different industrial relations systems. In many cases, even if it exists, the sectoral level is under-developed. In other cases, there is simply no social dialogue at this level. The weakness of current sector-level actors, structures and bargaining processes in many new Member States and candidate countries not only increases the diversity of national systems within the enlarged Europe, but actually jeopardises the feasibility and relevance of developing sector-level industrial relations in the enlarged Europe.

The second challenge takes place at European level and derives from the first one. The lack of institutionalised sector-level industrial relations in the new Member States and candidate countries introduces greater complexity and increased difficulties into the possible linkages between national structures and the European sectoral social dialogue committees.

Both types of challenge are examined one by one in this chapter, in the light of recent data collected for the European Commission.

For the first challenge, we summarise the current situation of sector-level collective bargaining in the new Member States and in Bulgaria, Romania and Turkey. This section aims, on the one hand, to identify to what extent the sector constitutes a significant bargaining level in these countries and, on the other, to evaluate whether sector-level industrial relations in these countries could be reinforced as a consequence of their integration into the EU.

Second, this chapter concentrates on the specific difficulties that the European sectoral social dialogue committees have to face with the greater diversity generated by enlargement, in terms of socio-economic interests and the social partners' readiness to cooperate in the European social dialogue, but also with the lack of institutionalised sector-level industrial relations in the countries concerned. This second part of the chapter shows how enlargement generates questions of efficiency and legitimacy for European sectoral committees.

Before that, the section below gives some details on the sources of empirical data used in the chapter and on the perspective adopted.

I. Sources, Data and Perspective

The empirical data presented in this chapter are principally derived from studies conducted over the last five years, for DG Employment and Social Affairs of the European Commission, by a network of national researchers. This network has progressively enlarged to represent all current Member States and three candidate countries – Bulgaria, Romania and Turkey (see note at end of chapter). Croatia has been left aside for the purpose of this chapter as we currently have no comparative data on sectoral bargaining there. The research network has compiled data on the actors, the structures and the processes of collective bargaining in a series of sectors, most often the sectors for which there is a social dialogue committee at European level. Comparable data have been collected over the years, covering nearly thirty branches, ranging from electricity to road transport, and including for instance such sectors as temporary agency work, commerce, industrial cleaning, culture and media (see UCL-IST 2003a, 2003b, 2004a, 2004b and 2004c).

Data on a small number of selected sector cases are presented here. Systematic comparative sectoral data for the new Member States and candidate countries are rare in the literature, and we have seen fit to present information on "sector cases" for which it was possible to obtain recent and comparable information from all the countries. We have also chosen sectors that are illustrative, even if each sector has its own dynamics and cannot be considered as representative of all branches of the economy in each country (Marginson and Traxler, 2005). Finally, we have tried to cover contrasting branches, from industry and services, with a majority of large companies or with a large proportion of small and medium-sized enterprises, with a large or small proportion of undeclared work, as well as former public services and private activities.

In terms of theoretical perspective, this chapter focuses on structures and institutions of collective bargaining, rather than on actors' strategies and ideologies. There are three reasons for this.

The first is that the relevance and potential development of sector-level collective bargaining in the new Member States and candidate countries are currently being heightened by their integration into the European Union. This has increased the heterogeneity among Member States and, moreover, it has introduced into the European Union national systems that contrast strongly with the majority of the existing ones: in thirteen of the fifteen old Member States, the sector plays a dominant or an important role (Visser in CEC, 2004; Schulten, 2005). The entry of the new players modifies this situation, with bargaining structures that are very different, and where the sector level plays a much weaker role. This in turn places new pressures on collective bargaining in branches of industry and services in the EU-15, as these are confronted by changing conditions of competitiveness associated with new challenges for collective bargaining on wages, working time, working conditions and employment (Marginson and Traxler, 2005). This is the first reason why it is interesting to draw a comparative picture of the current situation of sector-level bargaining structures in the new Member States and candidate countries.

There is, secondly, a more political reason. Sector-level bargaining is considered by the European Commission as an important layer of social dialogue at European level but also in the Member States. Additionally, since 1999, more than thirty sectoral social dialogue committees have been set up; their representativeness, their capacity to negotiate, but also their capacity to implement the results of their discussions, depend on their relationships with national actors and bargaining structures in the branches in each country. The fairly recent constitution of sectoral social dialogue committees in their current institutional form follows on from pre-existing joint committees or informal working groups for most sectors (see chapter 2 in this volume). In any event it gives them a similar institutional existence, created in a context where sector-level bargaining played a key role in the majority of Member States. Enlargement has changed this situation and, therefore, raises the question of institutional capacity at sector level in the new Member States: are actors constituted and structured at this level, and if so, what are their characteristics? Do social dialogue committees have counterparts in the new Member States? Are there bargaining arenas in the different sectors that are able to produce collective agreements? What are the relationships between the various bargaining levels in each country?

Thirdly and finally, from a theoretical point of view, it would of course be interesting to focus on the actors' strategies, ideologies, action and relationships. However, structures and actors' strategies develop inter-dependently (Reynaud, 1989): employers' organisations and trade unions create and develop structures, rules and mechanisms to support their action, but they also need structures and institutions to develop their strategies and action. In any case, if one wants to examine the situation of branch-level bargaining in the new Member States, the necessary starting point is to identify the players in the sectors in each country and their potential role in bargaining systems. Besides, the national institutional structures can also be easily observed, and these are interesting because they reveal the previous industrial relations processes, the actors' capacity, strategies and relationships that have progressively contributed – or not contributed – to the constitution of arenas at sector level. In the context of a multi-level analysis (see Hollingsworth, 2002), trying to understand the potential connections between European sectoral committees and national situations, it is interesting to look at the institutional arenas in which unions and employers' organisations negotiate – or do not negotiate – in a comparative way across all the countries. Furthermore, empirical data are available for all the new Member States, while a study on actors' positions and strategies would require a specific research programme.

II. Sector-level Bargaining in the New Member States and Candidate Countries

A. Sectoral Actors

The role of sector-level collective bargaining has been much debated already, especially after Calmfors and Driffill (1988) produced their curve showing that, in economic terms, decentralised or centralised bargaining systems are more efficient, while the intermediary level has adverse effects on economic performance.

Their approach has been much criticised but in fact since then several authors have underlined the importance of the sector in national industrial relations (IR) systems. According to Lallement (1998), the sector has become a more and more relevant intermediary level of negotiation due to the evolution of labour structures, public policy and technological improvements. Marginson and Sisson (2004) also show that increased economic and political interdependence across borders favours some kind of convergence in the same sector in several countries, while there is greater divergence between sectors within a given country.

From a more political point of view, the European Commission and the Council have adopted positions in favour of sector-level bargaining as a key dimension of national IR systems: in the European Commission's words, "the sectoral level is often the most appropriate level for the discussion of many labour market issues, which is why it has traditionally been the predominant level of collective bargaining in many Member States" (CEC, 2004: 71).

However, if sector-level bargaining prevails in a majority of EU-15 countries, this is not the case in the new Member States, and European political support is not sufficient to change actors and structures inherited from the specific historical dynamics within each national industrial relations system.

A number of conditions are required for sector-level collective bargaining to play a significant role in a national system of industrial relations: organisations must be structured, able and willing to act and to negotiate at sectoral level; structures or "arenas" where actors can negotiate – such as joint committees – must have been established; in addition, trade unions and employers' organisations must be endowed with the capacity to sign agreements that define binding rules applicable to companies and workers in the sector, which in turn requires a capacity of enforcement. These rules will be more binding where there is a process for extension, making it possible for a given agreement to become applicable to all companies and workers in the sector, thereby increasing the coverage rate of agreements concluded.

Specific historical dynamics have generated very different actors, structures and strategies within the traditional political, economic and social context of each country. In the majority of EU-15 countries, trade unions and employers' organisations are structured at sectoral level and have a strategy at this level, with bargaining institutions responding to actors' capacity and strategies. Strong bargaining arenas at sectoral level, in turn, reinforce the role that actors wish to play at this level and, accordingly, their own structures and strategies oriented towards sector-level regulation.

By contrast, most of the new Member States and candidate countries are characterised by weak or simply non-existent sector-level bargaining institutions, whereas centralised cross-industry or, at the opposite end of the spectrum, decentralised company-level bargaining prevails. In some of them, sector-level structures exist but with no real bargaining capacity, acting only to exchange points of view.

There are several reasons for this. The first ones have to do with the actors' capacity. In the new Member States, trade unions and employers' organisations are generally not structured or only weakly organised on a sectoral basis, and they have no or few resources to act at this level. Besides, as noted by Cremers (2005) about the construction industry, the autonomy of social partners in these countries is weak and this is related to the predominant role of the State. In Cremers' approach this refers to the construction industry, but the same applies to most other sectors, as studies conducted recently in sectors such as commerce or textiles show (UCL-IST, 2003a and b; 2004a, b and c). Other reasons derive from the actors' strategies. Employers often prefer to maintain negotiations at company level and are consequently reluctant to develop sectoral bargaining and to empower the employers' organisation with the capacity to conclude sector-level agreements. Similarly, the autonomy of company unions may undermine any mandate for negotiation above plant level (Cremers, 2005). In addition, the recognition of freedom of association in the new Member States, which accompanied their economic and political transition, has led in some countries to the emergence of an industrial relations landscape characterised by (extreme) plurality, in contrast with the former "unitarism" (Lado and Vaughan-Whitehead, 2003). This fragmentation does not make multi-employer bargaining any easier. It favours the emergence of inter-union disputes and is "not favourable for moving towards more coordinated, coherent bargaining that would cover an increasing number of workers" (Lado and Vaughan-Whitehead, 2003: 75). Fragmentation itself scatters scarce human and financial resources between the organisations, which reduces their possibility to better structure and organise at this level. As a result, the sector is not a level where strong social dialogue arenas have been set up: as Keller (2005) sums up the situation, the existing organisations are weak in terms of available resources and compete with each other, density ratios are low, coverage rates of sectoral agreements are low on average, and there is no well-developed tradition or practice of collective bargaining at sectoral level in the majority of new Member States.

To give an idea of the sectoral organisations existing in the new Member States and candidate countries, tables 1 and 2 contain a list of social partner organisations – trade unions in table 1 and employers organisations in table 2 – that are active in the road transport sector. The identification of those players was based on the NACE delimitation of economic activity in the road transport sector, namely activities corresponding to NACE code 60.2 entitled "other land transport", covering scheduled passenger land transport, taxi operations, non-scheduled passenger road transport such as occasional coach services or excursions, and freight transport by road. This corresponds to the delimitation of the sector as used at European level by the members of the sectoral social dialogue committee.

The tables also identify the number of members each organisation has and, more interestingly, whether the organisation is organised across the whole sector as defined by the NACE code – and consequently by the European sectoral social dialogue committee – or differently. There are be three possibilities here: a given organisation may play a role for the sector as defined "theoretically" ("sector" column), it may play a role only for part of it ("sub-sector" column), or it may be active in the road transport sector but also for employers or workers from one or more other sectors ("several branches" column).

It is clear from the tables that, in the new Member States and candidate countries, the organisations rarely match the delimitation of NACE 60.2 used at European level. Social partners are generally structured at a lower level: at sub-sector level, one finds organisations covering exclusively either electric tramway, buses, taxi operations, international freight transport or public companies. Or else they cover a broader range of activities, including for example transport by air, water and road.

Table 1: Trade Unions in the Road Transport Sector

Country	Workers' Organisations	Number of Members	Level of Organisation		
		Total (and in Sector)	Sector	Sub-sector	Several Branches
NEW MEMBER STATES					
Cyprus	SEGDAMELIN PEO (Cyprus Agricultural, Forestry, Transport, Port, Seamen and Allied Occupations Trade Union)	8,300 (500)			X
	OMEPEYE – SEK (Federation of Transport, Petroleum and Agricultural Workers – SEK)	6,000 (4,500)			X
Czech Republic	DOSIA (Trade Union of Workers in Transport, Road and Car Repair Services)	19,882 (17,282)			X
	OSD (Transport Workers' Union)	21,250 (19,720)			X
	OSPEA (Trade Union Federation of Electric Tramway and Bus Workers)	700		X	
Estonia	ETTA (Estonian Transport and Road Workers' Trade Union)	4,757 (3,100)			X
Hungary	Road Transport Trade Union	16, 000		X	
	National Organisation of International and Professional Car Drivers	ND		X	
	LIGA Road Transport Trade Unions	ND		X	
	Transportation Workers' Council Association	ND			X
Latvia	No trade union representing road transport workers				
Lithuania	The Lithuanian Federation of Road Transport Workers' Trade Unions	2,081 (1,100)			X
Malta	GWU (General Workers' Union)	47,254 (170)			X
Poland	Trade Union Federation of Transport and Equipment Employees in Construction "Transbud"	1,050		X	
	Federation of Independent Self-Governing Trade Unions of Employees of Polish Bus Service PKS in the Republic of Poland	5,000		X	
	Federation of Independent Self-Governing Trade Unions of Employees of Car Transport in Communication	ND		X	
	PKS Bus Workers' National Section – NSZZ Solidarnosc	17,326		X	
	Transporters' Secretariat of NSZZ "Solidarnosc"	ND	ND	ND	ND
	City Transport Workers' National Section – NSZZ "Solidarnosc"	12,500		X	

Poland	Drivers' Independent Trade Union	ND		X	
	Polish Drivers' Trade Union	5,000		X	
	National Section of Transport – "Solidarnosc 80"	500		X	
	City Transport Workers' Trade Union in Poland	3,687		X	
	Drivers' Independent Trade Union Pekaes Transport	170		X	
	Federation of Trade Unions of City Transport Workers in Poland	4,500		X	
Slovakia	NOZVCD (Independent Trade Union of Public Road Transport)	11,221		X	
	Odborovy zvaz DOPRAVA (Transport Trade Union)	2,928			X
Slovenia	Trade Union for Transport and Communications of Slovenia	10,050			X
CANDIDATE COUNTRIES					
Bulgaria	UTWSB (Union of Transport Workers' Syndicates in Bulgaria)	16,551 (6,093)			X
	Syndicate of Autotransport Workers in Bulgaria	3,300 (3,300)			X
	Federation of Transport Workers "Podkrepa"	6,171 (4,100)			X
Romania	CSNTR (National Trade Union Convention of Transporters from Romania)	150,000 (ND)			X
	STAR (Federation of Romanian Vehicle Transporters' Trade Unions)	30,000	X		
	FNSSR (National Federation of Drivers' Trade Unions from Romania)	15,000		X	
	TRANSLOC Federation	26,000		X	
	Union of Subway and Aviation Trade Unions	5,200 (ND)			X
Turkey	TUMTIS (Turkish Motor Vehicle Workers' Union)	13,271	X		
	Nakliyat-Is (Turkish Progressive Road Transport Workers' Union)	13,746		X	
	Karsan-Is (Union of Transport and Cargo Industry Workers)	759 (ND)			X

Source: UCL-IST (2004c).

Table 2: Employers' Organisations in the Road Transport Sector

Country	Workers' Organisations	Number of Members	Level of Organisation		
		Total (and in Sector)	Sector	Sub-sector	Several Branches
New Member States					
Cyprus	SEAK (Confederation of Professional Motorists of Cyprus)	900		X	
	PEAA (Pancyprian Professional Motorists' Union)	850		X	
	Transport Development Association	52		X	
Czech Republic	SD CR (Transport Union)	143 (64)			X
	SDP CR (Association of Transit Companies of the Czech Republic)	118		X	
Estonia	AL (Union of Estonian Automobile Enterprises)	46	X		
	ERAA (Association of Estonian International Road Hauliers)	450		X	
Hungary	Association of Road Transportation Enterprises	63		X	
	National Association of Haulage	5,500		X	
	National Road Haulage Association	1,750		X	
	Federation of International Transporters	5,000		X	
Latvia	Latvian Association of International Road Hauliers	785		X	
Lithuania	Lithuanian National Road Hauliers' Association "Linava"	630		X	
Malta	Unscheduled Bus Service	32		X	
	Public Transport Association	430		X	
	Coop Services Limited	ND		X	
	Hauliers' Cooperative	45		X	
	GRTU (Association of General Retailers and Traders)	7,000 (90)			X
	White Taxis Amalgamated	170		X	
	Rent-a-car Association	95		X	
Poland	All-Poland Motor Transport Employers' Federation	132		X	
	All-Poland Union of Road Transport Employers	3,670		X	
	Association of International Road Hauliers	4,300		X	

Slovakia	ZAD (Union of Bus and Coach Transport)	17		X	
	Union of City Transport Employers in Bratislava, Kosice and Presov	3		X	
	ADCP (Association of Road Transport Organisations)	26		X	
	Taxi Guild Bratislava	12		X	
	SZZ (Association of Entrepreneurs in Road Car Transportation of the Slovak Republic)	ND		X	
	CESMAD SLOVAKIA (Road Transport Association of the Slovak Republic)	1,600		X	
Slovenia	Transport and Communications Association	2,071 (ND)			X
CANDIDATE COUNTRIES					
Bulgaria	Chamber of National Transport	>500			X
	Bulgarian Autotransport Union	72		X	
Romania	ARTRI (Romanian Association for International Road Transport)	2,058		X	
	UNTRR (National Union of Road Hauliers from Romania)	7,424		X	
	URTP (Romanian Union of Public Transport)	55		X	
	FNPTRR (Romanian Road Transport Employers' National Federation)	3,052		X	
Turkey	Road Transport Carriers, Transport Commission Agents and Transport Contractors Employers' Association	132		X	

ND: No data
Source: UCL-IST (2004c).

The road transport example shows how fragmented social partners can be, and to what extent they may cover circumstances that differ widely from one country to another. In such an apparently well-defined sector, one finds for instance twelve workers' organisations in Poland or seven employers' organisations in Malta, and most organisations cover specific sub-sectors or even, sometimes, one single public enterprise.

Overall, there is a very limited number of organisations that cover the theoretical definition of road transport activity, either because they cover only one sub-sector, as is the case in Malta or Latvia, or because they cover a much wider range of activities, as can be observed for trade unions in Cyprus and Slovenia.

The road transport example is not necessarily representative of all economic activities. Nevertheless it illustrates a situation that can also be found in commerce, telecommunications, textiles and other sectors.

One must add that the partners do not necessarily have the same organisational demarcation lines from one country to another, or between their national and European organisational structures. In the construction sector, for example, employers' organisations may be a federation of individual employers or entrepreneurs or else a confederation. On the workers' side, the organisation may be active at national level as an umbrella body of in-company unions or of organisations for the different trades. The structure can also vary: unions may be organised along industry lines or represent several industries; they may be structured according to occupational categories (see Visser in CEC, 2004). Thus, individual workers may either be affiliated directly or via company or regional structures (Clarke *et al.*, 2003).

In sum, referring to "sectoral social partners" can be misleading, as it may suggest an image of well-structured players who have a similar role and identity in the different national situations. Beyond a general label identifying "one sector", or beyond the economic delimitation given by the NACE codes, there is a variety of organisational realities. This must be kept in mind as we turn our attention to bargaining processes and outcomes.

B. Bargaining Levels and Outcomes

Looking at the various bargaining levels in the new Member States and candidate countries, the data from the literature generally show that in most countries, the sector is of minor relevance in bargaining, whereas the company is the most significant arena. Table 3 below is compiled from two recent reports published by the European Commission (Visser in CEC, 2004) and the European Foundation (Schulten, 2005), and indicates the relative importance of each level for wage bargaining in the different countries.

Table 3: Levels of Collective Wage Bargaining

Country	Intersectoral Level	Sectoral Level	Company Level
NEW MEMBER STATES (Sources: Visser in CEC, 2004; Schulten, 2005)			
Cyprus			
– Visser		***	*
– Schulten		*	***
Czech Republic		*	***
Estonia		*	***
Hungary	*	*	***
Latvia		*	***
Lithuania		*	***
Malta		*	***
Poland		*	***
Slovakia			
– Visser	*	**	**
– Schulten		***	*
Slovenia			
– Visser	**	**	*
– Schulten	***	*	*
CANDIDATE COUNTRIES (Sources: Schulten 2005 for Bulgaria and Romania; own research for Turkey)			
Bulgaria	*	***	*
Romania		*	***
Turkey			***

Note: * = existing level; ** = important but not dominant level: *** = dominant level of wage bargaining. For some countries (Cyprus, Slovak Republic, Slovenia), the two sources show divergent data; we have indicated both findings wherever they are different. For Bulgaria and Romania, the data come from Schulten 2005 only.

Even if there is some divergence in interpretation between the sources, the main observation is clear: in the new Member States, sector-level bargaining is clearly not the dominant level, except in two countries – Cyprus and Slovakia – where it may be of more importance; even in these cases, the data are not convergent. Of the three candidate countries, Bulgaria is the only one where the sector plays a key role in the structure of the industrial relations system. In eight other countries – Czech Republic, Estonia, Hungary, Latvia, Lithuania, Malta, Poland and Romania – the sectoral level simply co-exists with another dominant level which, in all cases, is the company level. In Turkey, the sector is simply not mentioned as an existing bargaining level. Finally, Slovenia is the exception, with both cross-industry and sector-level bargaining.

This concerns wage bargaining only, and in some countries the findings have to be considered in the light of tripartite processes that operate at national level but do not cover wage issues.

Looking at a specific sector gives us a clearer picture of the situation. Table 4 presents the situation in the textile industry, based on data collected in 2003. The textile example indicates that, even where actors are structured at sectoral level, it does not mean that collective bargaining takes place and leads to agreements at this level.

Table 4: Bargaining and Outcomes at Sectoral Level in the Textile Industry

Country	Countries where …					
	There are organisations structured at sectoral level	There is a sectoral arena for bargaining	At least one organisation on each side has a formal capacity to negotiate at sectoral level	Social dialogue takes place	Collective agreements are signed	Coverage rate of agreements in the sector (%)
New Member States						
Cyprus	X	X	X	X	X	70
Czech Rep.	X	X	X	X	X	93
Estonia	X	X				
Hungary	X	X	X	X		
Latvia	X					
Lithuania	X					
Malta						
Poland	X	X		X		
Slovakia	X	X	X	X	X	56 (estimate)
Slovenia	X	X	X	X	X	100
Candidate countries						
Bulgaria	X	X	X	X	X	15
Romania	X	X	X	X	X	100
Turkey	X	X	X	X	X	< 30

Source: UCL-IST (2003b).

For this sector, in all the countries except three – Latvia, Lithuania and Malta – there are structures where social partners can meet at sectoral level. However, in the new Member States collective agreements are concluded in only four countries – Cyprus, Czech Republic, Slovakia and Slovenia – and with a coverage rate of over 50% in the sector. In the candidate countries, by contrast, sectoral structures produce agreements in all three countries listed here, but in Bulgaria and Turkey they cover a minority of workers in the sector.

Electricity affords another interesting example, different from the textile industry in that it is a former publicly owned activity, with a concentration of large companies and no or very marginal undeclared work. Here our information shows that, even in a sector as institutionalised as electricity, company-level bargaining is more frequent than sectoral bargaining, and in five of the thirteen countries considered in the table there are no collective agreements concluded at sectoral level.

Table 5: Collective Bargaining in the Electricity Sector

Country	Level(s) of Bipartite Social Dialogue			Countries where agreements have been concluded at sectoral level
	Sector	Company	Other	
NEW MEMBER STATES				
Cyprus		X (only 1 company in sector)		X
Czech Republic	X	X		X
Estonia		X		
Hungary	X	X		X
Latvia		X		
Lithuania		X		
Malta		X		
Poland	X	X	Region	X
Slovakia	X	X		X
Slovenia	X	X	Sub-sector	X
CANDIDATE COUNTRIES				
Bulgaria		X	Sub-sector	X
Romania	X	X		X
Turkey		X	Workplace	

Source: UCL-IST (2004b).

It is clear from the tables above that in some countries branch-level industrial relations are not only "under-developed", as stated by the European Commission (CEC, 2004), but much more than that: in some countries they are quasi or totally non-existent.

Accordingly, if we look at bargaining levels, the role played by the sectoral level varies across a very wide range of possibilities:

– at one end of the continuum, we find a "classic" sector-level social dialogue, with trade unions and employers' organisations that are structured at sectoral level and have the capacity and willingness to negotiate at this level, with bargaining processes that lead to the conclusion of collective agreements laying down binding rules that must be implemented in all or some workplaces in the sector. This is the case, typically, in Slovenia, generally considered as constituting an exception in the IR systems of the new Member States.

– at the other end of the continuum, the actors are not structured at sectoral level, or they are structured but do not have the capacity to negotiate at this level, there is no joint committee or arena where they could negotiate, and as a result no agreements are negotiated or (obviously) concluded. In this case, collective bargaining takes place at national central level, either on a bipartite cross-industry basis, or in tripartite processes. Several new Member States have inherited such a centralised system from their former regime. In other countries, the key point for bargaining is at company or even plant level, with very decentralised and ultimately weakly coordinated bargaining systems. Estonia illustrates such a situation where sector-level social dialogue is nearly absent.

C. Prospects for Reinforcement?

Is there any potential for future reinforcement of branch-level bargaining in the new Member States and candidate countries? Their integration into the European Union brings new exogenous factors that are likely to favour transformation. These factors are of two different but complementary kinds: they derive from European integration as such, that generates new rules and practices for economic activities as well as for social dialogue, notably by means of strong support for capacity-building by sector-level actors and for the activities of European sectoral social dialogue committees. They also derive from the new interactions between countries, and especially, for sector-level economic and social actors, greater interdependence between countries (Lallement, 1998; Marginson and Sisson, 2004) and trade union attempts to increase coordination (Marginson and Traxler, 2005). This increased interdependence generates convergence at sectoral level across countries, but not harmonisation across all countries and sectors.

The question here is, then, to what extent are there in the new Member States and candidate countries existing sector-level structures that could be strengthened through European support or could converge towards a European model? Conversely, this raises a political issue: is it relevant, and furthermore, is it realistic, to try to promote, or reinforce, sectoral social dialogue in the new Member States and candidate countries? If, in the course of history, for various reasons the unions and employers' organisations have not considered it fruitful to negotiate on a sectoral basis, or have not reached a consensus on this, or else have not had the possibility to do so, is it realistic to consider that they will change their behaviour and suddenly find the capacity to organise and negotiate at this level, perhaps at the cost of scaling down the role that other bargaining levels traditionally play? In other words, is there any potential for future convergence of IR systems in the new Member States towards greater importance for sector-level social dialogue?

National IR systems have not developed like a building would, progressively growing step by step following a nicely pre-defined architectural plan. They have developed, like any social system, through the action of their players, that is, their capacity to organise and to act, their strategies, the different competing strategies of the actors involved, their relationships to other actors – and specifically the State – in one word, through socio-historical dynamics. And until the recent process of European integration, this had happened within the specific dynamics of each national system.

In this context, the integration of newcomers into the European Union might give fresh impetus to the structuring or strengthening of sector-level social dialogue. Access to a free market first of all leads to a redefinition of competition and economic conditions in sectors that used to be strongly embedded within national boundaries. Such common economic pressures could favour the convergence of national industrial relations towards a common model. Perhaps surprisingly, liberalisation brings some factors for convergence, for instance in the greater role of some multinational companies that have bought former publicly-owned companies and tend to import their bargaining tradition from abroad. However, it generates divergence too, as economic activity changes with different trends, depending on markets, public policies, wages, etc. Liberalisation also contributes to strengthening employers' reluctance to engage into multi-employer bargaining that would reduce their room for manoeuvre, or more simply to engage into bargaining as such.

Beyond changes in the economic context, other factors such as the activities of European sectoral social dialogue committees, support from the European trade unions and employers' organisations, and European political promotion of social dialogue in the Member States, could all favour convergence towards a sector-level model that has long prevailed in the older Member States.

Nevertheless, even if there are similar exogenous factors, the convergence hypothesis has already lost a lot of influence now that it is clear that convergence has not happened in the "old" Member States of the EU-15. Although common processes are at work and tend to generate some kind of convergence in a given sector across national boundaries, in fact industrial relations remain nationally embedded and preserve their own dynamics.

It is unrealistic, for instance, to imagine that social partners in Turkey will, in the medium term, constitute industry-level bargaining, especially as there is strong resistance from the employers but also political reluctance to engage in any kind of multi-employer bargaining (UCL-IST, 2003a, 2003b, 2004a, 2004b and 2004c). So while there are factors for convergence, the endogenous factors specific to each national IR system remain at work and contribute to maintaining diversity.

This can be observed, once again, in the case of the construction industry. Some national governments do currently encourage the promotion of bipartite social dialogue within the sector, as is the case in Bulgaria and Hungary, while in some other countries (Lithuania, Poland, Romania) there is no active encouragement for social dialogue from the public authorities. Indeed, Cremers (2005) points to a lack of serious political backing for more partnership in the sector. Another point which could be due to divergences between countries is the relationships between the actors themselves. Cooperation or conflict-prone relationships between workers' and employers' organisations can lead to diverse situations and may influence the social dialogue and its results. From a more general point of view, the historical background to the social dialogue must also been taken into account. Countries where, a few years ago, employees were at the same time the owners of the means of production and where the State was the collective employer have a different background and reality than countries which never experienced the planned economy.

In sum, enlargement not only brings greater heterogeneity, with sector-level patterns now varying from one extreme of a continuum to the other, between institutionalised IR at this level and … nothing. It also challenges the coherence across national systems of industrial relations and raises questions about the feasibility, and moreover the legitimacy, of EC projects for the development of sector-level bargaining in the new Member States.

III. Challenges for European Sectoral Social Dialogue

Enlargement also generates new challenges for sectoral social dialogue at European level. The first and most obvious challenge is greater diversity. The second can be described in terms of coordination of multi-level governance, ranging from the European social dialogue committees to in-company practices in the different countries.

A. Diversity and Complexity

Diversity starts with an often underestimated issue, namely the delimitation of each sector as such. For instance, as has been mentioned before, the term "road transport" does not reflect the same reality in Poland, Hungary, Cyprus or the Czech Republic. And this is even more problematical with complex sectors like "personal services" or "live performance". The precise delimitation of a given sector may differ from one country to another, and its definition may moreover vary between the European level and the countries themselves.

This is the case for instance in the textile sector. Basically, the textile industry can be defined as the manufacture of textiles and the manufacture of clothing and furs (NACE DB 17 and 18). However, in some countries – Bulgaria, Czech Republic, Malta, Romania, Slovakia, Slovenia – the manufacture of leather and leather products (NACE DC 19) is also included, which in industrial relations terms means that trade union and employers' organisations tend to be structured so that their scope of activity includes companies classified under sub-section DC 19. Consequently, this sub-section is included in social dialogue in the "textile" sector (UCL-IST, 2003b).

The heterogeneity in the delimitation of a specific sector not only creates complexity because it increases the number of different situations that European social partners have to represent, but also because unions and employers' organisations at both European and national level deal with contrasting situations. How can a consensus be reached when the different actors speak about different realities? That is one of the reasons why Keller (2005) argues that at European level sub-sectoral dialogues might be more promising, as actors' interests would be more homogeneous and easier to aggregate.

However, heterogeneity not only stems from the actors but also from the diverse trajectories that a similar sector can follow from one country to another. This is not the case for all sectors, but some are currently developing in very different ways. The construction industry provides an interesting example here. Cremers considers that "in general there is a rather homogenous definition across Europe of what belongs to the sector" (Cremers, 2005: 359). Circumstances may be similar across countries but they develop differently, posing challenges that are important in a given country but not in the one next door where developments are very different. In the case of the construction industry, the sector is in deep economic crisis in some countries, while it is booming in others (see table 6). Moreover, the sector is composed of a multitude of small companies, as the majority have fewer than ten employees; in some countries such as Cyprus, the Czech Republic, Malta and Slovakia, between 65% and 90% of all enterprises in the sector have no employees at all, and work only with self-employment. In this sector and in these countries, there is a large proportion of undeclared work. In all of them, privatisation is almost total. In such a context, issues such as wages, working time, training and education, or health and safety, are viewed differently, and trying to reach common solutions on a European basis constitutes a highly complex challenge.

It is becoming more and more difficult to envisage common solutions on a European basis.

Table 6: Socio-economic Characteristics in the Construction Sector

Country	Economic trend	Predominant companies (size)
NEW MEMBER STATES		
Cyprus	Decline	Self-employed
Czech Republic	Decline	Self-employed companies*
Estonia	Growth	Companies with <20 employees
Hungary	Growth	Companies with <5 employees
Latvia	Growth	Companies with <50 employees
Lithuania	Growth	ND
Malta	Growth	Self-employed companies
Poland	Decline	Companies with <10 employees
Slovakia	Decline	Self-employed companies
Slovenia	Growth	Companies with <50 employees
CANDIDATE COUNTRIES		
Bulgaria	Growth	Companies with <10 employees
Romania	Growth	Companies with <10 employees
Turkey	Decline	Companies with <10 employees

* Data available only on the structure of registered units in construction (Sector F) according to the following three forms: self-employed, commercial companies and cooperatives, State firms and miscellaneous (as at 31/12/2003).

Source: UCL-IST (2004a).

Lastly, the different degrees of capacity or readiness of national trade unions and employers' organisations to participate in developing European social dialogue can also contribute to the huge diversity between Member States. Indeed, some governments had difficulty in convincing their public opinion of the importance for the country of joining the European Union. Beyond the socio-economic interest – or lack of it – in acceding to the European Union, employers' and workers' organisations can be reluctant to develop new institutions that would erode their newly-gained sovereignty. Some sections of the public in the new Member States and candidates countries have a negative opinion about the European Union as regards specific topics like agricultural policies or religion for instance. It is unrealistic to believe that all social partners – or at least most of them – in the new Member States and candidate countries will adopt an attitude in favour of "more Europe", and specifically in favour of further developments in European social dialogue, if one considers the anti-Europe ideology present in some countries. Accepting, and even more, supporting, European sectoral social dialogue requires that organisations within the country go along with both European integration and multi-employer industrial relations, which is clearly not the case in all trade unions and all employers' organisations in those countries.

B. Coordination of Multi-level Governance

The second challenge for European sectoral committees concerns coordination of multi-level social dialogue, from European to local company level. This can be divided into three questions.

First, to what extent are the European sectoral social partners representative of national actors? Do European trade unions and employers' organisations represent members in all the countries and, moreover, do they have national counterparts who are organised on a sectoral basis? The Commission has already identified a difficulty here, particularly on employers' side:

> While some European social partners organisations have members in virtually all of the new Member States, others have none at all. In general, the trade unions have found it easier to identify counterparts than employers, partly as a result of the fact that following the dismantling of the former planned economies, employers' organisations are a new phenomenon in many of these countries. Indeed, historically, the legitimate actors on the employer side were the chambers of commerce and industry (CEC, 2004: 87).

One must note here that many workers' organisations already existed in the last century – before being restored in the early 1990s in most cases. In Lithuania for instance, while the trade union organisation of construction workers began to be established at the end of the 19th century and was registered in 1921, the builders' federation was formally registered in 1995, after the 24 largest construction companies joined forces in 1993 with the approval of the Lithuanian Government.

Tables 7 and 8 give an indication of the situation in the commerce sector, country by country. Due to the great difficulty of collecting reliable data in most of the new Member States and in the candidate countries, the information in the tables should be read very cautiously, and particularly the figures on the number of members, since these are most often an estimation. Even with this restriction in mind though, the tables indicate the huge diversity among organisations, and the diverse situation in terms of national organisations' affiliation to European social partners. On the employers' side in particular the situation is highly complex, with organisations – chambers of commerce, craft associations or employers' federations – playing different roles in collective bargaining and in industrial relations in general; their members also include very different types of companies, ranging from self-employed and very small enterprises to large retail groups, and they are affiliated to different European organisations. The commerce example illustrates the structural difficulty of organising supranational representation covering both large multinational retail groups and archipelagos of very small companies (on employers' organisations, see also chapter 9 in this volume). Independently of any political strategy or of organisations' strategies, the actors' structure and identity make European-scale coordination considerably more complex. The fact that national organisations are affiliated to European social partners, moreover, does not mean that they are ready to give a mandate to European players to determine regulation that would have an impact in each country.

Table 7: Commerce – Trade Unions and Their Affiliation to European Social Partners

Country	Organisation	English translation of name	Number of members	Number of members in the sector	European affiliation(s)
NEW MEMBER STATES					
Cyprus	SEBETTYK	Cyprus industrial, commercial, press-printing and general service workers' trade union	7,000	5,000	UNI-Europa
	SEK	Federation of clerical and commercial employees	6,500	4,000	UNI-Europa
	DEOK	Democratic trade union of commercial and industrial employees	1,000	100	/
Czech Republic	OSPO	Union of commercial employees	17,678	ND	UNI-Europa
	CMOS PHCR	Czech-Moravian trade union of catering, hotels and tourism	2,721	ND	EFFAT
Estonia	ETKA	Estonian trade union of commercial and servicing employees	840	840	UNI-Europa
Hungary	KASZ	Commercial employees' trade union	21,000 (+9,000 inactive)	18,000	UNI-Europa
Latvia	LTUC	Latvian trade union of commerce	3,806	3,806	UNI-Europa

Lithuania	Lietuvos komercijos ir kooperacijos darbuotoju profesine sajunga	Lithuanian trade union of commercial and cooperative employees	2,666	2,666	UNI-Europa NFU HK Danish Funktionfor-bund Swedish confederations Handel HTF
Malta	/	/	/	/	/
Poland	No data for the Commerce sector				
Slovakia	OZPOCR SR	Trade union of employees in commerce and tourism	20,000	20,000	UNI-Europa
Slovenia	Sindikat delavcev trgovine Slovenije	Trade union of commerce of Slovenia	28,000 (+ unemployed)	28,000	UNI-Europa
	Konfederacija 90	Confederation 90	40,000	ND	/
CANDIDATE COUNTRIES					
Bulgaria	Nezavisima SindiKalna Federatzia na Turgoviata, Kooperatziite, Turisma, Kredita I Obshtestvenoto Obsluzhvane	Independent trade union federation of commerce, cooperatives, tourism, credit and social services	About 6,000	2,502	UNI-Europa
	Federatzia Turgovia KT "Podkrepa"	Federation of commerce "Podkrepa" CL	2,100	2,100	UNI-Europa
Romania	FSLC	Federation of free trade unions of commerce	ND	ND	UNI-Europa
	CONSINCOOP	National confederation of trade unions from consumer cooperatives	17,197	17,197	/
Turkey	Tez-Koop-Is	Union of commerce, cooperatives, education, office and fine arts workers of Turkey	62,377	2,200	UNI-Europa

	Türkiye Kooperatif ve Büro Isçileri Sendikası (Koop-Is)	Union of cooperative and office workers of Turkey	46,157	ND	/
	Türkiye Sosyal Sigortalar, Egitim, Büro, Ticaret, Kooperatif ve Güzel Sanatlar Isçileri Sendikası (Sosyal-Is)	Union of social insurance, education, office, commerce, cooperative and fine arts workers of Turkey	43,914	ND	/

Source: UCL-IST (2003a).

Table 8: Commerce – Employers' Organisations and Their Affiliation to European Social Partners

Country	Organisation	English translation of name	Number of members	Number of members in the sector	European affiliation(s)
New Member States					
Cyprus	KEVE	Cyprus chamber of commerce and industry	8,000	255,000	Eurochambres ABC UEAPME ETPO
	OEV	Employers' and manufacturers' federation	4,500	155,000	UNICE
	POVEK	Cyprus federation of small-scale industry, craftsmen and shopkeepers	8,000	ND	Applied in 2003 to UEAPME
Czech Republic	SOCR CR	Czech confederation of commerce and tourism	4,020	ND	UGAL EUROMETAL EuroHandel Institut
Estonia	EKL	Estonian society of merchants	35	ND	/
Hungary	AFEOSZ	National federation of general consumer cooperatives	1,317	100,000	EURO-COOP
	KISOSZ	National federation of traders and caterers	35,000	20,000	/
	Orsàgos Kereskedelmi Szövetség	National trade association	300	100,000	Euro-Commerce
Latvia	LTA	Latvian traders' association	1,000	ND	ND

Lithuania	Lietuvos prekybos imoniu asociacija	Lithuanian association of trade undertakings	53	15,000-18,000	/
Malta	GRTU	Association of general retailers and traders	Mainly self-employed	Mainly self-employed	Eurocommerce UEAPME
Poland	No data for the Commerce sector				
Slovakia	Zvaz obchodu SR	Association of trade companies and training organisations	64	ND	Eurocommerce
	Coop Jednota Slovensko	Association of cooperatives	ND	13,500	EURO-COOP
Slovenia	Zdruzenje za trgovino	The trade association	ND	ND	/
Candidate countries					
Bulgaria	Suyuz na Targovtzite v Bulgaria	Federation of traders in Bulgaria	35	2,000	/
Romania	ANPACT.RO	National association of owners and administrators of commercial complexes, fairs and markets of Romania	500	5,400	/
	ANPCDI	National association of employers' organisations from commerce, distribution and real estate activities	ND	ND	/
Turkey	Kamu Isletmeleri Isverenleri Sendikası (KAMU-Is)	Union of employers of public enterprises	1	ND	/

Source: UCL-IST (2003a).

The second question stems directly from the first one: how can sectoral social dialogue committees negotiate for widely diverse situations and produce agreements, or at least joint declarations that go beyond very general guidelines? As Pochet shows after analysing 353 documents issued by the sectoral committees, a vast majority of them are common positions or declarations: "Therefore, if we interpret the social dialogue restrictively as the negotiation of binding agreements, "agreements" constitute fewer than 2% of all texts" (Pochet, 2005: 321).

Thirdly and finally, how can the rules – be they of a soft or hard nature – emerging from the European sector-level social dialogue be implemented within the countries, especially where there are no equivalent sector-level organisational structures? The concrete translation of joint texts and declarations in the reality of one sector's activity needs some form of coordination with national structures. This difficulty has been acknowledged by the European Commission already:

> These weaknesses [in IR in new Member States] pose a challenge in terms of the effective participation of the social partners from the new Member States in the European social dialogue, including their ability to implement and monitor new generation texts effectively, and their capacity to make use of the possibility provided in some EU directives for certain provisions to be implemented by collective bargaining (CEC, 2004: 76).

Here again, the fact that many new Member States have no significant structures for sector-level bargaining constitutes an obstacle. And it is obvious that national players are not necessarily aware of the existence of those texts, they are not necessarily willing to implement them, and they do not necessarily agree with their national counterparts to do so, all of this generating a very high degree of uncertainty about implementation.

In sum, enlargement brings new challenges for the development and vitality of the European sectoral social dialogue. Enlargement has in fact been conducted in parallel with the development since 1999 of the "new-look" European social dialogue committees. With enlargement, these committees face greater heterogeneity in the national situations that they have to cover. Enlargement, therefore, poses challenges for European sectoral committees in terms of their capacity for action, given the great difficulty of defining a common agenda likely to be relevant enough to reflect apples and pears. In addition, the absence of sectoral bargaining mechanisms in some new Member States can weaken the European sectoral social dialogue because it impedes the implementation of European sectoral agreements at national level. This also jeopardises the representativeness of organisations belonging to the committees at European level. Analysing the construction industry, Cremers concludes that the development of social dialogue at EU level "has to be based on effective national organisations that have the mandate and capacity to talk to and negotiate with each other at supranational level" (Cremers, 2005: 362). Although to some extent the development of sectoral social dialogue committees confirms the importance of branch-level industrial relations in Europe, their efficiency, but also their legitimacy, depends on the support they receive from structures at national level. And these structures, once again, have very different roles or even, in some countries, simply do not exist.

Conclusion

Along with current developments in the European sectoral social dialogue, enlargement brings new challenges, with the integration into the EU of national IR systems with weak or non-existent sector-level industrial relations.

The first challenge for sectoral industrial relations in Europe concerns the relevance and feasibility of sector-level industrial relations as a key level of bargaining within countries. The picture for all new Member States is generally very pessimistic, sectoral social dialogue being considered "weak", "under-developed", "poor" or "rare". In reality, the situation of sector-level bargaining varies between the two extreme ends of a continuum: at one end, structured and active social dialogue resulting in agreements covering a significant part of a sector's population; at the other, no sector-level actors or weak actors, no bargaining, no agreements.

The first end of the continuum, however, is the exception rather than the rule. In most countries, sectoral social dialogue is hampered by the characteristics of the actors themselves: they are often weak and fragmented, they do not have sufficient resources and capacity, their autonomy is restricted by the role of the State, they do not have the willingness or strategy to negotiate at sectoral level, they lack the tradition and "know-how required to do so, and finally there are conflicting views between unions and employers, but also between the different trade unions and the various employers' organisations. Accordingly, sectoral bargaining structures theoretically exist in all countries except Turkey, but in practice they are not very active, or produce no agreements, or else only result in agreements with low coverage rates.

Consequently, this generates a very uncertain interaction between European social dialogue committees and national industrial relations structures. This constitutes the second challenge: a challenge to the efficiency of European social dialogue. On the one hand, it is obviously confronted by greater diversity: specific historical dynamics have generated very different actors, structures and strategies within the traditional political, economic and social context specific to each country. This affects the very definition of what is known as "sectoral social dialogue". Indeed, differences can occur in the delimitation of the activities belonging to the sector, a similar sector can follow diverse trajectories from one country to another, the characteristics of organisations taking part in collective bargaining vary considerably, and more generally, bargaining structures in the different contexts do not correspond to one another.

This produces greater complexity and increased difficulties in the possible linkages between national structures and the European sectoral social dialogue committees. Enlargement has brought at least four new difficulties into the equation: European social partners now have to deal with very divergent economic and social situations in one and the same sector across all the countries; they can hardly get a clear and strong mandate from fragmented, weak and potentially reluctant national organisations; they face greater difficulty in coordinating disparate organisations that face, themselves, very contrasting situations; finally, the implementation of the texts issued by the sectoral social dialogue committees faces huge uncertainty if it depends on an active role being played by the corresponding national bodies.

Sector-level collective bargaining is weak in the new Member States and candidate countries: this much is clear, but an optimist would consider that European integration will favour convergence towards a more "EU-15 style" of industrial relations. Common exogenous factors could favour some convergence. However, this has not been the case for the EU-15 countries, which have not lost the most specific features of their industrial relations. Why would new the Member States and candidate countries, starting from an even more diverse and much weaker sectoral bargaining situation, converge towards a common sector-level approach? Similarly, promotion, information and training will not be sufficient to change national dynamics, as actors and structures are deeply embedded in national socio-economic and political contexts. The challenges will remain for a few more years.

Note

The network collecting the data on which this chapter is based was composed, from 2003 to 2005, of the following members in the new Member States and candidate countries:

- Bulgaria: Rumiana Gladicheva, Institute for Social Analyses and Policies;
- Cyprus: Evros I. Demetriades, Department of Economics, University of Cyprus;
- Czech Republic: Ales Kroupa and Jaroslav Hala, Research Institute for Labour and Social Affairs;
- Estonia: Kaia Philips and Raul Eamets, Institute of Economics, University of Tartu;
- Hungary: Andras Toth, Institute of Political Sciences, Hungarian Academy of Sciences (in 2004); Csaba Makó, Péter Csizmadia and Miklós Illéssy, Hungarian Academy of Sciences Institute of Sociology, Research Group for Organisation and Work;
- Latvia: Alf Vanags, Svetlana Sevcenko and Julia Pobyarzina, Baltic International Centre for Economic Policy Studies (BICEPS);
- Lithuania: Mark Chandler, Stockholm School of Economics in Riga and Baltic International Centre for Economic Policy Studies (BICEPS);
- Malta: Saviour Rizzo and Manwel Debono, Centre for Labour Studies, University of Malta;

- Poland: Pierre Grega, DRIS (Développement, Réhabilitation, Intégration et Sécurité) sprl;
- Romania: Ion Glodeanu, Institute of Sociology, Romanian Academy;
- Slovak Republic: Lubica Bajzikova and Helena Sajgalikova, Faculty of Management, Comenius University in Bratislava;
- Slovenia: Alenka Krasovec and Miroslav Stanojevic, Faculty of Social Sciences, University of Ljubljana;
- Turkey: Engin Yildirim and Suayyip Calis, Faculty of Economics and Administrative Sciences, Department of Labour Economics and Industrial Relations, Sakarya University.

References

Calmfors, L. and Driffill, J. (1988), "Bargaining Structure, Corporatism and Macroeconomic Performance", *Economic Policy*, No.6, April 1988, pp.16-61.

CEC (2004), *Industrial Relations in Europe 2004*, Office for the Official Publications of the European Communities, Luxembourg.

Clarke, L., Cremers, J. and Janssen, J. (2003), "EU Enlargement, Construction Labour Relations as a Pilot", *CLR Studies*, No.1, European Institute for Construction Labour Research, Reed Business Information, The Hague.

Cremers, J. (2005), "Social Dialogue in the European Construction Industry", *Transfer*, Vol.11, No.3, Autumn 2005, pp.359-362.

Hollingsworth, J. R. (2002) "On Multi-level Analysis" in Hollingsworth, J. R., Muller, K. H. and Hollingsworth, E. J. (eds.), *Advancing Socio-economics, An Institutionalist Perspective*, Rowman & Littlefield, Lantham, MD, pp.19-35.

Keller, B. (2005), "Europeanisation at Sectoral Level. Empirical Findings and Missing Perspectives", *Transfer*, Vol.11, No.3, Autumn 2005, pp.398-408.

Lado, M. and Vaughan-Whitehead, D. (2003), "Social Dialogue in Candidate Countries: What For?", *Transfer*, Vol.9, No.1, pp.64-87.

Lallement, M. (1998), "Relations professionnelles et emploi: du niveau à la configuration", *Sociologie du Travail*, No.2/98, pp.209-231.

Marginson, P. and Sisson, K. (2004), *European Integration and Industrial Relations, Multi-level Governance in the Making*, Palgrave Macmillan, Basingstoke.

Marginson, P. and Traxler, F. (2005) "After Enlargement: Preconditions and Prospects for Bargaining Coordination", *Transfer*, Vol.11, No.3, Autumn 2005, pp.423-438.

Pochet, P. (2005), "Sectoral Social Dialogue. A Quantitative Analysis", *Transfer*, Vol.11, No.3, Autumn 2005, pp.313-332.

Reynaud, J.-D. (1989), *Les règles du jeu. L'action collective et la régulation sociale*, Armand Colin, Paris.

Schulten, T. (2005), "Changes in National Collective Bargaining Systems Since 1990", *Eironline* (http://www.eiro.eurofound.eu.int/print/2005/03/study/tn0503102s.html).

UCL-IST (2003a), "Monographs on the Situation of Social Partners in Acceding and Candidate Countries: Commerce", Research project conducted on behalf of DG Employment and Social Affairs of the European Commission,

Institut des Sciences du Travail, Université catholique de Louvain (online at http://www.trav.ucl.ac.be/research/presentation.html).

UCL-IST (2003b), "Monographs on the Situation of Social Partners in Acceding and Candidate Countries: Textiles", Research project conducted on behalf of DG Employment and Social Affairs of the European Commission, Institut des Sciences du Travail, Université catholique de Louvain (online at http://www.trav.ucl.ac.be/research/presentation.html).

UCL-IST (2004a), "Monographs on the Situation of Social Partners in the New Member States and Candidate countries: Construction", Research project conducted on behalf of DG Employment and Social Affairs of the European Commission, Institut des Sciences du Travail, Université catholique de Louvain (online at http://www.trav.ucl.ac.be/research/presentation.html).

UCL-IST (2004b), "Monographs on the Situation of Social Partners in the New Member States and Candidate Countries: Electricity", Research project conducted on behalf of DG Employment and Social Affairs of the European Commission, Institut des Sciences du Travail, Université catholique de Louvain (online at http://www.trav.ucl.ac.be/research/presentation.html).

UCL-IST (2004c), "Monographs on the Situation of Social Partners in the New Member States and Candidate Countries: Road Transport", Research project conducted on behalf of DG Employment and Social Affairs of the European Commission, Institut des Sciences du Travail, Université catholique de Louvain (online at: http://www.trav.ucl.ac.be/research/presentation.html).

Conclusion

Christophe DEGRYSE and Philippe POCHET

The analysis of the sectoral social dialogue which we have attempted to conduct in this volume has enabled us to highlight the headway made in this dialogue but also, and above all, its limitations. We have concentrated mainly on the output of joint texts and established a typology of five groups of sectors, each of which produces a particular type of document. The players in sectors which are in decline and heavily exposed to international competition handle the industrial and employment crisis by producing "codes of conduct"; those in sectors covered by integrated Community policies attempt to build a European tier of industrial relations, in some cases even managing to sign agreements (in the narrow sense of the term). The players in sectors forced to interconnect with one another, where there is a tradition of partnership, manage deregulation/privatisation by opening up space for negotiation and producing mostly recommendations. Traditional sectors confine themselves to a more "conservative" social dialogue while searching for some truly European "substance". Finally, those sectors seeking to enhance their image construct such European "substance" with varying degrees of success, in certain instances by creating a sort of European quality label, trying to devise codes of conduct not based on ILO standards (ethical, for example). The commerce sector (and to a lesser extent local government) is a separate case, experimenting with a variety of social dialogue instruments in a bid to better highlight its specific characteristics.

These findings do not deal exhaustively with the question of the creation of transnational players – far from it. Mobilisation capacity (strikes, joint activities, coordinated action) has not been explored in this volume; nor has the coordination of wage bargaining, an important activity in certain sectors, especially metalworking. Furthermore, the effectiveness of lobbying work aimed at influencing the Community agenda and sectoral policies has been addressed only in passing. These themes will be the subject of a forthcoming volume. By focusing on the joint documents stored in our database, we have been able to identify trends common to certain sectors and overall trends noticeable in all sectors.

Our analysis has also brought to light a number of issues which we shall examine by way of a provisional conclusion. This conclusion is by necessity provisional because, as the different chapters have shown, the diverse circumstances of each sector, the factors determining their potential for development, the players' strategies, etc. are such that no definitive pronouncements can be made. We shall describe below the procedural, structural and substantive issues which struck us in the course of our research.

I. Procedural Issues

These issues apply to all sectors. They mainly concern:

- methods of approving joint texts;
- clarification of the scope of these texts;
- follow-up;
- verification of national-level implementation.

This set of issues has to do with the rules of the game as regards drafting, approving and implementing documents. One particular feature of the sectoral social dialogue is that each party is in a position to determine its own rules of procedure on the negotiating mandate and the approval of any negotiated outcomes. Whereas the European Treaties are evolving in the direction of increased qualified majority voting (QMV) in the social policy field, many sectors are still at the stage of adopting decisions by consensus. This might be nothing but a technical detail, were it not for the fact that it gives the employers' side considerable scope to block progress. Indeed, the employers' organisations can always exert pressure in negotiations by arguing that one or other of their members objects. Looking back at the former joint committees, where texts were adopted by a vote, our informants tell us that voting was a way of alleviating tension within the employers' group (see chapter 1). It seems to us that the sectoral players ought to follow the European rules to the letter, approving by a qualified majority joint documents covering fields which are subject to QMV at European level (e.g. unanimity for social protection but QMV for working conditions). Having laid down this principle, individual employers' organisations and sectors alike could determine the type of qualified majority (weighted or not depending on the country, etc.). In order to ensure a harmonised approach on the trade union side, the rules adopted by the ETUC to approve agreements with UNICE/UEAPME and CEEP could serve as a basis for individual sectors.

In several cases we have also encountered confusion as to the actual scope of texts adopted: are they binding or are they optional? This lack of clarity raises the question of follow-up and implementation which, it seems to us, should be explicitly and systematically dealt with by Sectoral Social Dialogue Committees. The notion of a "voluntary agreement" should in particular be clarified. What exactly is voluntary: the opening of negotiations, the signature of an agreement or its implementation nationally? Are the national players bound by an agreement, or is it in effect merely a recommendation whose application is optional? The risk in the latter case is that rights will be defined but subsequently not observed in a uniform manner throughout the sector and throughout Europe. What could happen is that, where national trade union organisations were strong, they would have sufficient clout to ensure rigorous application of the European-level agreement concluded. But where trade unions were weaker they would not be able to do so, because these agreements are not guaranteed in law. This issue has arisen in no uncertain terms at cross-industry level, and one of the items in the social partners' new programme of action for the period 2006-2008 relates specifically to clarifying the texts already adopted. Over and above such clarification, the chapter in this volume concerning the implementation of European social dialogue texts in Sweden likewise suggests that there is a degree of confusion in the minds of national trade unionists about what is really meant by implementation. Implementation can in fact take place *de facto* without those concerned either considering or presenting it as such.

Lastly, we would emphasise the key role needing to be played by the European Commission. We should not forget that, pursuant to the Treaties, its task is "promoting the consultation of management and labour at Community level" and taking "any relevant measure to facilitate their dialogue by ensuring balanced support for the parties" (Article 138). Unless the Commission becomes more actively involved in supporting sectoral social dialogue, and unless it makes more of a contribution to shaping the dialogue and following up joint texts, we think it unlikely that any further steps can be taken.

II. Structural Issues

The structural issues thrown up by the European sectoral social dialogue relate mainly to two elements: first, EU enlargement to take in the central and eastern European countries; second, the linking of the sectoral and cross-industry dialogues to create a well-structured arena for social dialogue[1].

Let us begin with enlargement. The absence of a sectoral bargaining level, the weakness or non-existence of trade unions and/or employers'

1 We would not attach the label "collective bargaining" to this arena, given the low-level commitments currently being entered into by those concerned.

organisations – or else their declining numbers – are not just problems in most of the new Member States. They likewise constitute a problem across the entire European Union in terms of the social partners' representativeness and legitimacy. A variety of initiatives exists, of course: cross-industry (in the new programme of action), sectoral (in many action programmes), in works councils, national trade unions, etc. However, there do not seem to be any strategic links between these diverse initiatives up to now. In addition, the relevant chapter demonstrates the potential importance of the European sectoral dialogue as a reference point for a sectoral social dialogue yet to be constructed or invented in most of the new Member States. This question will, in our opinion, very soon become central to the European debate. What is the point of strengthening European sectoral social dialogue if its effects within Europe are asymmetrical because the players in certain countries are too weak for any European-level outcomes to be implemented nationally?

The links among all the sectors currently organised, as well as between the sectoral and cross-industry levels, appear to be weak. All the players of course quite rightly emphasise their particularities, their independence and the existence of informal or formal cooperation with one or other related sector, but we cannot envisage a coherent European social arena emerging on this basis. So, even though these structural issues are equally pressing in all sectors, they seem not to be the subject of any joint deliberations and strategies. We have noted, for example, that headway made in one sector has no knock-on effect in others.

The fact that several sectors are structured around European or global multinationals has major consequences for the sectoral social dialogue and the interaction between national and transnational negotiations (works councils or sectors). Finally, it should also be pointed out that the restructuring of national and European trade unions has had an impact on the demarcation and definition of sectors.

III. Substantive Issues

While the first two types of issues cut across all sectors, it seems to us that these substantive issues depend to a large extent on the particularities of each sector. Besides, as we showed in chapter 4, the substantive issues specific to a sector or group of sectors are contingent on the players' ability to "push them up" to the European level, because they are not usually given but have to be constructed in a context of transnational diversity.

These issues have to do with sectoral specifics and with the answers to questions such as: is the sector heavily exposed to international competition? is it closely integrated at European level? what national traditions exist? what is the extent of trade union membership? does enlargement have any particular new implications for the sector? Clearly the trade unions' strategies in hairdressing, private security and even telecoms and postal services are partly determined by the specific structural nature of the sector. The employers' strategies in no way favour the emergence of a European negotiating arena. Indeed, the employers have no interest in any such development. Yet they do go further under certain circumstances, mainly for one of two reasons. Firstly, for fear of internal competition between employers' organisations: for instance, UNICE signed up to the first joint agreement with the ETUC partly because it was afraid that the sectors might gain the ascendancy. The other reason is that a joint stance may be adopted in opposition to other employers' factions. This applies for example to the strategy taken up by Eurocommerce in the face of hard discounters (and the Wal-Mart threat).

A caricature of the social dialogue's limitations would have the employers shouldering full responsibility every time it is deadlocked. However, while the employers' reservations have been pretty much constant, it is also a fact that the trade union organisations in some sectors do not appear to thoroughly exploit their European-level opportunities. We are thinking here, for instance, of matters such as common social standards, competition between sites, the threat of relocation and outsourcing, etc. This may perhaps be attributable to the lack of any coordinated strategies on the part of national organisations – which brings us back to the question of national trade union strategies. More generally, can there be effective sectoral social dialogue without the emergence of coordinated demands at European level? Wage coordination, or rather the attempts to achieve it, is a case that demonstrates the complexity of such an approach.

We saw in the chapter on UNI-Europa that there are a number of differences between the ideal social dialogue scenario and the current one. Can dialogue progress to a further stage if national trade unions are not convinced by the strategic importance of the European transnational level? Should the issues traditionally underpinning the very existence of trade unions, namely wages and working conditions, remain exclusively in the national domain? And is the most effective course of action on wages or reducing working time to coordinate national collective bargaining in accordance with jointly adopted objectives? Or is this, rather, a staging-post on the way to negotiations with the employers? Should only relatively consensual topics, such as training and non-discrimination or new topics such as stress, violence at work and telework, be assigned to Europe? In other words, in what ways should the European and national levels complement each other?

Last of all, as we stated in our Introduction, the purpose assigned to social dialogue depends partly on our vision of Europe. According to a classic federalist vision, its purpose is to take up or coordinate the key elements of national trade union objectives. According to a more experimental-type vision, European social dialogue is aimed more at innovating, in respect of both themes and instruments. For the time being, the European sectoral social dialogue is manifestly following the latter approach. This would be all very well as long as it was what the players desired (but it is not what the trade unions want: they would prefer to have more classic, binding instruments, and would like the effects not to be confined just to a few representatives meeting in Brussels). It is at this interface between national and transnational action that the significance of the outcomes may perhaps become clear. But that will be the subject of our next volume.

Notes on the Contributors

Christophe Degryse

Christophe Degryse is a journalist and author of several volumes on the European Union. His main contributions to the work of the Observatoire social européen are in the field of cross-industry and sectoral social dialogue. In particular, he is joint editor of "Social Developments in the European Union", an annual volume published by the ETUI-REHS in cooperation with the Observatoire social européen and the Swedish programme SALTSA.

Anne Dufresne

Anne Dufresne is a social economist and has been a researcher at the Observatoire social européen (Brussels) since 1999. She is currently studying for a doctorate in sociology at the University of Paris X-Nanterre and the Free University of Brussels (ULB) where she is part of GRAID (Research group on institutional actors and their discourse). Her research mainly concerns macro-economic issues linked to economic and monetary union as well as the European social dialogue and coordination of collective bargaining (cross-industry and sectoral).

Nadia Hilal

Nadia Hilal is a political scientist (Institut d'études politiques, Paris). She works at the Institut des Sciences du Travail (IST) at the Catholic University of Louvain (UCL). She studies the representativeness of the sectoral-level social partners in the European Union. Her main research fields are the social dimension of the European Union, trade union cooperation, European collective action and the European transport sector. She has recently edited "Déréglementations économiques européennes: quels effets pervers? Le cas du transport routier de marchandises" (Sociologie du travail, February 2006, volume 48, IRESCO).

Évelyne Léonard

Évelyne Léonard is a professor at the Institut d'Administration et de Gestion (IAG) of the Catholic University of Louvain (UCL). Since 2004 she has been president of the Institut des Sciences du Travail (IST) at UCL. Her teaching includes human resource management and industrial relations. One of her current research activities is the coordination of comparative studies for the European Commission on the representativeness of trade unions and employers' organisations in specific sectors in all the Member States and candidate countries.

Sofia Murhem

Sofia Murhem received her PhD in economic history from Uppsala University in 2003 for the thesis "Turning to Europe. A new Swedish industrial relations regime in the 1990s". She has written on a number of industrial relations topics, such as European works councils, the service sector, small and medium enterprises, the effects of privatisation and Europeanisation, "flexicurity" etc. She is currently a researcher in industrial relations at the Swedish National Institute for Working Life and a lecturer at Uppsala University.

Philippe Pochet

Philippe Pochet, a political scientist, is Director of the Observatoire social européen. He is the Digest Editor of the Journal of European Social Policy, an affiliate at the Centre of European Studies (Free University of Brussels) and also an invited lecturer at the Catholic University of Louvain-la-Neuve, where he co-chairs the study group on the Active Welfare State with Pascale Vielle. His main research fields are the social impacts of monetary union, the social dimension of the European Union and challenges of the globalisation process. He has recently edited "The Open Method of Co-ordination in Action. The European Employment and Social Inclusion Strategies", with J. Zeitlin and L. Magnusson (P.I.E.-Peter Lang, 2005).

Delphine Rochet

Delphine Rochet has a degree in political science and is a graduate of the European Master in labour studies. Since 2004 she has been a researcher at the Institut des Sciences du Travail (IST) of the Catholic University of Louvain (UCL). Her research mainly concerns European sectoral social dialogue and the institutional representativeness of trade unions and employers' organisations in specific sectors in all the Member States and candidate countries. She is also part of the EIRO (European Industrial Relations Observatory) network of the European Foundation for the Improvement of Living and Working Conditions as a Belgian national correspondent.

Isabelle Vandenbussche

Isabelle Vandenbussche has a degree in labour studies and is a graduate of the Département des sciences de la population et du développement. Since 2004 she has been a researcher at the Institut des Sciences du Travail (IST) of the Catholic University of Louvain (UCL). Her research mainly concerns European sectoral dialogue and the institutional representativeness of trade unions and employers' organisations in the European Union and candidate countries. She is also part of the European Industrial Relations Observatory (EIRO) network of the European Foundation for the Improvement of Living and Working Conditions as a Belgian national correspondent.

"Work & Society"

The series "Work & Society" analyses the development of employment and social policies, as well as the strategies of the different social actors, both at national and European levels. It puts forward a multi-disciplinary approach – political, sociological, economic, legal and historical – in a bid for dialogue and complementarity.

The series is not confined to the social field *stricto sensu*, but also aims to illustrate the indirect social impacts of economic and monetary policies. It endeavours to clarify social developments, from a comparative and a historical perspective, thus portraying the process of convergence and divergence in the diverse national societal contexts. The manner in which European integration impacts on employment and social policies constitutes the backbone of the analyses.

Series Editor: Philippe POCHET, Director of the Observatoire Social Européen (Brussels) and Digest Editor of the Journal of European Social Policy.

Recent Titles

No.55 – *The European Sectoral Social Dialogue. Actors, Developments and Challenges*, Anne DUFRESNE, Christophe DEGRYSE and Philippe POCHET (eds.), SALTSA/Observatoire social européen, 2006, 342 p., ISBN 90-5201-052-8.

No.54 – *Reshaping Welfare States and Activation Regimes in Europe*, Amparo SERRANO PASCUAL, Lars MAGNUSSON (eds.), SALTSA, 2006, 313 p., forthcoming.

No.53 – *Shaping Pay in Europe. A Stakeholder Approach*, Conny Herbert ANTONI, Xavier BAETEN, Ben EMANS, Mari KIRA (eds.), forthcoming.

No.52 – *Les relations sociales dans les petites entreprises. Une comparaison France, Suède, Allemagne*, Christian DUFOUR, Adelheid HEGE, Sofia MURHEM, Wolfgang RUDOLPH & Wolfram WASSERMANN, 2006, 243 p., ISBN 90-5201-323-3.

No.51 – *Politiques sociales. Enjeux méthodologiques et épistémologiques des comparaisons internationales / Social Policies. Epistemological and Methodological Issues in Cross-National Comparison*, Jean-Claude BARBIER & Marie-Thérèse LETABLIER (eds.), 2005, 2nd printing 2006, 295 p., ISBN 90-5201-294-6.

No.50 – *The Ethics of Workplace Privacy*, Sven Ove HANSSON & Elin PALM (eds.), SALTSA, 2005, 186 p., ISBN 90-5201-293-8.

No.49 – *The Open Method of Co-ordination in Action. The European Employment and Social Inclusion Strategies*, Jonathan ZEITLIN & Philippe POCHET (eds.), with Lars MAGNUSSON, SALTSA/Observatoire social européen, 2005, 2nd printing 2005, 511 p., ISBN 90-5201-280-6.

N° 48 – *Le Moment Delors. Les syndicats au cœur de l'Europe sociale*, Claude DIDRY & Arnaud MIAS, 2005, 2nd printing 2005, 349 p., ISBN 90-5201-274-1.

No.47 – *A European Social Citizenship? Preconditions for Future Policies from a Historical Perspective*, Lars MAGNUSSON & Bo STRÅTH (eds.), SALTSA, 2004, 361 p., ISBN 90-5201-269-5.

No.46 – *Restructuring Representation. The Merger Process and Trade Union Structural Development in Ten Countries*, Jeremy WADDINGTON (ed.), 2004, 414 p., ISBN 90-5201-253-9.

No.45 – *Labour and Employment Regulation in Europe*, Jens LIND, Herman KNUDSEN & Henning JØRGENSEN (eds.), SALTSA, 2004, 408 p., ISBN 90-5201-246-6.

N° 44 – *L'État social actif. Vers un changement de paradigme ?*, Pascale VIELLE, Philippe POCHET & Isabelle CASSIERS (dir.), 2005, 2e tirage 2006, ISBN 90-5201-227-X.

No.43 – *Wage and Welfare. New Perspectives on Employment and Social Rights in Europe*, Bernadette CLASQUIN, Nathalie MONCEL, Mark HARVEY & Bernard FRIOT (eds.), 2004, 2e tirage 2005/2nd printing 2005, 206 p., ISBN 90-5201-214-8.

No.42 – *Job Insecurity and Union Membership. European Unions in the Wake of Flexible Production*, M. SVERKE, J. HELLGREN, K. NÄSWELL, A. CHIRUMBOLO, H. DE WITTE & S. GOSLINGA (eds.), SALTSA, 2004, 202 p., ISBN 90-5201-202-4.

N° 41 – *L'aide au conditionnel. La contrepartie dans les mesures envers les personnes sans emploi en Europe et en Amérique du Nord*, Pascale DUFOUR, Gérard BOISMENU & Alain NOËL, 2003, en coéd. avec les PUM, 248 p., ISBN 90-5201-198-2

N° 40 – *Protection sociale et fédéralism*e, Bruno THÉRET, 2002, 495 p., ISBN 90-5201-107-9.

No.39 – *The Impact of EU Law on Health Care System*s, Martin MCKEE, Elias MOSSIALOS & Rita BAETEN (eds.), 2002, 314 p., ISBN 90-5201-106-0.

No.38 – *EU Law and the Social Character of Health Car*e, Elias MOSSIALOS & Martin MCKEE, 2002, 259 p., ISBN 90-5201-110-9.

No.37 – *Wage Policy in the Eurozon*e, Philippe POCHET (ed.), Observatoire social européen, 2002, 286 p., ISBN 90-5201-101-X.